Tastefully VEGAN

CREATIVE VEGETARIAN COOKING

FOURTH EDITION

Kathryn McLane, RN
Gerard McLane, DrPH

The recipes and information in this cookbook have been written and published for informational and educational purposes. This book should not be used as a substitute for recommendations from your own physician or other health care professionals. The authors and publisher are providing you with these recipes and information so that you can have the knowledge and can choose, at your own risk, to act on that knowledge.

Design and layout: Gerard and Kathryn McLane
Nutritional Analysis: Judy Jamison, PhD, RD & Gerard McLane, DrPH, CNS
Photography: Multi-media Creations
Food Styling: Mark Corliss

First Edition: First Printing— April 1995
Second Printing— December 1997

Second Edition: First Printing— May 1998

Third Edition, Revised: First Printing— May 2001

Fourth Edition, Revised: First Printing— October 2005
Second Printing—July 2010

Published by: TEACH Services, Inc.,
www.TEACHServices.com

ISBN-13: 978-1-57258-641-3 (Paperback)
ISBN-13: 978-1-57258-642-0 (Hardback)
Library of Congress Catalog Card Number: 2005931873

Written permission has been received and/or credit given where appropriate for all other copyrighted material presented in this book. We wish to give special thanks and recognition to Dr. Don Hall and Wellsource, Inc. for A New Food Pyramid and the Healthy Eating Self Test.

Dedication

To our children, the joy of our lives:
Melissa, Stephen, and Jonathan, who happily and willingly became the official taste testers for ***Tastefully Vegan***.

Acknowledgments

The authors would like to express their heart-felt thanks and gratefully acknowledge the contributions made by the following family and friends.

Bea Hadley, Kathryn's mother, for her inspiration to prepare delicious food and for the many hours she unselfishly stood by Kathryn's side to help her chop, cut, cook and clean up during the years of recipe development.

Carroll Hadley, Kathryn's dad, for his continual support and encouragement to push forward with this project.

Sylvia Mayer, for sharing her exquisite artistic talent to help create the scenes for the food photography.

JoDee Crandall, for assisting Kathryn in Cooking School at The Lifestyle Center of America and for demonstrating a mutual joy in teaching.

Pastor Barry and Lilly Tryon, our next door neighbors whose friendship and loving kindness have blessed us tremendously. Special thanks to Lilly, one of the best cooks in the country, for her input on several of the recipes.

Judy Jamison, for her help with the difficult task of nutritional analysis.

Pastor Dale and Kathy Martin, special friends who share in our vision to promote the health ministry. Kathy, an English major and an accomplished cook and instructor of vegetarian cooking classes, has graciously donated many hours to proofreading for which we are very grateful.

Ricky and Vivian Seiler, caring neighbors who were always willing to help out in a pinch whenever needed during the final months before publishing.

Friends in Guam and the Guam SDA Clinic, for sponsoring and supporting our monthly vegetarian fiesta dinner demonstrations.

Staff and guests of The Lifestyle Center of America, who have tasted, tested and enjoyed many of the recipes in this book.

CONTENTS

1st Foreword

It is obvious that there is an upsurge in healthful living throughout our society. Americans are interested in improving the quality of their lives. They want to live longer and be healthier. Diet plays a major role in health. A significant number of the diseases that are killing Americans—heart disease, stroke, cancer, diabetes, high blood pressure—all have a relationship to diet. An improved diet means improved health.

You may be seeking a new lifestyle. The reason you have picked up this book is because you want to improve the quality of your health by improving your diet. Let me commend you for this intelligent step. As the speaker for *It Is Written Television*, my wife and I live an enormously hectic lifestyle. We travel thousands of miles every year by plane. Yet we are extremely conscious of our diet. We are convinced that good nutrition, a vegetarian diet of fruits, nuts, grains and vegetables, gives us the nutrition and the energy necessary to function at optimum levels. We heartily endorse a vegetarian diet. We believe that the diet recommended in this book will reduce disease, increase longevity and dramatically improve the quality of life.

Dr. Gerard McLane and his wife, Kathryn, are health professionals. The diet they recommend is not some faddish, way-out, quack diet. It is solidly based in science and buttressed by formidable medical authorities. These recipes have been tested in the kitchen of the Lifestyle Center of America in Sulphur, Oklahoma. The food is not only healthy but it's also delicious. My wife and I have eaten in the dining room at the Lifestyle Center on numerous occasions. We have rarely eaten food that is as healthfully tasty as this. We heartily recommend the recipes in this book. As you put them into practice with your family, you will make a significant contribution to their long-term health and happiness.

Yours for better health,

Mark and Ernestine Finley
It Is Written Television

2nd Foreword

Perhaps nothing captures the essence of Kathryn McLane's cooking better than a particularly revealing experience. One of Kathryn's more outspoken cooking school students publicly declared that he had to eat his words. He was making good on a boisterous promise to do just that if Kathryn could duplicate the taste of one of his favorite recipes—without her using any of the "unhealthful" ingredients it called for. Needless to say, Kathryn had marvelously succeeded!

That incident provides a window into Kathryn McLane's unusual talent of making healthy foods taste good. This book is a testimony to that skill. As my patients have attended her classes at the Lifestyle Center of America, they find that Kathryn's recipes supply an abundance of options for those hard-to-find special dishes that still honor the highest principles of health. This book provides tangible evidence that individuals desiring better health can adopt the healthiest eating-style—a vegan diet—and yet not sacrifice taste. Having personally enjoyed many of Kathryn's recipes, and seen the physical benefits that come to my patients from a diet that includes her creations, I can heartily endorse this book.

My enthusiasm for this edition is increased by Dr. Gerard McLane's contributions. Gerard is a much appreciated colleague who has used his editorial skills and health education expertise to make this book even more practical and "user friendly."

A promise of better health as well as good eating await you as you embark on your journey through **Tastefully Vegan.**

David DeRose, MD, MPH
Lifestyle Center of America

3rd Foreword

"Without continually exercising ingenuity, no one can excel in healthy cooking, but those whose hearts are open to impressions and suggestions from the Great Teacher, will also learn many things and will be able also to teach others; for He will give them skill and understanding."

Nineteenth Century Author

This is the first time that I have been asked to review and comment on a cookbook; but, of course, with my vast experience as an *eater* I am sure mine will be the LAST WORD on the subject.

This is no *ordinary* cookbook! I have seen and used many cookbooks when I was a bachelor and was well known for the many scrumptious delicacies that I would prepare on weekends after exams while I was in college in Montreal. That was gourmet cooking and I was a budding gourmet chef. Yet, never in my wildest imaginings would I, in those days, associate the words "gourmet" with "healthy!" Kathryn, this book surpasses your first edition and places you among the unique group of persons "wise in the kitchen."

This book is not a collection of healthy, esoteric recipes…the kind found in some health books which include recipes…far from it! What you have created is a truly GOURMET vegetarian cookbook that expands the envelope of meal preparation without the use of animal products. To this, you and Gerard have added the health principles that were used in the formulation of recipes and as the foundation for food preparation.

So now, no one needs be compelled to a life of tasteless, albeit nutritious, vegan meals on those special occasions which beg for more pleasure to the palate. There is, through this book, a tasty option in which otherwise healthy people can prepare exotic, mouth-watering vegan, gourmet meals without abandoning health practices. This is a cookbook-*plus*…a masterfully crafted resource: ***Tastefully Vegan.***

Zeno Charles-Marcel, MD
Medical Director
Lifestyle Center of America

Introduction

Welcome to the adventure of **TASTEFULLY VEGAN,** a cookbook with a new approach to creative vegetarian cooking. You will find examples of beautifully planned vegetarian meals organized to help you easily plan and prepare delicious no-cholesterol meals in your home. This cookbook is divided into twelve sections each representing a different theme popular to vegetarians today who enjoy a wide variety of flavors.

Each menu theme offers an assortment of entrée, vegetable, bread, salad and dessert recipes to select. You can quickly plan an entire meal and save precious time. Specific meal themes are demonstrated which would be appropriate for any special occasion or celebration for each month of the year. For example, you might choose the "Sweetheart's Banquet" for Valentine's Day, "Stars and Stripes Sizzler" on the 4th of July, "Summertime Breeze" for those hot August days and of course the "Thanksgiving Tradition" and "Jingle Bells Buffet" for your holiday entertaining. There are over 440 recipes included to help you create your own favorite combination of delicious and "HEALTHY" meals any time of year.

The idea for this cookbook grew following a series of "Vegetarian Fiestas" conducted at the Governor's Mansion in the country of Guam. Each month, over 100 people attended and were offered a healthy full course meal. We wanted our guests to experience the joy of fine vegetarian cooking, one of life's simple pleasures!

This cookbook offers another unique bonus. It's VEGAN too! That means the recipes use no animal products including milk, cheese or eggs. We have also replaced the potentially "Bad Fats" for "Good Fats," given healthy substitutes for the harmful and irritating spices and created a variety of "guilt free" desserts for you to enjoy.

You may ask, "How can it still taste good?" There are few cookbooks that offer vegetarian recipes that are vegan, nutritious and delicious too. Our goal is to offer healthy recipes without sacrificing the pleasure of eating. This has been an interesting task to accomplish. The recipes found here have been tested and tasted by hundreds of people who now enjoy preparing them in their own homes. You will realize it is possible for healthy food to taste delicious with just a little extra work. Good health results from consistent good eating and good living habits. Be creative. Be smart. Provide the best for the ones you love and give them a gift that will last for a lifetime.

About the Authors

Kathryn's background as a nursing health professional and wife of a Preventive Care Specialist has opened for her opportunities she had never anticipated. Traveling to different countries of the world with her husband to conduct health seminars, she began to see the need to help people learn how to cook great vegetarian food that was both healthful and delicious.

Kathryn has taught thousands of cooking school participants how to prepare tasteful and nutritious vegan vegetarian recipes which are low in fat and cholesterol free.

Cooking school participants experienced hands-on cooking techniques in preparing a wide variety of recipes from exquisite vegetarian cuisine to quick and easy "on-the-go" meals. Her goal was to prepare and educate each person with enough experience and knowledge of vegetarian cookery before completing the class to ensure an easier transition when returning home. Kathryn believes confidence and a high level of comfort when preparing meals are the keys to success in continuing this very important lifestyle change.

Kathryn began conducting cooking schools in Singapore as a part of the health seminars offered at Youngberg Adventist Hospital. She and Gerard also conducted cooking demonstrations and health seminars in Thailand but their work in Guam became the cornerstone for the development of "Tastefully Vegan." Once a month, Kathryn and Gerard conducted a vegetarian fiesta in the governor's mansion in Guam regularly attended by over 100 participants. In the United States, they have conducted cooking schools and presented health seminars in several states for large church groups and hundreds of people at camp meetings. During the years Kathryn served as cooking school instructor for the Lifestyle Center of America in southern Oklahoma, these recipes were thoroughly tested in the cooking school lab and served in the main dining room.

Dr. McLane has been a professional of preventive care since receiving his doctorate in 1977. He is a specialist in the therapeutic and motivational approaches to health risk management, disease prevention and lifestyle interventions and brings those skills to his role as President of The Preventive Care Group in Asheville, North Carolina.

Dr. McLane earned both his Master's and Doctor of Public Health degrees from Loma Linda University School of Public Health, Loma Linda, CA. He is a Founding Member of the American College of Lifestyle Medicine, a Certified Nutrition Specialist, and a Certified Health Education Specialist. Kathryn earned her nursing degree from Southern Missionary College in 1975. After working in hospitals for 14 years, she branched out into community health education. She now provides consultation for health products and serves as a trainer and recruiter for FreeLife International, Total Health Company.

Dr. McLane and his wife Kathryn worked at Hinsdale Hospital for 10 years prior to serving as medical missionaries in the Far East from 1989 to 1994, with service in Singapore, Thailand, the Philippines, Indonesia, Guam, Chuuk and Palau.

While on Guam, Dr. McLane hosted "Health Talk Today," a twice-weekly program on public radio.

Kathryn McLane, RN
Gerard McLane, DrPH, CHES, CNS
The Preventive Care Group
P.O. Box 940
Candler, NC 28715

For seminar information or questions about this book, you may contact the authors at the address above or at the website and E-mail addresses noted below.

www.tastefullyvegan.com

TastefullyVegan@aol.com

Position of the American Dietetic Association: Vegetarian Diets (1997)

This paper is reproduced in full on the Internet at the address located at http://www.eatright.org/Member/PolicyInitiatives/index_21026.cfm and with the permission of the American Dietetic Association, (ADA). This position paper by the ADA has been published in The Journal of the American Dietetic Association, 2003; 103: 748–765.

Scientific data suggest positive relationships between a vegetarian diet and reduced risk for several chronic degenerative diseases and conditions, including obesity, coronary artery disease, hypertension, diabetes mellitus, and some types of cancer. Vegetarian diets, like all diets, need to be planned appropriately to be nutritionally adequate.

POSITION STATEMENT

It is the position of The American Dietetic Association (ADA) and Dietitians of Canada that appropriately planned vegetarian diets are healthful, are nutritionally adequate, and provide health benefits in the prevention and treatment of certain diseases.

Vegetarianism in Perspective

The eating patterns of vegetarians vary considerably. The lacto-ovo-vegetarian eating pattern is based on grains, vegetables, fruits, legumes, seeds, nuts, dairy products, and eggs, and excludes meat, fish, and fowl. The vegan, or total vegetarian, eating pattern is similar to the lacto-ovo-vegetarian pattern except for the additional exclusion of eggs, dairy, and other animal products. Even within these patterns, considerable variation may exist in the extent to which animal products are avoided. Therefore, individual assessment is required to accurately evaluate the nutritional quality of a vegetarian's dietary intake.

Studies indicate that vegetarians often have lower morbidity (1) and mortality (2) rates from several chronic degenerative diseases than do non-vegetarians. Although non-dietary factors, including physical activity and abstinence from smoking and alcohol, may play a role, diet is clearly a contributing factor.

Please visit the website mentioned above to read the remainder of this paper published by the American Dietetic Association (ADA).

The Vegan Diet Philosophy

Pure and Simple
vs
Variety-The Spice of Life

There are two approaches to eating a vegan diet. One would consist of a diet that is pure and simple filled with the foods nature has to offer in its most natural state. The other would be taking these same foods, giving them a new look and enhancing their flavors with the help of sweet herbs and spices, creative mixtures of ingredients and some specially prepared health foods. This would ultimately broaden the "variety" to which a tasteful vegan diet can offer.

The simple "quick and easy" method has its place in today's fast pace world. But unfortunately, most rely on "convenience foods" or "prepared foods" to meet these demands that in most cases immediately raises a red flag when healthful eating is a priority. If one can be satisfied with a diet requiring only basic cooking skills and consisting only of raw nuts and seeds, raw or steamed vegetables, whole fruits and grains, then that individual must be well aware of the benefit reaped from a simple, wholesome and uncomplicated diet. I believe people should also be taught how to do the little extras that provide variety in the simple vegan diet while maintaining a healthy standard. To accomplish a vegan diet with "variety" without compromising the recommended guidelines of daily fat, protein, fiber and sodium content requires without any question a commitment to some extra time spent in the kitchen. It cannot always compete with the ease, speed and simplicity of TV dinners or convenience foods, but surpasses all in quality and taste while consistently promoting health. Without question, a vegan diet is not and cannot be an effortless task. The truly dedicated believers of health promotion who also enjoy knowing how to do all the little "extras" welcome variety in the diet. Preparation becomes a joy rather than a chore. As with all things in life, moderation should also be practiced in time spent for preparation. We believe our diets should consist of a realistic combination of the simple wholesome foods always available to us as well as the flavorful recipes we devote our time to in preparation. Our objective is to supply you with those recipes in ***Tastefully Vegan*** that will assist you in preparing meals that will add "variety" and "spice" to your life.

Vegetarianism
The key to good health

What is a Vegetarian?

The term "vegetarian" has been loosely used over the years to incorporate everything from those who eat solely of a plant-based diet to those who incorporate some foods of animal sources in their diets. There are three types of vegetarians who do not eat animal flesh.

Vegetarians avoid the use of meat, fish, and poultry. **Actually, we prefer the term vegetarian to mean avoiding the use of all animal products as food.** However, those that use some animal products such as milk, cheese and eggs, are called lacto-ovo vegetarians. Lacto vegetarians use dairy products but not eggs. Webster's Collegiate Dictionary defines vegetarianism as the theory or practice of living on a diet made up of vegetables, fruits, grains, nuts, and sometimes eggs or dairy products. Also, in Webster's Dictionary, "herbivore" is used as a second definition for vegetarianism, being defined as a plant-eating animal.

A "Vegan," a term used to denote a strict vegetarian, is one who consumes no animal or dairy products whatsoever. Some vegans will also avoid the use of animal products for clothing as well.

Whatever type of vegetarian you are now or wish to become, you will find exciting and innovative recipes included in this book. Some are simple, some are more involved. Choosing to eat vegetarian is a goal that can be accomplished even in this fast food world we now live in.

Guidelines for a Balanced Vegetarian Diet

1. Eat a variety of whole grains, legumes (beans), vegetables, nuts and fruits. A vegetarian diet will be based on these foods.

2. Limit sweets, high fat foods, junk foods, and highly processed foods. These foods add additional calories and are lacking in nutrients and fiber.

3. Choose soy milks and nut milks along with non-dairy cheeses in place of dairy products.

4. Vegans should supplement their diet with a reliable vitamin B-12 source unless sufficient amounts of B-12 fortified foods are included

in the diet, (many cereals, soymilks, and soy-meat analogs are fortified with vitamin B-12).

Reasons why people don't eat meat

1. **Longer, healthier life:** Vegetarians are at lower risk for heart disease, cancer, diabetes, high blood pressure and obesity. *Only animal products contain cholesterol.*

2. **Environment:** Meat production takes more resources, causing soil erosion, water depletion, pollution from pesticides and animal waste.

3. **Economy:** Raising grain and vegetables is cheaper than raising livestock, so it costs less to eat.

4. **World hunger:** The amount of grain needed to produce an 8 oz. Steak could feed 40 people a cup of grain each.

5. **Other reasons:** Some protest the cruel treatment of animals mass-produced for their meat while others will not eat meat for religious reasons.

Debunking the Myths of Vegetarianism

Vegetarians eat chicken and fish. Total vegetarians will not eat any flesh.

Starch is fattening. Actually, carbohydrates are low in fat. Dairy foods and meat, however, are high in fat. In fact, fat has over twice the calories as carbohydrates.

Meat is the only good source of protein. Grains, vegetables and legumes can supply all the protein we need. The key is choosing variety and consuming enough calories to meet energy needs.

Vegetarians don't get enough vitamins and minerals. Well-planned vegetarian diets supply all the nutritional requirements. The American Dietetic Association has confirmed this to be true.

Vegetarians have to carefully mix proteins in each meal. A mixture of proteins from plant sources will naturally complement each other over a day's time. It is not a major nutritional concern.

Vegetarian food is not good tasting. Not true! Vegetarian meals can be diverse, colorful, and delicious. Try these recipes and check with the multitude of chefs who create exciting vegetarian dishes at many restaurants across the nation.

Tips for transitioning to a Vegetarian Diet

1. Start by limiting your meat, poultry or fish intake to one meal a day, then once a week. You don't have to go cold turkey. Remember, serving sizes are only 2 - 3 ounces.

2. Try to make one of your favorite meals vegetarian by replacing the meat with beans, tofu or a soybean analog (textured vegetable protein). A visit to the health food store, where you will find new products available, might be a good place to start. However, large supermarkets are now featuring many of these same products.

3. Begin increasing the fiber content in your meals. This should be done slowly if you were previously on a low fiber diet but your body will adapt to the higher levels of fiber and your digestion will be improved.

4. Read labels to understand the list of ingredients. Things to look for are fat content, undesirable ingredients, and sodium content if you are on a sodium restricted diet. Other helpful information on a label includes total calories, sugar content and fiber content.

5. Clean out your cupboards, refrigerator and freezer to include only foods that are healthy. Purchase only items which will promote health and well-being for family members and guests alike.

6. Many foreign cuisines offer interesting meatless dishes. Look for these types of restaurants when eating out. Also, many family style restaurants will make up a vegetable plate when requested to do so.

7. Avoid fast-food establishments as few offer meatless choices. However, salad bars, potato bars, and veggie burgers are becoming more popular.

8. Connect with others who can help you to become a vegetarian. The Vegetarian Resource Group is on the Internet at www.vrg.com to help you. Many books and magazines are also available on the subject. Get together with friends who also want to cook vegetarian and share ideas.

9. Visit your local health food stores. If they do not carry products you

want, they will usually order them for you.

10. Contact the manager of your favorite grocery store. If you inform them of the specialty items you wish to purchase on a regular basis, they will often order them for you.

11. Join up with a food cooperative. They carry most of the specialty foods you will need. Often they will deliver right to your door.

Setting Up A Vegan Kitchen

"The Basics"

LEGUMES:
(Dry, canned or frozen)
Black beans
Black-eyed peas
Garbanzos (chick peas)
Kidney beans
Lentils, brown and red
Lima beans
Navy beans
Pinto beans
Red beans
Soy beans

GRAINS:
Barley, pearled
Barley, rolled
Brown rice, long grain
Brown rice, instant
Millet
Oats, rolled (old fashioned)
Oats, quick
Wheat, bulgur (cracked)
Wheat germ
Wheat, hard winter
Wheat, rolled

FROZEN FRUITS & JUICES:
Apple juice concentrate
Blackberries
Blueberries
Grape juice concentrates
(purple, white, white/peach)
Lemon juice
Orange juice concentrate
Peaches
Pineapple juice concentrate
Raspberries
Strawberries

DRIED FRUITS:
Apples
Apricots
Currants
Dates
Figs
Mango
Papaya
Pineapple
Prunes
Raisins

RAW NUTS:
Almonds (sliced, slivered, whole)
Almond butter
Cashews (pieces, halves, whole)
Peanuts
Peanut Butter
Pecans (chopped, halves)
Walnuts, English

RAW SEEDS:
Flax
Poppy
Pumpkin
Sesame, hulled or whole
Sesame butter (Tahini)
Sunflower

"The Basics"

BAKING SUPPLIES:

Arrowroot (or cornstarch)
Baking powder, Rumford (non-aluminum)
Bran, oat
Bran, wheat
Brown sugar, dark and light
Carob powder
Citric acid, crystals
Coconut, unsweetened grated (dry)
Coconut, unsweetened grated (fresh, frozen)
Coconut milk, "lite" canned, unsweetened
Coffee substitute (Roma®)
Cooking sprays, variety of flavors
Flavoring, almond extract
Flavoring, maple extract
Flavoring, natural butter (non-dairy)
Flavoring, natural maple (alcohol free)
Flavoring, natural vanilla (alcohol free)
Flavoring, strawberry extract
Flavoring, vanilla extract (pure)
Flavoring, walnut
Flour, barley
Flour, garbanzo
Flour, oat
Flour, rye
Flour, soy
Flour, unbleached white or all purpose
Flour, vital wheat gluten
Flour, whole wheat and pastry wheat
Honey, liquid or spun
Maple syrup, pure
Molasses, mild
Olive oil, "extra light"
Olive oil, "extra virgin-cold pressed"
Powdered sugar
Sesame oil
Sunflower oil
Tapioca, minute or pearled
Tofu, aseptic boxed (soft, firm, extra-firm)
Tofu, water-packed (silken, soft, firm, extra-firm)
Yeast, active and rapid rise

DRIED HERBS / SPICES:

Allspice
Basil
Cardamom
Celery salt
Chives
Cinnamon, ground
Coriander, ground
Cumin, ground
Cumin seed, whole
Dill weed
Garlic powder
Garlic salt
Italian seasoning
Marjoram
Nutmeg
Nutritional yeast
Onion, chopped
Onion, minced
Onion powder
Onion salt
Oregano
Paprika
Parsley
Pumpkin pie spice
Rosemary
Sage
Salt
Savory
Thyme
Turmeric

Setting Up A Vegan Kitchen

"Specialty Items"

Specific company name brands of specialty items are not "always" named in the recipes. The following list consists of those products that have been tested and used for the recipes in ***Tastefully Vegan***. If the listed name brands are not available in your location, similar substitutions are recommended.

COOKING SPRAYS:

A. Pam®
  1. Butter
  2. Garlic
  3. Original
  4. Olive oil

MEAT SUBSTITUTES:

A. Companion
  1. Mock Chicken
  2. Mock Duck

B. Morningstar Farms
  1. Better 'n Burgers
  2. Burger-Style Crumbles
  3. Ground Meatless, burger
  4. Ground Meatless, sausage

C. Natural Touch
  1. Vegan Burger Crumbles
  2. Vegan Sausage Crumbles

D. Worthington®
  1. Chic-Ketts™, frozen "chicken"
  2. Choplets™, canned
  3. Granburger™, dehydrated (TVP)
  4. Multigrain Cutlets™, canned
  5. Vegetarian Burger™, canned

E. Yves Veggie Cuisine
  1. Canadian Veggie Bacon
  2. Veggie Wieners, "low fat"
  3. Veggie Wieners, "fat free"
  4. Deli Slices
  5. Just Like Ground

SEASONINGS:

7A. Bernard Jensons
  1. Vegetable seasoning

B. Bragg®
  1. Liquid Aminos

C. Cook's or McCormick®
  1. Vanilla powder

D. Frontier
  1. Beef-style Seasoning
  2. Chicken-style Seasoning
  3. Pumpkin Pie Spice
  4. Vegetable Broth Seasoning

E. McCormick® (or) Schilling
  1. Garlic & Herb "Salt-Free"
  2. Imitation Butter Flavored Salt
  3. Pizza Seasoning

F. McKay's®
  1. Beef-style Seasoning, no MSG
  2. Chicken-style Seasoning, (no MSG, no whey, no lactose)

G. Modern Products, Inc.
  1. Spike, "Original" All Purpose
  2. Vege-Sal, All Purpose

H. Old El Paso®
  1. Mild green chilies

I. Spicery Shoppe
  1. Natural Butter Flavoring
  2. Natural Maple Flavoring
  3. Natural Vanilla Flavoring

"Specialty Items" (continued)

NATURAL SWEETENERS:

A. Lundberg Grain Syrup
(brown rice syrup)

B. Date Sugar (any brand)
(granulated dates)

C. Fructose
(fruit sugar)

D. Fruitsouce
(grain and fruit sweetener)

E. Stevia, extract or powdered
(natural herb sweetener)

F. Sucanat®
(dehydrated cane juice)

BAKING AIDS:

A. Emes Kosher Jel®, plain
(vegetable "gelatin")

B. ENER-G®
1. Baking Powder Substitute
2. Baking Soda Substitute
3. Egg Replacer

C. Instant Clear Jel®
(instant food thickener)

D. Lighter Bake®
(fat and egg substitute)

E. Wonderslim®
(fat and egg substitute)

MILK ALTERNATIVES:

A. Almond Mylk, beverage

B. Dari-Free, powdered
(potato milk)

C. Better Than Milk™, powdered
(soymilk, plain or vanilla*)
(rice milk)

D. Silk®, beverage (ready to drink)
(soymilk, plain or vanilla)

E. Soyagen, powdered
(soymilk, plain)

F. Soy Good, powdered
(soymilk, plain or vanilla)

G. Soy Supreme, powdered
(soymilk, plain)

H. West Soy "Plus," beverage
(soymilk, plain or vanilla)

CHEESE ALTERNATIVES:

A. SoyaKass® (block)
1. Cheddar
2. Jack
3. Mozzarella

B. Galaxy Foods, slices & shreds
1. Large variety of flavors
2. Parmesan, grated

C. SoyCo
1. Parmesan, grated
2. Veggy Singles

D. Tofutti®, Better 'N Cream Cheese
1. French Onion
2. Herb
3. Plain

*Recipes in this book often call for the milk alternative "Better Than Milk™." The "original-plain, caseinate free" formula is the recommended choice for the recipes because of its flavor. It is available in powdered or ready to drink formulas. The "light" formula resembles skim milk and is not as suitable for the recipes in most cases.

Eating is one of life's great pleasures

Making unwise food choices can increase your risk of a heart attack, stroke, diabetes, cancer, obesity, osteoporosis, high blood pressure, and a host of other serious health problems.

It seems obvious that if you want good health you need to choose foods that promote health and avoid those that promote disease. Fortunately, health and nutrition research has identified key guidelines that can help you make wise food choices.

Here are 10 healthy eating guidelines to help you achieve optimum health

1. Eat predominantly from whole, plant-based foods

The U.S. Dietary Guidelines state,[1] "Eating a variety of whole grains, fruits, and vegetables is the basis of healthy eating." These foods are packed with nutrients and phytochemicals that protect the body from heart disease, cancer, and high blood pressure. They are cholesterol free and low in calories. Emphasize plant-based foods in your diet.

2. Maintain a healthy weight

This is not an easy task for most people. Two out of three people today are either overweight or obese! If you don't consciously plan to maintain a healthy weight, chances are you will be overweight in time.

Here are eating tips to consider:

- Learn to enjoy lower calorie foods
- Limit high calorie desserts and treats to special occasions only
- Drink water in place of soda pop, beer, and other high calorie drinks
- Limit fast food and high fat restaurant meals
- Keep portion sizes moderate and avoid second helpings
- Eliminate junk foods and frequent snacking
- Eat slowly and enjoy your meals
- If you need help in losing weight, join a reliable program with a support group, see your doctor, or visit a dietitian

A healthy weight is defined as a body mass index (BMI) less than 25. Check the BMI chart to see how you rate.

Height	Healthy BMI 23	OverWt BMI 25	Obese BMI 30+
4' 10"	110	119+	143+
5' 0"	118	128+	153+
5' 2"	126	136+	164+
5' 4"	134	145+	174+
5' 6"	142	155+	186
5' 8"	151	164+	197+
5' 10"	160	174+	209+
6' 0"	169	184+	221+
6' 2"	179	194+	233+
6' 4"	189	205+	246+

BMI chart from National Center for Health Statistics

Are You Overweight?

1. Locate your nearest height in the left column.
2. If your BMI is 25–29, you are overweight.
3. If your BMI is 30 or greater, your are obese.
4. A BMI of 23 has the best longevity in women.

3. Aim for 30–60 minutes of physical activity daily

Activity balances calorie intake to help you maintain a healthy weight. Choose moderate activities such as brisk walking, active gardening, mowing the lawn, aerobics to music, biking, and active sports.

Start at levels you can complete without undue strain or fatigue. Gradually increase your time and/or intensity until you can complete at least 30 minutes daily. Two 15-minute sessions per day is fine.

Keep it fun. Think of physical activity as play! Take time to play or be active every day. For best health, the Institute of Medicine (IOM)[2] recommends up to 60 minutes of activity on most days, especially if weight control is a problem.

If you have health problems, get your doctor's guidance before starting to exercise.

4. Eat fresh fruits and vegetables in abundance

They help maintain your weight and promote good health. The National Institute of Health (NIH) DASH Diet[3] for cardiovascular health recommends eating 8–10 servings of fruits and vegetables daily. These foods help lower blood pressure and cholesterol. They also add color, texture, taste, and enjoyment to any meal.

These include:

- Citrus fruits
- Raw veggies
- Salads and leafy greens
- Berries and melons
- Onions, scallions, leeks, and garlic
- Broccoli and cabbage
- Tomatoes and peppers
- Apples and bananas

They taste great and are good for your health!

5. Choose healthy fats

Not all fats are bad. Some are essential for health. You will live longer and have less heart disease if you eat moderately of healthy fats every day. Include healthy fats at most meals:

- Unhydrogenated vegetable oils such as canola, olive, soy, corn, and peanut
- Trans-fat free margarine (read the labels)
- n-3 fatty acids (found in flax meal, walnuts, soy foods, canola oil, and fish)
- Olives, avocado, and nuts (good sources of healthy fats)

Limit the intake of saturated and trans fats. The IOM recommends as low an intake of trans fats and cholesterol as possible (zero is ideal).[2] NIH recommends less than 7% of calories from saturated fat.[4]

Reading food labels and the ingredient list can help you evaluate fats in foods. Look for trans fat content. If "hydrogenated fat" or "partially hydrogenated fat" is listed, then trans fat is present. Sources of trans fat include most margarines, shortening, and foods made with hydrogenated fats.

6. Choose whole grains

Nutrition studies show that whole wheat bread, brown rice, oatmeal, and other whole grains actually lower the risk of heart attacks, strokes, and certain cancers. In the Nurses' Health Study[5] non-smoking women who ate at least three servings of whole grains daily cut their risk of heart disease in half and had lower risk for diabetes than those eating refined grains.

When choosing breads and cereals, read the food label. Look for the phrase "100% whole wheat" or other grain. The ingredient list should say "entire," "whole," or "100%" of a grain. Brown rice is a healthier choice than white rice.

7. Eat nuts/legumes daily

Legumes are rich in protein, high in fiber, and are cholesterol free. Nuts are rich in protein and healthy fats. When eaten daily, they help lower cholesterol and risk of heart disease. In the Nurses' Health Study,[6] women who ate nuts daily had 35% fewer heart attacks than those who seldom ate nuts.

Foods such as hummus and nut butters make healthy alternatives to butter or margarine.

8. Choose healthy protein foods

Limit red meats. They are high in protein but also high in saturated fat. Limit eggs to one in a day. Look for eggs high in omega-3 fats. You need 0.8 grams (g) of protein/kilogram of body weight/day. A 130-pound woman needs 47 g/day. A 200-pound man needs 73 g/day. Very active people and athletes need 1.0 to 1.2 g of protein/kg body weight/day. One kg is equal to approximately 2.2 pounds.

Healthier sources of protein include foods such as legumes, tofu, soy, Gardenburgers©, and other vegetable protein foods. They are cholesterol free and low in saturated fat. Skinless poultry and fish are also healthier alternatives to red meat.

9. Limit high fat dairy products

Dairy is a good source of protein and calcium but is often high in saturated fat and cholesterol. The DASH diet found low fat dairy helpful in lowering blood pressure. Limit intake of butter, cream, and high fat cheese. Soymilk is a healthy alternative for those who prefer not to drink milk. Choose brands low in added sugar and with 8 g of protein/cup. If you don't drink milk, be sure you get adequate calcium and vitamin B-12 from other sources or take a supplement.

10. Choose healthy carbohydrates

Refined carbohydrates such as snack foods, sugar, soda pop, white bread, white rice, and potatoes are absorbed rapidly. This results in high blood sugar, high insulin levels, and increased risk for obesity, diabetes, and heart disease. Limit high glycemic foods. Choose unrefined carbohydrates high in dietary fiber.

Use the New Food Pyramid[7] as a guide for healthy eating!

New Food Pyramid

What is a Serving Size?

Dairy—1 C milk or yogurt, 1/2 C cottage cheese, 1 oz. low fat cheese

Plant oils—1 tsp vegetable oil or trans fat free margarine

Vegetables—1 C salad, 1 C fresh veggies or 1/2 C cooked, 6 oz. juice

Legumes—1/2 C cooked beans, peas, lentils, or garbanzos

Grains—1 slice bread, 2/3 C dry cereal , 1/2 C cooked cereal, rice, or pasta

Protein foods—1 egg, 1/4 block tofu, 1 soy or Garden-burger®, 2 oz. fish or meat

Fruit—1 medium fresh fruit or 1/2 C canned, 1 C berries or melon, 6 oz. pure fruit juice

Nuts—1 oz. nuts or seeds, 2 T nut butter

Other Nutrition Guidelines

- Drink plenty of water. It's good for the circulation and urinary system.
- Use salt moderately, no more than 1500 mg of sodium/ day; especially important if blood pressure is high.
- Eat plenty of dietary fiber, women 25 g/day and men 38 g/day.
- Multiple vitamin-mineral supplements may help young women, dieters, the elderly, and those with poor eating habits.

Practical Ideas for Improving Nutrition

Choose more of these	Eat less of these
Fresh salads and veggies	Creamed vegetables
Fresh fruits—citrus, berries, melons	Canned, highly sweetened fruit
Pure fruit juice—orange, apple, grape	Soda pop, sweetened drinks
Whole grain breads, brown rice, whole grain cereals	White bread, sweetened cereals, pastries, white rice
Legumes—peas, beans, lentils, soy	Pork and beans, chili, beef
Low fat milk, yogurt, cheese, soymilk, low in sugar with 8+ g protein	Whole milk, yogurt, high fat cheeses, cream, ice cream
Soy or Gardenburgers©, bean burritos	Hamburgers, hot dogs, beef tacos
Vegetable oils, unhydrogenated, e.g., canola, soy, olive oil, salad dressing	Lard, shortening, hydrogenated vegetable oils
Trans-fat free margarine	Margarine or butter
Tofu, soy meat alternates, legumes, peanut butter, egg whites	Bacon, sausage, limit whole eggs to one in a day, look for "high omega-3" eggs
Baked or boiled potatoes in smaller portions and occasional use	Hash browns, French fries, huge baked potatoes
Fish, skinless poultry, soy alternates	Red meats— beef, pork, lamb
Nuts, almond or peanut butter, sunflower seeds	Snack foods, chips, candy
Fruit salad and low calorie desserts in place of traditional desserts	High calorie desserts, cheese cake, custards, creamy desserts, full-fat ice cream

References

1. HHS, Dietary Guidelines, 2000
2. NAS, Inst. of Medicine, DRIs, 2002
3. JAMA 289:2083-93, Apr 23/30, 2003
4. NIH, ATP3 Heart Report, 2000
5. Amer J of Clin Nutr 70:412-19, 1999
6. BMJ, Nov 14, 1998
7. W Willett, Sci Amer, Rebuilding the Food Pyramid, Dec 17, 2002

Replacing Nutrients

Vegetarians eating no animal products may need to be more aware of the dietary reference intakes (DRI)[a] of some nutrient sources.

- Calcium: **Adults need 1000—1200 mg/ day**
  Source: tofu processed with calcium, broccoli, seeds, nuts, kale, bok choy, legumes, greens, lime-processed tortillas, fortified soy beverages, grain products

- Folic acid: **Adults need 400 mcg/ day**
  Source: dark green leafy vegetables, asparagus, broccoli, whole wheat, bran, yeast, lentils, tomato juice, oranges

- Iron: **Adults need 8—18 mg/day**
  Source: legumes, tofu, green leafy vegetables, dried fruit, whole grains, and iron-fortified cereals and whole wheat bread

(Absorption of iron is improved by the vitamin C found in citrus fruits & juices, tomatoes, strawberries, broccoli, peppers, dark-green leafy vegetables, and potatoes with skins.)

- Protein: **Adults need 46—63 g/day**
  Source: tofu and other soy based products, legumes, seeds, nuts, grains, gluten, and vegetables

- Vitamin B-12: **Adults need 2.4 mcg/day**
  Source: fortified cereals, soy beverages, nutritional yeast, meat analogs

- Vitamin D: **Adults need 5—15 mcg/day**
  Source: fortified cereals, soy beverages and sunshine

- Zinc: **Adults need 8—11 mg/day**
  Source: flaxseed, brewers yeast, tahini, whole grains (especially the germ and bran), whole wheat bread, legumes, nuts, seeds, and tofu

---

[a] The DRI estimated range for an average man and woman

The Bottom Line

Eat a wide **variety** of **unrefined** plant based foods in sufficient quantity to maintain ideal weight. Follow the daily food guide pyramid with the recommended servings to assure a good balance of all the nutrients. Each group in the pyramid provides a variety of plant-based foods in which to make healthy food choices. Extra servings of grains, vegetables and fruits are allowed to satisfy hunger. Extra servings for the remaining food groups is discouraged.

Recommendations for Vegetarians

Consult a registered dietitian or other qualified nutrition professional especially during periods of growth, breast-feeding, pregnancy, or recovery from illness.

1. Minimize intake of less nutritious foods such as sweets and fatty foods.

2. Choose whole or unrefined grain products instead of refined products.

3. Choose a **variety** of nuts, seeds, legumes, grains, fruits, and vegetables, including good sources of vitamin C to improve iron absorption.

4. For infants, children and teenagers, ensure adequate intakes of calories, foods fortified with vitamin D, calcium, iron, B12, protein, and zinc (Intakes of vitamin D, calcium, iron, protein, and zinc are usually adequate when a variety of foods and sufficient calories are consumed).

5. Take iron and folate (folic acid) supplements during pregnancy under most circumstances.

6. Use fortified food sources of vitamin B12.

7. If sunlight is inadequate, take a vitamin D supplement.

Plant Sources of Calcium

Vegetables, 1 c *	**mg**		**mg**
Collards	357	Broccoli pieces	177
Turnip greens	249	Okra	176
Kale	179	Mustard greens	104
Cooked Beans, 1 c			
Soybeans	131	Garbanzos	80
Navy	128	Black-eyed peas	106
Pinto	86	Lentils	37
Dried Fruits			
Figs, 3 large	78	Apricots, 1/2 c	50
Currants, 1/2 c	62	Raisins, 2 oz	36
Pitted dates, 1/2 c	58	Prunes, 1/2 c	30
Others			
Fortified soymilk, 1 c	100–500	Tofu, 4 oz	110
Tofu (precipitated with calcium salts, 4 oz)	300	Almonds, 1 oz	75
		Sweet potato, 1 med	72
Blackstrap molasses, 1 T	137	Med orange, 1 med	55
Tahini, 1/2 oz	115	Bread, 2 slices	45

Dairy Products for Comparison	
Fruit-flavored, low-fat yogurt, 8 oz with added milk solids	345 mg
Milk, low-fat, 1 c	300
Cheddar cheese, 1 oz	204
Cottage cheese, low-fat 1/2 c	77

* While 1 cup of Spinach has 167 mg of calcium, spinach is not regarded as a good source of calcium due to its high content of oxalates that diminish calcium absorption.

Reference: **Bowes & Church's - Food Values of Portions Commonly Used,** edited by Jean A. T. Pennington, PhD, RD., 15th Edition, 1989.

Nutrition for the Eighties by Winston J. Craig, PhD, RD, 1992.

Plant Sources of Zinc

Soy Bean Products	**mg**		**mg**
Miso, 1/2 c	4.58	Tempeh, 1/2 c	1.50
Soybean flour, defatted, 1 c	2.46	Soybeans, mature	0.99
Tofu, firm, 1/2 c	1.98	Soymilk, 1 c	0.54
Vegetables, cooked, 1/2 c			
Lentils	2.25	Pinto Beans	0.81
Lima beans	0.37	Potato, baked with skin	0.65
Kidney beans	0.95	Collards	0.61
Corn, yellow	0.39	Artichoke, 1 med	0.43
Black beans	0.96	Squash	0.35
Nuts			
Pecans, dry roasted, 1 oz	1.61	Almond, whole, 1 oz.	0.95
Cashews, dry roasted, 1 oz.,		Walnuts, English, 14 halves	0.78
18 pieces	1.59	Sesame butter, 1 T	0.69
Cashew butter, 1 oz	1.47	Almond butter, 1 T	0.49
Seeds			
Sunflower, 1oz.	1.44	Sesame, 1 T	0.70
Pumpkin, 1/2 oz., 71 seeds	1.06		
Grains			
Ralston® cereal, 3/4 c	1.06	Whole wheat, 1 slice	0.42
Oatmeal cereal, 3/4 c	1.00	Mixed grain, 1 slice	0.30
Wheat bran, 2 T	1.00	White, 1 slice	0.15

Reference: **Bowes & Church's - Food Values of Portions Commonly Used,** edited by Jean A. T. Pennington, PhD, RD., 15th Edition, 1989.

Plant Sources of Iron

Soybean Products, 1/2 c	**mg**		**mg**
Tofu, firm	13.19	Tempeh	1.88
Tofu	6.65	Soymilk, 1 c	1.38
Miso	3.78		
Cereal, 3/4 c			
Cream of wheat	9.0	Ralston, cooked	1.24
Bran Flakes	8.1	Oatmeal, cooked	1.08
All Bran	4.5	Grits, white hominy	1.02
Rice, white, enriched, 1 c	1.8	Rice, brown, 1 c	1.00
Other Vegetables, cooked, 1/2 c			
Soybeans, mature	4.42	Lima beans	2.25
Lentils	3.30	Black-eyed peas	2.14
Potato, baked with skin, 6.5 oz	2.75	Artichoke, 1 med	1.62
Kidney beans	2.60	Peas, green	1.24
Navy beans, canned	2.42	Brussels sprouts	0.94
Garbanzos	2.37	Broccoli	0.89
Soybeans, green	2.25	Squash	0.32
Leafy Vegetables, 1/2 c			
Spinach, cooked	3.21	Dandelion greens	0.94
Swiss chard, cooked	1.99	Mustard greens	0.84
Turnip greens	1.59	Kale, cooked	0.59
Collards	0.95	Lettuce, Romaine	0.31
Seeds			
Pumpkin, 1/2 oz., 71 seeds	2.12	Sesame, whole, 1 T	1.31
Sunflower, 1 oz.	1.92		
Fruit			
Raisins, seedless, 2/3 c	2.08	Tomato juice, 1/2 c	0.80
Avocado, 1 med	2.04	Apricots, raw, 3 med	0.58
Prune juice, 1/2 c	1.51	Grapes, 1 c	0.41
Papaya nectar, 8 oz.	0.86	Banana, raw, 1 med	0.35

Plant Sources of Iron
(continued)

Nuts	**mg**		**mg**
Cashews, dry roasted, 1 oz., 18 pieces	1.70	Walnuts, black, 1 oz., 14 halves	0.87
Cashew butter, 1 oz.	1.43	Walnuts, English, 14 halves	0.69
Sesame butter, 1 T	1.34	Pecans, dry roasted, 1 oz.	0.62
Almond, whole, 1 oz.	1.30	Almond butter, 1 T	0.59

Bread, 1 slice			
Mixed grain	0.82	White bread	0.68
Whole wheat	0.80	Cracked wheat	0.67

Animal products for Comparison			
T-bone steak, 3.5 oz.	2.54	Halibut, 3 oz.	0.91
Hamburger, lean, 3.5 oz.	2.35	Bacon, 3 med pieces	0.31
Chicken, 3.5 oz.	1.21	Ham, 1 oz.	0.28
Egg, whole, 1 large	1.04	Milk, 2%, 8 oz.	0.12

Reference: **Bowes & Church's - Food Values of Portions Commonly Used,** edited by Jean A. T. Pennington, PhD, RD., 15th Edition, 1989.

Plant Sources of Protein

Legumes, 1/2 cup cooked	grams		grams
Soybeans	14.25	Garbanzos	7.25
Lentils	9.0	Black eyed peas	7.0
Split peas	8.25	Mung beans	7.0
Red kidney beans	8.0	Pinto beans	7.0
Navy beans	8.0	Lima beans	6.0
Great northern beans	7.5		

Nuts, 2 oz.			
Peanuts, dry roasted	4.0	Brazil nuts, dried	8.2
Walnuts dried	13.8	Pumpkin seeds	6.8
Pistachios	11.6	Pine nuts	6.6
Almonds	11.2	Pecans, dried	4.4
Cashews, dry roasted	8.6		

Vegetables, 1/2 cup cooked			
Artichoke, medium	10.4	Collards	2.5
Potato with skin	5.0	Corn	2.5
Green peas	4.0	Turnips	2.5
Spinach	3.0	Kale	2.0
Avocado, medium, raw	2.5	Tomato puree	2.0
Broccoli	2.5		

Spreads, 2 T			
Peanut butter	8.0	Sesame butter	5.0
Cashew butter	5.0	Almond butter	4.8

Bread			
Pita, whole wheat, 1-6" diameter	6.3	Whole wheat, 1 slice	3.0
Pita, white, 1-6" diameter	5.5	French, 1 slice (1oz)	2.7
English muffin	4.0	White, 1 slice (1oz)	2.0
Whole wheat-homemade, 1 slice	3.9		

Plant Sources of Protein
(continued)

Crackers	**grams**		**grams**
Triscuits, 7 crackers	3.0	Saltines, low sodium,	
Wheat thins, 24 crackers	2.0	3 crackers	1.6

Meat Analogues, 1 patty			
Prime Patties, Frozen,			
Morningstar Farms	19.5	Chik Patties,	
Staklets, 1 piece	12.3	Morningstar Farms	7.3
Garden Vege Patties,		Leanies, Worthington®,	
Morningstar Farms	11.2	1 link	7.3
Frichik, Worthington®,		Bacon simulated meat	
2 pieces	9.9	product-1-strip	0.9

Animal Sources of Protein
(for comparison)

Milk, skim, 8 oz	8.4	Bacon, 2 slices	11.7
Milk, whole, 8 oz	8.0	Bologna, Beef, 1 slice	2.8
		Corned beef, 3.5 oz	18.2
Cheese, American, 1 oz	6.3	Ground beef, 3.5 oz	23.0
Cheese, Cheddar, 1 oz	7.1	Ham, 3.5 oz	21.2
Cheese, Cottage Cheese, 4 oz	14.1	Liver, Beef, 3.5 oz	24.4
Cheese. Mozzarella, 1 oz	5.5	Steak, T-bone, 3.5 oz	24.0
Cheese, Swiss, 1 oz	8.1		
Bass, Black, 4 oz	23.6	Boiled Egg, 1 large	6.1
Catfish, 3 oz	15.4		
Salmon, Smoked, 3 oz	15.5		
Trout, 3 oz	22.4		
Tuna, 3 oz	24.8		

References:

1. **Bowes and Church's, Food Values of Portions Commonly Used**, 15th edition, 1989

2. **Nutritive Value of Foods**, USDA, Home and Garden Bulletin #72

Fats that Heal, Fats that Kill

Fats that Heal, Fats that Kill, The complete guide to fats, oils, cholesterol and human health, Udo Erasmus, PhD, ***alive*** books, 1993

Popular books on nutrition that tackle fats, oils, and cholesterol contain many contradictory statements of 'fact'. The reason is that most writers are not knowledgeable in this field. Some of their 'facts' tell only half the story, the part about the fats that kill. Some of their 'Facts' about fats and oils are the half-truths that industries disseminate in order to market fat and oil products for profit. Also, authors often copy each other's mistaken 'facts' because they have not invested the time and effort required to extract truths from the research literature. This book departs from that lazy practice.

All aspects of how fats, oils, cholesterol, and essential nutrients affect our health are covered in this book, including:

- The properties of fats, fatty acids, sugars, and cholesterol; the healing and the killing fats;
- How fats and oils are made into marketable consumer products; the health effects of applying technical skills (processing) to foods without regard for human health;
- The body's ways of dealing with fats and foods; fats and cholesterol found in foods; how food preparation affects health; research findings;
- How to make and use oils with human health in mind; new and therapeutic products; other important nutrients;
- Degenerative diseases;
- The politics of health; and
- A consideration of the basis of human health.

You will end up with a broad understanding of the topic, have specific, detailed information at your fingertips, and gain insights that will make it easier to optimize health and avoid degenerative diseases. This book separates fact from advertising fiction, and equips you to assess future developments in the field.

We highly recommend this book as a reference for beginning and maintaining positive lifestyle changes.

Importance of Fats

Fats in our diets are necessary in reasonable amounts for good health. They provide a good source of food energy and also help make our food taste good. Fats also help us from getting hungry too soon after a meal by delaying rapid emptying of the stomach. They also carry the fat-soluble vitamins A, D, E, and K. Essential fatty acids (essential means we must obtain them in our diet since we can not manufacture them) are required for growth, reproduction, and maintenance of the health of tissue membranes and skin.

These essential fatty acids are converted into very important substances vital for regulation of many body processes including the immune response, inflammatory reactions, regulation of blood pressure and blood clotting, the maintenance of hormonal balance, the regulation of blood cholesterol, the regulation of our energy levels, and maintenance of healthy skin tone and smoothness to name a few.

We are probably not reducing the harmful fats in our diets as much as we think. With our dependence on fast foods we still consume too much saturated fats and trans fats. Trans fats are also referred to as partially hydrogenated vegetable oils.

To achieve a healthy balance of fats in our diet we need to consume less or none of the harmful saturated fats from animal origin. We also need to consume adequate amounts of the beneficial fats, especially the Omega 3's, found in nuts, seeds, legumes, and grains. It would also be wise to reduce our intake of the harmful fats by using food preparation methods that add little, if any, fat.

For a detailed discussion of fats read Dr. Udo Erasmus's book, **Fats that Heal, Fats that Kill** discussed on page 36. Also read Dr. Winston Craig's book, **Nutrition and Wellness – A vegetarian way to better health**.

All Fats Are Not Equal

Cholesterol: A complex fatty substance found in body cells. Cholesterol differs from fat in that cholesterol may be present in all animal tissue, while fat deposits are mainly found under skin and around organs. Cholesterol in high concentrations is unwanted for it may be deleterious to overall health and well-being. Oxidized cholesterol may damage arteries and be deposited in the arterial wall. Although cholesterol is needed to form hormones, cell membranes, and other body substances, the body will naturally produce enough to meet its needs without incorporation of it into the diet. *Only foods from animal sources contain cholesterol. Plant foods are free of cholesterol.*

Fat: All fat contains 9 calories per gram (more than twice the 4 calories contained in a gram of carbohydrate or protein). Fat can be solid (butter, margarine, lard or shortening) or liquid (vegetable oils). The difference in the fat is due to its fatty acid composition. Fats are a mixture of mono, poly, and saturated fatty acids.

Fatty Acids: The basic chemical unit of fat which are made up of_chains of carbon atoms to which hydrogen atoms are attached. Fatty acids are categorized into saturated, monounsaturated, or polyunsaturated based on how many hydrogen atoms are attached in relation to the maximum they can hold. **Essential Fatty Acids** cannot be manufactured by the body, therefore must be acquired from our food sources. They are involved with deriving energy from food and moving that energy around so our bodies can utilize it.

Hydrogenated Fat: A fat commercially processed from unsaturated liquid oil. By adding hydrogen to the oil (hydrogenation) it becomes more saturated. Examples of hydrogenated fat, also called "trans fats," are spreadable fats such as margarine, shortening, and smooth and creamy peanut butter.

HDL-C: Known as the "good" cholesterol since it returns excess cholesterol to the liver. HDL-C is made up of proteins and lipids (fats), and because it has a higher percentage of protein to fat, it is thought to help rid the blood of excess cholesterol. Higher HDL levels are desirable because of their association with lower rates of heart disease. Caloric restriction has been shown to raise HDL levels.

LDL-C: Known as the "bad" cholesterol. LDL-C is made up of protein and lipid, however, the lipid component is greater than that of the protein component. LDL's are associated with an elevated risk of coronary heart disease because of their connection with high level of blood cholesterol. Caloric restriction has been shown to lower LDL levels.

Lipids: The technical name for substances commonly referred to as fats, oils, cholesterol and triglycerides.

Mono-Unsaturated Fats: Fats containing one double bond and usually liquid at room temperature. Examples are olive, peanut, sesame and canola oils, as well as oils from most nuts and seeds. Monounsaturated fats appear to have positive effects on blood fat levels by lowering total blood cholesterol, lowering LDL or bad cholesterol, and showing little or no effect on HDL.

Poly-Unsaturated Fats and Oils: Fats and oils containing one or more double bonds, commonly liquid at room temperature, and primarily of plant origin. Examples are soybean, corn, cottonseed, safflower, and sunflower oils. Polyunsaturated fats tend to reduce total cholesterol. Long-term effects of diets rich in poly-unsaturated fats are uncertain at this time; however, some studies have actually shown an increased cancer risk with diets high in polyunsaturated fats.

Saturated Fats: Fats that have no double bonds and which are usually solid at room temperature. Saturated fats are derived primarily from animal sources. Examples are red meat, poultry products, dairy (butter, cheese), and lard. Note that palm oil, coconut oil, cocoa butter and partially hydrogenated vegetable oils too are also considered saturated fats. These fats raise total blood cholesterol and are more related to high lipid levels in the blood than are foods high in cholesterol. However, foods high in both cholesterol and saturated fat cause more damage to the arteries than when saturated fat is found alone, such as in plant foods.

Trans-Fatty Acids: Appear to be the most harmful to blood cholesterol because they raise LDL-C and lower HDL-C. Trans fatty acids are found in hydrogenated vegetable oils such as margarines and shortenings and in many commercially made products such as cookies, crackers, chips, and fried foods like French fries. Unfortunately, trans fatty acids are not required to be included on the ingredient list found on food labels. Although the amount of these fats may be small in some products, the only defense for consumers is to avoid products that contain partially hydrogenated vegetable fat including most margarines and smooth and creamy peanut butter.

Triglycerides: The primary type of fat found in the body and visible in the blood. This is the form in which fatty acids are stored in the body's fat tissues and in the seeds of plants.

Plant Sources of Fat

	Total Fat grams	Sat Fat grams	Mono Fat grams	Poly Fat grams	Chol Fat Mg
Nuts and Seeds - 1/4 c					
Peanuts, roasted	17.6	3.1	8.0	4.0	0.0
Sesame seeds	17.5	2.5	7.0	8.0	0.0
Pecans	17.0	1.0	11.0	4.5	0.0
Sunflower seeds	16.8	3.2	3.0	9.5	0.0
Almonds	16.0	1.0	10.0	3.5	0.0
Peanut butter, 2T	15.3	2.8	7.8	5.0	0.0
Walnuts	13.5	1.5	4.0	8.0	0.0
Cashews	13.0	2.5	8.0	2.0	0.0
Pumpkin seeds	13.0	2.5	4.0	6.0	0.0
Vegetable Oils - 1 T					
Corn	13.6	1.7	3.9	8.0	0.0
Cottonseed	13.6	3.5	3.0	7.1	0.0
Safflower	13.6	1.2	2.3	10.1	0.0
Soybean	13.6	2.0	3.7	7.9	0.0
Sunflower	13.6	1.4	3.3	8.9	0.0
Coconut	13.6	11.8	1.6	0.2	0.0
Palm	13.6	6.7	5.6	1.3	0.0
Olive	13.5	1.8	10.6	1.1	0.0
Peanut	13.5	2.3	6.9	4.3	0.0
Margarine - 1T					
Veg. shortening	12.8	3.9	7.1	1.8	0.0
Hard (stick)	11.4	2.1	5.7	3.6	0.0
Soft (tub)	11.4	1.8	4.8	4.8	0.0
Soy Products - 1/2 c					
Miso	6.5	0.9	1.3	3.65	0.0
Tofu, (2½" x 2¾" x 1")	5.0	0.7	1.0	2.9	0.0
Beans - 1/2 c					
Soybean	5.0	0.65	0.95	2.65	0.0
Chickpeas	2.0	0.2	0.45	0.95	0.0
Lima	0.5	0.1	0.05	0.25	0.0
Lentils	0.5	0.05	0.1	0.25	0.0
Peas	0.5	0.05	0.05	0.15	0.0

Animal Sources of Fat
(for comparison)

	Total Fat grams	Sat Fat grams	Mono Fat grams	Poly Fat grams	Chol Fat Mg
Salad Dressings -1 T (with egg or dairy except for Italian and French)					
Mayonnaise	11.0	1.6	3.7	5.7	8.0
Blue Cheese	8.0	1.5	2.2	4.3	3.0
Italian	7.1	1.0	2.0	4.1	0.0
French	6.4	1.5	1.5	4.9	0.0
Thousand Island	5.6	0.9	1.6	3.1	4.0
Mayo, Lo-Cal	3.0	0.5	0.7	1.6	4.0
Animal Fats- 1 T					
Beef fat	12.8	6.4	5.9	0.5	14
Chicken fat	12.8	3.8	6.3	2.7	11
Lard	12.8	5.0	6.4	1.4	12
Butter	11.5	7.2	3.9	0.4	31
Meat, Poultry, Fish - 2 oz.					
Ground beef	11.7	4.6	6.7	0.4	51
Beef rump	8.9	3.5	5.1	0.3	47
Beef liver	4.5	1.6	1.9	0.0	273
Chicken, w skin	6.2	1.7	3.2	1.3	48
Turkey, w/o skin	1.8	0.6	0.7	0.5	39
Tuna in oil	4.6	1.2	0.4	0.4	117
Shrimp	0.9	0.1	0.4	0.4	117
Eggs					
Egg yolk	5.6	1.7	3.2	0.7	274
Egg white	trace	0.0	0.0	0.0	0.0
Dairy Products – **c**heddar cheese, 1 oz and cottage cheese, ½ c					
Cheddar cheese,	9.4	6.0	2.7	0.3	30
Whole milk, 8 oz	8.2	5.1	2.4	0.2	34
2% milk, 8 oz	4.7	2.9	1.4	0.2	18
Skim milk, 8 oz	0.6	0.4	0.1	0.0	5
Cottage cheese	5.2	3.3	1.5	0.2	17

Reference: **Bowes & Church's - Food Values of Portions Commonly Used,** ed. by Jean A. T. Pennington, PhD, RD., 15th Edition, 1989 **Nutritive Value of Foods,** USDA, Home & Garden Bulletin # 72

Selecting Cooking Oils

Why Be Choosy?

As terms like "monounsaturated fats," "essential fatty acids" (EFA's), or "trans fatty acids" become more common in today's vocabulary, the concern for selecting the proper oil plays an important role in good health and fine cooking. More people today have begun to understand that all fats are not forbidden and that some actually support good health. Our bodies welcome good fats as a means of transporting the fat soluble vitamins (A, D, E and K) to key areas of the body, as contributors of EFA's in regulating and maintaining cell growth, and even in assisting with the development of healthy bones, nerves, skin and cell membranes. While we depend primarily on the good fats in wholesome foods to provide our bodies with the necessary tools of good health, it would be difficult and even unnecessary to completely exclude the use of cooking oils from our diets. Even small allowances of free oils add tremendously to the flavor and textures of carefully planned meals.

Like all fats, oils differ in their molecular structure and are categorized by their degree of saturation, basically defined as the arrangement of carbon atoms linked with hydrogen and oxygen. While all oils contain various ratios of saturated to unsaturated fats, the type of fat that is most concentrated in its composition classifies them.

There are four main categories of interest:

1. **Highly saturated oils,** which impose definite heart health risks, are those oils that remain solid at room temperature. Commercially prepared foods containing coconut and palm oil fall into this category and are not recommended for use.

2. **Monounsaturated oils,** (oils containing only one double carbon bond) remain liquid at room temperature but cloud and thicken when chilled. Because of the molecular structure of monounsaturated fats, oils remain stable when exposed to higher temperatures. Olive, canola, almond, peanut and avocado oil are the most common oils available in this group. Monounsaturated oils also tend to reduce total blood cholesterol, including the "bad" low-density lipoproteins (LDL), without affecting the "good," high-density lipoproteins (HDL), levels.

1. **Polyunsaturated oils,** (oils containing two double carbon bonds) remain liquid even when chilled. Examples include corn, safflower, soybean and

sunflower oils. These oils lower total cholesterol and LDL but unfortunately also lower HDL. Also, polyunsaturated oils are unstable when exposed to higher heat and are highly susceptible to attack by "free radicals" or un-bonded oxygen molecules. Polyunsaturated oils can also be hydrogenated to improve their shelf life and use in packaged or processed foods producing a harmful by-product called "trans fatty acids" which can promote cancer and heart disease. However, some polyunsaturated oil is necessary to obtain EFA's. Therefore, these oils, (when not exposed to high heat) are recommended for use, in limited amounts, in foods such as salad dressings, sauces, dips and spreads.

4. **Super-unsaturated oils,** (oils containing 3 double carbon bonds) remain liquid no matter how cold and contain EFA's including omega-3. Flaxseed oil is the most common in this group and is often used as a dietary supplement. Because it is extremely unstable in heat, it should never be used in cooking over 210° F.

In summary, when cooking with oils, choose the monounsaturated oil group most frequently, polyunsaturated oils occasionally and saturated oils rarely. When teaching people how to cook healthfully, we urge them to use olive oil as their principal cooking fat. The best olive oils are greenish yellow in color and represent the first pressing of the olive. To add a delightful, rich flavor with a savory aroma, use "extra-virgin" olive oil in sautéed foods, entrees, gravies, marinades and some salad dressings. Olive oil is an especially delicious compliment to Italian cooking. For times when a neutral tasting oil is needed for baked goods or when making desserts, sweet toppings and sauces, choose "extra-light" olive oil. Although this type is somewhat refined, it has almost no flavor, making it a good option. Sunflower oil may also be used when a light tasting oil is desired as long as the recipe does not require much heat exposure. Your best quality oils will be found in health food stores, specialty supermarkets and gourmet shops. Looking on the label for the words "Cold Pressed" is advisable to assure prevention of any over-exposure to heat during processing. Some less expensive brands found in grocery stores may be extracted with heat and solvents in such a way that is damaging to the fatty acid chemistry. However, wherever you purchase cooking oil, it is important to keep it fresh and good tasting as long as possible. To prevent oils from becoming rancid, store in the refrigerator and take them out just long enough to use them. All oils are sensitive to heat, light, and exposure to oxygen. Expose all oils to as little heat as is possible. This means we would not recommend the use of deep fat frying or frying over high heat. Use oils sparingly and only when necessary to enhance the delightful flavors of "Tastefully" prepared "Vegan" meals.

Importance of Fiber

Men and women everywhere are now purchasing fiber-fortified breads and cereals. Many are adding oat bran to their homemade cookies and cereals. For some, dietary fiber is synonymous with bulk or roughage. Actually, fiber comprises those parts of the plant cell and cell wall that resist digestion by enzymes of the stomach and the small intestine. This indigestible dietary fiber provides the bulk in our foods that softens our stool, along with water and some exercise, to prevent constipation.

Read Dr. Winston Craig's book, **Nutrition and Wellness – a vegetarian way to better health**, for a more complete understanding of the role fiber plays in our diet. Our goal is to include 20–35 grams of fiber in our food each day. To accomplish this we should enjoy at least 2–3 good sources of fiber at each meal. The following tips may help you to achieve this goal:

1. Eat **breakfast.** This is a good time to eat fiber-containing foods such as bran or whole grain cereals, bran or whole grain muffins, oatmeal, whole grain bread, fruit and potatoes. Some breakfast cereals may contain as much as 14 grams of dietary fiber per serving, providing at least half of the daily recommendation.
2. Add **bran cereals** to quick breads, yeast breads, pancakes, casseroles and pie crusts.
3. Eat your **fruit** don't drink it. Fruit is also an excellent choice as a daily dessert.
4. Substitute **whole grain flour** for refined flour in many recipes.
5. Choose **whole grain** products.
6. **Legumes (beans)** are excellent sources of fiber and may substitute for meat in burritos, chili, casseroles, soups and stews, and pasta dishes.
7. **Nuts and seeds** are good sources of fiber and may be consumed daily in small amounts. For those consuming a low fat diet, only small amounts of nuts or plant oils should be consumed.
8. **Dried fruit** is typically high in fiber and provides a concentrated source of calories.
9. **Vegetables** are good sources of fiber, antioxidants and phytochemicals.
10. Any prepared or processed food with **3 or more grams of dietary fiber per serving** is considered a good source of fiber. Any food with **5 or more grams of dietary fiber per serving** is considered an excellent source of fiber.
11. Remember to **increase your water intake** as you gradually increase your fiber intake.

Plant Sources of Fiber

Legumes, ½ cup cooked	grams
Baked beans	10.9
Chick peas	6.3
Soybeans	5.6
Red Kidney	4.8
Lentils	4.2
Lima beans	1.4
Split peas	1.4

Vegetables, ½ cup cooked	
Artichoke, medium	8.4
Pumpkin, canned	5.4
Green Peas	5.2
Broccoli, 2/3 c	4.1
Potato, sweet	4.0
Beet greens	3.9
Popcorn, 3 ½ c	3.5
Squash, winter	3.5
Potato	3.1
Spinach, canned	3.0
Tomatoes, fresh, 2 med	2.8
Squash, summer	2.2
Carrots	2.2
Mushroom, canned	2.1
Lettuce, 2 c raw	2.0
Cabbage, boiled	1.6
Celery, 4, 5 in stalks	1.6
Asparagus	1.2

Nuts and Seeds	
Almonds, whole 1 oz (24)	3.5
Sunflower seeds, 1 oz	3.3
Pistachios, 1 oz	3.1
Peanuts, raw, 1 oz	2.4
Pecans, halves, 1 oz	2.2
Brazil nuts, 8 med	1.5
Walnuts, 1 oz (14 halves)	1.4
Cashews, 1 oz (12-18 med)	1.1
Sesame seeds, whole, 1 T	1.1

Bread	grams
Bran muffin, 2	7.0
Whole wheat muffin, 2	6.0
Whole-wheat bread, 2 slices	4.4
Pancake, buckwheat, 2 (4 inch)	2.0
White bread, 2 slices	1.2
French bread, 2 slices	0.6
Danish pastry, no nuts	0.5
Doughnut, plain yeast	0.4
Doughnut, cake	0.2

Crackers	
Rye-crisp, 6	4.6
Saltine, 6	0.7
Butter, 6	0.6
Graham, 2 sq	0.1

Flours	
Bran, 4 T	8.8
Rye, 4 T	3.6
Whole-wheat, 4 T	3.2
White, 70%, 4 T	1.0

Cereals	
All Bran, ½ c	9.3
Puffed Wheat, 1 c	4.0
Granola, homemade, ½ c	4.0
Raisin Bran, ¾ c	3.5
Shredded Wheat, 4 lg biscuits	3.4
Wheat Flakes, ¾ c	3.0
Grapenuts, ¾ c	2.0
Rice Krispies, 1 c	1.8
Oatmeal, cooked, ½ c	1.6
Cheerios, ½ c	1.5

Rice & Pasta, 1 c	
Brown rice, cooked	2.0
White rice, cooked	1.0
Spaghetti, cooked	0.5

Plant Sources of Fiber
(continued)

Fruits	grams
Currants, dried, ¼ c	8.8
Apple, flesh & skin	8.0
Figs, dried, 2 small	6.4
Persimmon, 1 med	6.4
Raspberries, fresh, ⅓ c	5.2
Raspberries, canned, ¼ c	5.2
Blackberries, fresh, ⅓ c	3.7
Dates, 4	3.6
Pear, flesh & skin, 1 whole	3.6
Prune, dried, 6 large	3.6
Figs, fresh, 2 small	3.2
Raisins, dried & seedless, 8 T	3.2
Orange, 1 med	3.1
Pineapple, canned, 3 med slices	3.0
Plums, fresh, 3 med	2.7
Strawberries, cooked, 1 c	2.7
Banana, 1 small 6-inch	2.5

	grams
Honeydew melon, ¼ of 5-inch	2.4
Nectarine, fresh, 2 large	2.4
Rhubarb, cooked, ½ c	2.4
Peach, fresh, 1 large	2.25
Strawberries, fresh, 10 med	2.1
Applesauce, ½ c	2.0
Grapes, 16 med	2.0
Plums, canned, 3 med	2.0
Watermelon balls, ¾ c	1.8
Cantaloupe, ⅓ of 5-inch	1.6
Pineapple, fresh, 1 c	1.3
Grapefruit, ½	1.3
Cherries, sour, fresh, 10	1.1
Avocado, ⅛ of 3 ¼ x 4-inch	1.0
Apple juice, 4 oz	0.4
Grape juice, 4 oz	0.4
Orange juice, 4 oz	0.4

Miscellaneous	
Pickle, 1 large dill	1.53
Jam (plum or strawberry), 1 T	0.2
Marmalade, 1 T	0.03

How to Use This Book

This book is primarily a cookbook with delicious vegan vegetarian recipes. The ADA position paper on vegetarianism on page 23 supports the viewpoint that you can be healthy eating a well-planned vegan dietary. This book is not a book which discusses all of the nutritional concerns involved with eating a balanced vegan diet. There are abundant sources of information available for you to pursue this avenue of knowledge. We have presented some of the key pieces of information you may need to improve your eating habits which we have found to be useful to individuals while attending our seminars.

The Recipe Section

The recipe section in this book is divided into 12 chapters with specific recipe choices for each section to assist in menu planning.

The recipes will speak for themselves. Try them. Test them. We have found them to be tasteful and nutritious. You of course may also want to make changes. We invite you to be creative and have fun.

Nutritional Analysis

You will find an alphabetized recipe nutritional analysis chart. The Food Processor V6.11 from ***esha*** **Research** was utilized. The nutrient analyses are approximate values for calories, protein, carbohydrate, fiber, fat, Vitamins B12 and D, Calcium, iron, sodium and zinc; Cholesterol, which will always be 0 in vegan cooking was not included.

Use of Abbreviations

The following abbreviations are utilized to name ingredient amounts in recipes or to give directions:

T = tablespoon
tsp = teaspoon
c = cup
oz = ounce
qt = quart
lb = pound
F = Fahrenheit
env = envelope
rec = recipe
pkt = packet
sm = small
med = medium
lg = large
p = page

Secrets and Tips For Successful Baking

1. **Measure Exactly:** Use liquid measuring cups for liquids. Use dry measuring cups for dry ingredients. Check liquid measurements by setting the measuring cup on a level countertop. Spoon (don't pour or scoop) flour and other dry ingredients into the measuring cup. Overfill the cup, and gently tap the side of the cup once to assure all air pockets are filled. Then level off ingredients at the top with a knife. It is easy to skimp with measuring spoons. Always make sure to fill measuring spoons right to the top.

2. **Excess:** Don't add extra liquid or dry ingredients to a recipe even if you have just a little left over. It does make a difference.

3. **Substitutions:** Always replace a liquid or dry ingredient you wish to omit with a similar product. Some spices can be omitted without altering the texture or quality of the recipe but it is always best to replace disliked flavors with an alternative to maintain full flavor.

4. **Baking:** Baked recipes should be positioned on the center of the middle rack in the oven. With the exception of bread, avoid baking more than one recipe at a time. Filling the oven space with several recipes on one rack or layered on several racks will alter the air circulation and heat distribution, therefore increasing the likelihood of burning or uneven baking.

5. **Bake Ware:** To avoid burning the bottom of cookies, muffins, biscuits, rolls, cakes or granola etc., only use bake ware that is advertised as "heavy duty." This would include bake ware made with stainless steel or heavy tin. Stone bake ware will also provides you with excellent results Look for these products in department stores, discount chains like Wal-Mart and kitchen specialty stores. You will probably have to pay more for the better quality but the results will more than pay you back for your investment. If you have to use the lighter, less expensive bake ware you may need to shorten the baking time or lower the temperature 25 degrees half way through the baking time.

6. **Study the Recipe:** Start by reading through the whole recipe in order to understand any unanticipated directions or to know if any "sub-recipes" need to be prepared ahead of time before beginning the main recipe, i.e. sour cream, cheese, mayonnaise etc.

Garbanzo Olive Salad
Italian Bread Sticks
Almond Cheesecake Delight
Fat-Free Italian Dressing
Tofu Lasagna

Italian At Its Best

Featuring

This dinner evokes the spirit of Italian cooking at its very best—with healthful sauces and "cheese" for the pasta, fresh vegetables, whole wheat garlic bread, and special desserts you won't forget.

TOFU LASAGNA

BASIC ITALIAN SAUCE:

2 T	Olive oil	1 tsp	Salt
1 med	Onion, chopped	14.5 oz	Tomato sauce w/herbs (3 cans)
½ sm	Bell pepper, chopped	6 oz	Tomato paste
2 lg	Garlic cloves, minced	6 oz	Water or "olive broth"
2 T	Sucanat® or honey	1 c	Burger-style crumbles
1 ½ T	Nutritional yeast flakes	2 to 4 c	Assortment of vegetables, ie sliced olives, mushrooms, fresh steamed spinach, grated carrots or zucchini
1 T	Dried minced onion		
2 ½ tsp	Italian seasoning		
2 tsp	Beef-style seasoning		

Sauté onions, bell pepper, and garlic in olive oil or water. Add seasonings, sauces, liquids and burger-style crumbles (may also use sausage flavored crumbles) and simmer 10 minutes. Prepare vegetables of choice, add to sauce or set aside as a separate layer during the assembling process. (See below.)

NOODLES:

It is not necessary to cook the noodles in this recipe. Just allow ½ inch spaces between the noodles when arranging them in the baking dish to provide enough room for the noodles to expand. May use whole grain or spinach noodles as desired but you may need to allow extra baking time.

RICOTTA-STYLE FILLING:

2 tubs	Water-packed tofu, extra firm	2 tsp	Basil, dried
3 T	Fresh lemon juice	2 tsp	Honey
2 ½ T	Olive oil, "extra virgin"	1 ½ tsp	Garlic powder
1 T	ENER-G® Egg Replacer	1 ¼ tsp	Salt

Press excess water out of tofu. Crumble tofu in a large bowl until it resembles ricotta cheese. Stir in remaining ingredients. Set aside (reserve ½ cup for top).

METHOD:

Prepare a 9 x 13 baking dish with cooking spray. Pour a thin layer of sauce in the bottom of the dish. Arrange thin layers of ingredients in this order: 1)Noodles 2)Filling 3)Sauce 4)Vegetables. Make 3 layers but end the third layer with sauce and sprinkle the reserved filling on top. Bake at 350°F, about 60 minutes. Garnish top with Parmesan and/or Mozzarella cheese (see page 51). Cook 10 more minutes until cheese is bubbly. Cool 10 minutes. Serve.

Note: I prefer using SoyCo® Lite & Less™ Parmesan Cheese Alternative.

Yield: 14 cups

NON-DAIRY PARMESAN CHEESE

MIX:

⅓ c	Nutritional yeast flakes	½ c	Ground almonds, w/o skins

ADD:

2 T	Soymilk powder, plain*	1 tsp	Garlic powder
2 tsp	Chicken-style seasoning (McKay's®)	1 tsp	Onion powder

COAT OR SPRAY EVENLY WITH:

2 tsp Fresh lemon juice mixed with 1 tsp water

Mix with hands until crumbs are very small. Toast on a cookie sheet at 200° F, stirring every 30 minutes until dry and crispy. Avoid browning. If desired, return toasted "parmesan cheese" to the blender and process until mixture resembles fine crumbs. Store in a closed container. Keeps for many weeks in the refrigerator.

* Better Than Milk™, Original is recommended for this recipe.

Yield: ¾ cup

MOZZARELLA "CHEESE"

1 c	Soymilk beverage, plain (or water)	4 tsp	Fresh lemon juice
1 c	Cooked rice, brown or white	1 ½ tsp	Salt
¾ c	Water-packed tofu, extra firm	1 tsp	Onion powder
½ c	Raw cashews, rinsed	¼ tsp	Garlic powder
4 T	Emes Kosher Jel® (plain)		

In a blender, combine all ingredients and process on high speed, stopping and stirring as necessary, until completely smooth and creamy (3 to 5 minutes). The sauce will heat up and appear "shiny" when completed. Pour into a container coated with cooking spray. Refrigerate 2 to 4 hours until set. Gently shake out to slice cheese.

Note: To shred cheese easily, freeze mixture at least 2 hours first. For a creamy sauce to pour over vegetables or noodles, do not refrigerate mixture after blending, but heat and serve immediately. Or, if using previously "set" leftover cheese, heat mixture slowly over low to medium heat, stirring frequently until melted.

Tip: May substitute cashews with slivered blanched almonds (w/o skins).

Yield: 3 cups

ANGEL HAIR GOURMET PASTA CASSEROLE

8 oz	Angel hair pasta, uncooked
1 ½ tsp	Olive oil
½ tsp	Onion salt (to taste)
10 ¾ oz	Tomato soup, condensed
2 c	Water-packed tofu, extra firm
¾ tsp	Salt
1 recipe	Soy Good Sour Cream (p.111)
2 c	Soy cheddar cheese, shredded
1 ½ c	Burger-style crumbles
1 ½ c	Onions, chopped
1 c	Green bell peppers, diced
½ c	Mushrooms, chopped
2 T	Olive oil
2 tsp	Beef-style seasoning
½ tsp	Garlic powder
2 T	Soy Parmesan cheese

Break angel hair pasta into 1-inch pieces and cook in salted water according to directions on the package. Drain and rinse pasta. Drizzle with 1 ½ tsp olive oil and season with onion salt. Set noodles and soup aside. Crumble tofu in a bowl and sprinkle with salt. Prepare sour cream recipe and add to tofu. Stir gently until well mixed. Shred cheese and set aside. In a large frying pan, sauté burger, onion, bell pepper and mushrooms in oil until vegetables are tender and burger is lightly browned. Sprinkle burger mixture with beef-style seasoning and garlic powder and mix well. Prepare a 9" x 11" casserole dish with cooking spray. Spread half of the noodle mixture evenly in the bottom of the dish. Next, sprinkle half of the burger mixture over the noodles. Then spread half of the sour cream/tofu mixture over the burger. Cover the sour cream/tofu mixture with half the can of tomato soup. Finally, sprinkle 1 cup shredded soy cheese over the soup. Repeat layers with remaining ingredients once more, except do not sprinkle the remaining cheese on top yet. Bake uncovered at 350° F, 35 minutes. Now sprinkle remaining soy cheese and soy Parmesan cheese on top, return to oven and bake 10 minutes more. Cool 10 to 15 minutes and when set, cut into squares and serve.

Yield: 12 cups

BETTER 'N MEATBALLS

1 pkg Morningstar Farms® Better 'n Burgers (4 patties per pkg)

Thaw burgers completely. Lightly oil or spray hands with cooking spray. Quarter the patties and re-shape each quarter into 1-inch balls. Arrange on a cookie sheet and bake at 350° F, 10 to 15 minutes. Serve with spaghetti.

Tip: For a quick & easy appetizer, try Better 'N Meatballs served with the Barbecue Sauce on page 164. Serve with fringed toothpicks.

Yield: 16 balls

SPAGHETTI FLORENTINE *with* BETTER 'N MEATBALLS

4 c	Fresh spinach, stems removed	¼ c	Black olives, sliced
1 c	Onions, chopped	¼ c	Mushrooms, sliced
2 med	Garlic cloves, minced	1 T	Nutritional yeast flakes
1 T	Olive oil	1 T	Brown sugar or Sucanat®
2 jars	Spaghetti sauce, vegan	1 tsp	Beef-style seasoning
1 c	Burger-style crumbles	16–18	Better 'n Meatballs (p. 52)

Chop spinach and steam or simmer in a small amount of water until tender. In a large pot, sauté onions and garlic in olive oil. Add spinach and remaining ingredients, except meatballs, and simmer 5 to 10 minutes. Serve sauce with spaghetti noodles and Better 'N Meatballs or Italian-style Meatless Balls (recipe following).

Yield: 10 cups

ITALIAN-STYLE GROUND MEATLESS BALLS

1 c	Vegetarian burger (or)	2 T	Nutritional yeast flakes
1 c	GranBurger® ground and rehydrated in ¾ c hot water	1T	Beef-Style seasoning
		2 tsp	Basil, dried
1 c	Mashed potatoes, cooked	1 tsp	Italian seasoning
1 c	Onions, minced	1 tsp	Garlic powder
1 c	Pecans or walnuts, finely chopped	1 c	Water-packed tofu, firm
½ c	Quick oats	1 c	Black olives
½ c	Wheat germ	2 T	Olive oil
1 env	Onion-mushroom soup mix, (Lipton®)	1 T	ENER-G® Egg Replacer
½ c	Seasoned bread crumbs or stuffing mix		

Combine Vegeburger (or GranBurger), mashed potatoes, onion, nuts, oats, wheat germ, soup mix, bread crumbs and seasonings. Set aside. In a blender, combine tofu, olives, oil and egg replacer and process until well mixed. Stir blender ingredients into dry ingredients. Shape into 1 inch balls and place on baking sheet prepared with cooking spray. Bake at 350° F, 35-40 minutes. Turn half way through cooking time to assure even browning. Serve with spaghetti sauce.

Yield: 5 cups / 40 to 60 balls

RIGATONI
with
PESTO SAUCE

12 oz	Rigatoni pasta, dry	¼ c	Pine nuts
1 c	Fresh basil leaves, packed	4 med	Garlic cloves
½ c	Soy Parmesan cheese, grated	⅛ tsp	Salt
⅓ c	Olive oil, "extra virgin"		

Cook pasta in salted water according to directions on package. To prepare pesto sauce, combine remaining ingredients in a blender and process on high speed until puréed. Drain and rinse pasta. Spoon pesto sauce over pasta and stir until evenly mixed. Reheat if necessary. If desired, garnish with additional Parmesan cheese before serving.

Variation: Substitute penne pasta for rigatoni. Pine nuts may be substituted with blanched slivered almonds, hazel nuts (without skins), or raw pumpkin seeds.

Yield: 7 cups

MAFALDA SURPRISE
(Instead of Spaghetti)

4 c	Mafalda pasta, uncooked	½ c	Vegetarian burger
1 c	Fresh mushrooms, sliced	1 T	Nutritional yeast flakes
½ c	Onions, chopped	1 tsp	Brown sugar or Sucanat®
1 lg	Garlic clove, minced	2 c	Soy cheddar cheese, shredded (SoyaKass®)
2 tsp	Olive oil		
1 jar	Spaghetti sauce (26 oz)	(opt)	Soy Parmesan cheese, grated

Cook pasta in salted water according to directions. While pasta is cooking, sauté mushrooms, onions, and garlic in olive oil until tender. Add spaghetti sauce, burger, yeast flakes, and sweetener. Simmer, covered, 5 to 10 minutes. Drain pasta when tender, rinse and toss with a little olive oil. For each serving, spoon spaghetti sauce over the pasta and sprinkle about ¼ cup shredded soy cheddar cheese over the sauce. If desired, garnish with soy Parmesan cheese also. Serve as cheese softens or melts.

Note: Mafalda is "mini lasagna" and very appealing when served this way.

Yield: 12 cups

BAKED EGGPLANT PARMESAN

1 lg	Eggplant	½ tsp	Marjoram, ground
2 c	Corn bread stuffing mix	½ tsp	Thyme, dried
½ tsp	Paprika	½ tsp	Salt
½ tsp	Onion powder	½ c	Garbanzo Mayonnaise (see recipe below)
½ tsp	Garlic salt		

Wash eggplant (peeling is optional). Slice eggplant into ½ inch thick pieces. In a blender, process stuffing mix and spices to make fine crumbs. Coat both sides of eggplant with Garbanzo Mayonnaise (see recipe below) and then dip into the corn bread stuffing mixture. Prepare a baking sheet with cooking spray. Spread eggplant out evenly and bake at 375° F, at least 20 minutes. Slices need to be turned to have them evenly browned. Place a single layer of eggplant slightly overlapping in a casserole dish. Pour Italian sauce (page 50) or spaghetti sauce over center strip of eggplants. Garnish with shredded Mozzarella and Parmesan cheeses (recipes on page 51). If available, you may prefer using SoyCo® Lite & Less™ "Grated Parmesan Cheese Alternative." Bake at 350° F, 10 to 15 minutes until sauce is bubbly. Serve while hot.

Yield: 18 to 20 slices

GARBANZO MAYONNAISE

2 c	Water	1 tsp	Salt
½ c	Raw cashews, rinsed well	½ tsp	Onion salt
6 T	Garbanzo flour	½ tsp	Garlic powder
¼ c	Fresh lemon juice	2 T	Instant Clear Jel®
4 tsp	Apple juice, frozen concentrate		

In a blender, combine all ingredients except Instant Clear Jel®. Process until very smooth. While blender is running, add Clear Jel® 1 tablespoon at a time through the lid spout to thicken mayonnaise. Use the same day if possible. The thickened state is temporary (about 6 hours). For a long-term effect, omit Instant Clear Jel® and instead use 2 to 2 ½ T cornstarch and cook, stirring constantly until thickened. Refrigerate.

Yield: 2 ½ cups

CARROTS WITH ORANGE SAUCE

1 lb	Fresh carrots	⅓ c	Water
½ c	Pineapple juice	1 T	Cornstarch
3 T	Honey or ¼ c fructose, granular	⅛ tsp	Salt
3 T	Frozen orange juice, concentrate		

Julienne carrots or slice diagonally. Microwave, steam or boil carrots in a small amount of water. Carrots should remain crisp-tender for improved flavor and color. In a saucepan, combine the pineapple juice, sweetener and orange juice concentrate. Mix water with the cornstarch and salt and stir until dissolved. Add to the saucepan and bring to a boil stirring constantly. Cook until thickened and clear. Pour orange sauce over carrots and serve.

Yield: 4 cups

BROCCOLI IN LEMON SAUCE

Prepare lemon sauce and bell pepper garnish.

LEMON SAUCE:

2 T	Oil	1 T	Fresh lemon juice
1 T	All purpose flour	½ tsp	Lemon zest, grated
½ c	Soymilk beverage, plain (Better Than Milk™ Original)	¼ tsp	Salt

Combine oil and flour in a small saucepan. Blend well. Add remaining ingredients. Cook over medium heat, stirring constantly, until thickened.

Note: For a creamier sauce, prepare powdered soymilk in double strength proportions of powder and water.

BELL PEPPER GARNISH:

⅛ c	Red bell pepper, slivered	1 tsp	Fresh lemon juice
1 tsp	Oil		

Sauté peppers in oil and lemon juice about 2 minutes. Set aside.

STEAMED BROCCOLI:

1 lb Fresh broccoli spears

Steam or microwave broccoli. Avoid overcooking to retain flavor and color. Pour lemon sauce over broccoli and garnish with sautéed red bell pepper.

Yield: 6 cups

GARBANZO-OLIVE SALAD

Romaine lettuce
Fresh spinach leaves
Canned garbanzos
Black olives
Cherry tomatoes
Carrots
Bell peppers
Red onion rings
Artichokes, canned
Avocado
Sunflower seeds
Soy Feta Cheese
Alfalfa sprouts
Croutons

Combine any of the above ingredients to your own preference. Serve with "Fat Free" or "Lite" Italian Dressing (recipes following).

Yield: Variable

SPINACH & PASTA SALAD

1 c	Spiral or bow tie pasta		1 c	Artichoke hearts (opt)
8 c	Fresh spinach, rinsed		2 T	Fresh cilantro, snipped
1 c	Red cabbage, finely sliced		1 c	Fat-Free Italian Dressing (see below)
1 c	Green onion, sliced			

Cook pasta according to directions, rinse and chill. Break spinach leaves and remove any large stems. Chop sliced cabbage into 1-inch pieces. Slice green onion stems diagonally into 1-inch pieces. Add remaining ingredients and toss lightly.

Yield: 12 cups

"FAT-FREE" ITALIAN DRESSING

Add to one 1.05 oz package Good Seasons® "Fat-Free" Italian Dressing Mix:

¼ c	Fresh lemon juice		6 T	Pineapple juice
2 T	Frozen apple juice, concentrate		⅓ c	Water

Mix together in a cruet or a container with a tight fitting lid. Shake well. Refrigerate 30 minutes before using. Shake again before serving.

Variation: For a stronger Italian flavor, decrease water to ¼ cup.

Yield: 1 ⅛ cups

"LITE" ITALIAN DRESSING

Add to one 0.7 oz package of Good Seasons® "Lite" Italian dressing mix:

3 T	Fresh lemon juice	⅓ c	Water (+ 2 T opt)
3 T	Pineapple juice, concentrate	¼ c	Olive oil, "light"

Mix together in a cruet or a container with a tight fitting lid. (Add an additional 2 T of water if you prefer a thinner and milder dressing.) Shake well and refrigerate. Shake again before serving.

Yield: 1 cup

"LOW-FAT" CREAMY ITALIAN DRESSING

Add to one 0.7 oz package of Good Seasons® Italian dressing mix:

1 c	Mori-Nu® Tofu, firm	½ tsp	Garlic & Herb seasoning (McCormick® "salt free")
½ c	Pineapple juice, unsweetened	¼ tsp	Salt
2 T	Olive oil, "light"	⅛ tsp	Citric acid, rounded
2 T	Soy parmesan cheese (opt)		

Combine all ingredients in a blender and process until well mixed.

Yield: 1 cup

RASPBERRY VINAIGRETTE

Add to one 1.05 oz package Good Seasons® "Fat-Free" Italian Dressing Mix:

½ c	Water	¼ c	White grape / raspberry (frozen juice concentrate)
¼ c	Fresh lemon juice		

Mix together in a cruet or a container with a tight fitting lid. Shake well. Store refrigerated up to 2 weeks.

Yield: 1 cup

MINESTRONE SOUP

1 c	Onions, chopped	1 tsp	Onion powder
½ c	Celery, sliced	½ tsp	Coriander, ground
2 med	Garlic cloves, minced	⅛ tsp	Oregano, dried (flakes)
1 T	Olive oil	1 sm	Bay leaf
6 c	Water	1 ½ c	Kidney or red beans, canned
1 T	Chicken-style seasoning	2 c	Diced tomatoes, canned
2 tsp	Basil, (or) 2 T fresh basil	¾ c	Macaroni, elbow or shell
1 ½ tsp	Lawry's® Seasoned Salt	2 c	Zucchini, sliced or quartered
1 ½ tsp	Sucanat®, sweetener	1 c	Carrots, sliced

In a large saucepan, sauté onion, celery and garlic in oil until tender. Add water, seasonings and beans. Bring to a boil. Lower heat, cover and simmer about 20 minutes. Add tomatoes and macaroni, cover and simmer about 10 minutes. Add zucchini and carrots and simmer 5 to 10 minutes more or until pasta and vegetables are tender. Remove bay leaf before serving.

Yield: 14 cups

ITALIAN BREAD STICKS

7 oz	Warm water	1 c	Unbleached white flour
⅔ c	Raw cashews, rinsed	½ tsp	Italian seasonings, (opt)
1 T	Olive oil	½ tsp	Salt
1 T	Active yeast, rapid-rise	1 tsp	Garlic purée, (mixed in 1 T water)
1 T	Honey		
1 c	Whole-wheat pastry flour	1 T	Sesame seeds

In a blender, combine water, cashews, and oil and process on high speed until smooth and creamy. Pour blended mixture into a bowl and stir in yeast and honey. Wait 5 minutes. In a separate bowl, combine flours, Italian seasoning (opt) and salt. Pour the blender mixture into the flour and stir until dough forms. Knead lightly. Pinch off pieces of dough (about ¼ c) and roll between hands to form a long thin roll about ½ inch thick. Prepare a cookie sheet with cooking spray and lay each bread sticks down 1 inch apart. Twist each bread stick into desired shape. Lightly brush with warm water (or opt garlic water) and sprinkle with sesame seeds and pat into dough gently. Pre-heat oven to 350° F. Let rise 10 minutes or until double in size. Bake 15 to 20 minutes or until golden brown, light and crispy.

Yield: 1 dozen

GARLIC BREAD

Spread garlic butter (recipes below) generously on fresh whole grain French bread. If desired, sprinkle with additional granulated garlic powder and fresh or dried herbs of choice. Wrap with foil and bake at 400° F, 15 minutes until warm and moist. For a crispy crust, open foil at the top and bake an additional 5 minutes.

Yield: 16-inch loaf

GARLIC BUTTER

1 c	Cold water	1 T	Emes Kosher Jel® (plain)
¼ c	Yellow corn meal	1 T	Cooked carrot (opt for color)
½ c	Mori-Nu® Tofu, extra firm	2 tsp	Garlic powder
½ c	Warm water	1 tsp	Honey
¼ c	Almonds	1 tsp	Imitation butter flavored salt
3 T	Natural Butter Flavor, vegan (Spicery Shoppe®)	½ tsp	Salt
2 T	Olive oil, "light"	pinch	Citric acid

Combine cold water and corn meal in a small saucepan and bring to a boil stirring constantly. Reduce heat to low, cover and simmer 10 minutes. Refrigerate until completely cool and "set." In a blender, combine water, almonds, butter flavoring, oil and Emes®. Process on high speed until no longer "gritty." Spoon chilled corn meal mush into the blender mixture and all remaining ingredients and process until smooth and creamy. Bits of carrot should not be visible. Refrigerate several hours before serving until "butter" thickens to a spreadable consistency.

Yield: 3 cups

QUICK & EASY GARLIC BUTTER

10 oz	Spectrum® Naturals, Spread (or 8 oz Smart Balance® "Light")	1 tsp	Garlic powder (or 2 tsp garlic purée)
(opt)	Salt to taste (suggest ⅛ to ¼ tsp)		

Combine ingredients and stir until well mixed. Spread on bread as needed and wrap loaf in foil. Bake at 400° F, 15 minutes. For a crispy crust, open foil at the top and bake an additional 5 minutes.

Yield: 1 ¼ cup

ITALIAN-STYLE PIZZA

CORN MEAL CRUST:

1 T	Active dry yeast	1 tsp	Italian seasoning (opt)
1 T	Honey or brown sugar	2 T	Vital wheat gluten
1 ¼ c	Warm water	¾ c	Yellow corn meal
1 ½ T	Olive oil	2 c	Unbleached white flour
1 tsp	Salt	½ c	Whole-wheat flour

Dissolve yeast and honey in water. Yeast should bubble in 5 to 10 minutes. When ready, add oil, salt and (opt) Italian seasoning. Beat in gluten flour by hand. Stir in cornmeal. Add flours gradually and with oiled hands knead dough gently forming dough into a ball. Place in oiled bowl and let rise 20 to 30 minutes until double. Punch down and knead briefly. Divide dough into two equal parts. Prepare two pizza pans with cooking spray and sprinkle with cornmeal. Using a lightly floured rolling pin, roll dough out to 1 cm thick and ½ inch wider than the pizza pan. Transfer to pizza pan and make the dough thicker around the border to form an edge.

ITALIAN PIZZA SAUCE:

1 tsp	Garlic, purée	½ tsp	Onion powder
1 T	Olive oil	½ tsp	Parsley, dried flakes
1 can	Italian plum tomatoes (14 oz)	¼ tsp	Basil, dried
6 oz	Hunt's® tomato paste	½ tsp	Salt
1 ½ tsp	Sucanat®, sweetener	2 tsp	Soy Parmesan cheese (SoyCo® "Lite & Less")
¾ tsp	Oregano, ground		

Sauté garlic in oil. Add tomatoes with juice and mash until smooth. Stir in tomato paste. Add remaining ingredients and simmer 15 minutes.

METHOD:

Spoon pizza sauce over entire crust. For added flavor, sprinkle additional commercial pizza seasonings over sauce. Cover with shredded soy mozzarella cheese, your choice of favorite vegetable toppings and SoyCo® Lite & Less™ "Grated Parmesan Cheese Alternative." Bake at 450° F, 10 minutes. Reduce heat to 375° F, (400° F if using a round baking stone) and continue baking 15 to 20 minutes until crust is lightly browned and toppings are cooked.

Note: When short on time, may substitute Italian Pizza Sauce with your favorite commercial brand pizza sauce.

Yield: (2) 12-inch pizzas

ONE OF A KIND MINI PIZZAS

Whole-wheat pita bread, uncut
Garlic purée (opt)
Pizza sauce
Pizza seasoning
Soy Parmesan cheese, grated
Soy mozzarella cheese, (see page 51)
Sausage-style crumbles (opt)
Vegetables toppings of choice (olives, mushrooms, onions, tomatoes, green peppers etc.)
Parsley, dried

Personalize each mini pizza with choice of above ingredients. Turn pita bread up side down and if desired, spread with a thin layer of garlic before covering "crust" with pizza sauce. Season with pizza seasoning or any vegetable herb seasoning mix. Sprinkle with mozzarella and Parmesan cheese, vegan crumbles and add veggies of choice. Cover with additional mozzarella and/or parmesan cheese. Garnish with parsley. Arrange pizzas on a cookie sheet or pizza stone and bake at 375° F, 15 to 20 minutes or until crust is crispy and veggies are tender.

Variation: Replace pita bread with whole-wheat English muffins.

Yield: Variable

HOT ITALIAN OPEN FACED SUB SANDWICH

1	Whole-wheat hoagie bun	2 T	Black olives, sliced (opt)
1	Garlic clove, crushed (puréed)	¼ c	Soy cheese, shredded
½ c	Spaghetti or pizza sauce	1 tsp	Soy Parmesan cheese, grated

Split bun. Spread a thin layer of garlic over inside of bun. Cover with sauce, olives and cheeses. Bake open faced on a cookie sheet at 350° F, 10 to 15 minutes or until cheese is bubbly.

Yield: (2) open faced buns

CARROT CAKE

1 ½ c	Sucanat® or fructose, granular	2 c	Whole-wheat pastry flour
8 oz	Canned crushed pineapple, (undrained)	1 c	Unbleached white flour
		1 ½ T	ENER-G® Baking Powder
½ c	Oil	1 ½ T	ENER-G® Baking Soda
3 c	Carrots, finely grated	1 tsp	Salt
¼ c	Grated coconut, unsweetened	1 tsp	Coriander, ground
½ c	Water	¼ tsp	Cardamom, ground (heaping)
2 tsp	Vanilla extract	½ tsp	Cinnamon, ground (heaping)
1 c	Raisins	½ c	Walnuts, chopped (opt)

In a large bowl, combine sweetener of choice, crushed pineapple and oil, and mix together well until the sweetener is completely dissolved. Add carrots, coconut, water, vanilla and raisins and mix until well blended. In a separate bowl, combine remaining ingredients. Then add gradually to the wet ingredients, mixing until well blended. Prepare 2 cake pans or one oblong baking pan with cooking spray and lightly flour before adding batter. Bake at 350° F, 30 to 35 minutes if using cake pans or 45 to 55 minutes for the oblong pan. Cool. Cover with frosting of choice. (See recipes following.)

Note: If using the traditional form of baking powder and baking soda, reduce amount to 2 tsp (each) or use 1 T baking powder and 1 tsp baking soda.

Yield: 9 x 13 sheet cake (or) two 9-inch round cakes

"BETTER THAN CREAM CHEESE" FROSTING

12 oz	Soy cream cheese, plain (Tofutti®)	1 ½ tsp	Instant Clear Jel® (food thickener)
6 T	Powdered sugar		
3 T	Vanilla, powdered *	⅓ c	Pecans, chopped

Using an electric beater, whip cream cheese with sugar and vanilla until smooth and fluffy. Sprinkle the Clear Jel® into the mixture while beating on medium speed and continue 15 seconds until thickened. Stir in nuts. Spread on completely cooled cake. May garnish with additional pecans.

* May substitute powdered vanilla with 1 T natural vanilla flavoring.

Note: Double recipe to frost a 9-inch layered cake.

Yield: 2 cups (scant)

ORANGE FLUFF
TOFU WHIPPED TOPPING

1 box	Mori-Nu® Tofu, extra firm (12.3 oz)	1 tsp	Natural vanilla flavoring
⅓ c	Orange juice, concentrate	¼ tsp	Salt
⅓ c	Water	2 T	Instant Clear Jel®
¼ c	Powdered sugar		(instant food thickener)

In a blender, combine all ingredients except Instant Clear Jel®. Process until smooth and creamy. Set the blender on medium speed, remove the lid spout and add Clear Jel® one tablespoon at a time until thickened. Chill before spreading on cake. May garnish with choice of sliced orange wedges, orange twists or grated orange peel and fresh mint leaves.

Note: Double recipe to cover a layered cake.

Yield: Approx 2 cups

PISTACHIO ICE CREAM

2 c	Soymilk creamer, plain (Silk®)	½ tsp	Vanilla extract
1 c	Soymilk beverage, vanilla	½ tsp	Almond extract
1 c	Better Than Milk™ powder, plain	6 drops	Green food coloring
¼ c	Fructose, granular	1 c	Pistachios, unsalted, chopped

In a blender, combine all ingredients except nuts and process until creamy. Pour mixture into an ice cream maker and operate according to directions. (If desired, may double recipe to fit a larger ice cream maker.) Add nuts to the ice cream when nearly set or during the last 5 minutes of churning.

Yield: 1 quart

FROZEN FRUIT
ICE CREAM

Freeze 4 cups fresh or canned fruit, in any combination. In a blender, process the frozen fruit with ½ cup Better Than Milk™ "Original" soymilk powder. Add a small amount of fruit juice concentrate, only if necessary to assist in the blending process. For a sweeter taste, add fructose or a few drops of Stevia extract. Serve at once as soft ice cream or return to the freezer several hours for firmer ice cream. Scoop up, garnish with toppings and serve immediately.

Toppings: Sprinkle with grated coconut, chopped nuts, carob chips, sunflower seeds, or fresh chopped fruit for added flavor.

Yield: 3 cups

ALMOND CHEESECAKE DELIGHT

CRUST:

1 c	Freshly ground pecans	⅛ tsp	Salt
1 c	Graham cracker crumbs	3 T	Water
3 T	Vital wheat gluten (Do-Pep®)		

Process raw pecans in a food processor or blender until finely ground. Combine pecans with remaining ingredients. Work mixture with hands until the water has evenly moistened the dry ingredients and mixture is slightly sticky. Pour into an 8-inch pie pan or spring form mold and press mixture out to edges evenly. Bake 10 minutes at 325° F. Set aside to cool.

FILLING:

½ c	Water	¼ c	Unbleached white flour
½ c	White grape/peach juice, (frozen juice concentrate)	2 ½ T	Emes Kosher Jel® (plain)
		2 T	Honey, fructose or sugar
½ c	Slivered almonds, (w/o skins)	1 T	Fresh lemon juice
1 c	Water-packed tofu, extra firm	1 T	Natural vanilla, flavoring
1 c	Cooked white rice, packed	⅛ tsp	Salt
¼ c	Better Than Milk™ powder		

Combine water, juice (Welch's® 100%), and almonds in a blender and process on high speed until almonds are completely liquefied and mixture does not taste "gritty." Add remaining ingredients and process until smooth and creamy. It may be necessary to stop and stir mixture as needed during processing. Pour blender ingredients into a saucepan and heat over med/low stirring constantly until thickened. Pour mixture into a pre-baked and cooled crust. Refrigerate 2 to 3 hours until set. Serve with berry topping of choice. (Recipes follow.)

Yield: 4 cups

BLUEBERRY TOPPING

3 c	Blueberries (fresh or frozen)	¼ c	White grape juice (frozen concentrate)
¼ c	FruitSource® (or honey)	1 ½ T	Cornstarch

Bring 2 c blueberries and FruitSource® or honey to a boil in a heavy saucepan. Mix the (Welch's® 100%) white grape juice and cornstarch together and stir until dissolved. Pour the cornstarch-juice mixture into the boiling berries, stirring constantly. Reduce heat, continue stirring and simmer until mixture is thickened and clear. Remove from heat. Stir in remaining blueberries. Chill.

Yield: 3 cups

STRAWBERRY-RASPBERRY TOPPING

1 c	Birds Eye® frozen raspberries	1 T	Cornstarch
¼ c	White grape juice, frozen concentrate	2 c	Fresh strawberries
3 T	FruitSource® (or 2 T honey)		

Combine thawed raspberries, un-drained, (Welch's® 100%) white grape juice, FruitSource® and cornstarch in a blender and process until smooth. Strain the puréed mixture through a sieve to remove seeds. Pour into a saucepan and simmer, stirring constantly until thick and clear. Cool. Slice strawberries and stir into mixture. Refrigerate until needed.

Yield: 3 cups

LEMON CUSTARD PIE

¾ c	Pineapple chunks	3 T	Fresh lemon juice
½ c	Water	2 c	Pineapple juice
½ c	Raw cashews, rinsed	⅓ c	Fructose, granular
½ c	Minute® Tapioca	1 tsp	Natural vanilla, flavoring
¼ c	White grape/peach juice (frozen juice concentrate)	¼ tsp	Lemon zest
		⅛ tsp	Salt
¼ c	Soymilk powder, plain (Better Than Milk™ Original)	pinch	Turmeric, ground

In a blender, combine pineapple chunks, water, cashews, tapioca, juice concentrate, milk powder, and lemon juice. Process on high speed until smooth and creamy. Add remaining ingredients and blend again until well mixed. Pour mixture into a heavy non-stick sauce pan or double boiler pan and bring to a boil stirring constantly. Reduce heat slightly and simmer until thick and tapioca dissolves. Cool 5 minutes. Pour into a "9-inch" graham cracker or granola crust. Refrigerate until set, about 6 hours. Garnish with lightly toasted shredded coconut before serving if desired.

Yield: 9-inch pie

LEMON CHIFFON PIE

½ c	Water	2 c	Pineapple juice
½ c	Raw cashews, rinsed	⅓ c	Fructose, granular
½ c	Pineapple chunks	3 T	Fresh lemon juice
¼ c	White grape/peach juice (frozen juice concentrate)	2 tsp	Natural vanilla, flavoring
¼ c	Soymilk powder, plain (Better Than Milk™ Original)	½ tsp	Lemon zest, grated
3 T	Emes Kosher Jel® (plain)	⅛ tsp	Salt
		pinch	Turmeric, ground

In a blender, combine water, cashews, pineapple chunks, juice concentrate, milk powder and Emes®. Process until completely smooth and creamy. Add remaining ingredients and blend again until well mixed. Pour mixture into a saucepan and simmer, stirring constantly until yellow color develops. Cool to lukewarm. Fill a "9-inch" graham cracker or granola crust half full, transfer crust to your refrigerator shelf and fill to the top with remaining filling. (This procedure will avoid spilling since the filling is in a very liquid form before it is chilled and set.) Refrigerate until set, about 6 hours. Garnish with lightly toasted shredded coconut or fresh mint leaves if desired.

Yield: 9-inch pie

GRANOLA PIE CRUST

2 c	Granola	2 T	Water (more or less as needed)
1 T	Unbleached white flour		

In a blender, combine granola and flour and grind until only fine crumbs are left. Moisten with water, pour into a pie pan and pat into shape.

Yield: 1 ½ cups

FROSTED GRAPES

Wash and freeze red seedless grapes. Cut into clusters and arrange on a decorative platter. Serve immediately before grapes lose the "frosty look."

Yield: Variable

Sweetheart's Banquet

Featuring

French Cuisine. Prepare a candlelight dinner for two, ideal for any special occasion. Show your valentine how much you care by sharing a beautifully presented meal and by expressing your concern for the health of the one you love.

OAT CRÊPES NON-DAIRY BATTER

2 c	Soymilk beverage, plain	1 T	Oil
¾ c	Whole-wheat pastry flour	1 tsp	Honey
¾ c	Quick oats	½ tsp	Salt
1 T	ENER-G® Egg Replacer		

Combine all ingredients in a blender and process until smooth. Let stand 10 minutes. Cook according to electric crêpe pan instructions. Or, coat a 10-inch non-stick frying pan with no-stick cooking spray. Preheat pan over med-hi heat. Remove pan from heat and pour a scant ⅓ cup batter into the middle of the pan. Quickly tilt the pan in a circular motion until the batter evenly forms an 8-inch crêpe. Return the pan to the heat for about 1 minute or until the bottom of the crêpe is lightly browned. Flip the crêpe over and lightly brown the other side for about 30 seconds.

Yield: 12 crêpes

ASPARAGUS-ALMOND CRÊPES

5 c	Frozen asparagus "cuts" or "tips"	1 T	Onion powder
1 med	Onion, chopped	1 T	Nutritional yeast flakes
½ c	Water	1 tsp	Salt
4 c	Almond cream (see page 71)	1 T	Fresh lemon juice
½ c	Unbleached white flour	1 rec	Oat Crêpes (see above)
2 T	Chicken-style seasoning	dash	Paprika to garnish

Simmer asparagus and onions in water for 10 minutes or until onions are translucent. Meanwhile, prepare almond cream. Combine almond cream, flour, seasonings, and lemon juice and mix together well. Reserve ½ cup cream sauce and set aside to be used later for topping. Pour remaining cream sauce into cooked asparagus, bring to a boil and cook 1 or 2 minutes until thick. Prepare crêpes. Spoon filling into crêpes and roll up. Place seam side down in a baking dish prepared with cooking spray. Cook reserved ½ cup cream sauce until thick. Pour sauce down center of crêpes. Garnish with paprika and serve.

Yield: 12 crêpes

ALMOND CREAM

3 ½ c	Water	1 tsp	Vanilla extract
⅔ c	Blanched almonds (w/o skins)	¼ tsp	Salt

In a blender, combine a portion of the water to cover almonds (about 1 cup) and process until thoroughly liquefied. Add remaining water, (plus or minus to make a total volume of 4 cups), vanilla and salt and blend well.

Yield: 4 cups

SPINACH-POTATO CRÊPES

1 c	Cooked fresh spinach	½ tsp	Savory, dried
1 c	Raw shredded potatoes	½ tsp	Chicken-style seasoning
½ c	Onions, chopped	½ c	Jack Cheese Sauce
1 clove	Garlic, minced	1 rec	Oat Crêpes (see page 70)
2 T	Olive oil	Dash	Paprika to garnish
1 tsp	Seasoned salt		

Drain cooked spinach, squeeze out excess liquid, chop finely and set aside. Shred and rinse potatoes. Drain well. Using a non-stick frying pan, sauté potatoes, onions, and garlic in oil. While the vegetables are cooking, add seasoned salt, savory and chicken flavored seasoning. When vegetables are tender, add spinach and continue cooking over med-lo heat 5 minutes longer. Stir in ½ cup cheese sauce (see recipe below) and mix until well blended. Prepare crêpes. Spoon filling into crêpes and roll up. Place seam side down in an oblong baking dish prepared with cooking spray. Garnish with additional cheese sauce and paprika. Serve immediately.

Variation: If preferred, replace spinach with chopped broccoli florets.

Yield: 12 crêpes

JACK CHEESE SAUCE

1 c	Water	1 ½ T	Fresh lemon juice
1 c	Cooked brown or white rice	1 ½ tsp	Salt
½ c	Raw cashews, rinsed	1 tsp	Onion powder
1 T	Nutritional yeast flakes	¼ tsp	Garlic powder

In a blender, combine water, rice and cashews and process until smooth and creamy. Add remaining ingredients and blend well.

Yield: 2 cups

"CHICKEN"- MUSHROOM CRÊPES

3 c	Creamy Mushroom Sauce	2 med	Garlic cloves, minced
¾ c	Sour Cream Supreme	½ tsp	Beef-style seasoning
2 T	Olive oil	½ c	Jicama, julienned
2 c	Mock chicken, diced *	1 rec	Oat Crêpes (see page 70)
1 c	Spanish onions, chopped	dash	Paprika, to garnish
1 c	Fresh mushrooms, sliced		

Prepare Mushroom Sauce and Sour Cream Supreme (recipes following) and set aside. Sauté "chicken," onions, mushrooms, garlic and beef-style seasoning together in olive oil until vegetables are tender. Combine mushroom sauce and sour cream. Pour 2 ½ cups sauce mixture over mock chicken and vegetables. Reserve remaining sauce and set aside. Add jicama and stir all together well. Prepare crêpes. Spoon filling into crêpes and roll up. Place seam side down in an oblong baking dish prepared with cooking spray. Pour reserved mushroom sauce down center of crêpes. Cover with foil and bake at 325° F, 10 to 15 minutes. Garnish with paprika before serving.

* ***Note:*** I recommend using Worthington® "Chic-Ketts™" available in the frozen foods section of some health food stores.

Yield: 12 crêpes

CREAMY MUSHROOM SAUCE

1 ½ c	Onions, chopped	⅔ c	Unbleached white flour
2 T	Olive oil	⅓ c	Soymilk powder, plain *
2 c	Fresh mushrooms	2 tsp	Nutritional yeast flakes
1 c	Water	2 tsp	Chicken-style seasoning
¼ tsp	Onion salt	1 ½ tsp	Salt
3 c	Water	½ tsp	Basil, dried

Sauté onions in oil until golden. Coarse chop mushrooms and add to the onions with (1 cup) water and onion salt and simmer until mushrooms are tender. Set aside 1 cup sautéed mushrooms. In a blender, combine (3 cups) water, flour, milk powder, and seasonings and process until smooth and creamy. Add reserved 1 cup mushrooms to the blender and "flash blend" ingredients together a few times. Pour blender ingredients into a saucepan and bring to a boil stirring constantly until thickened. Stir remaining onion and mushroom mixture into sauce and mix all together well.

****Note:*** Better Than Milk™ "Original" is the recommended product.

Yield: 4 cups

SOUR CREAM SUPREME

1 ¼ c	Mori-Nu® Tofu, firm (10.5 oz)	1 tsp	Honey
¼ c	Sunflower oil or extra light olive oil	½ tsp	Salt
2 ½ T	Fresh lemon juice		

Process all ingredients in a blender until smooth and creamy.

Yield: 1 ½ cups

CHAMPAGNE "CHICKEN"

1 ½ c	Mock chicken, chunks*	2 ½ c	Fresh mushrooms, sliced
1 or 2 T	Olive oil		

Tear "chicken" into large bite size pieces. Sauté "chicken" in oil until nicely browned. Add mushrooms and sauté until tender.

GRAVY:

3 c	Water	3 T	Bragg® Liquid Aminos
½ c	Raw cashews, rinsed	1 ½ T	Nutritional yeast flakes
⅓ c	Soymilk powder, plain**	1 T	Onion powder
3 T	Cornstarch	1 T	Chicken-style seasoning

In a blender, process cashews with a portion of the water (1 cup) until very smooth. Add remaining water and other ingredients and continue blending until thoroughly mixed. Pour over mock chicken and mushroom mixture and simmer until thickened.

CHAMPAGNE:

¼ c Non-alcoholic champagne (Catawba®)

Pour Catawba® into gravy/chicken mixture and mix well. Serve hot with rice.

* I recommend using Worthington® "Chic-Ketts™" available in the frozen food section of some health food stores.

** Better Than Milk™ "Soy Original" is the recommended product.

Yield: 8 cups

GREEN BEANS ALMONDINE

1 lb	Fresh or frozen green beans	1 T	Nutritional yeast flakes
(opt)	Salt or garlic salt to taste	1 T	Sesame seeds
⅓ c	Sliced or slivered almonds		

Snap or French cut green beans. Simmer, covered, in a large skillet with a small amount of water until tender. Sprinkle lightly with salt if desired. Meanwhile, prepare almonds by placing them on a cookie sheet in the oven at 250° F, and roast until lightly toasted. Or, heat in a frying pan without oil over med-lo heat, stirring often until lightly browned. Watch carefully to prevent burning. When beans have completed cooking, add yeast to water remaining in the skillet and stir until dissolved. Add more water if necessary until it has the appearance of melted butter. Spoon green beans into a shallow serving dish and garnish with almonds and sesame seeds.

Yield: 4 cups

RICE-BARLEY PILAF

3 c	Water	¼ c	Wheat germ, toasted
1 c	Brown rice	½ tsp	Beef-style seasoning
1 tsp	Salt	½ tsp	Chicken-style seasoning
⅓ c	Barley, whole grain	2 T	Fresh parsley, snipped
1 c	Onions, finely chopped	⅓ c	Sliced almonds, lightly toasted
1 c	Celery, finely chopped	2 T	Sesame seeds, toasted
1 c	Carrots, shredded	(opt)	Soy Parmesan cheese, grated*
2 T	Olive oil		

In a medium saucepan, bring water to boiling. Add rice and salt; return to boiling. Reduce heat, cover and simmer 15 minutes. Then add barley to the rice and continue cooking 15 minutes more. Do not drain. Meanwhile, sauté onions, celery, and carrots in olive oil until tender. Combine the rice-barley mixture and sautéed vegetables with wheat germ, and the beef and chicken-style seasonings. Pour into a large casserole dish coated with cooking spray. Bake uncovered at 350° F, 20 minutes or until grains are tender and lightly browned. Fluff with a fork and stir in parsley. Garnish with almonds, sesame seeds, and soy Parmesan cheese for added flavor.

****Note:*** "SoyCo® Lite & Less™ Grated Parmesan Cheese Alternative" is the recommended product.

Yield: 6 cups

FRENCH ONION SOUP

2 lg	Spanish onions, sliced	2 T	Bragg® Liquid Aminos
3 T	Olive oil	1 env	Onion soup mix, (Lipton®)
4 c	Water	2 T	Beef-style seasoning
½ c	Ginger ale, soft drink	1 T	Unbleached white flour
½ tsp	Worcestershire sauce (vegetarian brand)	1 rec	Alpine cheese (see below)

In a saucepan, sauté onions in oil until golden brown. Reserve one cup of water. Pour remaining water and liquid ingredients into the saucepan. Combine the reserved water with the soup mix and beef-style seasoning to make a broth and set aside. Brown the flour in a small dry frying pan. Cool. Add flour to the broth mixture and stir until dissolved. Slowly pour broth into the saucepan with the onions and simmer 5 minutes stirring frequently until thoroughly blended. Fill soup mugs and top with a slice of toasted French bread and Alpine Cheese and broil 1 to 2 minutes until cheese is bubbly. Or, toast bread on a cookie sheet. Remove from oven and place a slice of Alpine cheese over bread. Return to oven and bake at 350° F, 5 minutes or until cheese is soft and bubbly. Drop one slice of bread into each bowl and serve immediately.

Yield: 7 cups

ALPINE CHEESE

1 c	Water	1 T	Nutritional yeast flakes
1 c	Cooked white or brown rice	1 T	Fresh lemon juice
½ c	Raw cashews, rinsed	1 ½ tsp	Salt
½ c	Ginger ale, soft drink	1 tsp	Onion powder
3 T	Emes Kosher Jel® (plain)	¼ tsp	Garlic powder

In a blender, combine water, rice, cashews, ginger ale and Emes Kosher Jel® and process on high speed until smooth and creamy. Add remaining ingredients and blend well. Pour into a container coated with cooking spray. Refrigerate 2 to 4 hours until set. Gently shake out of container and slice as needed.

Yield: 2 ½ cups

TOMATO-LENTIL COUSCOUS

1 ½ c	Water	¼ tsp	Celery salt
2 T	Olive oil	¼ tsp	Garlic salt
1 tsp	Onion powder	1 c	Whole-wheat couscous
1 tsp	Parsley flakes	½ c	Canned lentils, drained
1 tsp	Nutritional yeast flakes	3 T	Sun-dried tomatoes, diced (packed in olive oil and herbs)
½ tsp	Salt, rounded		

Combine water, oil, and seasonings in a medium saucepan and bring to boil. Add couscous and stir. Return to boil, then lower heat and cover. Simmer 1 to 2 minutes or until all the water has been absorbed. Remove from heat and allow to stand 5 minutes. Fluff with fork. Drain lentils and add to couscous. Add the sun-dried tomatoes and gently stir entire mixture. Best if served immediately. Nice when garnished with fresh parsley or chives and fresh tomatoes, diced.

Yield: 3 ½ cups

VEGETABLE BOUQUET SALAD

12	Cherry tomatoes, halved	4 T	Fresh parsley, chopped
3	Celery stalks, thinly sliced	2 T	Green onion, diced (opt)
3	Carrots, thinly sliced	1 head	Leafy lettuce
2	Cucumbers, thinly sliced	2 c	Alfalfa sprouts

Combine all vegetables except lettuce and sprouts in a large bowl. Chill. Arrange lettuce leaves on a salad plate with the leafy edges facing out. Mound vegetables in center of plate or arrange vegetables in a decorative flower design. Garnish with alfalfa sprouts and additional parsley sprigs. Serve with French Dressing, Thousand Island Dressing or Raspberry Vinaigrette. (See recipes following.)

Yield: 12 cups

FRENCH DRESSING

½ c	Water	½ tsp	Salt
3 T	Apple juice, frozen concentrate	½ tsp	Paprika
3 T	Fresh lemon juice	½ tsp	Onion powder
2 T	Tomato purée	½ tsp	Garlic powder
2 T	Orange juice	⅛ tsp	Dill weed (opt)
¼ tsp	Mixed herbs or salad herbs	1 T	Cornstarch

Mix all ingredients except cornstarch in a blender. Pour mixture into a saucepan. Add cornstarch and stir to dissolve. Bring to a boil, stirring constantly until thickened. Remove from heat and chill before serving.

Yield: 1 cup

THOUSAND ISLAND DRESSING

1 c	Soy Mayonnaise (page 166)	½ c	Quick Vinegarless Ketchup (see page 170)
⅓ c	PA's® Sweet Pickle Relish, (vinegarless)	½ tsp	Onion powder

Combine all ingredients and chill before serving.

Note: May substitute homemade mayonnaise with Nayonaise®

Yield: 2 cups (scant)

RASPBERRY VINAIGRETTE

Add to one 1.05 oz package Good Seasons® "Fat-Free" Italian Dressing Mix:

½ c	Water	¼ c	White grape / raspberry (frozen juice concentrate)
¼ c	Fresh lemon juice		

Combine all ingredients in a cruet or a container with a tight fitting lid and shake gently until well mixed. Refrigerate 30 minutes before using. Stores well when refrigerated up to 2 weeks.

Yield: 1 cup

FRESH HERBED SAVORY GARLIC BREAD

Prepare or purchase "whole-wheat" French bread. Slice diagonally into 1-inch wide pieces. Spread the following mixture on each slice.

5 T	Spectrum® Naturals Spread (or) Smart Balance®, "Light" Spread	1 stem	Green onion, finely chopped
1 T	Fresh parsley, minced	¼ tsp	Garlic powder
2 tsp	Fresh basil, minced (¼ tsp dried)	⅛ tsp	Salt (to taste)

Wrap loaf in foil and bake at 400° F, 15 minutes. Open foil and bake an additional 3 to 5 minutes for a crispy crust.

Yield: 1 loaf

GARLIC BREAD

Spread garlic butter (recipe below) generously on fresh whole grain French bread. Sprinkle with granulated garlic powder and herbs of choice. Wrap with foil and bake at 400° F, 15 minutes until warm and moist. For a crispy crust, open foil at the top and bake an additional 5 minutes.

Variable

"QUICK & EASY" GARLIC BUTTER

10 oz	Spectrum® "non-dairy" Spread (or 8 oz Smart Balance® "Light")	1 tsp	Garlic powder (or 2 tsp garlic purée)
(opt)	Salt to taste (suggest ⅛ to ¼ tsp)		

Combine ingredients and stir until well mixed. Spread on bread as needed and wrap loaf in foil. Bake at 400° F, 15 minutes. For a crispy crust, open foil at the top and bake an additional 5 minutes.

Yield: 1 ¼ cup

CAROB PUDDING PARFAIT

2 c	"Instant" Whipped Topping (see below)	¼ c	Carob powder
1 ¼ c	Mori-Nu® Tofu, extra-firm, (10.5 oz)	3 T	Cornstarch
1 c	Almond Mylk™ beverage, vanilla	1 tsp	Vanilla extract
½ c	Sucanat® or fructose, granular		

In a blender, combine all ingredients and process until smooth. Pour mixture into a saucepan and simmer until thick. Cool. Refrigerate until set. Spoon alternate layers of pudding and "Instant" Whipped Topping (see below) into a parfait glass. Finish layering process with whipped topping on the top layer. If desired, garnish with chopped nuts or a cherry etc.

Variation: Add sliced bananas between the pudding layers and "Instant" Whipped Topping for a delicious Carob-Banana Pudding Parfait.

Tip: Mori-Nu® "Lite" Tofu also works well in this recipe.

Yield: 6 parfaits

"INSTANT" WHIPPED TOPPING

1 ½ c	Water	⅓ c	Coconut milk, canned ("lite," unsweetened)
⅔ c	Soymilk powder, plain*		
½ c	Blanched almonds (w/o skins)	2 tsp	Natural vanilla, flavoring
3 ½ T	Emes Kosher Jel® (plain)	¼ tsp	Salt
3 T	Fructose, honey or powdered sugar		Ice

In a blender, combine the water, milk powder, almonds and Emes Jel and process until the almonds are liquefied completely. Add remaining ingredients and process briefly. Finally, begin adding ice slowly through the lid spout and continue processing on high speed to make a total volume equal to 5 cups. Turn blender off and wait briefly. Mixture should now be light and fluffy. Best when served immediately. If stored, and mixture becomes too firm, hand whip or beat gently with an electric beater before serving.

* Recommend Better Than Milk™ Soy Original.

Yield: 5 cups

FRENCH TARTS

TART PASTRY:

1 c	Whole-wheat pastry flour	¼ c	Hot water
1 c	All purpose flour	3 T	Orange juice
¼ c	Wheat germ	1 T	Honey
1 tsp	Salt	½ c	Raw cashew butter
¼ c	Olive oil, "extra light"		

Combine the flours, wheat germ and salt. In a separate bowl, mix oil, water, orange juice and honey together. Add the cashew butter and stir together until well blended. Pour into the flour mixture and stir until dough is moist. Knead into a ball. Roll out ball between 2 pieces of wax paper. Remove wax paper and cut dough into circles 1-inch larger than tart tins. Press pastry circles into tart tins and crimp edges. Bake at 350° F, 10 to 12 minutes. Cool.

CUSTARD:

2 ½ c	Water	5 T	Cornstarch
½ c	Cooked rice	¼ c	Coconut, grated
⅓ c	Blanched almonds (w/o skins)	1 tsp	Vanilla extract
⅓ c	Honey	¼ tsp	Salt
3 T	Better Than Milk™ soymilk, powder		

In a blender, combine half the water with all remaining ingredients and process until completely smooth. Add remaining water and blend until mixed well. Pour into a saucepan and bring to a boil, stirring constantly until thick. Fill tart tins ¾ full and chill. When chilled, garnish with thinly sliced fresh fruits of choice. Pour Berry Shine Glaze (see recipe below) over fruit.

BERRY SHINE GLAZE:

⅔ c	Frozen apple juice, concentrate	4 tsp	Cornstarch
⅓ c	Strawberries or raspberries		

In a blender, process all ingredients on high for one minute until creamy. Pour into saucepan and cook over medium-high heat stirring constantly until thick and clear. Cool until lukewarm and pour over fresh fruit. Chill before serving.

Yield: 24 tarts

Better Than Milk Combo
Barley Nut Waffles
Very Berry Fruit Soup
"Instant" Whipped Topping
Scrambled Tofu "Eggs"
Breakfast Banana Crisp

A Breakfast Bash

Featuring

Waffles, pancakes, French toast, fruit soups, scrambled "eggs," and more. Breakfast is the most important meal of the day. It can also be the healthiest when it is low in fat and cholesterol free. Start your day out right. Try a wide selection of fabulous and delightfully healthy recipes.

HEARTY "MULTI-GRAIN" WAFFLES

2 ¾ c	Water	¼ c	Honey
1 ½ c	Old fashioned oats	2 T	Sunflower seeds
1 c	Rolled barley	1 T	Oil
¾ c	Cornmeal	2 tsp	Maple flavoring
⅔ c	Wheat germ	2 tsp	Vanilla extract
½ c	Soymilk powder, plain	1 tsp	Salt
¼ c	Pecans or walnuts		

Combine all ingredients in a blender and process until smooth and creamy. Let stand to thicken while waffle iron is heating. If your waffle iron has a temperature control knob, set a little below the regular waffle setting to allow waffles to bake a few minutes longer than egg waffles. Blend batter again briefly and pour into a waffle iron that has been prepared with cooking spray. Bake waffles 11 minutes or until golden brown. Set waffles on a cooling rack a few minutes before serving.

Tip: Store extra waffles in the refrigerator or freezer. To reheat, just toast in an oven or toaster until hot and crispy.

Yield: 10 (4-inch square) waffles

LIGHT 'N CRISPY OAT WAFFLES

2 ¼ c	Water	¼ c	Sucanat®, sweetener
2 c	Quick oats	1 T	Liquid lecithin
⅓ c	Barley flour	2 tsp	Vanilla extract
¼ c	Raw wheat germ	1 ½ tsp	Maple flavoring
¼ c	Cornmeal	¾ tsp	Salt
¼ c	Raw cashew pieces		

In a blender, combine all ingredients and process on high speed until smooth and creamy. Set mixture aside about 5 minutes while you pre-heat the waffle iron. Spray the waffle iron with cooking spray and then pour batter into the center of the iron and fill out to the edges. Bake 12 minutes. Cool on a baker's rack several minutes before serving for crispier waffles.

Yield: 8 (4-inch square) waffles

BARLEY-NUT WAFFLES

2 c	Water	¼ c	Cornmeal
1 ½ c	Rolled barley	¼ c	Pure maple syrup
½ c	Old fashioned oats	1 T	Oil
½ c	Soymilk powder, plain	2 tsp	Vanilla
½ c	Almonds, slivered	1 tsp	Maple flavoring
½ c	Wheat bran	1 tsp	Salt
¼ c	Raw wheat germ	½ tsp	Almond extract

Combine all ingredients in a blender and process on high speed until smooth. Pre-heat a waffle iron, coat surface with cooking spray and pour batter into the center of the waffle iron. Spread batter out evenly to the edges. Gently close the lid and cook 10 minutes. (Don't peak.) Serve with fruit soup, nut butter and applesauce or your favorite topping.

Note: Some brands of rolled barley have higher fiber content than others requiring more water in the recipe. If batter seems too thick after blending, add up to ¼ cup more water.

Yield: 8 (4-inch square) waffles

SOY-OAT WAFFLES

1 c	Soaked soybeans (½ c dried)*	¼ c	Whole-wheat flour
5 c	Water	¼ c	Pecans or walnuts
4 ½ c	Quick oats	1 T	Oil
½ c	Cornmeal	1 T	Vanilla, extract
½ c	Seven-grain cereal, uncooked	2 tsp	Salt
⅓ c	Date sugar	2 tsp	Maple flavoring

In a blender, combine half of all ingredients at a time and process until smooth. Mix both batters together in a large pitcher for pouring convenience. Pre-heat a waffle iron, coat surface with cooking spray and pour batter into the center of the waffle iron. Spread batter out to the edges. Gently close lid and cook 11 minutes. Set waffles on a cooling rack a few minutes before serving.

****Note:*** To prepare soybeans, cover dried soybeans generously with water and soak overnight. Drain and discard water. You can prepare soybeans ahead and keep them in your freezer until needed.

Yield: 16 (4-inch square) waffles

RICE WAFFLES

1 ⅓ c	Rice flour
1 c	Cooked brown rice, soft (prepared with a 3:1 ratio)
1 c	Water
1 half	Pear, canned or fresh (ripe)
¼ c	Pear juice
2 T	Syrup, maple or rice
1 tsp	Liquid lecithin
1 tsp	Vanilla extract
½ tsp	Maple flavoring
½ tsp	Salt

Preheat your waffle iron. In a blender, combine all ingredients and process until smooth. Spray the waffle iron with cooking spray. Pour the batter into the center of the lower iron plate and spread mixture out evenly. Wait 15 seconds and gently close lid. Bake 12 minutes (don't lift lid sooner).

Yield: 6 (4-inch) waffles

MILLET WAFFLES

2 c	Cooked millet (4:1 ratio)
1 c	Millet flour
½ c	Water
1 half	Pear, canned or fresh (ripe)
2 T	Maple syrup or Sucanat®
1 ½ tsp	Maple flavoring
1 tsp	Vanilla extract
1 tsp	Salt

Preheat your waffle iron. In a blender, combine all ingredients and process until smooth. Spray the waffle iron with cooking spray. Pour the batter into the center of the lower iron plate and spread mixture out evenly. Wait 15 seconds and gently close lid. Bake 12 minutes (don't lift lid sooner).

Yield: 6 (4-inch) waffles

HONEY BUTTER

½ c	Smart Balance® "Light," softened (non-hydrogenated spread)
¼ c	Spun honey (Sue Bee®)

Stir Smart Balance® and honey together until well mixed and serve promptly.

Tip: Serve with pancakes, waffles, French toast, biscuits, corn bread or muffins.

Yield: ¾ cup

NICE 'N EASY WHOLE GRAIN PANCAKES

1 ⅔ c Soymilk beverage, plain or vanilla
½ c Water-packed tofu, silken (softest) (or Mori-Nu® boxed tofu, soft)
2 c Whole-wheat pancake mix (Aunt Jemima®)

Combine soymilk and tofu in a blender and process until creamy. Pour into pancake mix and stir gently until evenly moistened and large lumps disappear. Let stand 1 or 2 minutes to thicken. Cook on a lightly oiled griddle pre-heated at 400° F, approximately 2 minutes on each side or until golden brown and cooked through in the middle.

Note: Choose a pancake mix that is not the "complete" type. Complete mixes contain dairy products and "oxidized" cholesterol. Any brand pancake mix can be used, however, due to differences in fiber content, the milk/pancake mix ratio may need to be adjusted to obtain the proper batter consistency.

Tip: This pancake recipe also works great for waffles!

Yield: 10 (4-inch) pancakes

TASTY & TENDER BUCK-WHEAT PANCAKES

1 ¾ c Soymilk beverage, plain ("Silk®" or "West Soy Plus")
½ c Water-packed tofu, silken (or Mori-Nu® boxed tofu, soft)
1 ½ c Whole-wheat pancake mix (Aunt Jemima®)
½ c Buckwheat pancake mix (Aunt Jemima®)

Combine soymilk and tofu in a blender and process until creamy. Combine both pancake mixes. Pour blender ingredients into pancake mix and stir gently until evenly moistened and large lumps disappear. Let stand 1 or 2 minutes to thicken. Cook on a lightly oiled griddle pre-heated at 400° F approximately 2 minutes on each side or until golden brown and cooked through in the middle.

Tip: Buckwheat pancakes taste especially good when served with "Roddenbery's® Cane Patch Syrup." Look for this unique syrup in grocery stores located in most Southeastern states. It's an extraordinary flavor treat!

Yield: 10 (4-inch) pancakes

"LOVE YOUR HEART" OAT-BRAN PANCAKES (Yeast-raised)

3 c	Soymilk beverage, warmed	⅓ c	Brown sugar or Sucanat®
1 ¾ c	Quick oats	¼ c	Oat bran
1 ½ c	Wheat bran	1 T	Yeast, rapid rise (¼ oz pkt)
1 c	Whole-wheat flour	1 T	Oil
½ c	Unbleached white flour	1 ½ tsp	Salt

Combine all ingredients in a blender and process on high speed until smooth. Let sit 10 to 15 minutes to activate the yeast or until batter rises to the top of the blender. Pre-heat a griddle to 350° F. Pour out enough batter to form 5-inch pancakes. Cook each pancake about 3 minutes. Flip over and cook 3 minutes more on the other side. Cool completely on a baker's rack. Reheat before serving in a toaster or wrap in foil and reheat in the oven.

Note: Although it is not mandatory, it is still best to wait and eat yeast-raised products the day after preparation.

Tip: Individually wrap pancakes and place in an air-tight container to freeze.

Yield: 14 (5-inch) pancakes

WHEAT 'N BRAN HEART HEALTHY PANCAKES

2 c	Whole-wheat flour	2 c	Soymilk beverage, plain
⅔ c	Wheat bran	1 c	Water-packed tofu, silken
2 tsp	Baking powder	3 T	Fructose or brown sugar
½ tsp	Baking soda	1 tsp	Lemon juice
1 tsp	Salt		

Combine first five dry ingredients in a bowl and mix well. Combine soymilk, tofu, sweetener and lemon juice in a blender and process until creamy. Add to dry ingredients and stir gently until evenly moistened and large lumps disappear. Let stand 1 or 2 minutes to thicken. Cook on a lightly oiled griddle at 400° F. Turn when bubbly and golden brown. Cook an additional 2 minutes or until browned and cooked all the way through the middle.

Yield: 12 (4-inch) pancakes

"WHEAT-FREE" BROWN RICE PANCAKES

1 c	Soymilk beverage, vanilla	½ tsp	Lemon juice
1 c	Applesauce, unsweetened	2 c	Brown rice flour
½ c	Water-packed tofu, silken (softest)	1 tsp	Baking powder
2 T	Fructose granules or brown sugar	¾ tsp	Salt
1 tsp	Vanilla extract	¼ tsp	Baking soda

In a blender, combine soymilk, applesauce, tofu, sugar, vanilla and lemon juice. Process until smooth and creamy. Combine dry ingredients in a bowl and mix well. Pour blender ingredients into the flour mixture and stir gently until evenly moistened. Let stand 1 or 2 minutes to thicken. Cook on a lightly oiled griddle pre-heated at 400° F. Turn when golden brown and "puffy" (will not bubble). Cook two minutes more on the other side until done in the middle.

Tip: Makes a great waffle too!

Yield: 8 (4-inch) pancakes

COCONUT SYRUP

15 oz	Cream of Coconut, canned	1 T	Smart Balance®, "Light"
15 oz	Water	1 tsp	Coconut flavoring
2 ½ T	Cornstarch	1 tsp	Vanilla extract
½ c	Coconut milk "lite," canned	pinch	Salt

Pour Cream of Coconut into a saucepan. Fill the can with water and pour half into the saucepan. Add cornstarch to remaining water and stir until dissolved. Set aside. Add coconut milk, Smart Balance®, flavorings and salt to the saucepan and bring to a boil. Add remaining cornstarch/water and return to boiling, stirring constantly. Remove from heat. Syrup will thicken as it cools.

Tip: Serve over pancakes, waffles or French toast.

Yield: 4 cups

MAPLE SYRUP TOPPING

¼ c	Maple syrup	1 T	Fresh lemon juice
3 T	Brown sugar	¼ c	Hot water

Cook maple syrup, sugar and lemon juice in a heavy covered saucepan over medium heat until sugar dissolves and mixture begins to boil. Uncover and cook an additional 5 minutes until syrup becomes dark brown and very thick. Remove from heat and slowly add hot water, stirring constantly. Serve warm.

Yield: 2/3 cup

CASHEW-BANANA FRENCH TOAST

1 c	Water	1 T	Frozen O.J. concentrate
⅔ c	Raw cashews	½ tsp	Salt
½ med	Ripened banana	½ tsp	Vanilla extract
¼ c	Unbleached white flour	¼ tsp	Cinnamon, ground
1 T	Honey	8 slices	Whole grain bread

Combine all ingredients, except bread, in a blender and process on high speed until smooth and creamy. Pour mixture into a shallow bowl. Lightly oil or coat a non-stick griddle or frying pan with cooking spray. Quickly dip and coat both sides of sliced bread with the batter. Fry over med-lo temperature. Avoid turning until first side is well "set" and golden brown. If French toast seems too "soggy," lightly toast bread before dipping into batter. Or, as another method, dip frozen bread slices. Older bread that has become dry also works great in this recipe. Serve with fruit soup, applesauce, "all-fruit" jam, Coconut Syrup (see recipe on page 87) or topping of choice.

Yield: 8 slices

CASHEW-APPLE FRENCH TOAST

1 ½ c	Water	1 ½ T	Apple juice, concentrate
1 c	Raw cashews	¾ tsp	Salt
¾ med	Apple, peeled	1 tsp	Vanilla extract
⅜ c	Unbleached white flour	⅜ tsp	Cinnamon, ground
1 ½ T	Honey	8 slices	Apple or raisin bread

Combine all ingredients (except bread) in a blender and process on high speed until smooth and creamy. Pour mixture into a shallow bowl. Lightly oil or coat a non-stick griddle or frying pan with cooking spray. Quickly dip and coat both sides of sliced bread with the batter. Fry over med-lo temperature. Avoid turning until first side is well "set" and golden brown. If French toast seems too "soggy," lightly toast bread before dipping into batter. Or, as another method, dip frozen bread slices. Older bread that has become dry also works great in this recipe. Serve with fruit soup, applesauce, "all-fruit" jam, Coconut Syrup (see recipe on page 87) or topping of choice.

Yield: 8 slices

VERY-BERRY FRUIT SOUP

12 oz Chiquita® "Raspberry Passion" (frozen juice concentrate)
2 tsp Vanilla extract
16 oz Canned peaches, unsweetened (drained, reserve juice)
1 c Pineapple chunks, unsweetened (drained, reserve juice)
3 T Cornstarch, arrowroot or tapioca powder
4 c Frozen mixed berries (blueberries, strawberries blackberries, raspberries)
2 Bananas, sliced

Combine the juice concentrate, vanilla, and the reserved fruit juice from the cans of pineapple and peaches in a large saucepan. Add cornstarch and stir to dissolve starch. Bring to a boil over med-hi heat, stirring mixture constantly. Reduce heat, continue stirring and simmer until juice thickens and clears. Stir in the canned and frozen fruits. Return to a boil and cook 2 or 3 minutes longer. Remove from heat and allow to cool 5 minutes. Add sliced bananas before serving. Serve over waffles, pancakes or toast. Garnish with coconut and/or "Instant" Whipped Topping (recipe on page 90) if desired.

Yield: 12 cups

TROPICAL FRUIT SOUP

12 oz Dole® "Pineapple-Banana" (frozen juice concentrate)
1 ¼ c White grape juice
2 tsp Vanilla extract
3 ½ T Cornstarch or tapioca starch
4 c Frozen mixed fruit, (peaches, pineapple, melon balls, grapes)
2 Bananas, sliced
2 Kiwi, sliced

Combine the juice concentrate, white grape juice, vanilla, and cornstarch in a large saucepan. Stir to dissolve starch. Bring to a boil, stirring constantly. Reduce heat to simmer and continue stirring until mixture clears and thickens. Cut frozen fruit into smaller chunks. Add frozen fruit to the juice mixture and cook a few minutes more. Stir in sliced bananas and kiwi last before serving. Serve over waffles, pancakes or toast. Garnish with coconut and/or Whipped Topping (see recipe on page 90) if desired.

Yield: 10 cups

"INSTANT" WHIPPED TOPPING

1 ½ c	Water	⅓ c	Coconut milk, canned ("lite," unsweetened)
⅔ c	Soymilk powder, plain*	2 tsp	Natural vanilla, flavoring
½ c	Blanched almonds (w/o skins)	¼ tsp	Salt
3 ½ T	Emes Kosher Jel® (plain)		Ice
3 T	Fructose, honey or powdered sugar		

In a blender, combine the water, milk powder, almonds and Emes Jel and process until the almonds are liquefied completely. Add remaining ingredients and process briefly. Finally, begin adding ice slowly through the lid spout and continue processing on high speed to make a total volume equal to 5 cups. Turn blender off and wait briefly. Mixture should now be light and fluffy. Best when served immediately. If stored, and mixture becomes too firm, hand whip or beat gently with an electric beater before serving.

* Recommend Better Than Milk™ "Original."

Yield: 5 cups

MILLET PORRIDGE

4 c	Water	½ c	Coconut, grated
1 c	Millet	½ c	Dates, chopped
1 tsp	Salt	2 tsp	Natural vanilla, flavoring

In a saucepan, combine water, millet and salt. Bring to a boil, stirring constantly. Reduce heat, cover and simmer 30 minutes. Add remaining ingredients and simmer 10 minutes more. Garnish with granola if desired.

Variation: Add 1 c diced apples and ¼ tsp cinnamon.

Yield: 6 cups

PRACTICALLY PERFECT STUFFED PRUNES

1 bag	Sunsweet® "Orange Essence" prunes	2 c	English walnut halves

Press walnut halves into the indented side of each prune and enjoy!

Tip: To serve as hors d'oeuvres, place prunes on a paper doily and a silver platter.

Yield: 40 stuffed prunes

BAKED "APPLE-WALNUT" OATMEAL

4 c	Soymilk beverage, plain	½ tsp	Salt
½ c	Fructose, granules	2 c	Old fashioned oats, dry
2 T	Smart Balance®, "Light" (non-hydrogenated spread)	2 c	Tart apples, peeled, diced
		1 c	Walnuts, chopped
1 ½ tsp	Cinnamon, ground	¾ c	Currants

Preheat oven to 350° F. In a large saucepan, combine soymilk, sweetener, Smart Balance®, cinnamon and salt. Bring to a boil and remove from heat. Stir in oat, apples, walnuts and currants. Prepare a casserole dish with cooking spray. Pour oatmeal mixture into dish and bake uncovered 35 minutes. Serve alone or with soymilk.

Yield: 8 cups

FAST & EASY APPLE-NUT COUSCOUS

2 c	Apple juice	1 c	Whole-wheat couscous
2 T	Smart Balance®, "Light" (non-hydrogenated spread)	¼ c	Currants or raisins
		¼ c	Walnuts, chopped
¼ tsp	Cinnamon, ground		

Bring apple juice, Smart Balance® and cinnamon to a boil. Stir in couscous, currants or raisins and walnuts. Reduce heat, cover and simmer 5 minutes or until liquid is absorbed. Fluff with a fork before serving.

Variation: May substitute walnuts with pecans or raw sunflower seeds. If preferred, add nuts or seeds as a topping after couscous is cooked.

Yield: 3 cups

"QUICK" BREAKFAST TOAST

1 slice	Whole grain bread	3 T	Applesauce
1 T	Natural peanut butter		

Toast bread and spread with peanut butter and top with applesauce.

Variation: Substitute applesauce with mashed or puréed pears.

Yield: 1 slice toast

QUICK-COOKING 2-GRAIN HOT CEREAL

2 c	Water	½ c	Soymilk beverage, plain
⅔ c	Quick oats	2 tsp	Butter-style sprinkles
⅓ c	Ralston® (uncooked) (100% wheat, hot cereal)	¼ tsp	Salt (to taste)

Bring water to a boil. Combine oats and Ralston and pour into water stirring constantly. Reduce heat and simmer 1 minute. Remove from heat, stir in soymilk, butter sprinkles (opt), and salt. Cover and let sit one minute to thicken. Add toppings of choice.

Suggested toppings: Raisins, currants, wheat germ (plain or honey crunch), granola, sunflower seeds, Sucanat®, brown sugar, or try BaKon® Seasoning for a savory flavor.

Yield: 3 cups

BREAKFAST BANANA CRISP

4 c	Water	1 ½ tsp	Salt
1 c	Millet, dry	1 tsp	Lemon zest, grated
12 oz	Pineapple juice, frozen concentrate	3 T	Soymilk powder *
12 oz	Water	4 c	Sliced bananas
1 T	Vanilla, powdered (or 1 ½ tsp clear vanilla extract)	4 c	Granola, low fat

In a saucepan, combine (4 cups) water and millet. Bring to a boil. Reduce heat, cover and simmer 20 to 25 minutes until millet is soft. Remove from heat. Combine pineapple juice concentrate and water for a 1:1 ratio dilution. In a blender, combine half of the cooked millet, juice mixture, vanilla, salt, lemon zest and milk powder and process on high speed until creamy. Pour mixture out into a bowl and repeat procedure for the remaining half of ingredients. Spread 2 cups granola on the bottom of a 9" x 13" pan. Layer enough bananas over top of granola to cover. Pour ⅓ millet cream over the bananas. Repeat layering of bananas and cream procedure two more times. Top with remaining 2 c granola.

* Recommend Better Than Milk™ Original, plain

Yield: 12 cups

FRUIT-FILLED SWEET ROLLS, TWISTS or BRAIDS

DOUGH:

1 c	Warm water	1 tsp	Salt
1 c	Whole-wheat flour	1 c	Unbleached white flour
2 T	Honey or brown sugar	¼ c	Whole-wheat flour
2 tsp	Yeast	¼ c	Quick oats
4 tsp	Oil	1 T	Vital wheat gluten

In a bowl, combine water, 1 c flour, honey and yeast to make a "sponge." Let rest 15 minutes. Stir in oil, salt and remaining ingredients. Turn out onto a floured surface and knead about 10 min. If needed, add up to ¼ c additional whole-wheat flour. Cover and let rise 10 minutes. Then proceed with recipe.

FILLING:

1 c	Dates (or favorite dried fruit)	½ c	Pecans or walnuts, chopped
¾ c	Water	½ c	Raisins or currants
1 tsp	Maple flavoring	¼ tsp	Cinnamon, ground

Simmer dates in water and maple flavoring until soft. Cool. Transfer to a blender and process until smooth. Set remaining ingredients aside.

SWEET ROLLS: Place dough on a floured surface and roll out a 9" x 15" rectangle about ¼ inch thick. Spread date purée evenly over dough to within ½ inch of edges. Sprinkle generously with nuts, raisins and cinnamon. Roll up into a log and pinch seams together. Cut into 1-inch slices and place on a baking sheet prepared with cooking spray. Let rise 15 min. or until double. Bake at 350° F, 18-20 min. While hot from the oven, brush rolls with apple or white grape juice concentrate to give rolls a "glazed" look. Yield: 16 rolls

DATE-NUT TWIST: Follow direction for sweet rolls until dough is rolled up. Place log on a prepared baking sheet and cut in half lengthwise except for one inch in the middle. Lift, cross and twist from the middle to the end on both sides. Let rise until double. Bake at 350° F, 20 to 25 min. Brush with juice as explained above to give the twist a "glazed look." Yield: 16-inch twist

DATE-NUT BRAID: Place dough on a floured surface and roll out a 9" x 15" rectangle and about ¼ inch thick. Transfer dough to a baking sheet prepared with cooking spray. Spread date purée down the center of the dough. Sprinkle generously with nuts, raisins and cinnamon. Using shears or a sharp knife, cut diagonal strips in dough, at 2-inch intervals on each side of filling. Starting at one end, fold strips alternately from each side to make a criss-cross braid. Tuck under any excess dough at the end. Let rise until double. Bake at 350° F, 20 to 25 minutes. Brush with juice. Yield: 16-inch braid

SCRAMBLED TOFU "EGGS"

1 lb	Water-packed tofu, firm	2 tsp	Chicken-style seasoning
½ c	Onions, chopped	1 T	Nutritional yeast flakes
½ c	Mushrooms, sliced	½ tsp	Salt (scant)
¼ c	Bell peppers, chopped	½ tsp	Onion powder
2 T	Green onions, sliced (or fresh chives, chopped)	¼ tsp	Garlic powder
1 T	Olive oil	⅛ tsp	Turmeric (or less for a lighter yellow color)

Crumble tofu into chunks and set aside to drain. In a large skillet, sauté fresh vegetables in oil until tender. Add tofu to skillet. Combine spices and sprinkle evenly over tofu. Mix well. Cook scrambled "eggs" over medium heat 5-10 minutes or until liquids evaporate and yellow color becomes prominent.

Yield: 4 cups

CREAMED TOFU "EGGS"
Over Toast

1 recipe	Scrambled Tofu "Eggs" (see above)	1 recipe	Jiffy Mushroom Soup (see page 204)

Prepare Tofu "Eggs" according to directions, with or without vegetables added. In a large saucepan, prepare Jiffy Mushroom Soup. Add "eggs" to the soup and stir gently to combine both recipes. Reheat and serve over toast, English muffins, biscuits or rice as preferred.

Yield: 7 cups

HASH BROWNS

4 c	Raw potatoes, shredded	1 T	Nutritional yeast flakes
2 T	Olive oil	1 ½ tsp	Garlic salt
2 T	Dried parsley	½ tsp	Chicken-style seasoning
1 T	Onion powder	½ tsp	Spike® Seasoning (or) (Nature's Blend, page 95)
1 T	Fresh chives, chopped		

Rinse shredded potatoes in a colander and drain well. Mix all ingredients together. Pour hash browns into a non-stick frying pan and cook over medium heat 10 to 15 minutes stirring every 2 minutes until browned.

Yield: 4 cups

"QUICK" VINEGARLESS KETCHUP

1 ½ c	Tomato sauce	2 T	Fruit-Fresh®, powder (or) ⅛ tsp citric acid
1 c	Tomato paste	1 ½	tsp Salt
½ c	Pineapple juice	1 tsp	Onion powder
¼ c	Fresh lemon juice	½ tsp	Garlic salt
1 tsp	Lime juice	½ tsp	Paprika
3 T	Date butter (page 236)	¼ tsp	Worcestershire sauce (opt) (any vegetarian brand)
2 T	Pineapple/orange juice (frozen concentrate)		
2 T	Fructose or honey		

Combine all ingredients in a blender and process until smooth. Refrigerate. Freeze extras not used within two weeks.

Variation: For thicker ketchup, decrease tomato sauce to 1 cup and increase tomato paste to 1 ½ cups.

Yield: 4 cups

NATURE'S BLEND ALL PURPOSE HERBAL SEASONING

¼ c	Granulated onion	2 tsp	Parsley, dried (flakes)
¼ c	Beef-style seasoning	2 tsp	Savory, dried (flakes)
¼ c	Sesame seeds	2 tsp	Coriander, ground
3 T	Garlic salt	1 tsp	Marjoram, dried (flakes)
4 tsp	Basil, dried	1 tsp	Sucanat®, sweetener
2 tsp	Oregano, dried (flakes)	½ tsp	Dried orange peel, ground

Combine all dried herbs in a jar or an air-tight container and shake to mix well. Keep out of light or store in the refrigerator.

Yield: 1 ¼ cups

COUNTRY BISCUITS
"Yeast-raised"

1 ½ c	Warm water	1 ½ c	Whole-wheat pastry flour
1 T	Rapid-rise yeast	⅔ c	Soymilk powder, Soyagen® (may also use Soy Supreme)
6 T	Oil (⅓ c + ½ T)	1 ½ tsp	Salt
2 c	Unbleached white flour		

In a large bowl, combine water, yeast and oil. In a separate bowl, combine dry ingredients. Pour wet ingredients into dry ingredients and stir quickly but as little as possible until dough is well moistened and holds together. Mixture will be a bit sticky and look "fluffy." Turn out onto a well-floured board. Push together into a ball but do not knead mixture. With a floured rolling pin, roll out 1 inch thick and cut with a biscuit cutter. Place biscuits side by side or up to ½ inch apart on a baking sheet prepared with cooking spray. Let rise in a warm oven ¼ inch only. (No more than this or biscuits will have a bun texture.) Do not remove biscuits from oven and turn heat on to 425° F. Bake until golden brown or about 12 to 15 minutes.

Note: For a crisp crust, place biscuits in a paper bag, sprinkle with water and place in a warm oven before serving.

Yield: 20 biscuits

SAUSAGE-STYLE GRAVY

2 ½ c	Water	¼ c	Cornstarch
¾ tsp	Salt	1 T	Beef-style seasoning
1 c	Water	¾ c	Sausage-style crumbles
½ c	Raw cashews	1 T	Green onion or chives, sliced

Combine (2 ½ cups) water and salt in a large saucepan. In a blender, combine (1 cup) water, cashews, cornstarch and beef-style seasoning and process until smooth and creamy. Add blender ingredients to the pot of salt water and bring to a boil stirring constantly. Add sausage crumbles and cook until thick and creamy. Add green onion or chives and cook one more minute. Serve over biscuits, toast or rice.

Variation: For Burger-style Gravy, replace sausage crumbles with burger-style crumbles or Morningstar Farms "Ground Meatless."

Yield: 5 cups

CHIPPED "BEEF" GRAVY

2 ½ T	Unbleached white flour	1 tsp	Chicken-style seasoning
1 ¾ c	Soymilk beverage, plain (Silk®)	½ tsp	Salt
⅓ c	Water-packed tofu, silken	4 slices	Veggie "beef or bacon"

Stir flour in a dry frying pan over med-hi heat until lightly browned or appears "off-white" in color. Cool. In a blender, combine flour with soymilk, tofu and seasonings and process until smooth and creamy. Pour the blender ingredients into the frying pan and bring to a boil, stirring constantly until thickened. Dice the vegetarian deli-slices and add to the gravy. Simmer about a minute. Serve over biscuits, mashed potatoes or rice.

Yield: 2 cups

BREAKFAST SCONES
"Yeast-raised"

1 c	Quick oats	4 tsp	Active yeast, rapid rise
1 c	Hot water	½ c	Warm water
¼ c	Oil	1 ½ c	Whole-wheat flour
¼ c	Soymilk powder, plain	1 ¼ c	Unbleached white flour
2 T	Fructose or brown sugar	½ c	Raisins or currants (opt)
1 tsp	Salt		

Combine oats, hot water, oil, soymilk powder, sweetener and salt in a bowl and soak about 30 minutes. Dissolve yeast in the warm water and add to the oat mixture. Combine the two flours. Take out ¼ cup of the flour mixture and spread it out on a clean counter or a kneading board. Add remaining flour and raisins to the oat mixture and stir to form a large ball. Place dough on the floured surface and knead briefly and gently to coat all sides with flour. Roll dough out with a rolling pin to ¾ inch thickness or into a 10-inch diameter circle. Prepare a cookie sheet with cooking spray. Cut dough with a biscuit cutter, shape into scones and position each one about 1 inch apart on the cookie sheet. Let scones rise about 10 minutes. Bake at 350° F, 25 to 30 minutes or until lightly browned and scones sound hollow when tapped. Cool. Store in an airtight container.

Tip: Scones can be made ahead several days. Wrap in foil and reheat before serving. Scones are also great in "lunches to go" or traveling.

Yield: 18 scones

MAPLE-PECAN SCONES

1 ¼ c	Whole-wheat pastry flour	½ c	Soymilk beverage, (Silk®)
1 c	Unbleached all purpose flour	⅓ c	Smart Balance®, "Light"
⅓ c	Pecans, chopped	⅓ c	Pure maple syrup
1 T	Baking powder	1 tsp	Vanilla extract
1 T	Flax seeds, ground	½ tsp	Maple flavoring
½ tsp	Salt	1 tsp	Sucanat®, sweetener

In a mixing bowl, combine flour, pecans, baking powder and ground flax seeds. Cut in Smart Balance® with a pastry blender until mixture resembles coarse crumbs. Combine the soymilk with the maple syrup and extracts. Add to the dry ingredients and mix lightly to form a soft dough. Turn dough onto a lightly floured surface and knead gently a few times to shape dough into a ball. Place on an un-greased round baking stone. Press ball into an 8-inch circle, 1-inch thick. Spray a knife with cooking spray and score dough nearly through into 8 wedges; do not separate. Brush top with maple syrup, sprinkle with Sucanat® and press it gently into the dough. Bake at 425° F, 15 to 18 minutes.

Tip: Scones are best when served freshly made and still warm. Serve plain or with maple syrup, applesauce, or Smart Balance® "Light."

Yield: 8 scones

HONEY-WHEAT CURRANT SCONES

1 ¼ c	Whole-wheat pastry flour	½ tsp	Cinnamon, ground (opt)
1 c	Unbleached white flour	¾ c	Soymilk beverage, (Silk®)
⅔ c	Currants	⅓ c	Honey
1 T	Baking powder	¼ c	Olive oil, "extra light"
1 T	Flax seeds, ground	1 tsp	Vanilla extract
½ tsp	Salt	1 tsp	Sucanat®, sweetener

In a mixing bowl, combine flour, currants, baking powder, flax seeds, salt and if desired, cinnamon. Combine soymilk, honey, oil and vanilla and add to the dry ingredients. Mix lightly to form a soft dough. Turn dough out onto a lightly floured surface and knead gently 5 or 6 times to shape dough into a ball. Place on an un-greased round baking stone. Press ball into an 8-inch circle, about 1-inch thick. Spray a knife with cooking spray and score dough nearly through into 8 wedges; do not separate. Moisten top of dough with water, sprinkle evenly with Sucanat® and press it gently into the dough. Bake at 400° F, 18 minutes. Serve warm with Smart Balance®, honey or applesauce.

Variation: Omit currants, add ¾ c blueberries and ½ tsp grated lemon zest.

Yield: 8 scones

HOMEMADE MUESLI

- 6 c Low sugar "flake" style cereal (multigrain, bran or corn flakes, etc)
- 2 c Rolled barley or oats
- ½ c Raisins
- ½ c Dates, chopped
- ½ c Raw sunflower seeds
- ½ c Pecans, chopped
- ½ c Coconut flakes (opt) (unsweetened)

Choose your favorite "flake" cereal or any combination of several low fat and low sugar dry cereals in a bowl. Then add all remaining ingredients and store in an airtight container. Serve with milk alternative beverage of choice. If a sweeter cereal is desired, add fresh fruits such as bananas and peaches or drizzle with honey or brown rice syrup.

Yield: 11 cups

"HEART SMART" GRANOLA

- 6 c Quick oats
- 1 c Oat bran
- 1 c Soymilk powder, plain or vanilla
- ⅓ c Sliced almonds or walnuts
- 2 T Sesame seeds
- ¾ c Honey or maple syrup
- ¼ c Water
- 2 tsp Vanilla extract
- 1 tsp Maple flavoring (opt)

Combine oats, oat bran, milk powder, nuts and seeds. In a separate bowl, combine honey, water and flavorings. Pour liquids over oat mixture and mix until evenly moistened. Prepare two cookie sheets with cooking spray and spread granola out evenly over both cookie sheets. Do not mash or press granola down. Bake at 225° F, 1½ hours, stirring every 30 minutes. Cool completely before storing.

Variation: Replace the water with apple juice for a fruitier flavor. For a reduced sugar recipe, decrease honey or syrup to ⅓ cup and increase water to ⅔ cup.

Yield: 9 cups

FRUIT-SWEETENED GRANOLA

DRY INGREDIENTS:

6 c	Rolled grains, any combination (Oats, barley, wheat)	1 c	Almonds, sliced (or slivered)
1 c	Whole grain flour	1 c	Sesame seeds
½ c	Pecans or walnuts, chopped	1 c	Coconut flakes (opt)

BLENDER INGREDIENTS:

¾ c	Water	2 med	Bananas, ripened
½ c	Apple juice, frozen concentrate	1 T	Vanilla extract
½ c	Raw cashews	1 ½ tsp	Maple flavoring
½ c	Dates	1 tsp	Salt

Combine dry ingredients in a large bowl. Combine blender ingredients and process until smooth and creamy. Pour liquid over dry ingredients. Stir and mix together with hands until entire mixture is evenly moistened and crumbly. Spread granola out on cookie sheets. Bake 2 to 3 hours at 225° F, stirring mixture every 45 minutes until lightly browned. Cool completely before storing. Granola becomes crispier as it cools.

Yield: 12 cups

HONEY GRANOLA

DRY INGREDIENTS:

3 c	Quick oats	1 c	Wheat germ
2 c	Rolled barley flakes	1 c	Almonds, sliced
1 c	Rolled wheat flakes	½ c	Pecans, chopped
1 c	Soymilk powder	½ c	Sesame seeds
1 c	Whole wheat flour	1 c	Coconut, shredded (opt)

LIQUID INGREDIENTS:

¾ c	Hot water	1 T	Vanilla extract
¾ c	Creamy "spun" honey	1 tsp	Maple flavoring
½ c	Olive oil, "extra light"	½ tsp	Salt (opt)

Combine dry ingredients in a large bowl. Combine liquid ingredients and pour over dry ingredients. Stir and mix together with hands until entire mixture is evenly moistened and crumbly. Spread granola out on 2 cookie sheets. Bake for 2 to 3 hours at 225° F, stirring mixture every 45 minutes until dry or very lightly browned. Remove from oven and cool completely before storing. Granola becomes crispier as it cools.

Yield: 10 cups

MAPLE-NUT GRANOLA

7 c	Oats (5 c quick, 2 c old fashioned)	1 c	Pure maple syrup
1 c	Raw wheat germ	¼ c	Olive oil, "extra light"
1 c	Chopped or sliced nuts, (Pecans, walnuts, almonds)	1 tsp	Vanilla extract
		1 tsp	Maple flavoring
½ c	Sesame seeds	¼ tsp	Almond extract
1 tsp	Salt	¼ tsp	Coconut extract (opt)

Mix dry ingredients together in a large bowl. Combine maple syrup, oil and flavorings in a measuring cup, stirring well to emulsify. Pour syrup mixture over dry ingredients and stir until evenly moistened. Spread granola out on 2 cookie sheets and bake at 225° F about 1 ½ hours (less in some pans), stirring every 30 minutes until very lightly browned and nearly dry. Remove from oven and store when completely cooled and crisp.

Variation: Add 1 cup unsweetened coconut in addition to or as a substitute for sesame seeds. Keep in mind that coconut is a saturated fat food, and although it is not as harmful as an animal saturated fat, it still should be used sparingly. May also add raisins or other dried fruit of choice after baking.

Tip: No time to watch and stir? Try baking overnight in a 200° F oven. Or, combine all ingredients in a large 2" deep baking pan and stir until well mixed. Bake at 250° F for 2 to 3 hours, stirring once.

Yield: 10 cups

BETTER MILK COMBO

½ c	Better Than Milk™ powder*	1 c	West Soy "Plus," soymilk
3 T	DariFree® Potato Milk, powder	5 c	Water

In a blender, combine all ingredients and process until well mixed. Refrigerate until cold before serving. Stir again each time before serving.

***Note:** Recommend Better Than Milk™ "Soy Original" for this recipe.

Variation: Decrease water to 4½ cups for a richer flavor. May substitute any brand "ready to drink" soymilk beverage for WestSoy. For a "creamier" milk taste, process milk powders in the blender with 1 cup "warm" water before adding remaining 4 cups water and soymilk beverage.

Yield: 6 cups

BASIC NUT MILK

1 c	Water	4 c	Water
¾ c	Raw nuts, (cashews, almonds or pecans, etc.)	1 tsp	Vanilla extract
1 or 2 T	Fructose or honey	¼ tsp	Salt

In a blender, combine 1 c water with nuts and process on high speed several minutes until completely liquefied or no longer "gritty." Stop blender and add remaining ingredients. Blend briefly. Pour into a pitcher and chill and stir again before serving.

Tip: Pour milk through a cheese-cloth to remove extra pulp to produce a thinner consistency. Use pulp in casseroles, cookies or pie crusts.

Yield: 6 cups (scant)

CAROB-PECAN MILK

1 recipe	Basic "Pecan" Milk (see above)	½ tsp	Maple flavoring
3 T	Fructose or Sucanat®	½ tsp	Roma® or Caffix® (coffee substitutes)
¼ c	Carob powder		
⅓ c	Soymilk powder, plain or vanilla		

Combine above ingredients in a blender and process until well mixed.

Note: Add 3 cups soy or potato milk to above recipe to decrease fat grams per serving.

Yield: 6 ½ cups

ROMA® CAPPUCCINO

½ c	Soymilk beverage, plain (Silk®)	1 tsp	Carob powder
½ c	Water	¼ tsp	Vanilla extract
1 ½ tsp	Fructose or Sucanat®	⅛ tsp	Maple flavoring
1 tsp	Roma®, rounded		

Combine all ingredients in a blender and process on low speed until well mixed. Heat in a saucepan on the stovetop, or in a microwave oven.

Yield: 1 cup

Brunch with "A Twist"

Featuring

An assortment of quiches, potatoes, pastas, breads, and fruits. All have the appearance of a typical morning brunch. However, there is a surprising difference. These recipes taste delicious without adding the usual eggs, cheese, and milk. Give your health a boost. Experience a satisfying meal you can serve and enjoy anytime of day.

"CHICKEN" DIVAN

4 c	Water	1 T	Olive oil
2 c	Brown rice	2 pkt	Gravy Quik® (chicken-style)
1 tsp	Salt	2 c	Fresh broccoli florets
2 c	Mock chicken*	1 T	Fresh parsley, snipped
¼ c	Breading Meal # 2	1 T	Sesame seeds, lightly toasted

Combine water, brown rice and salt in a saucepan. Simmer, covered, until rice is tender. Tear mock chicken into bite-size pieces and moisten with water. Place "chicken" and Breading Meal #2 (see page 114) in a plastic bag and shake to coat "chicken" evenly. Brown "chicken" in oil and set aside. Prepare gravy according to directions on the package except increase water to 1 ¼ cups. (May substitute ½ cup water with ½ c soymilk for a richer flavor.) Steam or microwave broccoli 3 minutes or until crisp-tender. Arrange rice on a large platter. Top with the broccoli and "chicken" and pour the gravy over all evenly. Garnish with the parsley and sesame seeds.

Note: I recommend using Worthington® "Chic-Ketts™" available in the frozen foods section of some health food stores.

Yield: 10 cups

SAUSAGE-STYLE MUSHROOM & ONION QUICHE

1 rec	Potato, Oat or Wheat Crust	2 T	ENER-G® Egg Replacer
2 c	Onions, chopped	1 T	Water
2 c	Mushrooms, chopped	2 tsp	Beef-style seasoning
1 c	Bell peppers, diced	1 tsp	Spike® or Nature's Blend
2 lg	Garlic cloves, minced	1 tsp	Basil, dried
1 c	Sausage-style crumbles	1 tsp	Onion powder
2 T	Olive oil	½ tsp	Salt
2 c	Mori-Nu® Tofu, extra firm	3 T	Corn bread stuffing, crushed (Pepperidge Farm®)
3 T	Cornstarch		
2 T	Nutritional yeast flakes		

Prepare choice of Potato, Oat or Wheat Quiche Crust (recipes following) and set aside. In a large non-stick frying pan, sauté vegetables and sausage in oil until vegetables are tender. Remove from heat and set aside. In a blender, combine tofu and all remaining ingredients, except stuffing mix, and process until smooth and creamy. Pour over vegetable mixture and stir until well mixed. Pour into a 10-inch quiche dish with the prepared crust. Cover top with stuffing mix and bake at 350° F, 50 to 60 minutes or until center of quiche is set.

Yield: 10-inch quiche

MIXED VEGETABLE QUICHE

1 recipe	Potato, Oat or Wheat Crust
1 c	Onions, chopped
1 clove	Garlic, minced
1 tsp	Olive oil
1 c	Broccoli, finely sliced
½ c	Carrots, finely sliced
½ c	Cauliflower, finely sliced
1 c	Cheese Sauce (see below)
2 boxes	Mori-Nu® Tofu, extra firm (12.3 oz each)
3 T	Cornstarch
2 T	Water
2 T	ENER-G® Egg Replacer
1 T	Dry minced onion
2 tsp	Chicken-style seasoning
½ tsp	Salt
¼ tsp	Lawry's® Seasoned Salt
¼ tsp	Garlic salt
¼ tsp	Spike® Seasoning
¼ tsp	Basil, dried
¼ c	Corn bread stuffing mix (Pepperidge Farm®) (opt)

Prepare choice of Potato, Oat or Wheat Quiche Crust (recipes following) and set aside. In a non-stick frying pan, sauté onions and garlic in oil or a small amount of water until onions are translucent and set aside. Steam or microwave vegetables until crisp-tender. Drain if necessary and set aside. Prepare Cheese Sauce and set aside one cup for the recipe. (This step can be done well in advance to save time on the day it is needed.) In a blender, combine (1 cup) cheese sauce, tofu, cornstarch, water and Egg Replacer. Process until smooth and creamy. Pour out into a bowl. Add onions, mixed vegetables and all seasonings, except stuffing mix, to the tofu/cheese sauce mixture and mix well. Pour into a 10-inch quiche dish with the prepared crust. Sprinkle stuffing mix on top and bake at 350° F, 50 to 60 minutes or until center of quiche is set.

Yield: 10-inch quiche

"CHEESE" SAUCE

1 c	Cooked rice or millet
1 c	Hot water
¾ c	Raw cashews or almonds
¼ c	Carrots, cooked
2 T	Nutritional yeast flakes
1 T	Fresh lemon juice
1 tsp	Onion powder
1 tsp	Salt
½ tsp	Lawry's® Seasoned Salt
¼ tsp	Garlic powder

In a blender, combine rice, water, nuts and carrots and process on high speed until smooth and creamy. Add all other ingredients and blend again briefly.

Yield: 2 ½ cups

SPINACH-POTATO QUICHE

1 recipe	Potato, Oat or Wheat Crust	3 T	Cornstarch
1 c	Onions, chopped	2 T	Water
1 c	Fresh mushrooms, chopped	2 T	ENER-G® Egg Replacer
1 clove	Garlic, minced	1 T	Dry minced onion
1 T	Olive oil	1 tsp	Chicken-style seasoning
10 oz	Fresh spinach, coarsely chopped	1 tsp	Salt
1 c	Raw potatoes, shredded	1 tsp	Basil
4 oz	Chopped green chilies, canned	¼ tsp	Lawry's® Seasoned Salt
1 c	Cheese Sauce (see page 107)		Paprika to garnish
2 boxes	Mori-Nu® Tofu, extra firm (12.3 oz each)		

Prepare choice of Potato, Oat or Wheat Quiche Crust (recipes following) and set aside. In a non-stick frying pan, sauté onions, mushrooms and garlic in oil or 2 T water until onions are translucent. Remove from heat. Remove large stems from spinach, cut into 2 inch pieces and place in a large pot with 1 c water. Simmer until tender. Drain, cool and squeeze dry. Add spinach, potatoes and chopped chilies to onion-mushroom mixture, cook 1 or 2 more minutes and remove from heat. Prepare Cheese Sauce and set aside one cup for the recipe. (This step can be done well in advance to save time on the day it is needed.) In a blender, combine (1 c) cheese sauce, tofu, cornstarch, water and egg replacer. Process until smooth and creamy. Pour out into a bowl. Add the spinach-potato mixture, and all seasonings, except paprika, to the tofu/cheese sauce mixture and mix well. Pour into a 10-inch quiche dish with the prepared crust and garnish with paprika. Bake at 350° F, 50–60 min. or until center of quiche is set.

Yield: 10-inch quiche

POTATO QUICHE CRUST

⅓ c	Potatoes, cooked	⅓ c	Water
1 c	Unbleached white flour	3 T	Olive oil, "extra light"
1 T	Soymilk powder, plain	1 tsp	Sesame seeds
½ tsp	Salt		

Peel, cube and boil 2 potatoes. Mash enough potatoes to equal ⅓ cup and set aside. Combine flour, soy milk powder and salt. Mix water and oil together and pour into the dry ingredients. Stir until just moistened. Add mashed potatoes to the dough. Knead mixture together until a soft, pliable dough is formed. Let dough rest several minutes. Roll dough out on a floured surface. Then press dough into a 10-inch quiche dish. Flute edges. Press sesame seeds into bottom of crust.

Yield: 10-inch crust

OAT QUICHE CRUST

⅓ c	Potatoes, cooked	½ tsp	Salt
¾ c	Oat flour	⅓ c	Water
¼ c	Whole-wheat flour	3 T	Olive oil, "extra light"
1 T	Soymilk powder, plain	1 tsp	Sesame seeds

Peel, cube and boil 2 potatoes. Mash enough potatoes to equal ⅓ cup and set aside. Combine flour, soy milk powder and salt. Mix water and oil together and pour into the dry ingredients. Stir until just moistened. Add mashed potatoes to the dough. Knead mixture together until a soft, pliable dough is formed. Let dough rest several minutes. Roll dough out on a floured surface. Then press dough into a 10-inch quiche dish. Flute edges. Press sesame seeds into bottom of crust.

Yield: 10-inch crust

PASTRY-WHEAT QUICHE CRUST

¾ c	Whole-wheat pastry flour	⅓ c	Olive oil, "extra light"
¾ c	Unbleached all purpose flour	¼ c	Water
½ tsp	Salt	1 tsp	Sesame seeds

Spoon flours into measuring cups and combine in a mixing bowl. Add salt and stir until well mixed. Mix oil and water together, pour into flour mixture and stir lightly to form dough. Then knead gently to form a smooth ball. Place dough between two sheets of wax paper and roll out 2 inches larger than the pie plate. Remove top layer of wax paper, invert into 10-inch quiche dish and remove the other sheet of wax paper. Trim if necessary and flute edges. Press sesame seeds into bottom of crust.

Yield: 10-inch crust

SCRAMBLED TOFU CURRY-STYLE

VEGETABLES:

2 ½ c	Fresh mushrooms, sliced	1 T	Olive oil, "extra virgin"
2 c	Onions, chopped		

In a large frying pan, sauté mushroom and onions in oil until tender. Remove and set aside.

CURRY SAUCE:

3 c	Warm water	1 T	Chicken-style seasoning
½ c	Raw cashew pieces, rinsed	1 T	Onion powder
⅓ c	Soymilk powder, plain	1 tsp	Curry powder
3 T	Cornstarch	½ tsp	Onion salt
1½ T	Nutritional yeast flakes		

Pour one cup of the water into a blender and set the remaining water aside. Add cashews and process on high speed until completely smooth. Add the rest of the water and all remaining ingredients and blend until well mixed.

SCRAMBLED TOFU:

14 oz	Water-packed tofu, extra firm	½ tsp	Onion powder
1 T	Olive oil, "extra virgin"	½ tsp	Salt
1 T	Nutritional yeast flakes	¼ tsp	Garlic powder
2 tsp	Chicken-style seasoning	⅛ tsp	Turmeric, ground
1 tsp	Curry powder		

Press excess water out of tofu. Coat a non-stick frying pan with oil. Add tofu breaking it into bite-size pieces so it appears chunky. Combine all seasonings (may be done ahead) and sprinkle evenly over the tofu. Heat over medium heat and gently fold seasonings into tofu until well mixed. Avoid making tofu crumbly. Add mushroom and onion mixture. Simmer 3 to 5 minutes, stirring occasionally. Cover with curry sauce and gently stir until heated through and mixture thickens. Serve over rice, noodles, baked potatoes, biscuits or toast.

Yield: 8 cups

PASTA PRIMAVERA

2 c	Frozen sugar snap (or "petite" green peas)	1 tsp	Garlic & Herb seasoning ("salt free" recipe)
1½ c	Carrots, sliced	1 tsp	Onion powder
8 oz	Fettuccine noodles, dry	1 tsp	Parsley, dry
2 c	Water	½ tsp	Basil, dried
⅓ c	Soy cream cheese (Tofutti®)	½ tsp	Salt
¼ c	Soymilk powder, plain *	½ tsp	Spike® Seasoning (opt)
3 T	"Soy Good" Sour Cream (see below)	2 T	Toasted sesame seeds
2 T	Spectrum® (or) Smart Balance® "Light"	1 T	Fresh parsley, snipped
2 T	Unbleached white flour		

Simmer peas until crisp-tender. Microwave or steam carrots 2 to 3 minutes. Avoid overcooking. Set aside. Cook Fettuccine noodles according to package in 8 c salted water. Drain, rinse and drizzle with 1 tsp olive oil and stir to coat noodles. While noodles are cooking, combine water, cream cheese, soymilk powder, sour cream, Spectrum® or Smart Balance® Spread and flour in a blender. Process on medium speed until smooth and creamy. Pour mixture into a saucepan, add dry seasonings and simmer 5 to 10 minutes stirring frequently until thickened. Pour sauce over noodles, add pre-cooked vegetables and toss mixture lightly. May garnish with toasted sesame seeds and fresh parsley if desired. Serve immediately.

* Recommend Better Than Milk™ Soy "Original"

Yield: 6 cups

"SOY GOOD" TOFU SOUR CREAM

1 box	Mori-Nu® Tofu, firm (12.3 oz)	¼ tsp	Salt
3 T	Sunflower oil or extra light olive oil	¼ tsp	Honey
¼ tsp	Citric acid crystals		

In a blender, combine all ingredients and process until smooth and creamy.

Variation: Add 1 tsp fresh lemon juice for a stronger sour taste.

Yield: 1 ½ cups

MUSHROOM STROGANOFF

16 oz	Fettuccine, dry	½ tsp	Parsley, dried
1 tsp	Olive oil	¼ tsp	Salt
1 ½ c	Water-packed tofu, silken	⅛ tsp	Citric acid
1 c	Soymilk beverage, plain (Silk®)	1 can	Mock duck, (10 oz)
2 T	Unbleached white flour	2 T	Olive oil
1 T	Liquid Aminos or "lite" soy sauce	1 c	Onions, chopped
1 T	Onion powder	2 med	Garlic cloves, minced
1 ½ tsp	Beef-style seasoning	1 ½ c	Fresh mushrooms, sliced
1 tsp	Worcestershire sauce, vegetarian	(opt)	Fresh parsley, snipped

Cook pasta in salted water according to directions on the package. Drain, rinse and toss with a teaspoon of olive oil. Combine tofu, soymilk and flour in a blender and process until smooth and creamy. Pour into a saucepan and add liquid aminos, onion powder, beef-style seasoning, Worcestershire sauce, parsley, salt and citric acid. Cook, stirring constantly, until thickened and set aside. Slice mock duck (or vegetarian protein of choice) and braise in a large non-stick frying pan, with half of the olive oil until lightly browned. Remove from the pan and set aside. Add remaining oil to the frying pan and sauté onions until translucent. Add garlic and mushrooms, and sauté until tender. Add sautéed mixture and the mock duck to the cream sauce and stir to mix well. Before serving, re-heat sauce mixture and spoon desired amount over the fettuccine. Or, toss the sauce and the pasta together before serving. If desired, garnish with fresh parsley.

Variation: For vegetable stroganoff, delete mock duck. Add 1 cup each steamed sliced carrots, broccoli and cauliflower florets seasoned to taste.

Yield: 12 cups

PERFECT RICE (Oven to Table)

1 c	Brown rice, long grain	½ tsp	Salt
2 ½ c	Water	½ tsp	Chicken-style seasoning
1 T	Dried minced onion (opt)		

Heat rice in a dry skillet over med-hi heat. Stir-fry until rice begins to crackle and turns a light golden color. (This is called "dextrinizing" and conditions rice to cook up light and fluffy.) Coat a casserole dish with cooking spray. Pour in rice, water and seasoning and mix well. Cover with foil or a glass lid and bake at 350° F for 1 hour. Remove from oven, fluff with a fork and serve.

Yield: 3 cups

"CHICKEN" & CURRY STEW

1 c	Onions, chopped	1 T	Chicken-style seasoning
2 tsp	Olive oil	1 T	Curry powder, mild
4 c	Water	3	Cardamom seeds
1 c	Carrots, sliced	½ tsp	Salt
1 can	Tomatoes, diced (14.5 oz)	1 c	Frozen peas, thawed
16 oz	Vegetarian chicken protein (frozen or canned, 2–3 cups)	2 T	Fresh parsley, snipped
		¾ c	Coconut milk "lite," canned

Sauté onions in oil until tender. Add water and carrots and bring to a boil. Add canned tomatoes, and vegetarian chicken and return to simmering. Add chicken-style seasoning, curry powder, cardamom seeds and salt. Lower heat cover and simmer about 1 hour. Add peas and parsley and simmer 3 minutes. Add coconut milk and simmer 2 more minutes. Add more water if needed. Remove cardamom seeds before serving. Serve over seasoned brown rice.

Note: If you wish to prepare this recipe ahead of serving time, delay adding coconut milk until ready to reheat and serve.

Yield: 8 cups

CURRIED GARBANZOS
(Khatte Channa)

2 c	Onions, chopped	1 c	Garbanzo juice or liquid
3 T	Olive oil	1 T	Tamarind concentrate (pulp)
1 T	Garlic, minced	2 tsp	Massala curry powder
4 tsp	Fresh ginger, minced	1 ½ tsp	Cumin, ground
½ tsp	Turmeric, ground	1 ½ tsp	Salt or to taste
1 can	Tomatoes, diced (14.5 oz)	4 c	Garbanzos, canned

In a large pot, sauté onions in oil until lightly browned. Add garlic and cook a few minutes more. Add ginger, turmeric and tomatoes. Cover and simmer about 5 minutes. Add garbanzo liquid, tamarind, massala, cumin and salt. Simmer 2 minutes more. Add garbanzos, cover and simmer 10 more minutes. Serve with rice.

Yield: 8 cups

BREADING MEAL #2

½ c	Flour, wheat or white	1 T	Nutritional yeast flakes
¼ c	Cracker crumbs, finely blended	1 tsp	Onion powder
¼ c	Yellow corn meal	½ tsp	Salt
2 tsp	Beef or chicken-style seasoning	½ tsp	Garlic powder

Mix ingredients together and store in an air tight container.

Yield: 1 ⅛ cups

"QUICK BAKED" GOLDEN POTATO FRIES

Slice 2 large baking potatoes lengthwise into ½ inch wide sticks. Prepare a baking sheet with cooking spray. Spread potatoes out in a single layer. (To enhance flavor, drizzle 1 tsp olive oil over the potatoes and stir to coat evenly.) Sprinkle with any combination of seasonings to your taste i.e. dried parsley, herbs, chives, onion salt, garlic salt, Spike®, nutritional yeast etc. Broil on the top oven rack at 400° F. Stir after 10 minutes and then every 5 minutes for 15 minutes or until tender with golden brown crispy edges. You may also want to add onion rings to the fries during the last 5 minutes of baking time. Serve hot and, if desired, with Vinegarless Ketchup (see below) on the side.

Yield: 4 cups

"QUICK" VINEGARLESS KETCHUP

1 ½ c	Tomato sauce	2 T	Fruit-Fresh® powder (or) ⅛ tsp citric acid
1 c	Tomato paste	1 ½ tsp	Salt
½ c	Pineapple juice	1 tsp	Onion powder
¼ c	Fresh lemon juice	½ tsp	Garlic salt
1 tsp	Lime juice	½ tsp	Paprika
3 T	Date butter (see note, p. 251)	¼ tsp	Worcestershire sauce (Vegetarian brand) (opt)
2 T	Pineapple/orange juice (frozen concentrate)		
2 T	Fructose or honey		

Combine all ingredients in a blender and process until smooth. Refrigerate. Freeze extras not used within two weeks.

Variation: For thicker ketchup, decrease tomato sauce to 1 cup and increase tomato paste to 1 ½ cups.

Yield: 4 cups

VERY BERRY CREAM CHEESE SPREAD

4 oz Better Than Cream Cheese®, plain (Tofutti®)
¼ c All-fruit jam, (blueberry, strawberry or raspberry)

Gently stir and swirl mixture together. Spread on whole-wheat bagels or any whole grain bread of choice. Or, spread cream cheese on bread and top with jam.

Yield: ¾ cup

CREAM CHEESY SPREAD

8 oz Better Than Cream Cheese®, plain (Tofutti®)
⅛ tsp Citric acid

Sprinkle citric acid evenly over cream cheese and stir until well mixed. Use mixture to stuff celery, or as a sandwich filling with sliced olives, cucumbers, or onions etc.

Yield: 1 cup

DATE AND WALNUT BREAD

1 c Boiling water
1 c Dates, snipped finely
1 T Olive oil, "extra light"
½ c Fructose or brown sugar
1¾ c Whole-wheat flour
2 tsp Baking powder
1 tsp Baking soda
¾ tsp Salt
½ tsp Cinnamon, ground
½ c Walnuts, chopped
2 tsp ENER-G® Egg Replacer
2 T Water

Pour boiling water over dates and stir until cool. Add oil, and sweetener of choice. Mix well. Add dry ingredients (except Egg Replacer) and stir gently. Whisk Egg Replacer with water until foamy. Fold into batter. Pour into a loaf pan prepared with cooking spray and bake at 350° F, 55 to 60 minutes.

Yield: 1 loaf/12 slices

TOFU-BANANA BREAD #1

1 ⅓ c	Ripened bananas, mashed	1 c	Whole-wheat flour
¾ c	Water-packed tofu, silken	1 tsp	Baking powder
¾ c	Fructose or brown sugar	½ tsp	Baking soda
¼ c	Olive oil, "extra light"	½ tsp	Salt
1 tsp	Vanilla extract	¾ c	Walnut pieces
1 c	Unbleached white flour		

In a blender, combine bananas, tofu, sweetener, oil and vanilla and process until smooth and creamy. In another bowl, combine remaining ingredients. Pour blender ingredients into dry ingredients and mix well. Pour into a loaf pan prepared with cooking spray. Bake at 350° F, 52-55 minutes.

Yield: 1 loaf / 12 slices

HAWAIIAN BANANA-NUT BREAD

1 c	Ripened bananas, mashed	2 tsp	Baking powder
½ c	Water-packed tofu, firm	¾ tsp	Salt
¼ c	Olive oil, "extra light"	½ tsp	Baking soda
2 tsp	Vanilla extract	½ tsp	Cinnamon, ground
¾ c	Fructose or brown sugar	4 oz	Crushed pineapple, canned
1 c	Whole-wheat flour	1 T	ENER-G® Egg Replacer
¾ c	Grape Nuts® (cold cereal)	4 T	Water
½ c	Unbleached white flour	1 c	Walnuts or pecans, chopped

In a blender, combine bananas, tofu, oil, vanilla, and sweetener and process until smooth and creamy. Mix whole wheat flour, grape nuts, white flour, baking powder, salt, soda and cinnamon in a bowl. Add blender ingredients and well-drained pineapple to the dry ingredients and stir gently. Whisk Egg Replacer with water 2 or 3 minutes until foamy and fold into batter. Stir in the nuts last. Pour batter into a loaf pan prepared with cooking spray and bake at 350° F, 55 to 60 minutes.

Variation: To make Hawaiian Banana-Nut "Muffins," increase baking powder to 1 tablespoon, fill large "heavy duty" muffin tins ¾ full, and sprinkle additional finely chopped nuts on top. Bake at 375° F for 20 to 25 minutes.

Yield: 1 loaf / 12 slices

PEACH-NUT BREAD

2 ½ c	All purpose flour	¾ c	Honey
1 c	Wheat germ	¼ c	Dole® "Orchard Peach" (frozen juice concentrate)
1 T	Baking powder	¼ c	Olive oil, "extra light"
½ tsp	Baking soda	1 T	Lemon juice
½ tsp	Salt	1 tsp	Vanilla extract
1 c	Walnuts, chopped (reserve ¼ cup)	1 T	ENER-G® Egg Replacer
1 can	Peaches, juice packed (16 oz)		

Combine dry ingredients and set aside. Drain peaches, mash or chop finely and set aside. Combine honey, frozen juice concentrate, oil, lemon juice, vanilla and Egg Replacer and beat to dissolve Egg Replacer. Stir in peaches. Pour peach mixture into flour mixture; stir just until moistened. Pour into a loaf pan prepared with cooking spray. Sprinkle with reserved nuts. Bake at 350° F, approximately 1 hour and 10 minutes or until a toothpick comes out clean.

Variation: To make Peach-Nut "Spice" Bread, add 1 tsp cinnamon, ¼ tsp nutmeg, and ⅛ tsp cloves.

Yield: 1 loaf / 12 slices

RASPBERRY BRAN MUFFINS

1 c	Whole-wheat pastry flour	⅓ c	Honey
1 c	Wheat bran	¼ c	Olive oil, "extra light"
1 T	Baking powder	1 ½ tsp	ENER-G® Egg Replacer
½ tsp	Salt	1 c	Raspberries, fresh (or whole frozen berries)
¾ c	Soymilk beverage, plain		

Combine dry ingredients. In another bowl combine soymilk, honey, oil and Egg Replacer. Whisk to dissolve Egg Replacer. Combine liquid and dry ingredients and stir until just moistened. Gently fold in rinsed and drained raspberries. Prepare a heavy weight muffin tin with cooking spray. Fill cups nearly full. Bake at 400° F, 18 to 20 minutes or until lightly browned.

Note: If using light weight muffin tins, reduce heat to 375° F. If using a deep muffin tin designed for making 12 large muffins, double recipe.

Yield: 1 dozen (small) muffins

RAISIN BRAN MUFFINS
(Yeast-raised)

- 1 ¼ c Warm water
- 2 T Olive oil, "extra light"
- 2 T Wonderslim® or Lighter Bake® (Fat and Egg Substitute)
- 1 T Active yeast, rapid-rise
- 1 T Honey or molasses
- 1 tsp Vanilla extract
- ½ tsp Salt
- 1 ¼ c Whole-wheat flour
- ½ c Oat bran
- ½ c Wheat germ
- ½ c Date sugar
- ½ c Dates, diced
- ½ c Raisins
- ½ c Pecans, chopped (opt)

Combine water, oil, Wonderslim, yeast, honey, vanilla and salt. (Set aside while measuring dry ingredients.) Combine remaining ingredients in a separate bowl. Pour liquid ingredients into dry ingredients and stir gently until well mixed. Prepare a heavy weight deep muffin tin with cooking spray. Fill muffin tins with batter nearly full. Allow to rise in a warm draft-free place until over the top or about 30 minutes. Bake at 350° F, 25 minutes. Cool 10 to 15 minutes before trying to remove from pan. Set muffins on a cooling rack to cool completely before storing.

Yield: (12) large muffins

BRAN MUFFINS
(Quick-raised)

- 1 ½ c Whole-wheat flour
- 1 ½ c Wheat bran
- ½ c Oat bran
- ½ c Brown sugar
- 1 T Baking powder
- 1 tsp Carob powder
- ½ tsp Baking soda
- ½ tsp Salt
- ½ c Raisins
- ½ c Dates, chopped
- ½ c Pecans, chopped
- 1 ½ c Soymilk beverage
- ¼ c Olive oil, "extra light"
- ¼ c Molasses
- 1 T Lemon juice
- 1 T Vanilla extract

Combine all dry ingredients. In a separate bowl, combine tofu milk, oil, molasses, lemon juice and vanilla. Stir liquid ingredients gently into dry mixture and blend well. Prepare a heavy weight deep muffin tin with cooking spray and fill cups nearly full. Bake at 375° F, 25 to 28 minutes.

Yield: (12) large muffins

BLUEBERRY OAT BRAN MUFFINS

1 ½ c	All purpose flour	½ c	Honey
1 c	Oat bran	⅓ c	Olive oil, "extra light"
1 T	Baking powder	3 T	Applesauce
¾ tsp	Salt	1 tsp	Vanilla extract
½ tsp	Baking soda	1 T	ENER-G® Egg Replacer
½ tsp	Lemon zest, grated	2 T	Water
¾ c	Soymilk beverage, plain	¾ c	Fresh blueberries

Combine dry ingredients. In another bowl, combine soymilk, honey, oil, applesauce, and vanilla. Then add mixture to dry ingredients, stirring only until dry ingredients are moistened. Whisk Egg Replacer with water 2 or 3 minutes until foamy. Fold gently into batter. Rinse, drain, and blot blueberries dry and gently stir into the batter. Prepare a heavy weight muffin tin with cooking spray. Fill muffin cups ¾ full. Bake at 375° F, 20 to 25 minutes or until a light golden brown color.

Variation: For a "lower fat and sugar version", reduce oil to 3 T and increase applesauce to ⅓ cup. Also, decrease honey to ⅓ cup and increasevanilla to 1 T.

Yield: (12) large muffins

BLUEBERRY JAM

4 c	Frozen blueberries	½ c	Fructose, granular
12 oz	White grape juice, (100%) (frozen concentrate, undiluted)	1 ¾ oz	"Ball" Fruit Jell (1 box) ("low or no sugar" label)
½ c	Water	½ tsp	Fresh lemon juice

Combine all ingredients in a blender and process until berries and pectin are blended smooth. Pour into a saucepan and bring to a boil stirring constantly. Lower heat and cook one minute. Cool. Pour into small clean freezer jars. Leave ½ inch headspace. Screw caps on or place lid on jar and screw down band fingertip tight. Let stand until cool. Store in freezer or keeps well in refrigerator 3 to 4 weeks.

Variation: Substitute "white grape juice" with "white grape/peach juice" concentrate and omit lemon juice.

Yield: 4 cups

RASPBERRY JAM

4 c	Raspberries	5 T	Cornstarch, arrowroot, or tapioca powder
12 oz	White grape juice (frozen concentrate, undiluted)	½ tsp	Fresh lemon juice
12 oz	Water		

Purée raspberries in a blender. If desired, may strain puréed raspberries to remove seeds. In a saucepan, combine remaining ingredients and stir until cornstarch is dissolved. Bring to a boil and simmer until juice is clear. Add raspberry purée to juice and continue to cook stirring constantly until jam is thick. Cool and refrigerate.

Note: May also follow directions for "Blueberry Jam" using fruit pectin.

Yield: 5 cups

APPLE BUTTER

1 c	Purple grape juice, unsweetened	1 c	Frozen apple juice (concentrate, undiluted)
¾ c	Dark raisins	½ tsp	Cinnamon, ground
⅓ c	Dates, pitted	1 ⅓ c	Applesauce
5 T	Cornstarch		

Simmer grape juice, raisins and dates until soft. Pour mixture into a blender and process until smooth. In a saucepan, dissolve cornstarch in apple juice. Add grape juice mixture and cinnamon. Simmer, stirring constantly, until clear and thick. Stir in applesauce and refrigerate.

Yield: 4 cups

APPLE SPICE BUTTER

2 c	Dried apples, packed	½ c	Pineapple juice
2 c	Hot water	½ tsp	Cinnamon, ground

Soak apples in water 15 minutes. Pour into a blender and add remaining ingredients. Process on high speed until smooth. Chill.

Yield: 3 cups

"HEART SMART" CORN BUTTER

1 c	Cold water	2 T	Olive oil, "light"
¼ c	Yellow corn meal	1 T	Emes Kosher Jel® (plain)
½ c	Mori-Nu® Tofu, extra firm	1 T	Cooked carrot (opt for color)
½ c	Warm water	1 tsp	Honey
¼ c	Almonds	1 tsp	Imitation butter flavored salt
3 T	Natural Butter Flavor, vegan (Spicery Shoppe®)	½ tsp	Salt
		pinch	Citric acid

Combine cold water and corn meal in a small saucepan and bring to a boil stirring constantly. Reduce heat to low, cover and simmer 10 minutes. Refrigerate mixture until completely cool and "set." In a blender, combine tofu, water, almonds, butter flavoring, oil and Emes®. Process on high speed until no longer "gritty." Spoon chilled corn meal mush into the blender mixture and all remaining ingredients and process until smooth and creamy. Bits of carrot should not be visible. Refrigerate several hours before serving until "butter" thickens to a spreadable consistency.

Yield: 3 cups

ORANGE HONEY BUTTER

Add the following ingredients to 1 cup of cold, pre-set Corn Butter:

2 T	Creamy "Spun" honey (Sue Bee® or similar brand)	1 T	Orange juice concentrate
		½ tsp	Orange zest, grated

Whip at high speed until fluffy. Refrigerate before serving.

Yield: 1 ¼ cups

WALDORF APPLE SALAD

4 c	Apples, diced	½ c	Nayonaise® (soy mayonnaise)
1 c	Seedless red grapes, halved	2 T	Fructose, granular
½ c	Celery, diced	1 c	Non-dairy whipped topping (Cool Whip® or similar product)
½ c	Walnut or pecans, chopped		

Combine apples, grapes and celery. Lightly toast nuts on a baking sheet at 250° F for 10 minutes. (This step can be done ahead in larger quantities. Store nuts in the freezer until ready for use.) Add nuts to fruit mixture. Combine Nayonaise and fructose and gently stir into apple mixture. Fold whipped topping in last. Best if served immediately.

Yield: 6 cups

ENGLISH TRIFLE

BERRY FILLING:

1 c	Water	¼ c	Cornstarch
6 oz	White grape/raspberry (frozen juice concentrate)	2 c	Fresh or frozen berries (blueberries, cherries or raspberries)
1 tsp	Vanilla extract		
½ c	Water		

Combine 1 c water, juice concentrate and vanilla and bring mixture to a boil. Combine ½ cup water and cornstarch and stir until dissolved. Stirring constantly, add cornstarch-water to the boiling juice and continue stirring until mixture thickens and "clears." Add the berries and remove from heat. Set aside to cool.

CREAM FILLING:

1 box	Mori-Nu® Tofu, firm (12.3 oz)	½ tsp	Vanilla extract
⅓ c	Fructose, granular	¼ tsp	Salt
1 c	Soymilk beverage, plain (Better Than Milk™ Original)	2 T	Instant Clear Jel® (Instant food thickener)

In a blender, combine tofu, fructose, soymilk, vanilla and salt and process until smooth. Turn blender speed down to lowest setting, remove the lid and add Instant Clear Jel® food thickener. Replace lid, increase speed to highest setting and process briefly until mixture is thick.

CRUNCHY FILLING:

2 c Granola or graham crackers crushed until crumbly

PROCEDURE:

Layer above ingredients into parfait glasses in the following order:

1. Granola or graham crackers.
2. Berry filling
3. Cream filling
4. Repeat

End top layer with granola or graham crackers and a dollop of berry filling.

Yield: 8 parfaits

FRESH FRUIT *with* PUDDING COMPOTE

Prepare (12 c) of fresh fruit combinations; i.e. peaches, bananas, strawberries, grapes, blueberries, pineapple and kiwi. Set aside.

2 c	Water	½ c	Spun honey (Sue Bee®)
1 c	Water-packed tofu, silken	½ c	White flour
1 c	Cooked white rice	1 T	Fresh lemon juice
1 c	Coconut milk, canned ("lite," unsweetened)	2 tsp	Vanilla extract
		(opt)	Fresh mint leaves

In a blender, process water, tofu, rice, and coconut milk until smooth and creamy. Add remaining ingredients and blend until well mixed. Pour mixture into a saucepan and bring to a boil, stirring constantly until thick. Refrigerate pudding until cold before serving. Arrange half of fruit in a large serving bowl. Layer about three-fourths pudding mixture over fruit. Cover with remaining fruit. Spoon remaining pudding on top in the center, allowing fruit to show around the edges. Place a whole strawberry or small cluster of grapes on top. Garnish with mint leaves if desired.

Yield: 16 cups

ROMA® CAPPUCCINO

½ c	Soymilk beverage, plain (Silk®)	1 tsp	Carob powder
½ c	Water	¼ tsp	Vanilla extract
1 ½ tsp	Fructose or Sucanat®	⅛ tsp	Maple flavoring
1 tsp	Roma® (rounded)		

Combine all ingredients in a blender and process on low speed until well mixed. Heat in a saucepan on the stovetop or in a microwave oven.

Yield: 1 cup

Featuring

Tasty low-fat recipes bursting with all the natural flavors of Mexico without the added hot spices and oils.

QUESADILLAS

2 doz	Corn tortillas	1 c	Black olives, sliced
3 c	Enchilada sauce (see below)	4 oz	Canned green chilies, chopped (Old El Paso®)
2 c	Soy Mozzarella cheese, grated		

ENCHILADA SAUCE:

½ c	Onions, diced	1 ½ T	Chili Powder Substitute (see page 132)
2 med	Garlic cloves, minced	1 tsp	Cumin, ground
1 tsp	Olive oil	½ tsp	Salt
15 oz	Tomato sauce		
1 ⅛ c	Water		

In a saucepan, sauté onions and garlic in oil until translucent. Add remaining ingredients and simmer 30 minutes. Pour half of the sauce into a pie plate.

PREPARATION: Dip tortillas in enchilada sauce and transfer to a non-stick frying pan. Cover tortilla with 3 T mozzarella cheese, 2 T olives and 1 tsp chilies. Dip another tortilla in the sauce and place on top. Fry over medium heat until soft and slightly crispy. Flip and fry other side the same way. Serve with additional enchilada sauce, soy sour cream recipe of choice (see page 129 or page 131) and guacamole (see page 140).

Yield: 12 Quesadillas

"CHICKEN-STYLE" QUESADILLAS

1 ½ c	Mock chicken, shredded	¼ c	Canned green chilies, chopped
½ c	Onions, chopped	(opt)	Salsa or picante sauce, mild
1 T	Olive oil	8	Whole-wheat tortillas (8-inch)
2 c	Soy cheddar cheese, shredded		

Sauté mock chicken and onions in oil until onions are tender and chicken is golden brown. Remove from frying pan and set aside. Prepare frying pan with cooking spray. Spray a tortilla with a light coating of cooking spray and lay sprayed side down in the frying pan. Spread one fourth of the chicken mixture evenly over the tortilla. Sprinkle ½ c cheese over the chicken and spread about 2 tsp chilies over the cheese. Cover with another tortilla and spray the top with cooking spray. Cook over med/high heat until lightly browned. Flip over and cook the other side the same way.

Variation: Add blanched spinach to the recipe or substitute spinach in place of mock chicken.

Yield: 4 Quesadillas

CHILIQUILLAS

1 ½ c	Onions, chopped	1 tsp	Lawry's® Seasoned Salt
2 T	Olive oil	7 oz	Corn tortilla chips (low fat)
28 oz	Whole tomatoes, canned	2 c	Soy Jack cheese, shredded
1 pkt	Taco seasoning mix (1.25 oz)	1 c	Soy sour cream (or more)
4 oz	Canned green chilies, chopped	½ c	Soy cheddar cheese, shredded

Sauté onions in oil until tender. Add tomatoes, taco seasoning, chilies and seasoned salt. Mix well. Mash tomatoes and simmer mixture uncovered, 10 to 15 minutes. Set aside. Prepare a 9" x 13" casserole dish with cooking spray. Layer ingredients in this order, making two layers. 1) Tortilla chips 2) Sauce 3) Soy Jack cheese 4) Soy sour cream. Bake at 350° F, for 20 minutes. Top with the soy cheddar cheese, shredded, and bake 10 minutes more. Cool 10 to 15 minutes before serving. Cut into squares. Serve with a dollop of guacamole and soy sour cream. For a complete meal, serve with Spanish rice and refried beans on the side.

Variation: Add one layer of mashed chili beans or seasoned refried beans.

Yield: (12) 3-inch squares

BEAN BURRITOS SUPREME

8 lg	Flour tortillas, warmed	1 c	Sweet onions, diced
15 oz	Chili beans, canned	1 c	Black olives, sliced
15 oz	Refried beans, canned	8 oz	Ortega® Taco Sauce, mild
4 c	Lettuce, shredded	¼ c	Tomato sauce
4 c	Soy cheese, shredded	1 c	Soy sour cream
2 c	Tomatoes, diced (or salsa)	1 c	Guacamole
1 c	Cooked brown rice (opt)	(opt)	Black olives, sliced

Mash un-drained chili beans with refried beans in a frying pan. Heat until hot and bubbly. Fill tortilla with about ½ cup chili bean mixture, ¼ cup lettuce, ¼ cup soy cheese, 2 T tomatoes or salsa, 2 T rice (opt) and 1 T onions and olives. Roll up tortillas and place seam side down in a single serving augratin dish. Or, arrange burritos in an oblong casserole dish prepared with cooking spray. Mix taco sauce with tomato sauce and pour over burritos. Sprinkle with remaining cheese. Bake at 325° F, until cheese melts and burritos are heated through. Dollop 1 T sour cream and 1 T guacamole on top of each burrito and if desired, garnish with additional olives. Garnish with remaining shredded lettuce and diced tomatoes around the perimeter of each burrito.

Yield: 8 Burritos

SPINACH "CHEESE" ENCHILADAS

1 c	Onions, chopped	½ tsp	Lawry's® Seasoned Salt
4 lg	Garlic cloves, minced	8 oz	Ortega® Taco Sauce, mild
1 T	Olive oil	¼ c	Tomato sauce
8 c	Fresh spinach, chopped	10	Corn tortillas
2 tsp	Chicken-style seasoning	2 c	Soy cheddar cheese
1 tsp	Cumin, ground	¼ c	Green onions, sliced (opt)

In a large frying pan, sauté onions and garlic in oil until tender. Add spinach, and stir-fry until wilted. Add seasonings and stir until well mixed. Cover and simmer over med heat a few more minutes until tender. Combine taco sauce and tomato sauce. Pour ½ c sauce mixture in the bottom of an oblong casserole dish. Heat tortillas one at a time in a dry skillet over med/hi heat, turning frequently until tortillas are soft and pliable. Fill tortillas with about 2 T spinach mixture and 2 T soy cheese, shredded. Roll up and place seam side down in the casserole dish. Cover tortillas evenly with the remaining taco sauce. Bake uncovered at 375° F, about 20 minutes. Sprinkle remaining cheese on top and bake 10 minutes more until cheese is melted and begins to bubble. If desired, garnish with green onions. Serve with soy sour cream, and a side dish of rice and refried beans.

Yield: 10 Enchiladas

"CHICKEN" ENCHILADAS

2 c	Creamy Mushroom Sauce	2 tsp	Olive oil
1 c	Sour Cream Supreme	1 c	Onions, minced
1 ¼ c	Cashew Jack Cheese	¼ c	Green chilies, chopped
1 c	Mock chicken, cubed (Chic-Ketts™)	1 doz	Tortilla shells

Prepare Creamy Mushroom Sauce (page 129), Sour Cream Supreme (page 129) and Cashew Jack Cheese (see page 129, but do not add the Emes® Jel for this recipe). Combine the required amounts of mushroom sauce, sour cream and cheese in a large bowl. Sauté "chicken" in oil and add to the sauce mixture. Stir in onions and chilies and mix all together well. Fill shells, roll up and place in a baking dish, seam side down. Then add a little water to thin sauce enough to spoon remaining mixture over top. Bake at 350° F, about 30 minutes.

Yield: 12 Enchiladas

CREAMY MUSHROOM SAUCE

1 ½ c	Onions, chopped	⅔ c	Unbleached white flour
2 T	Olive oil	⅓ c	Soymilk powder, plain
2 c	Fresh white mushrooms	2 tsp	Nutritional yeast flakes
1 c	Water	2 tsp	Chicken-style seasoning
¼ tsp	Onion salt	1 ½ tsp	Salt
3 c	Water	½ tsp	Basil, dried

Sauté onions in oil until golden. Coarse chop mushrooms and add to the onions with 1 c water and onion salt and simmer until mushrooms are tender. Set aside 1 cup sautéed mushrooms. In a blender, combine 3 cups water, flour, soymilk powder, and seasonings and process until smooth and creamy. Add the reserved 1 cup mushrooms to the blender and "flash blend" ingredients together twice. Pour blender ingredients into a saucepan and bring to a boil stirring constantly until thickened. Add remaining onion and mushroom mixture and mix well.

Yield: 4 cups

SOUR CREAM SUPREME

1 ¼ c	Mori-Nu® Tofu, firm (10.5 oz)	1 tsp	Honey
¼ c	Sunflower oil or extra light olive oil	½ tsp	Salt
2 ½ T	Fresh lemon juice		

In a blender, combine all ingredients and process until smooth and creamy.

Yield: 1 ½ cups

CASHEW JACK "CHEESE"

1 c	Water	1 T	Fresh lemon juice
4 T	Emes Kosher Jel® (plain)	1 ½ tsp	Salt
1 c	Cooked rice, brown or white	1 tsp	Onion powder
½ c	Raw cashews, rinsed	¼ tsp	Garlic powder
1 T	Nutritional yeast flakes		

In a blender, combine water, Emes Jel, rice and cashews. Process on high speed until completely smooth and creamy. Add seasonings and blend again until well mixed. Pour into a container coated with cooking spray. Refrigerate several hours until set. Gently shake out of container to slice cheese as needed. To shred cheese easily, freeze mixture at least 2 hours first. Or, for a creamy sauce to serve over vegetables, slowly heat and melt cheese over lo-med heat stirring frequently.

Yield: 2 cups

TEX-MEX "CHEESE" ENCHILADAS

ENCHILADA SAUCE:

1 c	Onions, diced	2 ½ c	Water
5 med	Garlic cloves, minced	2 ½ T	Chili Powder Substitute*
2 tsp	Olive oil	2 tsp	Cumin, ground
2 cans	Tomato sauce (15 oz each)	1 tsp	Salt

In a 2 quart saucepan, sauté onions and garlic in oil until translucent. Add remaining ingredients and simmer 30 minutes. (* see recipe on page 132)

FILLING:

2 lb	Water-packed tofu, firm	1 ½ tsp	Onion powder
3 T	Soy sauce or liquid aminos	¾ tsp	Cumin, ground
1 ½ T	Tomato paste	2 tsp	Olive oil
1 ½ T	Peanut butter		

Freeze tofu ahead of time to change texture of tofu into a "bean curd". Thaw tofu and squeeze the excess water out. Tear the bean curd into bite-size pieces. Combine soy sauce, tomato paste, peanut butter, onion powder and cumin and mix with the tofu pieces. Pour into a large non-stick frying pan or skillet and brown in oil, turning often. Proceed with recipe.

1 ½ c	Soy mozzarella cheese, shredded	2 T	Green chilies, chopped (Old El Paso® chilies)
1 c	Black olives, sliced		
½ c	Onions, chopped	15	Corn tortillas

Stir the shredded cheese, olives, onions and chilies into the tofu mixture.

PREPARATION: Prepare a 9" x 13" casserole dish with cooking spray. Fill the bottom of the dish with enough enchilada sauce to cover. Heat tortillas in a frying pan over med heat until softened. Lay ⅓ c filling at the edge of the shell and roll it up tightly and place seam side down in rows. Continue procedure until pan is filled. Cover with sauce and bake uncovered at 350° F, about 25 minutes or until bubbling. Garnish with additional shredded soy mozzarella cheese and olives if desired and return to oven 5 more minutes.

Tip: Serve with "Soy Good" Tofu Sour Cream. (See page 131)

Yield: 15 enchiladas

MEXICAN ENCHILADAS

FILLING:

¼ c	GranBurger® (or TVP, beef flavored)	1 ½ c	Onions, chopped
¼ c	Warm water	½ c	Black olives, sliced
2 c	Pimiento Cheese, shredded (see p. 132) (or 2 c Soy cheddar cheese, shredded)	¼ c	Green chilies, chopped (Old El Paso® chilies)

Rehydrate Granburger or TVP in water. Combine all ingredients.

SAUCE:

2 cans	Hunt's® Ready Sauce, "Special"	2 T	Olive oil
6 oz	Tomato paste	1 T	Garlic purée
1 c	Water	1 tsp	Garlic powder
1½ T	Mild chili powder (or substitute*)	1 tsp	Cumin, ground
1 tsp	Beef-style seasoning (McKay's®)		

Combine Special Sauce and tomato paste. Stir in remaining ingredients.
(*See Chili Powder Substitute recipes on page 132)

SHELLS:

15 Fresh corn tortillas (Frozen tortillas break easily)

PROCEDURE:

Fill bottom of baking dish with enough sauce to cover. Heat tortillas one at a time in a frying pan until softened. Spoon ¼ c filling into tortilla shells, roll them up and place enchiladas seam side down in rows. Cover with remaining sauce. Top with shredded soy cheese, or Cashew Jack Cheese (page 129) or Pimiento Cheese (page 132) and olives. Bake uncovered, 325° F, 25 minutes.

Tip: Serve with "Soy Good" Tofu Sour Cream. (See below)

Yield: 15 enchiladas

"SOY GOOD" TOFU SOUR CREAM

1 ½ c	Mori-Nu® Tofu, firm (12.3 oz box)	¼ tsp	Salt
3 T	Sunflower oil or extra light olive oil	¼ tsp	Honey
¼ tsp	Citric acid crystals		

In a blender, combine all ingredients and process until smooth and creamy.

Variation: Add 1 tsp fresh lemon juice for a stronger sour taste.

Yield: 1 ½ cups

PIMIENTO "CHEESE"

1 ¼ c	Water	4 oz	Pimientos, canned
1 c	Cooked rice	2 T	Lemon juice
4 T	Emes Kosher Jel® (plain)	2 tsp	Onion powder
½ c	Water-packed tofu, extra firm	2 tsp	Salt
½ c	Raw cashews, rinsed	½ tsp	Garlic powder
3 T	Nutritional yeast flakes		

In a blender, combine water, rice, Emes Jel, tofu and cashews. Process on high speed until completely smooth and creamy. Add remaining ingredients and blend well. Pour into a container coated with cooking spray. Refrigerate several hours until set. Gently shake out to slice cheese.

Note: To shred cheese easily, freeze mixture at least 2 hours first. For a creamy sauce to serve over vegetables or noodles, do not refrigerate mixture after blending, but heat and serve immediately. Or, if using previously "set" leftovers, heat mixture slowly until cheese melts.

Yield: 3 cups

CHILI POWDER SUBSTITUTE

2 T	Paprika	1 tsp	Cumin, ground
1 T	Parsley flakes	1 tsp	Oregano, dried
1 T	Dried bell pepper	½ tsp	Dill, dried
1 T	Basil, dried	½ tsp	Savory, dried
1 T	Onion powder	¼ tsp	Garlic powder
2 sm	Bay leaves, dried		

Grind all in a blender until fine and powdery.

Yield: ½ cup

PUEBLO NACHOS

24	Tortilla chips, lower fat	⅓ c	Soy Good Sour Cream (see p.131)
½ c	Ortega® Taco sauce, mild	1 c	Soy cheddar cheese, shredded
(opt)	Chili, mashed (see p.138)	(opt)	Fresh cilantro or parsley

Prepare nachos by spreading tortilla chips on a baking sheet or on an oven-proof serving dish. Spoon about 1 tsp taco sauce on each chip followed by a spoonful of chili, if desired. Top with ½ tsp soy sour cream and sprinkle with soy cheddar cheese. Bake at 350° F, 10 minutes or long enough to melt cheese. If desired, garnish with snipped cilantro or parsley before serving.

Yield: 24 Nachos

TAMALE PIE

FILLING:

2 c	Onions, chopped	1 c	Cut corn, frozen or fresh
½ c	Green or red bell peppers, chopped	15 oz	Canned tomatoes, diced
2 T	Olive oil	2 tsp	Chili Powder substitute*
½ c	Burger-style crumbles (frozen or canned)	1 tsp	Beef-style seasoning
2 oz	Canned green chilies, chopped (Old El Paso®)	½ tsp	Cumin, ground
2 c	Canned beans, any combination (i.e. kidney, black and pinto beans)	½ tsp	Onion salt
		½ c	Soy cheese, shredded
		¼ c	Black olives, sliced

Sauté onions and bell peppers in olive oil until tender. Stir in burger and chilies. Add the beans, corn and tomatoes and mix well. Add the chili powder, beef-style seasoning, cumin and onion salt, stir until mixture begins to simmer and remove from heat. The cheese and olives will be added later.

CRUST:

2 ½ c	Cold water	1 ½ tsp	Chili Powder substitute*
1 ½ c	Yellow corn meal	1 tsp	Salt
2 oz	Canned green chilies, chopped (Old El Paso®)		

In a non-stick saucepan, combine above ingredients and bring to a boil, stirring constantly. Reduce heat, simmer and stir frequently until thick and sides pull away from the pan, about 5 minutes. Coat a 10-inch deep dish pie pan with cooking spray and pour about ⅔ of the corn meal mixture into the bottom of the pan. Spray a rubber spatula with no-stick cooking spray and press mixture over the bottom and sides of the pan. Pour filling into the pie pan and level. Sprinkle grated soy cheese over the filling. Top with sliced black olives. Drop remaining corn meal evenly over the filling and with fingers gently spread crust out to the edges. Flute the edges if desired. Bake at 350° F, 45 to 50 minutes or until golden brown.

Note: Our recipe for Chili Powder Substitute is found on page 132. If using commercial chili powder, reduce amounts listed in recipe by half.

Yield: 10-inch pie

VEGETARIAN FAJITAS

2 c	Onions, sliced	1 c	Zucchini, sliced diagonally and julienned
10 slices	Green bell pepper, (2 inch long strips)	5 oz	Fresh spinach, trimmed
6 slices	Red bell peppers, (2 inch long strips)	(opt)	Seasoned salt, garlic & herb seasoning, or liquid aminos
1 c	Fresh mushrooms, sliced	10 oz	Mock duck or veggie steaks, cut into strips (opt)
2 cloves	Garlic, minced	1 doz	Flour tortillas, 8-inch (wheat or white)
3 T	Olive oil		
1 c	Yellow summer squash, sliced diagonally		

In a large non-stick frying pan, sauté onions, peppers, mushrooms and garlic in oil. Add squash and stir-fry 5 minutes or until vegetables are tender. Add spinach and cover and steam until wilted. Season to taste. If desired, sauté mock duck or veggie steaks in another skillet until lightly browned. Add to stir-fry just before serving. Wrap tortillas in 2 packages of foil and place in a warm oven until ready to serve or heat in a covered tortilla dish.

Toppings: Sour cream (page 129 or 131), guacamole (page 140), salsa (page 137) and wedges of limes on the side.

Tip: For a full course Mexican dinner, serve vegetable fajitas with a side dish of Spanish rice and refried beans or frijoles.

Yield: 12 fajitas

HAYSTACKS

Seasoned Brown Rice *
Crispy Corn Chips *
Chili Beans *
Soy cheese, shredded
Shredded lettuce
Diced tomatoes
Chopped onions
Sliced black olives
Huevos Rancheros Salsa *
Guacamole *
"Soy Good" Sour Cream *
Ranch-Style Dressing *

Stack the above ingredients in the order given. For example, serve chips and/or rice on the plate first. Spoon beans on top next. Sprinkle cheese over beans. Add any or all of the other ingredients up to the top.

Note: For "quick" Haystacks, replace any of the above homemade ingredients for commercial products of choice.

* See recipes throughout chapter.

ARROZ MEXICANO (MEXICAN RICE)

1 ¾ c	Water	¼ tsp	Paprika
¾ c	Stewed tomatoes, undrained	¼ tsp	Cumin, ground
½ c	Onions, chopped	1 c	Carrots, diced
1 lg	Garlic clove, minced	¼ c	Green bell peppers, diced
2 T	Olive oil	¼ c	Red sweet peppers, diced
1 tsp	Chicken-style seasoning	1 ½ c	Instant brown rice
1 tsp	Parsley flakes	1 T	Fresh parsley, chopped
¾ tsp	Salt	1 T	Green chilies, chopped (Old El Paso®-canned chilies)
¼ tsp	Basil, dried		

In a blender, combine water, tomatoes, onion, garlic, seasonings and herbs. Add blender ingredients to the carrots and bell peppers and cook over medium heat, covered 20 minutes. Add the rice, cover and cook an additional 10 minutes until the liquid is absorbed and the rice is tender. Add the chilies and fresh parsley and stir until heated through.

Yield: 5 cups

SEASONED BROWN RICE

2 c	Water	½ tsp	Chicken-style seasoning
1 c	Brown rice	½ tsp	Salt
1 T	Dried minced onion		

Combine ingredients and cook in a rice cooker or cook on the stove top until rice is tender and water is absorbed, about 45 minutes.

Yield: 4 cups

CRISPY CORN CHIPS

6 Corn tortilla shells
Salt or seasoned salt (to taste)
Cooking Spray
(olive oil, garlic or butter flavored)

Place 6 corn tortillas in a stack. Cut into quarters, then cut quarters in half to make 8 wedge shaped stacks of chips. Arrange chips, one layer thick, on a baking sheet. Spray chips lightly on both sides with cooking spray and sprinkle with salt or seasoned salt. Bake in a preheated oven at 450° F, 8 to 10 minutes watching carefully to avoid browning.

Yield: 48 chips

FESTIVE SUN DRIED TOMATO "CHEESE" POLENTA

2 c	Water	½ c	Onions, diced
1 tsp	Salt	½ c	Black olives, sliced
1 c	Yellow cornmeal, fine	4 oz	Canned green chilies, chopped
1 c	Cold water	⅓ c	Sun dried tomatoes, diced (packed in olive oil and herbs)
½ tsp	Onion salt	1 ½ c	Soy cheddar cheese, shredded
1 c	Yellow cut corn, frozen		

Bring 2 c water and salt to a boil. Combine cornmeal with 1 c cold water and onion salt. Stir until well mixed. Pour cornmeal into boiling water stirring constantly until thickened or about 1 minute. Remove from heat. Stir in vegetables and 1 cup of the cheese. Spray a 10-inch baking dish with cooking spray. Pour mixture into dish, cover and bake at 350° F, one hour. Top with remaining shredded cheese and bake uncovered 10 minutes more. Chill until set and firm. Cut into squares and reheat in a warm oven or microwave before serving. Delicious served with salsa.

Yield: 9 (3-inch) squares

BAKED CORN FRITTERS

1 c	Warm water	¾ c	Yellow cornmeal
2 T	Honey	3 T	Soymilk powder, plain
1 T	Yeast	1 tsp	Salt
2 T	Light olive oil	¼ c	Pimientos, diced
1 ½ c	Unbleached white flour	2 T	Canned green chilies-chopped

Combine water, honey, yeast and oil. Let stand 3 to 5 minutes. Stir in flour, cornmeal, soymilk powder and salt. Add pimientos and green chilies and gently stir until evenly mixed. Prepare a "corn mold" pan with cooking spray. Fill with batter until ¾ full. Let rise until double. Bake at 350° F, 15 minutes or until golden brown. Remove from pan and arrange on a cookie sheet bottom side up. Return to oven and bake 5 minutes more to crisp the bottom side.

Note: If using a muffin tin, let rise until double and bake at 350° F, 20 minutes or until lightly browned.

Yield: 12 fritters

SASSY SALSA

1 can	Stewed tomatoes, (14.5 oz)	3 T	Fresh lemon juice
1 can	Zesty diced tomatoes, (14.5 oz) (with mild green chilies)	2 T	Fresh lime juice
1 can	Tomato sauce, seasoned (8 oz) (roasted garlic flavor)	2 tsp	Jalapeño peppers (deseeded and minced)
¼ c	Tomato paste	2 large	Garlic cloves, minced
¾ c	Sweet onions, diced	½ tsp	Garlic & Herb seasoning (McCormick® salt-free)
½ c	Roma tomatoes, diced	½ tsp	Onion powder
1 can	Green chilies, chopped (4 oz)	½ tsp	Salt
¼ to ½ c	Fresh cilantro, minced	½ tsp	Oregano, dried (opt)

Combine canned tomato products, onions, fresh tomatoes and canned chilies. Remove large stems from cilantro before mincing. Add cilantro and all remaining ingredients to the tomato mixture and mix well. Chill.

Yield: 7 cups

HUEVOS RANCHEROS SALSA

STEAM:

¾ c	Onions, chopped	½ tsp	Salt
½ c	Bell pepper, chopped	¼ tsp	Basil, dried
2 sm	Garlic cloves, minced	⅛ tsp	Oregano, dried
2 T	Fresh parsley or cilantro, minced	⅛ tsp	Cumin, ground

ADD:

4 oz Old El Paso® canned green chilies, chopped
2 c Fresh tomatoes, chopped (or 14.5 oz canned tomatoes, diced)

Combine ingredients. Microwave or cook until vegetables are blanched. Chill.

Yield: 3 cups

SEASONED SALT

¼ c	Celery salt	2 T	Onion powder
¼ c	Paprika	2 tsp	Garlic powder
2 T	Salt		

Mix all ingredients well. Store in an air-tight container.

Yield: ¾ cup

QUICK & SNAPPY 3 BEAN CHILI

1 can	Bush's® Chili Magic, (Traditional Recipe) (15.5 oz)	14.5 oz	Diced tomatoes, "no salt"
1 can	Red kidney beans, (15 oz) ("lower-sodium" variety)	⅔ c	Burger-style crumbles
1 can	Black beans, (15 oz)	2 T	Dried minced onions
		1 tsp	Beef-style seasoning
		¾ tsp	Cumin, ground

Lightly drain Chili Magic and pour into a saucepan. Lightly drain kidney beans and add to the saucepan. Do not drain black beans or tomatoes and add next. Stir in burger and seasonings. Cover and simmer chili 5 to 10 minutes. Serve hot.

Variation: For a richer tomato flavor, add 1 ½ T tomato paste.
Tip: Try a dollop of "Soy Good" Tofu Sour Cream (see page 131) or shredded soy cheddar or soy Mozzarella Cheese (see page 244) to top off this chili bean recipe.

Yield: 7 cups

CHILI BEANS

3 c	Dried pinto beans	1 qt	Diced tomatoes, canned
1 ½ c	Red kidney beans, canned	2 c	Burger-style crumbles (or 1 c TVP, beef flavored)
1 ½ c	Black beans, canned	1 T	Honey or Sucanat®
1 tsp	Salt, (or to taste)	1 T	Cumin, ground
2 c	Onions, chopped	1 T	Mild chili powder (or Chili Powder Substitute)
1 c	Red / green bell peppers, chopped	2 tsp	Beef-style seasoning
3 lg	Garlic cloves, minced		
1 T	Olive oil		

Sort, wash, and soak pinto beans overnight. Drain. In a large pot, simmer beans for 2 to 3 hours in only enough water to keep the beans covered. When tender, add kidney beans (drained), black beans and salt. In a non-stick frying pan, steam or sauté onions, bell pepper, and garlic in oil. Add sautéed mixture, tomatoes, burger, honey and seasonings to beans and simmer 30 minutes more stirring occasionally. (The longer the beans cook, the better the flavor.) Chili beans are also good cooked in a crock-pot, but with limited space, you will find it necessary to cut this recipe in half.

Yield: 12 cups

POZOLE SOUP

SOUP BASE:

1 T	Olive oil	1 qt	Water
1 clove	Garlic, minced	2 c	Crushed tomatoes, canned
1 stalk	Celery, thinly sliced	1 c	Tomato purée, canned
1 c	Onions, diced	1 c	Cilantro, chopped
1 c	Yellow squash, julienned	1T	Chicken-Style seasoning
1 c	Zucchini, julienned	1 tsp	Chili Powder Substitute (opt)
1 c	Carrots, diced		(see page 132)
1 ½ c	Hominy, canned	½ tsp	Salt

In a large pot, sauté garlic, celery, onions, squash and carrots in oil. Add remaining ingredients, (except hominy) and simmer until vegetables are tender. Add hominy just before serving to avoid overcooking. Fill soup bowls about half way with soup base before adding tortilla strips and garnishes listed below.

GARNISHES:

12	Corn tortillas strips, baked (see below)	1 c	Avocado, cubed
2 c	Purple cabbage, finely shredded	1 c	Black olives, sliced
2 c	Tomatoes, diced	2	Limes, quartered
1 c	Green onions, sliced	2	Lemons, wedged
1 can	Black beans, rinsed	(opt)	Soy cheese, shredded
1 c	Radishes, minced		

TORTILLA STRIPS: Stack tortillas and cut them into thin strips and then cut the strips in half. Prepare a baking sheet with cooking spray and spread tortilla strips out evenly. Bake at 250° F until crisp, turning as needed.

TO SERVE: Set baked tortilla strips and all garnishes out buffet style. Each person can then pick and choose. The tortilla strips should be added to the hot soup first followed by any or all of the garnishes. Lemon or lime juice squeezed over the top of the soup and garnish mixture adds a zesty flavor.

Yield: 3 quarts

GUACAMOLE

3 med	Ripe avocados	1 ¼ tsp	Salt or seasoned salt
¼ c	Soy mayonnaise	½ tsp	Garlic powder (opt)
1 c	Onions, minced	⅛ tsp	Cumin, ground (opt)
2 tsp	Fresh lemon juice	1 ½ c	Fresh tomatoes, diced

Mash avocado to desired consistency. Add mayonnaise of choice (recipes on page 165 or 166) and remaining ingredients, one at a time, mixing well after each addition. Add tomatoes last, stirring gently. Best if eaten the same day.

Yield: 5 cups

RANCH-STYLE DRESSING

1 box	Mori Nu® Tofu, firm (12.3 oz)	1 tsp	Onion powder
½ c	Water	1 tsp	Basil, dried
¼ c	Sunflower oil	½ tsp	Savory, dried
3 T	Fresh lemon juice	½ tsp	Parsley, dried
1 ¼ tsp	Salt	⅛ tsp	Citric acid crystals (to taste)
1 tsp	Honey	2 T	Fresh chives, minced (opt)
1 tsp	Garlic salt	1 T	Fresh parsley, minced (opt)

Combine all ingredients, except fresh herbs, in a blender and process until smooth and creamy. Stir in the optional fresh chives and parsley last. Chill before serving.

Yield: 2 ½ cups

RANCH DRESSING "QUICK and EASY"

1 pkg	Hidden Valley® Dressing Mix (Ranch® Buttermilk Recipe)	⅓ c	Olive oil, "extra light"
1 ¼ c	Mori-Nu® Tofu, firm	3 ½ T	Fresh lemon juice
½ c	Water	3 T	Soymilk powder, plain

Combine above ingredients in a blender and process until smooth and creamy. Chill before serving.

Variation: Add 2 T water and decrease oil to ¼ c for a lower fat version.
Note: Only the "Original" Ranch Dressing mix with the instructions to add "buttermilk and mayonnaise" is "vegan." The "add milk and mayonnaise" recipe has buttermilk powder in the ingredients.

Yield: 2 ½ cups

FRESH FRUIT PIE with ALMOND BARLEY CRUST

CRUST:

½ c Barley flour
½ c All purpose flour
1 T Wheat germ (opt)
½ tsp Salt
¼ c Raw almond butter
¼ c Hot water
2 ½ T Olive oil, "extra light"

Combine flours, wheat germ and salt. In a separate bowl, mix the almond butter, water and oil together. Pour into flour and stir until dough is moist. Knead into a ball and until smooth. (It won't get tough from too much handling.) Roll out between two sheets of waxed paper. Carefully remove wax paper and shape crust into a 9-inch pie plate. Pre-bake the crust before adding fresh fruit filling. Prick the bottom of the crust with a fork and bake at 350° F, 10 to 12 minutes. Over baking causes the crust to become tough.

Variation: May replace almond butter with raw cashew butter.

CUSTARD FILLING:

1 ¼ c Water
¼ c Cooked white rice
3 T Blanched almonds (w/o skins)
2 T Coconut, grated
3 T Honey
2 ½ T Cornstarch
2 T Soymilk powder
½ tsp Vanilla extract
⅛ tsp Salt

In a blender combine "half" the water, rice, almonds and coconut and process until smooth. Add remaining water and ingredients. Blend well. Place in saucepan and bring to a boil, stirring constantly. Pour into crust and refrigerate until cool. When chilled, cover with fresh fruits of choice, thinly sliced. Pour Berry Shine Glaze (recipe below) over fruit. Chill again. Top with "Instant" Whipped Topping (see recipe on page 90) before serving.

FRESH FRUIT: i.e. (Strawberries, banana, kiwi, mango, peaches, etc.)

BERRY SHINE GLAZE:

⅔ c Apple juice, frozen concentrate
⅓ c Strawberries or raspberries
4 tsp Cornstarch

In a blender, process all ingredients on high speed until creamy. Pour into a saucepan and bring to a boil, stirring constantly until thick and clear. Cool until lukewarm and pour over fresh fruit. Chill pie until ready to serve.

Yield: 9-inch pie

La FIESTA "SPLASH" SLUSHY DRINK

2 c	Fresh ripe mango, cubed	1 ½ c	Water
1 c	Fresh ripe papaya, cubed	1 c	Pineapple juice
½ c	Chiquita® "Caribbean Splash" (frozen juice concentrate)	1 tsp	Fresh lime juice
		½ tsp	Coconut flavoring (opt)

In a blender, combine all ingredients and process until smooth. Pour into a large shallow pan, cover and freeze several hours until slushy. Spoon into glasses and garnish with lime wedges.

Variation: Add 1 ripe banana. Also, may replace mango with ripe peaches.

Yield: 6 cups

VIRGIN PINA COLADA

1 ½ c	Crushed pineapple with juice	2 T	Cream of coconut
½ c	Canned coconut milk, unsweetened	3 c	Ice cubes
2 T	Pineapple juice, frozen concentrate		

Combine all ingredients in a blender. Blend on high speed until drink becomes slushy. Serve immediately.

Yield: 4 cups

VIRGIN STRAWBERRY DAIQUIRI

10 oz	Frozen strawberries	6 oz	Water
6 oz	Lemonade, frozen concentrate		

Combine ingredients in a blender. Process until well mixed. Add ice cubes until blender is full and blend again until mixture becomes slushy.

Note: If using unsweetened strawberries, add honey or fructose, if desired.

Yield: 2 ½ cups

SNAPPY TOMATO JUICE

1 qt	Tomato juice	½ tsp	Garlic purée
2 T	Fresh lemon juice	½ tsp	Dill weed
2 T	Vegetarian Worcestershire sauce	⅛ tsp	Cayenne pepper (opt)
1 T	Italian salad dressing, dry mix		

Combine all ingredients in a pitcher and mix well. Refrigerate until ready to serve. Serve in a tall glass over ice and garnish with a slice of lemon.

Yield: 34 oz

HOW TO COOK DRIED BEANS

Measure desired amount of beans (1 cup dried beans yields about 2 ½ cups of cooked beans). Wash several times with water, removing any spotted or discolored beans. Cover with water and soak overnight. Soybeans and garbanzos cook faster if frozen after being soaked. Other beans need not be frozen after being soaked, but, if you do this, it will shorten their cooking time.

To one cup of beans add 4 cups water (for lentils use 3 cups only). Bring to boiling point and reduce heat just to keep a constant simmer. Add more boiling water as necessary until beans are at desired tenderness. Lentils may be cooked in less than one hour, and should not be soaked, however, other beans may vary up to two hours or more. Soybeans and garbanzos will take 5 or more hours to be palatable and tender. When tender, add salt to taste, ½ tsp (more or less) to each cup of dried beans. Additional seasoning is advised as your taste indicates.

Many people do not eat beans because they cause flatus or gas. This can be overcome by preparing them properly. The substance in beans that produce gas, two unusual starches: stachyose and raffinose, are not broken down by the starch digesting enzymes normally present in the gut. Thus they remain in the digestive tract to come into contact with certain bacteria that react to break them down to carbon dioxide and hydrogen, which are the main components of gastrointestinal gas.

To break down these starches so they can be digested, wash the beans in the morning. Then place them in the amount of water needed for cooking. Let them soak all day. Before going to bed, place them in the freezer. The freezing process breaks up the starch molecules. Cook them in the same water that is now ice, but do not add any salt. Use the meat tenderizer that contains papain, which comes from papaya. This tenderizer contains salt, therefore it takes the place of salt. The papaya enzyme gets through to these starches and breaks them down. They will not cause any gas. If you cannot find meat tenderizer with papain then use six papaya enzyme tablets, crushed. These are equivalent to one teaspoon of meat tenderizer. Papaya enzymes do not contain salt. Therefore you will have to add salt. The INDO® meat tenderizer is available in most nutritional centers and is free from harmful additives. Be sure to check the label, as not all are acceptable.

Methods to help eliminate the distress from eating beans include the following:

1. Soak overnight, drain, cover with water and cook.
2. Soak overnight, drain and cover with water, bringing to a boil. Let set for one hour, then drain, add water and cook.
3. Soak overnight, drain and cover with water. Add 1-2 T fennel seed before cooking.
4. Soak overnight, drain and freeze beans. Rinse, add water and cook.

To all white beans at the time of salting add a few sprinkles of garlic salt. Lentils and black beans are good this way also. Simmer for 15 minutes. Red beans and soybeans are tasty with a sauce made of 1 cup onions, diced and sautéed in water until tender. Then add 1 clove of minced garlic, 1 T diced pimiento, and 2 T tomato paste. For soybeans use ½ c tomato paste, more onion and a bit of lemon juice. Simmer together and add to the beans. Cook beans until soupy thickness. A pinch of sweet basil, oregano or Italian seasoning may be added. Garbanzos are excellent when simmered with chopped onions, a little nutritional food yeast and salt.

Cooking Times for Legumes

There are two methods of pre-soaking legumes before cooking. Only lentils and split peas require no soaking before cooking.

1. Long Soak Method: Cover beans with about four times their volume of cold water and let stand to soak for 8 hours or longer.
2. Rapid Soak Method: Cover beans with about four times their volume. Bring to a boil, reduce heat and simmer 2 minutes. Remove from heat. Cover and let stand 1 hour before cooking.

Pressure cooking dramatically decreases the cooking times of dried beans. Use 4 cups water to 1 cup beans. Never fill the cooker more than half full. Add 1T oil to lessen frothing. Cook beans without salt at 15 lbs pressure.

Item:	Pressure Cooker:	Stove Top:
Lentils	5–10 minutes	45 minutes
Navy beans	20 minutes	1 hour
Green split peas	20 minutes	1 hour
Black-eyed peas	30 minutes	2 hours
Kidney beans	60 minutes	3 hours
Pinto beans	60 minutes	3 hours
Garbanzos	70 minutes	4–6 hours
Soybeans	70 minutes	4–6 hours

Siew Mai
Baked "Egg" Rolls
Vegetable Fried Rice
Lemon Wonton Soup
Sweet and Sour "Chicken"

A Taste of The Orient

Featuring

A selection of Asian recipes for you to enjoy which are popular in the countries of Singapore, China, Philippines, Guam and Thailand.

VEGETABLE FRIED RICE
(China)

1 c	Mock duck, canned	1 c	Sugar snap peas, frozen
1 c	Water-packed tofu, firm (cubed)	1 c	Carrots, julienned
1 tsp	Sesame oil	½ c	Baby corn, sliced
2 tsp	Soy sauce (or) Bragg™ aminos	½ tsp	Salt (or) 2 T Bragg™
2 tsp	Cornstarch dissolved in 2 T water	3 c	Cooked brown rice
½ c	Onions, diced	¼ c	Green onion, sliced
2 lg	Garlic cloves, minced	½ c	Cashews, lightly roasted
1 T	Olive oil, or water	2 T	Sesame seeds, toasted
1 c	Jicama, julienned	(opt)	Cherry tomato/parsley

Shred duck or gluten into small bite-size pieces and cube tofu. Place mixture into a non-stick wok or an extra large non-stick frying pan. Combine sesame oil, soy sauce and cornstarch-water. Pour sauce over duck-tofu mixture and set aside 5 minutes to marinate. Sauté mixture until tofu is nicely browned. Add onion, garlic and olive oil and stir-fry entire mixture together over medium heat until onion is transparent. Stir gently to avoid breaking up the tofu cubes. Add jicama, peas, carrots, baby corn and seasoning to the wok mixture and stir-fry 2 to 3 minutes until vegetables are crisp-tender. Stir in the pre-cooked rice and half of the green onions, cashews and sesame seeds and toss until well mixed. (Note: Rice should be light and fluffy in this recipe. Instant brown rice works well. For improved flavor, cook rice with salt, dried onion and/or with chicken-style seasoning.) Prepare a large serving platter with a border of lettuce. Mound rice mixture into the center of the platter and garnish with remaining green onion, cashews and sesame seeds. For added color, arrange fresh parsley and cherry tomatoes around the border and garnish with a feathered green onion stem on top.

Yield: 9 cups

MOCK DUCK IN BLACK BEAN SAUCE
(Singapore)

3 cloves	Garlic, minced	12 pods	Fresh snow peas
1 med	Onion, thinly sliced	1 can	Button mushrooms
¼ tsp	Fresh ginger, minced	2 c	Mock duck (10 oz can)
¼ c	Black beans, canned	½ tsp	Honey
1 T	Olive oil	3 T	Mushroom water

Sauté garlic, onions, ginger and beans (better if rinsed) in oil. Add snow peas and stir-fry 1 minute. Drain mushrooms (reserve water) and add to the stir-fry. Slice duck into strips, and stir-fry until braised. Mix honey with water, add to stir-fry, cover and simmer briefly. Serve with rice or noodles.

Yield: 5 cups

SWEET AND SOUR "CHICKEN" (China)

2 c	Mock chicken, pieces*	1 c	Red & green bell peppers
¼ tsp	Sesame oil	1 med	Carrot
2 tsp	Soy sauce or liquid aminos	½ sm	Cucumber
2 tsp	Cornstarch	3 sm	Roma tomatoes
2 T	Water	2 c	Sugar snap peas
1 tsp	Olive oil	¼ tsp	Salt or to taste
1 recipe	Sweet and Sour Sauce	1 stem	Green onion, sliced

Tear mock chicken into 1½ inch pieces. Combine sesame oil, soy sauce, cornstarch and water. Mix with "chicken" and stir until well coated. Allow to marinate for 5 minutes. In a large, non-stick frying pan, brown marinated "chicken" in oil and set aside. In a large saucepan, prepare Sweet and Sour Sauce (see recipe below). Cut peppers into chunky pieces. Cut carrot into thin diagonal slices. Add bell peppers and carrots to sauce. Cover and simmer until vegetables are crisp-tender. Peel cucumber, then quarter lengthwise. Remove seeds, divide strips in half again and then cut strips into 1-inch sticks. Quarter the tomatoes. Add the cucumber, tomatoes, peas and salt to the Sweet and Sour Sauce. Mix well, cover and simmer briefly. (Peas will lose color if over cooked.) Stir in chicken, cover and turn off heat. Remove from heat after 5 minutes. Pour Sweet and Sour "Chicken" into a shallow dish and garnish with a border of lettuce. Sprinkle green onion over the top. Serve with rice.

* *Note:* I recommend using Worthington® "Chic-Ketts™" available in the frozen foods section of some health food stores.

Yield: 8 cups

SWEET AND SOUR SAUCE

2 cloves	Garlic, minced	3 T	Tomato paste
1 ½ c	Onions, thinly sliced	2 T	Honey or fructose
1 T	Olive oil	1 T	Fresh lemon juice
1 tsp	Soy sauce, "lite"	1 T	Cornstarch
1 c	Pineapple juice	3 T	Water
1 c	Pineapple chunks		

In a large saucepan, sauté garlic and onions in oil and soy sauce until the onions are transparent. Combine pineapple juice, pineapple chunks, tomato paste, honey and lemon juice and add to the garlic-onion mixture. Cover and bring to a slow boil. Dissolve cornstarch in water and add to the sauce. Stir and simmer until sauce "clears."

Yield: 3 cups

SESAME "CHICKEN"

8 oz	Mock chicken, (Chic-Ketts®, ½ roll)

Breading Meal:

½ c	Corn bread stuffing, crushed	2 T	Unbleached white flour
¼ c	Sesame seeds, white	2 tsp	Fresh parsley, minced
3 T	Soy Parmesan cheese, grated		

Batter:

¾ c	Water	1 ½ T	Unbleached white flour
1 ½ T	Instant Clear Jel® (food thickener)	¼ tsp	Salt

Prepare breading meal and pour into a shallow bowl. Combine batter ingredients in a blender and process until smooth and pour into another shallow bowl. Tear mock chickens into chunks about 2 inches long by 1 inch wide. Dip into batter and coat all sides. Roll in breading meal. Prepare a baking sheet with cooking spray. Lay breaded "chicken" on the baking sheet allowing a little space between the pieces. Use a regular (plain), olive oil, butter, or garlic flavored cooking spray and spray directly on "chicken" to lightly coat each piece. Bake at 375° F, 10 minutes. Turn each piece over and bake 5 to 10 minutes more, or until golden brown.

Tip: Serve alone, or dip in ketchup or sweet & sour sauce on the side. Sesame "Chicken" is also very tasty when used to make a sandwich.

Yield: 8 pieces

PEKING NOODLE STIR-FRY

1 recipe	Scrambled Tofu "Eggs" (page 94)	½ c	Sliced almonds, (lightly toasted)
8 oz	Linguini "fini"(or) vermicelli pasta	2 T	Sesame seeds, white (or 1 T poppy seeds)
1 c	Frozen green "petite" peas		
½ tsp	Onion salt (to taste)		

Prepare "eggs" in a large skillet and set aside. Break noodles into 4 inch pieces and cook in boiling salted water according to directions on the package. While the noodles are cooking, simmer the green peas in a small amount of water until crisp-tender (about 2 minutes), remove from heat and drain. When ready, drain and rinse noodles and toss with a light coating of olive oil. Sprinkle onion salt evenly over noodles. Add noodles to the "eggs" and mix well. Stir in peas, almonds and sesame seeds. If desired, garnish with a stem of green onion, with tips frayed.

Yield: 8 cups

TOFU FOO YUNG

1 c	Onions, finely sliced	2 T	Bragg® Liquid Aminos
1 c	Fresh mushrooms, chopped	½ c	Water-packed tofu, extra firm
1 c	Snow peas, coarse chopped	¾ c	Unbleached white flour
1 c	Jicama, julienned	3 T	Nutritional yeast flakes
½ c	Bamboo shoots	1 T	ENER-G® Egg Replacer
1 T	Olive oil	2 tsp	ENER-G® Baking Soda
2 c	Bean sprouts, fresh	½ tsp	Salt
3 ½ c	Water-packed tofu, extra firm		

In a large skillet or wok, combine onions, mushrooms, peas, jicama, bamboo shoots and olive oil. Sauté over low to medium heat until crisp-tender. Add bean sprouts, stir briefly and remove from heat. In a blender, combine (3 ½ cups) tofu and liquid aminos and process until smooth and creamy. Pour out into a large bowl and add (½ cup) tofu. Mash the tofu, then add flour, yeast flakes, egg replacer, baking soda and salt. Stir mixture well. Add cooked vegetables to tofu mixture. Prepare a baking sheet with cooking spray and scoop ¼ c mixture onto baking sheet and flatten into a 3-inch circle. Leave a 1-inch space between each one. Bake at 350° F, 30 minutes, flip over and bake 15 minutes more. Serve hot with rice and Oriental Mushroom Gravy (recipe below).

Note: If using traditional baking soda, decrease amount to 1 tsp.

Yield: 18 patties

ORIENTAL MUSHROOM GRAVY

2 c	Cold water	4 T	"Lite" soy sauce
½ c	Fresh mushrooms, diced	2 T	Cornstarch

In a saucepan, combine all ingredients and stir until cornstarch dissolves. Cook over med-low heat until gravy thickens and clears.

Yield: 2 ¾ cups

ALMOND BROCCOLI STIR-FRY

4 c Broccoli, florets
¾ c Carrots, thinly sliced
½ c Water
⅛ tsp Salt

In a deep sauté pan or wok, combine vegetables with water and salt. Cover and bring to a boil, reduce heat and simmer 2 minutes. Remove lid for 30 seconds (to preserve the bright green color of the broccoli), cover again and simmer 2 to 3 minutes more until crisp-tender. Drain and reserve water for later use.

½ lb Water-packed tofu, extra firm
2 tsp Olive oil
1 c Onions, thinly sliced
½ c Fresh mushrooms, sliced
1 tsp Olive oil
1 c Reserved stock + water
2 tsp Chicken-style seasoning
1 T Cornstarch
(opt) Soy sauce to taste
½ c Slivered almonds, lightly toasted

Cut tofu into ½ inch cubes. In a non-stick frying pan, sauté tofu in 2 tsp oil over medium heat until golden brown on all sides. Add to broccoli. Next, sauté onions and mushrooms in 1 tsp oil until tender and the edges begin to brown. Add to broccoli. Combine reserved water with enough additional water to equal 1 cup. Add cornstarch and seasoning to water and mix well. Pour into frying pan and cook until bubbly and clear. Pour over broccoli mixture. Add almonds and stir-fry to reheat entire mixture before serving.

Yield: 7 cups

CABBAGE & WALNUT STIR-FRY

1 ¼ lb Cabbage, (½ head)
2 med Garlic cloves, minced
1 c Onions, sliced
1 ½ tsp Olive oil
½ c Water
¼ c Fresh parsley, chopped
¼ c Walnut pieces, toasted
2 tsp Chicken-style seasoning

Finely slice and cut cabbage into ½ inch pieces and set aside. In a wok or large frying pan, sauté garlic and onions in oil until tender. Add cabbage, water, parsley, walnuts, and seasoning. Stir-fry or cover and simmer about 15 minutes until cabbage is tender.

Yield: 8 cups

BROCCOLI-CHEESE RICE RING

4 c	Cooked rice, unseasoned	¼ c	Onions, minced
1 tsp	Chicken-style seasoning	¼ c	Black olives, sliced
¼ tsp	Onion salt	2 T	Green chilies, canned
2 c	Broccoli florets, small	1 T	Pimientos, diced
1 ½ c	Pimiento cheese (see p. 132)		

Combine rice, chicken-style seasoning and onion salt and mix well. Steam broccoli 2 minutes and stir into rice. In a small saucepan, heat cheese until melted. Add onions, olives, green chilies (chopped), and pimientos. Pour cheese mixture into rice mixture and stir until evenly coated. Spray a plastic ring mold prepared with cooking spray. Spoon mixture into the mold, packing lightly. Microwave, uncovered at high power 3 ½ to 5 minutes or until heated through. If you do not have a rotating tray, rotate mold halfway through cooking time. Cool several minutes and invert onto a round serving platter. May fill center of rice ring with additional steamed broccoli.

Yield: 8 cups

PERFECT RICE (Oven to Table)

1 c	Brown rice, long grain	½ tsp	Salt
2 ½ c	Water	½ tsp	Chicken-style seasoning
1 T	Dried onion, chopped (opt)		

Heat rice in a dry skillet over med-hi heat. Stir-fry until rice begins to crackle and turns a light golden color. (This is called "dextrinizing" and conditions rice to cook up light and fluffy.) Coat a casserole dish with cooking spray. Pour in rice, water and seasoning and mix well. Cover with a glass lid or foil and bake at 350° F for 1 hour. Remove from oven, fluff with a fork and serve.

Yield: 3 cups

SIEW MAI
(Singapore)

½ c	Onions, minced	1 T	Sesame oil
1 tsp	Garlic, minced	2 tsp	Dry bread crumbs
½ c	Mock duck, finely diced	4 tsp	Cornstarch
¼ c	Jicama or water chestnuts, diced	¼ c	Water
¼ c	Carrot, finely diced (reserve 1 T)	20	Wonton wrappers, (eggless variety)
1 T	Bragg® Liquid Aminos, (or "Lite" soy sauce)		

Sauté onions and garlic in a small amount of water until onion is translucent. Add mock duck and jicama or water chestnuts and stir-fry 2 minutes. Add liquid aminos or soy sauce, sesame oil and bread crumbs and mix lightly. Mix cornstarch with water and pour over duck mixture. Remove from heat and stir until well mixed. Lightly moisten round wonton wrapper on the top side. Place about one tablespoon of filling onto the center of each wrapper. Lift up all four corners of the wrapper, pinch and twist the sides together around the filling, leaving a little opening at the top. Then flatten the base. Press a few finely diced carrots inside the top for garnish. Place each Siew Mai on an oiled steamer tray and steam for 7 minutes.

Yield: 20 Pieces

PINAKBET
(Philippines)

1 c	Water-packed tofu, firm	2 c	Okra, sliced
4 med	Eggplant, chopped	1 c	Bitter melon (opt)
2 c	Fresh green beans, 2" cuts	1 c	Bell pepper, chopped
2 c	Squash, chopped	1 T	Soy sauce
1 c	Onions, chopped	2 tsp	Salt
2 T	Olive oil	1 tsp	Garlic powder
½ c	Water	2 tsp	Cornstarch in 2 T water

Cut tofu into strips and sauté in a non-stick frying pan coated with cooking spray until lightly browned. Set aside. Sauté eggplant, beans, squash and onions in oil. Add water and cover. Cook until vegetables are crisp-tender. Add okra, bitter melon (opt), bell pepper and seasonings and simmer until all vegetables are tender. Add cornstarch-water to thicken sauce if desired. Gently stir in tofu strips. Serve with rice and/or crispy noodles.

Yield: 12 cups

PAO
(Singapore)

DOUGH:

1 c + 2 T	Warm water	2 T	Oil
1 ½ T	Yeast	2 c	Whole-wheat flour
2 T	Brown sugar or honey	2 ½ c	All purpose flour
1 tsp	Salt		

Combine water, yeast and sugar in a bowl and let stand a few minutes until yeast begins to bubble. Add salt and oil to yeast mixture and stir to dissolve the salt. In a separate bowl, combine the two kinds of flour and set ½ c aside for later use. Pour yeast mixture into the bowl of flour. Stir with a big wooden spoon until the mixture is too difficult to work. Turn dough out unto a lightly floured surface and knead for about 8 to 10 minutes. Sprinkle additional reserved flour on the surface and onto hands if necessary to prevent sticking. Add more flour only when necessary to make a firm smooth dough. (The dough should be firmer than dough for baking bread.) Place dough in a large bowl, cover it with a damp cloth and let it rise until double in size. Punch the dough down with your fist. Return to the floured surface and knead until smooth. Divide into two parts. Shape each part into a long roll about 1 inch in diameter. Cut each roll into 14 small pieces. Form each roll into a ball. Cover all the rolls as you form them. Start with the first ball that you formed and flatten each ball with the palm of your hand. Roll each ball into a circle, 3 ½ inches in diameter. Place 2 tablespoons of Pao Filling (recipe below) into the center of each circle, form into a bun, and pinch top edges together. Place each bun on a piece of wax paper, cover and let buns rise 30 minutes.

PAO FILLING:

1 can	Mock duck, minced (10 oz)	1 c	Jicama, minced
1 can	Mock abalone, minced (10 oz)	4-5 tsp	Soy sauce
½ c	Onions (or green onions), minced	3 T	Cornstarch
1 tsp	Sesame oil		

Sauté minced mock duck, mock abalone, and onion in oil. Add jicama and soy sauce and stir-fry briefly. Stir in cornstarch and mix well. Let it cool.

TO STEAM: Arrange buns in a steamer, one inch apart. Bring water to a boil. Steam 12 minutes. Transfer steamed buns to a rack or cloth to cool.

TO BAKE: Arrange buns one inch apart on a cookie sheet coated with cooking spray. Bake in a pre-heated oven at 350° F, 15 minutes. Cover and cool. If you prefer to have the baked Pao buns to be as soft as the steamed Pao, store overnight in a plastic zip-lock bag.

Yield: 28 buns

FRESH SPRING ROLLS "POPIAH" (Singapore)

2 doz Lumpia wrappers (freshly made if possible)

FILLING:

¾ lb Water-packed tofu, firm
1 T Olive oil
1 clove Garlic, minced
½ c Onions, finely chopped
1 med Carrot, finely julienned
1 to 2 c Green beans, French cut
¼ head Cabbage, finely sliced
½ head Bangkuang (jicama), minced (or use water chestnuts)
2 c Fresh bean sprouts

SEASONING:

1 T Nutritional yeast flakes
1 T Soy sauce or Bragg® Liquid Aminos
2 tsp Chicken-style seasoning (McKay's®), or salt to taste
⅓ c Sweet Flour Sauce (or) molasses seasoned with salt or soy sauce

METHOD:

Dice tofu finely and brown in a non-stick frying pan with olive oil. Remove tofu and set aside. Sauté garlic and onions. Add carrots, green beans and cabbage, cover and cook 2 or 3 minutes over med-lo heat stirring frequently. Stir in Bangkuang, sprouts and tofu. Add yeast flakes, soy sauce and chicken-style seasoning and mix well. Remove from heat. Steam wrappers. Spread 1 teaspoon sweet sauce down the center of the wrapper. Put a lettuce leaf over the sweet sauce and spoon the filling onto the lettuce. Roll up and cut in half or in thirds. Serve on a bed of lettuce.

Tip: For a healthy sweet sauce, mix date butter with water, salt or soy sauce to taste, and a flour paste of equal parts flour and water. Cook over medium heat until thickened.

Yield: 24 rolls (whole)

BAKED "EGG" ROLLS

1 tsp	Garlic purée	1 c	Burger-style crumbles (or Mock duck, chopped)
2 T	Olive oil, "light"	1 T	Instant Clear Jel® (instant food thickener)
4 c	Carrots, finely julienned	3 T	Water
4 c	Cabbage, finely sliced	28	Egg roll skins, dairy-free
2 c	Bamboo shoots, julienned		
2 T	Soy sauce or liquid aminos		

Sauté garlic in oil. Add carrots, cabbage, bamboo shoots, soy sauce and burger. Stir-fry until crisp tender. Combine Clear Jel® and water and mix with beaters until mixture is smooth, then set aside. Place approximately 3 T of filling on each egg roll skin. Roll up firmly halfway, tuck ends under, then continue to roll to the edge. Use a small dab of the Clear Jel® mixture under the edge to "glue" the end of the wrapper shut. Place on a baking sheet prepared with cooking spray. Leave space between each egg roll. Spray each egg roll with olive oil flavored cooking spray. Bake at 350° F, 15 minutes. Remove from oven and turn egg rolls over and spray again. Bake an additional 15 minutes. Serve with Sweet & Sour Dip (see recipe below).

Yield: 28 rolls

SWEET & SOUR DIP

¼ c	Onions, minced	3–4 T	Honey or brown sugar
1 tsp	Oil	1 T	Lemon juice (or ⅛ tsp citric acid)
1 c	Pineapple juice	¼ tsp	Salt
½ c	Tomato sauce		
2 T	Cornstarch		

In a small saucepan, sauté onions in oil until transparent. Combine remaining ingredients in a bowl and stir until cornstarch is dissolved. Add to saucepan and cook over medium heat until clear. Add more pineapple juice or water if sauce is too thick.

Yield: 2 cups

RICE VERMICELLI "BEE HOON" or "PANCIT" (Philippines)

2 c	Mock chicken, (Chic-Ketts™)	5 c	Cabbage, thinly sliced
1 can	Mock duck, diced (10 oz)	6 c	Rice vermicelli, (rice stick) (presoaked in hot water)
12 oz	Water-packed tofu, firm (cubed)		
¼ tsp	Sesame oil	2 c	Baby corn, sliced
2 tsp	Soy sauce or liquid aminos	2 c	Fresh bean sprouts
2 tsp	Cornstarch in 2 T water	4 c	Fresh greens (i.e. spinach)
3 cloves	Garlic, minced	4 T	Soy sauce or liquid aminos
1 c	Onions, chopped	1 T	Chicken-style seasoning
1 tsp	Olive oil	3 T	Nutritional yeast flakes
2 c	Green beans, French cut	2 T	Vegetarian Oyster Sauce (opt)
2 med	Carrots, julienned	2 T	Toasted sesame seeds

Tear mock chicken into small pieces and combine with the mock duck and tofu. Marinate mixture for 5 minutes in sesame oil, soy sauce and cornstarch dissolved in water. In a non-stick wok, sauté mixture until browned. Pour into a bowl and set aside. Sauté garlic and onions in olive oil until onions are transparent. Add to the mixture which was set aside. Layer the next 7 ingredients (green beans thru fresh greens) in the wok in the order given. Sprinkle with water, cover and let cook over medium heat 3-5 minutes. Add seasonings and toss until well mixed. Gently stir in the prepared vegetarian protein, tofu, garlic and onion mixture. Garnish with sesame seeds and serve.

Yield: 16 cups

CHICKEN KELAGUEN (Guam)

1 ½ c	Mock chicken	2 T	Celery, chopped
1 tsp	Light olive oil	2 T	Bell pepper, chopped
¼ c	Onions, diced	¼ c	Green onion, chopped
1½ T	Fresh lemon juice	1 c	Fresh coconut, grated
¼ tsp	Salt	2 T	Red bell pepper, diced

Shred or pinch off small pieces of mock chicken and sauté in a non-stick frying pan with oil until golden. Chill. Combine onion, lemon juice and salt and pour this over the "chicken." Add the chopped vegetables and coconut and mix thoroughly. If needed add more salt to taste. Garnish with red bell pepper if desired. Serve cold on a bed of lettuce as a "chicken" salad.

Yield: 3 ½ cups

LEMON WONTON SOUP

WONTONS:

3 c	Zucchini, shredded
1 c	Onions, finely chopped
1 c	Fresh mushrooms, diced
⅓ c	Red bell pepper, finely diced
2 tsp	Oil
1 tsp	Sesame oil
2 T	Canned green chilies, chopped
1 T	Cilantro, minced
1 ½ tsp	Sesame seeds, white
1 tsp	Chicken-style seasoning
½ tsp	Salt
36	Round wonton wrappers (any "egg-less" brand) *

Sauté zucchini, onions, mushrooms and peppers in oils until tender. Add chilies, cilantro, sesame seeds and seasonings and mix well. To assemble wontons, cut into circles if necessary and brush surface of wonton wrapper with water. Place 2 or 3 teaspoons of filling onto center of the wrapper. Fold the top edge of the wrapper over to meet the opposite edge and press both edges together to seal. Continue until all filling and wrappers are used. Bring a pot of water to boil. Drop several wontons into the boiling water at a time and cook until they float to the surface, or about 3 minutes. Occasionally wontons break apart while boiling and will be wasted. Lay cooked wontons in a casserole dish sprayed with cooking spray until ready to use.

BROTH:

7 c	Water
¼ c	Vegetable broth powder
1 ½ T	Fresh lemon juice
1 ½ tsp	Lemon zest, grated
⅛ tsp	Sesame oil
1 c	Snow peas, julienned
¼ c	Green bell peppers, julienned
2 T	Cilantro, chopped

In a large pot, combine water, vegetable broth powder, lemon juice, lemon zest and sesame oil. Bring to a boil. After 3 minutes, add snow peas and turn off heat. To serve, place about 6 wontons in a shallow soup bowl with 1 cup broth. Garnish with bell peppers and cilantro.

* Vegan wonton wrapper can be found in most oriental grocery stores.

Yield: 36 Wontons in broth

VEGETABLE WILD RICE & MUSHROOM SOUP

2 c	Fresh mushrooms, sliced	2 T	Soy sauce, "Lite" (or Bragg® Liquid Aminos)
1 c	Onions, chopped	1 T	Beef-style seasoning
½ c	Celery, thinly sliced	1 T	Chicken-style seasoning
3 med	Garlic cloves, minced	2 tsp	Maggi® Liquid Seasoning
2 T	Olive oil	1 tsp	Garlic & Herb seasoning
3 qt	Water	1 tsp	Onion salt
2 c	Cabbage, finely sliced	1 tsp	Liquid smoke flavoring (opt)
1 c	Brown & Wild Rice mix	1 c	Frozen petite green peas
1 c	Carrots, sliced	¼ c	Fresh chives, sliced
3 T	Nutritional yeast flakes		

Sauté mushrooms, onions, celery and garlic in oil until tender. Add remaining ingredients, except peas and chives. Cover and simmer 25 minutes or until rice is tender. Add peas and chives. Simmer 2 to 3 minutes more. Serve hot.

Yield: 16 cups

BEAN THREAD SALAD "YAM WOON SEN" (Thailand)

8 oz pkg	Transparent bean thread (oriental noodles)	3 T	Lemon or tamarind juice
1 c	Onions, finely sliced	1 T	Bragg® Liquid Aminos
2 med	Tomatoes, cut in wedges	2 tsp	Honey
1 med	Cucumber, peeled & cubed	½ tsp	Garlic purée
¼ c	TVP, beef flavored (textured vegetable protein)	½ tsp	Lime juice (opt)
¼ c	Water	⅓ c	Green onion, diced
1 tsp	Beef-style seasoning	¼ c	Chinese parsley (cilantro)
		½ c	Roasted crushed peanuts

Bring 1 ½ quarts water to a boil. Remove from heat and add noodles. Soak 10 minutes or until soft. Drain well. Cut into 6-inch lengths. Slice onion into rings and then cut rings in half. Prepare tomatoes and cucumber and set aside. Rehydrate TVP in water with beef-style seasoning. Combine juice, liquid aminos, honey, garlic purée, and optional lime juice to make an "oriental dressing," then set aside. Place noodles on a large platter over a bed of leafy lettuce. Arrange onion, tomatoes, cucumber and softened TVP evenly over noodles. Pour dressing over mixture. Toss lightly. Garnish with a topping of green onions, parsley, and peanuts.

Yield: 8 cups

TOFU "COTTAGE CHEESE" SALAD

2 c	Water-packed tofu, extra firm	1 ½ tsp	Onion powder
½ c	Tomatoes, diced (opt)	¾ tsp	Salt
½ c	Cucumbers, diced (opt)	¼ tsp	Garlic salt
¼ c	Onions, finely diced (opt)	½ c	Sour Cream Supreme
¼ c	Green onion tops, minced	⅛ tsp	Citric acid
2 T	Dried chives	dash	Paprika

Squeeze excess water out of tofu by pressing block between hands. Crumble tofu into a bowl and add vegetables (opt), chives, and seasonings. Add citric acid to Sour Cream Supreme (see page 129) and gently stir into tofu mixture. Serve on a bed of lettuce and garnish with Paprika.

Note: If the optional vegetables are not used, decrease salt to ¼ tsp.

Yield: 5 cups

FUMI SALAD
(Japan)

6 c	Cabbage, thinly sliced	¼ c	Sesame seeds
1 c	Green onions with tops, sliced	1 pkg	Ramen® Noodles (discard broth mix)
½ c	Slivered almonds		

Mix cabbage and onions in a large bowl. Chill. Lightly toast the almonds and sesame seeds on a cookie sheet in the oven at 225° F. Cool and add to cabbage. When ready to serve, break the noodles into small pieces, add to the cabbage mixture and toss all ingredients together. Cover with "Oriental Dressing" recipe below.

Yield: 9 cups

ORIENTAL DRESSING

⅓ c	Pineapple juice	2 T	Olive oil, "light"
3 T	Apple juice, frozen concentrate	1 tsp	Sesame oil
2 T	Fresh lemon juice	¾ tsp	Salt

Mix or shake well and pour over salad when ready to serve. Toss lightly.

Yield: ¾ cup

BIT O' SUNSHINE LEMON PIE

2 c	Pineapple juice	7 T	Cornstarch
1 ¼ c	Orange juice	¼ tsp	Salt
¼ c	Fresh lemon juice	1 tsp	Lemon zest, grated
½ c	Honey	8-inch	Graham cracker crust
2 T	Fructose, granules		

In a blender, combine all juices, sweeteners, cornstarch and salt and process on low speed until well mixed and cornstarch is dissolved. Pour into a saucepan, add lemon zest and cook on med-hi heat, stirring constantly until thick. Pour into an 8-inch "ready to use" graham cracker crust or a 9-inch baked pie crust. Chill until cold and set in the middle. If desired, top with Soy-Creamy Dessert Topping (see page 198) or non-dairy whipped cream and lightly toasted pecans, finely chopped. Garnish with a small lemon twist.

Variation: Lime lovers may want to substitute half of the lemon juice with lime juice.

Yield: 1 (8-inch) pie

MAJA BLANKA (Philippines)

4 c	Coconut milk, canned ("lite," unsweetened)	½ tsp	Salt
1 c	Honey	1 c	Cornstarch
1 c	Creamed corn	1 c	Water
		½ c	Grated coconut, toasted

Boil coconut milk with honey, creamed corn and salt in a deep pot, stirring constantly. Mix cornstarch with water and add to the boiling mixture, stirring until thick. Pour into a Jello mold prepared with cooking spray and refrigerate until set. Then, turn out onto a serving platter and sprinkle top with the toasted grated coconut.

Note: To make fresh coconut milk, grate or shred 2 ripe coconuts. Put grated coconut into a large bowl and pour 1 quart water over the coconut and squeeze the coconut until all the "milk" is squeezed out. Drain coconut milk mixture in a colander and reserve the milk.

Yield: 7 cups

Barbecued
Vegetarian Kabobs
Blue Ribbon
Baked Beans
Classic Potato Salad

Stars & Stripes
Sizzler
Featuring
A variety of fun and tasty recipes combined to make your 4th of July picnic delightfully healthy and a smashing success.

BARBECUED VEGETARIAN KABOBS

24 cubes	Water-packed tofu, extra firm	2 sm	Zucchini, ¼-inch slices
12 pieces	Mock chicken, bite size*	12	Button mushrooms, whole
2 med	Carrots, ½ inch diagonal cuts	12	Cherry tomatoes, whole
1 med	Onion, cut in thick wedges	24	Pineapple chunks
1 sm	Bell pepper, 1-inch squares		

Cut tofu into 1-inch cubes. Cover tofu with Kabob Marinade (see page 163) and marinate in the refrigerator at least 4 to 24 hours before time of barbecue. Prepare Kabob Sauce or Tangy-Mayo (page 163) for the Kabob dressing. Prepare the Teriyaki Sauce (page 163). Tear mock chicken (or vegetable protein of choice) into large bite-size pieces and marinate in Teriyaki Sauce at least 20 minutes while preparing the vegetables.

Microwave or simmer carrots and onions in a small amount of water until crisp-tender. Add bell peppers and zucchini and cook 1 minute more. Sauté pre-marinated tofu in a non-stick fry pan with a small amount of left-over marinade. Be careful to brown all sides a few minutes until crispy to prevent tofu from falling off skewer. Set aside. Sauté pre-marinated "chicken" (or meat substitute of choice) in ⅓ cup Teriyaki Sauce until all the liquid has evaporated and the "chicken" is nicely browned.

Place vegetables, prepared tofu and gluten on kabob skewers in the following order: (Add or delete any ingredient according to preference.)

1. Mock chicken
2. Onion
3. Pineapple
4. Tofu
5. Zucchini
6. Carrot
7. Tomato
8. Bell pepper
9. Tofu
10. Pineapple
11. Onion
12. Mushroom

BARBECUE OPTION:
Place kabobs on a lightly oiled grill 4-6 inches above a solid bed of low-glowing coals. Grill, turning often and basting liberally with Kabob Sauce or Tangy Mayo Sauce until vegetables are tender.

OVEN OPTION:
Arrange kabobs on a baking sheet prepared with cooking spray. Baste kabobs liberally with choice of Kabob Sauce or Tangy Mayo and bake at 400° F, 20 to 25 minutes or until lightly browned. Turn once and baste several times with sauce during baking.

* Recommend "Chic-Ketts™," located in frozen foods at health food stores.

Yield: 12 vegetarian kabobs

KABOB MARINADE

¼ c	Olive oil	1 T	Sesame oil
¼ c	Lemon juice	1 tsp	Oregano, ground
¼ c	Bragg® Liquid Aminos (or "dark" soy sauce)	2 med	Garlic cloves, minced

Drain tofu, cube and let stand 15 min. while preparing marinade. Put the marinade and tofu into a plastic zip-lock bag, remove the air, seal and set the bag in a shallow pan so the tofu is covered by the marinade.

Yield: ¾ cups

KABOB SAUCE

1 ½ c	Tomato sauce	2 T	Honey
2 T	Lemon juice	2 T	Pineapple juice
3 T	Bragg® Liquid Aminos (or "lite" soy sauce)	¼ tsp	Garlic powder

Mix together and store in refrigerator until ready for use.

Yield: 2 ½ cups

"TANGY-MAYO" KABOB SAUCE

1 c	Soy mayonnaise, (p. 165 or 166)	½ tsp	Garlic purée
1 tsp	Oregano, ground	½ tsp	Paprika
1 tsp	Cumin, ground		

Mix together and store in refrigerator until ready for use.

Yield: 1 cup

TERIYAKI SAUCE

½ c	Water	1 ¼ tsp	Onion powder
2 tsp	Bragg® Liquid Aminos (or "lite" soy sauce)	¼ tsp	Garlic powder
1 tsp	Lemon juice	2 T	Honey
		2 T	Brown sugar

Mix together and store in refrigerator until ready for use.

Yield: ¾ cups

VEGETARIAN "MEATBALLS" with BARBECUE SAUCE

MEATBALLS:

2 c	Textured Vegetable Protein *	¼ c	Vital wheat gluten
1 ½ c	Boiling water	1 T	Nutritional yeast flakes
1 T	Soy sauce or Bragg® Aminos	1 tsp	Soymilk powder
1 T	Olive oil	1 tsp	Beef-style seasoning
½ c	Onions, chopped fine	½ tsp	Garlic powder
¼ c	Pecans, finely chopped	⅛ tsp	Basil or Italian seasoning
¼ c	Whole-wheat flour	pinch	Paprika

* (TVP)

Mix TVP with water, soy sauce and oil and let stand 10 minutes. Add remaining ingredients and mix thoroughly. Shape into 1-inch balls. Place meatballs" on a baking sheet prepared with cooking spray and bake at 350° F, 20 minutes or until lightly browned. Serve with barbecue sauce or spaghetti sauce and pasta.

Yield: 20 balls

BARBECUE SAUCE

1 ½ c	Tomato sauce	2 tsp	Fresh lemon juice
3 T	Molasses	½ tsp	Liquid smoke
2 T	Tomato paste	¼ tsp	Onion powder
1 T	Honey	⅛ tsp	Garlic powder
4 tsp	Soy sauce or liquid aminos	2 tsp	Instant Clear-Jel®

In a blender, combine all ingredients, except Clear-Jel,® and process until well mixed. Set blender on medium speed, remove lid spout and add Clear-Jel® to blender while in motion. Mixture will thicken in 5 to 10 seconds.

Yield: 2 cups

SIZZLIN' SOY BURGERS

1 lb	Burger-style crumbles, frozen	2 T	Water
1 pkt	Onion-mushroom soup mix (Lipton®)	⅓ c	Unbleached white flour
3 T	Ortega® Taco sauce, mild	⅓ c	Vital wheat gluten

Thaw burger, and mix with soup mix, taco sauce and water. Combine both flours and stir into burger mixture. Shape patties and fry on both sides over medium heat on a non-stick griddle or frying pan with a small amount of oil.

Note: These burgers can be easily reheated on a grill.

Yield: 8 burgers

BETTER 'N MAYONNAISE

1 box	Mori-Nu® Tofu, firm (12.3 oz)	1 tsp	Prepared mustard
⅓ c	Olive oil, "extra light"	½ tsp	Onion powder
¼ c	Soymilk beverage, plain (Silk®)	¼ tsp	Citric acid
2 T	Corn syrup, light (Karo®)	1 T	Instant Clear-Jel® (instant food thickener)
1 ¼ tsp	Salt		

Combine all ingredients except Instant Clear-Jel® in a blender and process until smooth and creamy. Lower the blender speed, remove the lid spout and add the Instant Clear-Jel® while the blender is running. Blend until thickened. Keep refrigerated.

Note: Substitute mustard with Better Mustard (see below) in this recipe. If the mayonnaise becomes too runny after 3 or 4 days, simply return mayo to a blender and add more Instant Clear-Jel® 1 tsp at a time to achieve desired consistency.

Yield: 2 ¼ cups

BETTER MUSTARD

¾ c	Water	½ tsp	Salt
⅓ c	Fresh lemon juice	1 clove	Garlic, mashed
¼ c	Unbleached white flour	½ tsp	Maggi® Seasoning
2 tsp	Turmeric	¼ c	Olive oil, "extra light"

In a blender, process first 5 ingredients on high until creamy. Pour into a saucepan and cook over boiling point temperature stirring constantly until thickened. Cool. Return to blender and add garlic and Maggi® Seasoning. Process on high, and slowly drizzle in oil through the lid spout. Continue to blend for one more minute. Spoon into a glass storage container. Chill before serving.

Yield: 1 ½ cups

CLASSIC POTATO SALAD

4 or 5 c	Potatoes, (cooked, peeled and cut into ¾ inch cubes)	2 T	Fresh parsley, minced
1 c	Celery, finely chopped	2 ½ tsp	Onion powder
1 c	Onions, finely chopped	1 ½ tsp	Dill weed
½ c	Pickles, chopped	1 tsp	Salt
½ c	Black olives, sliced	¼ tsp	Garlic powder
1 c	Soy Mayonnaise (recipe below)	⅛ tsp	Turmeric, ground

In a large bowl, combine vegetables, pickles (regular or vinegarless), olives and soy mayonnaise and stir gently until well mixed. Combine seasonings and stir evenly into the potato mixture. Serve hot or cold.

Yield: 8 cups

SOY MAYONNAISE

1 c	West Soy® Plus, soymilk	1 ¼ tsp	Salt
2 T	Cornstarch or arrowroot	½ tsp	Onion powder
½ c	Water	¼ tsp	Garlic powder
½ c	Soymilk powder, plain (Better than Milk™, "Original")	⅛ tsp	Citric acid
		2 T	Instant Clear-Jel®
¼ c	Slivered almonds, (w/o skins)	¼ c	Pineapple juice
⅓ c	Olive oil, "extra light"	¼ c	Fresh lemon juice

Dissolve starch in soymilk. Simmer over medium heat stirring constantly until thick. Cool. In a blender, combine water, milk powder, and almonds and process on high speed until completely smooth. Reduce blender speed and slowly dribble in oil through the lid spout. Turn the blender off, add the cooled soymilk and spices then blend again until well mixed. Keep the blender running at a high speed and add Instant Clear-Jel® powder one tablespoon at a time. It may be necessary to stop often and stir mixture to assist the blending process. Continue blending until completely smooth. Pour into a bowl and gently stir in the pineapple and lemon juice. (Do not add juices to the blender.) Refrigerate 1 to 2 hours before serving.

Note: As this recipe sits and ages 1 or 2 days, the consistency will become stiffer. Just add additional water a little at a time and whip with a wire whip to achieve desired thickness.

Yield: 2 ½ cups

PICNIC POTATO SALAD

2 lb	Red potatoes, boiled (about 1 qt)	1 c	Potato Salad Dressing (see below)
1 c	Onions, chopped	1 tsp	Salt
¾ c	Celery, sliced or diced	1 tsp	Dill weed
½ c	Pickles, chopped		

Cool potatoes and cut into bite size cubes. (Peeling is optional.) Add onions, celery, and pickles. Combine Potato Salad Dressing, salt and dill weed and stir gently into potato mixture. Chill before serving.

Yield: 7 cups

POTATO SALAD DRESSING

1 c	Soymilk beverage, plain	½ tsp	Salt
¼ c	Olive oil, "extra light"	2 T	Instant Clear-Jel® (instant food thickener)
2 T	Carrot, cooked	1 ½ T	Fresh lemon juice
1 ½ tsp	Onion powder		

In a blender, combine soymilk, oil, carrot, onion powder and salt. Process on high speed until carrots are liquefied. Add food thickener through the lid spout while blending on low speed. Increase speed as it thickens. Pour out into a bowl and add lemon juice. Stir until well mixed.

Yield: 1 ½ cups

MACARONI SALAD

4 c	Cooked elbow macaroni	¼ c	Sliced olives, black or green
¾ c	Red onions, chopped	½ c	Soy mayonnaise, (page 166)
¾ c	Celery, sliced	½ tsp	Garlic salt
¾ c	Dill pickles, chopped	⅛ tsp	Celery salt

Combine all ingredients and mix lightly. Chill before serving.

Yield: 7 cups

MOCK EGG SALAD

1 recipe	Scrambled Tofu "Eggs" (p. 94)	⅓ c	Black olives, sliced (opt)
½ c	Soy mayonnaise (p. 165 or 166)	⅓ c	Celery, sliced (opt)
½ c	Onions, chopped (opt)	⅓ c	Pickles, diced (opt)

Prepare tofu "eggs" according to directions, except omit onions, peppers, mushrooms and chives from the recipe. Chill. Prepare soy mayonnaise and refrigerate. When chilled, add mayonnaise, onions, olives, celery and pickles, (each more or less than specified according to preference) and stir gently into "eggs" until well mixed.

Note: For a "quick" mayonnaise substitute, use any commercially prepared soy mayonnaise, i.e. Nayonaise PA's® or Vegenaise®.

Yield: 4 cups

CHOICE COLESLAW

½ head	White cabbage	2 sm	Carrots, grated
¼ head	Red cabbage	1 med	Red apple, diced
2 stalks	Celery, sliced	1 c	Cooked spiral pasta (opt)

Thinly slice cabbage and place in a large bowl. Add celery, carrots, and apple to the cabbage. Cook pasta according to directions, rinse and drain well. Toss in with slaw. Add one recipe Coleslaw Dressing (recipe below) more or less according to taste.

Yield: 10 cups

COLESLAW DRESSING

1 c	Crushed pineapple, drained	⅛ tsp	Salt
¼ c	Honey	1 T	Instant Clear-Jel®
3 T	Fresh lemon juice	1 c	Soy mayonnaise

In a blender, whiz pineapple with honey, lemon juice, and salt. Add Clear Jel® through the lid spout while blender is running. Pour out into a bowl. Stir in soy mayonnaise (see recipes on page 165 or 166), then mix with well drained coleslaw. Adjust amount of dressing to your taste.

Yield: 2 ½ cups

BLUE RIBBON BAKED BEANS

1 lb	Dried navy beans or great northern beans
1 c	Onions, chopped
2 cloves	Garlic, minced
¼ c	Olive oil
¼ c	Date butter, brown sugar or Sucanat®
1 c	Ketchup (see vinegarless recipes on page 170)
1 or 2 tsp	Worcestershire sauce, (vegetarian brand)
6 T	Pure maple syrup
¼ c	Light molasses
14 oz can	Peeled tomatoes
20 oz can	Unsweetened pineapple tidbits, drained
2 c	Bell peppers, diced
(opt)	Salt or soy sauce to taste

Wash and sort beans. Soak overnight in a large pot of water. Rinse soaked beans well under cold water and place them in a large pot. Cover with water and bring to a boil. Reduce heat and simmer until tender (about 45 minutes to 1 hour). Drain, reserving ¾ cup cooking liquid.

In a 2-quart casserole dish or Dutch oven, over medium heat, sauté the onions and garlic in oil until onions are translucent (about 5 minutes). Add the date butter, brown sugar or Sucanat® and stir over medium-low heat until dissolved. Then stir in the ketchup and the remaining ingredients. Add salt, if desired to taste. Add the drained beans and mix well.

Preheat oven to 300° F. Cover the Dutch oven and transfer it to the oven, stirring occasionally for 2 ½ hours. Add the reserved bean liquid. Cover and bake 30 minutes more. Remove the cover and bake until the sauce is thick and syrupy (another 10 to 15 minutes). Serve hot.

Tip: Leftovers freeze well or you can divide the recipe in half for a smaller yield.

Yield: 4 quarts

"SPICY" VINEGARLESS TOMATO KETCHUP

½ c	Tomato purée
12 oz	Tomato paste
½ c	Tomato sauce
3 T	Pineapple juice, frozen concentrate
2 T	Orange juice, frozen concentrate
3 T	Fresh lemon juice
1 tsp	Calamansi lime or kumquat juice
½ tsp	Spike® All Purpose Seasoning
1 tsp	Onion powder
1 tsp	Salt
½ tsp	Basil, dried
½ tsp	Paprika
¼ tsp	Cumin, ground
¼ tsp	Garlic powder
1 T	Honey
2 T	Date butter (see page 251)

Combine all ingredients in a blender and process until smooth. Refrigerate. The flavor improves after 2 days. Freeze extras not used within two weeks. After thawing, blend again before using. Yield: 4 cups

"THICK & ZESTY" VINEGARLESS KETCHUP

12 oz	Tomato paste
1 c	Tomato sauce
¼ c	Fresh lemon juice
¼ c	Pineapple juice, frozen concentrate
2 T	Orange juice, frozen concentrate
1 tsp	Lime juice
¼ tsp	Citric acid crystals
1 tsp	Onion powder
1 tsp	Salt
½ tsp	Paprika
½ tsp	Garlic salt
⅛ tsp	Cumin, ground
2 T	Honey
3 T	Date butter (p. 251)

Process all ingredients in a blender until smooth. Refrigerate. The flavor improves after 2 days. Freeze extras not used within 2 weeks. Yield: 4 cups

"QUICK" VINEGARLESS KETCHUP

1 ½ c	Tomato sauce
1 c	Tomato paste
½ c	Pineapple juice
¼ c	Fresh lemon juice
1 tsp	Lime juice
3 T	Date butter (p. 251)
2 T	Pineapple/orange juice (frozen concentrate)
2 T	Fructose or honey
2 T	Fruit-Fresh®, powder (or ⅛ tsp citric acid)
1 ½ tsp	Salt
1 tsp	Onion powder
½ tsp	Garlic salt
½ tsp	Paprika
¼ tsp	Worcestershire sauce (opt) (Vegetarian brand)

Combine all ingredients in a blender and process until smooth. Refrigerate. Freeze extras not used within two weeks.

Yield: 4 cups

PURPLE PASSION FRUIT SALAD

6 c	Water or fruit juice
1 c	Tapioca pearls, small size (not "Minute®" type)
12 oz	Grape juice concentrate or a mixture of grape juice and passion fruit juice concentrates, undiluted
3 qts	Fruit assortment—canned, fresh, or frozen (Peaches, pears, grapes, apples, bananas, blueberries, etc.)

Combine water and tapioca in a large saucepan and cook over low heat about 45 minutes or until clear. Then refrigerate mixture until set. Pour out into a large salad bowl and add grape juice concentrate and stir until well mixed. Add fruit assortment, up to 3 quarts (more or less to your preference) stirring gently after each addition until desired thickness is achieved.

Yield: 5 quarts

ALMOND-APPLE BARS

3 c	Quick oats
1 ½ c	Old fashioned rolled oats
1 ½ c	Whole-wheat flour
1 ½ c	Unbleached white flour
1 ½ c	Sliced almonds
¾ c	Soymilk powder, plain
¾ c	Shredded coconut (opt)
1 ½ tsp	Salt
3 oz	Water (6 T)
1 ½ T	ENER-G® Egg Replacer
¾ c	Olive oil, "extra light"
¾ c	Apple juice, unsweetened (frozen concentrate)
½ c	Honey
2 tsp	Natural vanilla, flavoring
1 tsp	Maple flavoring

In a large bowl, combine all dry ingredients (1st column). In a separate bowl, combine water and egg replacer and whip until foamy. Add remaining liquids. Add liquid ingredients to dry ingredients and stir until well mixed. Prepare a cookie sheet with cooking spray. Spread mixture evenly onto the cookie sheet and press until flattened. Bake at 350° F, 18 to 20 minutes or until lightly browned. Remove from oven and score into squares or rectangles. Break at scored marks when cooled.

Yield: 48 squares

PEACH-RASPBERRY CRISP

FILLING:

1 qt	Canned or frozen peaches	1 tsp	Lemon juice
1 c	Frozen raspberries, drained	¼ tsp	Salt
1 can	Dole® "Orchard Peach" (frozen juice concentrate)	¼ tsp	Cinnamon, ground
		⅛ tsp	Nutmeg, ground
3 T	Minute® Tapioca	2 T	Fructose (opt)

Drain peaches and reserve juice. Chop peaches into bite-size pieces. Combine frozen juice concentrate with tapioca. Add lemon juice and salt. Bring juice to a boil over med-low heat, stirring often. Stir in peaches, raspberries, and spices when juice is thick and clear. Pour into a 9" x 13" baking dish prepared with cooking spray. For added sweetness, sprinkle fructose over mixture.

TOPPING:

1 c	Quick oats	½ tsp	Salt
½ c	Unbleached white flour	¼ tsp	Cinnamon, ground
½ c	Walnuts, chopped	⅓ c	Dates (or) ¼ c brown sugar*
¼ c	Old fashioned oats	3 T	Olive oil, "extra light"
¼ c	Shredded coconut	1 tsp	Vanilla extract

***DATE OPTION:**

Combine dry ingredients except dates and set aside. Cook dates over med-low heat with enough left over juice from peaches to cover dates. Simmer and stir until dates become a smooth paste. Process in a blender if necessary. Add oil and vanilla to the date mixture. Combine the date mixture and dry ingredients and mix together until topping is moist and crumbly. Cover fruit evenly with the topping. Bake at 350° F, about 20 minutes or just until topping is golden brown. Watch carefully.

***BROWN SUGAR OPTION:**

Combine dry ingredients except brown sugar. Combine brown sugar, oil and vanilla. Mix the dry and wet ingredients together until crumbly. Add 2T reserved peach juice or water to moisten topping. Cover fruit evenly with the topping. Bake at 350° F, 25 minutes or until golden brown.

Variation: For those who would prefer a cinnamon substitute; Combine 2 T ground coriander and 2 tsp ground anise or cardamom. Store in a covered container.

Note: For a lower sodium topping, reduce salt to ¼ tsp.

Tip: Serve with "Instant" Whipped Topping (see page 90).

Yield: 8 cups

CAROB CHIP COOKIES

1 c	Whole-wheat flour	¼ c	Spectrum® Naturals Spread®
½ c	Unbleached white flour	¼ c	Wonderslim® or Lighter Bake® (fat and egg substitutes)
½ c	Walnuts, chopped	2 tsp	Vanilla extract
⅓ c	Carob chips	½ tsp	Walnut flavoring
¼ tsp	Salt		
⅓ c	Honey		

Combine flour, walnuts, carob chips and salt. In a separate bowl, combine remaining ingredients. Pour liquids into dry ingredients and stir until well mixed. Cookie dough will seem sticky. Drop by spoonfuls onto a cookie sheet prepared with cooking spray. Oil fingers and lightly shape dough out into round cookies. Avoid mashing. Bake at 350° F, 18 to 20 minutes. Cookies will become crispier as they cool.

Variation: Replace half (2 T) of Spectrum® Spread with equal amounts raw natural nut butter (cashew, almond or peanut). Cookies will be crunchier with this method.

Yield: 15 to 18 cookies

CAROB CRISPIES

1 c	Carob chips, sweetened	4 c	Granola, dry
1 c	Peanut butter, natural	1 c	Currants or raisins
½ c	Maple syrup or honey	½ c	Nuts, chopped (walnuts, pecans, peanuts)
1 tsp	Roma®, coffee substitute	½ c	Dried coconut, grated (opt)
1 tsp	Vanilla extract		
½ tsp	Maple flavoring		

Combine carob chips, peanut butter, sweetener of choice, Roma® and flavorings in a small saucepan. Warm over medium heat stirring frequently until carob chips are melted. Mix granola, fruit and nuts together in a large bowl. Pour carob sauce over granola mixture and stir until well mixed. Prepare a 9" x 13" baking dish with cooking spray. Spread the warmed carob/granola mixture into the dish evenly and press mixture down. Spray a knife with cooking spray and cut mixture into squares. Refrigerate until cold. Break the squares apart and store in an airtight container in the refrigerator until ready to serve.

Yield: 48 squares

TOLL HOUSE COOKIE "LOOK-A-LIKES"

1 c	Whole-wheat flour	1 c	Light brown sugar, packed
1 c	Unbleached white flour	½ c	Mori-Nu® Tofu, firm
1 tsp	Salt	2 tsp	Vanilla extract
½ tsp	Baking soda	1 c	Walnuts, chopped
8 oz	Smart Balance® "Light" (non-hydrogenated spread)	⅔ c	Carob chips

Combine flours, salt and baking soda in a bowl and set aside. In a large mixing bowl, beat Smart Balance® (softened at room temperature), sugar, tofu, and vanilla at "cream" setting until smooth and creamy (about 1 minute). Lower speed and gradually beat in flour mixture. Resume high speed and beat 1 minute more. Stir in walnuts and carob chips. Drop by heaping tablespoons onto a cookie sheet prepared with cooking spray. Allow about one inch between cookies. Bake in a pre-heated oven on the center oven rack at 375° F, 14 minutes or until golden brown. Cool for 2 minutes. Using a spatula, transfer cookies to a wire rack to cool completely before storing.

Tip: For best results, use a heavyweight cookie sheet and bake only one pan full at a time.

Yield: 3 dozen

VANILLA ICE CREAM

2 c	Soymilk creamer, plain (Silk®)	1 c	Soymilk powder, plain*
2 c	Soymilk creamer, French vanilla (Silk®)	1 T	Clear vanilla, extract

Combine all ingredients in a blender and process until well mixed. Pour into an ice cream maker and operate according to manufacturer's directions.

* Better Than Milk™ Soy "Original" is the recommended product.

Tip: For a delicious treat, add ½ cup finely chopped carob chips and ¼ cup lightly toasted and finely chopped almonds (chilled) to the ice cream when nearly set or during the last 5 minutes of churning.

Note: This recipe can easily be doubled or tripled if necessary to fit the ice cream maker.

Yield: 1 quart

STRAWBERRY ICE CREAM

2 c	Frozen strawberries, packed	¼ c	Fructose, granules
2 c	Soymilk creamer, French vanilla (Silk®)	½ tsp	Strawberry extract
½ c	Soymilk powder, plain * (opt)		

Combine all ingredients in a blender and process until smooth and creamy. Pour into an ice cream maker and proceed according to the manufacturer's directions.

* Better Than Milk™ Soy "Original" is the recommended product.

Tip: This recipe can easily be doubled or tripled to fit the ice cream maker.

Yield: 1 quart

STRAWBERRY TROPIC DRINK

1 can	Frozen pineapple juice (diluted)	1 or 2	Ripened bananas
1 can	Frozen apple juice (diluted)	2 c	Strawberries
1 can	Frozen orange juice (diluted)		

Mix each can of juice concentrate with the amount of water listed on the can. Combine the bananas, strawberries and 1 c of the frozen juice mixture in a blender. Process until liquefied. Add blender mixture to the other juices and stir until well mixed. Chill if necessary and serve.

Yield: 5 quarts

QUICK PICNIC PUNCH

64 oz	Apple juice, unsweetened	32 oz	White grape juice
40 oz	Dole® "Orchard Peach" juice		

Combine juices and serve with crushed ice.

Note: May substitute Dole® "Orchard Peach" juice with any brand "white grape/peach" fruit juice if necessary.

Yield: 4 quarts

Summertime Breeze

Featuring

Quick and easy recipes to prepare in 30 minutes. A variety of delicious and healthy meals perfect for singles, weekdays, after work or when those unexpected guests drop by.

SAVORY LENTILS
Over Toast

2 c	Brown lentils, dried	½ tsp	Savory, dried
6 c	Hot water	½ tsp	Coriander, ground
2 T	Olive oil	1 ½ tsp	Cumin, ground
1 med	Onion, chopped	1 tsp	Thyme, dried
2 med	Garlic cloves, minced	½ tsp	Paprika
1 tsp	Basil, dried	1 ½ tsp	Salt
2 T	Nutritional yeast flakes	1 tsp	Garlic salt
2 tsp	Spike® All Purpose Seasoning	2 tsp	Honey (opt)

Rinse lentils well in water. Drain. In a saucepan, cover lentils with (6 cups) hot water and set aside. In a small frying pan, sauté onions and garlic in oil. Pour sautéed mixture into the water and lentils. Add all seasonings (except salt and garlic salt). Bring to a boil, cover and simmer 20 to 30 minutes or until lentils are tender. Finally, stir in salts and honey and continue cooking 1 to 2 minutes. Pour into a serving bowl and if desired, garnish with fresh herbs such as parsley, green onion, chives and chopped tomato. Serve over toasted whole wheat or pumpernickel bread. Garnish with shredded lettuce, carrots, cucumber, chopped tomato, avocado, sliced black olives, onions, roasted sunflower seeds, etc. Top with Ranch-Style Dressing, Ranch Dressing "Quick and Easy," or "Soy Good" Tofu Sour Cream. (Recipes on page 179.)

Variation: Serve lentils over brown rice and garnish as above for another delicious and healthy whole-meal idea.

Note: If you suffer from G.I. discomfort after eating legumes, try the following remedy. After thoroughly washing and rinsing the lentils, cover with water, bring to a boil and simmer 2-3 minutes. Remove from heat and let beans soak at least 1 hour or overnight, or all day while at work. Drain and thoroughly wash and rinse lentils again. Drain. Proceed with recipe. Unfortunately, this will also somewhat diminish the delicious flavor of the lentil. Also see article on how to cook beans on page 143.

Yield: 8 cups

RANCH-STYLE DRESSING

1 box	Mori Nu® Tofu, firm (12.3 oz)	1 tsp	Onion powder
½ c	Water	1 tsp	Basil, dried
¼ c	Sunflower oil	½ tsp	Savory, dried
3 T	Fresh lemon juice	½ tsp	Parsley, dried
1 ¼ tsp	Salt	⅛ tsp	Citric acid crystals (to taste)
1 tsp	Honey	2 T	Fresh chives, minced (opt)
1 tsp	Garlic salt	1 T	Fresh parsley, minced (opt)

Combine all ingredients, except fresh herbs, in a blender and process until smooth and creamy. Stir in the optional fresh chives and parsley last. Chill before serving.

Yield: 2 ½ cups

RANCH DRESSING "QUICK and EASY"

1 pkt	Hidden Valley® Dressing Mix (Ranch® Buttermilk Recipe)	⅓ c	Olive oil, "extra light"
1 ¼ c	Mori-Nu® Tofu, firm	3 ½ T	Fresh lemon juice
½ c	Water	3 T	Soymilk powder, plain

Combine above ingredients in a blender and process until smooth and creamy. Chill before serving.

Variation: Add 2 T water and decrease oil to ¼ cup for a lower fat version.

Note: Only the "Original" Ranch Dressing mix with the instructions to add "buttermilk and mayonnaise" is "vegan." The "add milk and mayonnaise" recipe has buttermilk powder in the ingredients.

Yield 2 ½ cups

"SOY GOOD" TOFU SOUR CREAM

1 ½ c	Mori-Nu® Tofu, firm (12.3 oz box)	¼ tsp	Salt
3 T	Sunflower oil or extra light olive oil	¼ tsp	Honey
¼ tsp	Citric acid crystals		

In a blender, combine all ingredients and process until smooth and creamy.

Variation: Add 1 tsp fresh lemon juice for a stronger sour taste.

Yield: 1 ½ cups

QUICK & SNAPPY 3 BEAN CHILI

1 can	Bush's® Chili Magic, (Traditional Recipe) (15.5 oz)	14.5 oz	Diced tomatoes, "no salt"
1 can	Red kidney beans, (15 oz) ("lower-sodium" variety)	⅔ c	Burger-style crumbles
1 can	Black beans, (15 oz)	2 T	Dried minced onions
		1 tsp	Beef-style seasoning
		¾ tsp	Cumin, ground

Lightly drain Chili Magic and pour into a saucepan. Lightly drain kidney beans and add to the saucepan. Do not drain black beans or tomatoes and add next. Stir in burger and seasonings. Cover and simmer chili 5 to 10 minutes. Serve hot.

Variation: For a richer tomato flavor, add 1 ½ T tomato paste.

Tip: Try a dollop of "Soy Good" Tofu Sour Cream (see page 179) or shredded soy cheddar cheese or Mozzarella Cheese (see page 244) to top off this chili bean recipe.

Yield: 7 cups

ONE OF A KIND MINI PIZZAS

Whole-wheat pita bread, uncut
Garlic purée (opt)
Pizza sauce
Pizza seasoning
Soy Parmesan cheese, grated
Soy mozzarella cheese (see page 244)
Sausage-style crumbles (opt)
Vegetables toppings of choice, (olives, mushrooms, onions, tomatoes, green peppers etc.)
Parsley, dried

Personalize each mini pizza with choice of above ingredients. Turn pita bread up side down and if desired, spread with a thin layer of garlic before covering "crust" with pizza sauce. Season with pizza seasoning or any vegetable herb seasoning mix. Sprinkle with mozzarella and Parmesan cheese, vegan crumbles and add veggies of choice. Cover with additional mozzarella and/or parmesan cheese. Garnish with parsley. Arrange pizzas on a cookie sheet or pizza stone and bake at 375° F, 15 to 20 minutes or until crust is crispy and veggies are tender.

Variation: Replace pita bread with whole-wheat English muffins.

Yield: Variable

TOFU "FISH" STICKS

1 lb	Water-packed tofu, extra firm

Slice the block of tofu from end to end into 10 slices of even thickness, (approximately 1 cm thick).

Broth:

2 c	Water	2 tsp	Onion salt
2 tsp	Chicken-style seasoning, (McKay's®)		

Prepare broth and bring to a boil. Add sliced tofu, reduce heat and simmer 5 to 10 minutes. (Use left over broth as a base for your favorite soup or gravy recipe.)

Breading Meal:

½ c	Unbleached white or wheat flour	1 T	Onion powder
½ c	Yellow corn meal	1 T	Parsley, dried
¼ c	Cracker crumbs, (opt)	½ tsp	Garlic powder
2 T	Nutritional yeast flakes	½ tsp	Salt
1 T	Chicken-style seasoning, (McKay's®)		
1 T	Garlic & Herb Seasoning, "salt-free"(McCormick®)		

Combine all ingredients in a pie plate. Dip the tofu into breading meal to coat both sides. Spray a non-stick frying pan with cooking oil or lightly coat the pan with olive oil and heat to medium temperature. Spray a light coating of cooking spray onto one side of the breaded tofu and gently lay the coated side into the pan. Then spray the other side. Fry both sides until golden brown and crispy. For an extra tasty treat, serve with ketchup (see page 190) or tartar sauce (see page 182).

Hint: Tofu "fish" sticks, tartar sauce and a whole wheat bun make a great sandwich too!

Yield: 10 fish sticks

"QUICK" TARTAR SAUCE

1 c	Nayonaise®, (eggless mayonnaise)	¾ tsp	Chicken-style seasoning
½ c	Onions, minced	¾ tsp	Onion powder
⅓ c	Sweet pickle relish (or) (PA's® Vinegarless Pickle Relish)	⅛ tsp	Garlic powder

Combine all ingredients and chill before serving.

Variation: Onions may be sautéed in a small amount of water if you prefer a less crunchy texture.

Yield: 1 ¾ cup

ORIGINAL TARTAR SAUCE

1 c	Better 'N Mayonnaise (see below)	1 tsp	Chicken-style seasoning
½ c	Onions, minced	½ tsp	Onion powder
⅓ c	Sweet pickle relish (or) (PA's® Vinegarless Pickle Relish)	1/16 tsp	Turmeric

Combine all ingredients and chill before serving.

Variation: Onions may be sautéed in a small amount of water if you prefer a less crunchy texture.

Yield: 1 ¾ cup

BETTER 'N MAYONNAISE

1 box	Mori-Nu® Tofu, firm (12.3 oz)	1 tsp	Prepared mustard
⅓ c	Olive oil, "extra light"	½ tsp	Onion powder
¼ c	Soymilk beverage, plain (Silk®)	¼ tsp	Citric acid
2 T	Corn syrup, light (Karo®)	1 T	Instant Clear Jel® (instant food thickener)
1 ¼ tsp	Salt		

Combine all ingredients except Instant Clear Jel® in a blender and process until smooth and creamy. Lower the blender speed, remove the lid spout and add the Instant Clear Jel® while the blender is running. Blend until thickened. Keep refrigerated.

Note: Substitute mustard with Better Mustard (see page 165) in this recipe. If the mayonnaise becomes too runny after 3 or 4 days, simply return mayo to a blender and add more Instant Clear Jel®, 1 tsp at a time to achieve desired consistency.

Yield: 2 ¼ cups

EASY SHREDDED POTATO CASSEROLE

30 oz	Frozen shredded potatoes (Ore Ida®)	⅔ c	Smart Balance® "Light," (melted)
1 ½ c	Soymilk beverage, plain (Silk®)	1 ½ tsp	Salt
1 c	Water-packed tofu, silken		

Prepare a 9" x 13" baking dish with cooking spray. Spread potatoes out evenly in the dish. Combine soymilk and tofu in a blender and process until creamy. Stir Smart Balance® and salt into the soymilk cream mixture. Pour cream over potatoes, stir until evenly mixed and bake uncovered at 375° F, 45 to 50 minutes or until tips of potatoes are golden. Garnish with parsley flakes (opt).

Variation: Garnish with shredded soy cheddar cheese and return to oven 5 to 10 minutes until cheese is bubbly.

Yield: 8 cups

CHEESY HASHBROWN CASSEROLE

32 oz	Frozen shredded potatoes, (Ore Ida®)	1 T	Chicken-style seasoning
1 c	Water	½ tsp	Salt
1 c	Pimiento Cheese Sauce (below)	2 c	Onions, chopped
½ c	Tofutti® Sour Cream (or)	1 T	Olive oil
	"Soy Good" Sour Cream (p. 179)	1 ½ tsp	Parsley, dried

Thaw potatoes in a large bowl. In a separate bowl, combine water, cheese sauce, sour cream, chicken-style seasoning and salt. Pour over potatoes and mix well. Sauté onions in oil until translucent and stir into potato mixture. Prepare a casserole dish with cooking spray. Spoon potato mixture into dish and spread out evenly. Garnish top with parsley. Bake uncovered at 350° F, 45 to 55 minutes.

Yield: 9 cups

PIMIENTO CHEESE SAUCE

2 c	Water	1 T	Fresh lemon juice
⅓ c	Raw cashews, rinsed	1 ½ tsp	Salt
¼ c	Nutritional yeast flakes	1 tsp	Onion powder
4 oz	Pimientos	¼ tsp	Garlic powder
3 T	Cornstarch		

In a blender, combine half the water, cashews, yeast flakes and pimientos and process on high speed until smooth and creamy. Add remaining water and ingredients and blend until well mixed. Pour out into a saucepan and cook over medium heat until thickened.

Yield: 3 cups

VEGETARIAN GOULASH

1 ½ c	Large elbow macaroni, uncooked	⅔ c	Burger-style crumbles
1 ½ c	Onions, chopped	1 tsp	Beef-style seasoning
½ c	Fresh mushrooms, sliced (opt)	2 cans	Stewed tomatoes (14.5 oz each)
¼ c	Green bell peppers, diced	½ tsp	Basil, dried
3 med	Garlic cloves, minced		
1 T	Olive oil		

Cook macaroni in salted water until tender. Drain and rinse well. While macaroni is cooking, sauté vegetables in oil until soft. Add burger crumbles, cover with beef-style seasoning and brown mixture slightly. Add tomatoes and basil, and simmer about 5 minutes. Stir in cooked macaroni and cook until heated through. May garnish with soy Parmesan cheese alternative.

Yield: 8 cups

MAFALDA SURPRISE
(Instead of Spaghetti)

4 c	Mafalda pasta, uncooked	½ c	Vegetarian burger
1 c	Fresh mushrooms, sliced	1 T	Nutritional yeast flakes
½ c	Onions, chopped	1 tsp	Brown sugar or Sucanat®
1 lg	Garlic clove, minced	2 c	Soy cheddar cheese, shredded (SoyaKass®)
2 tsp	Olive oil		
1 jar	Spaghetti sauce (26 oz)	(opt)	Soy Parmesan cheese, grated

Cook pasta in salted water according to directions. While pasta is cooking, sauté mushrooms, onions, and garlic in olive oil until tender. Add spaghetti sauce, burger, yeast flakes, and sweetener. Simmer, covered, 5 to 10 minutes. Drain pasta when tender, rinse and toss with a little olive oil. For each serving, spoon spaghetti sauce over the pasta and sprinkle about ¼ cup shredded soy cheddar cheese over the sauce. If desired, garnish with soy Parmesan cheese also. Serve as cheese softens or melts.

Note: Mafalda is "mini lasagna" and very appealing when served this way.

Yield: 12 cups

TABOULI SALAD

2 c	Water	¼ c	Olive oil, "extra virgin"
1 c	Bulgur wheat	2 T	Fresh lemon juice
1 ½ c	Fresh tomatoes, diced	2 lg	Garlic cloves, crushed
1 c	Green onions, diced	1 tsp	Salt
¾ c	Fresh parsley, minced		

In a saucepan, combine water and bulgur wheat. Bring to a boil, cover, remove from heat and let sit overnight or 6 to 8 hours. Add tomatoes, onions, and parsley to the bulgur wheat and stir gently. Combine oil and lemon juice and set aside. Combine garlic and salt and mash together to make a paste. Add garlic salt paste to the oil and lemon juice and mix well. Pour mixture over the other ingredients and stir until flavors are well mixed. Chill 1 or 2 hours before serving.

Yield: 5 cups

FRESH KALE SALAD with OMEGA DRESSING

3 c	Fresh kale, finely chopped	¼ c	Water
12	Cherry tomatoes, quartered	3 T	Fresh lemon juice
½ c	Sweet onions, diced	2 T	Bragg® Liquid Aminos
⅓ c	Black olives, sliced	2 T	Flax oil or Omega Oil blend
⅓ c	Pickling cucumber, diced	2 tsp	Honey
3 T	Sunflower seeds	½ tsp	Onion powder
2 T	Red bell peppers, diced	¼ tsp	Garlic powder
¼ c	Green onions, sliced		

Combine kale, tomatoes, onions, olives and cucumber in a serving bowl. Set aside the sunflower seeds, peppers, and green onions for later use. In a separate bowl or jar, combine water, lemon juice, liquid aminos, flax oil, honey and seasonings to make the "dressing" and mix well. Pour over salad and marinate in the refrigerator 2 hours. Add the sunflower seeds, red peppers and green onions just before serving.

Yield: 5 cups

HUMMUS
(A Middle Eastern Chickpea Puree)

2 ½ c	Cooked garbanzos, drained, (reserve broth)	4 cloves	Garlic
½ c	Tahini (sesame seed butter)	1 ½ tsp	Onion powder
7 T	Garbanzo broth or water	1 tsp	Salt
6 T	Fresh lemon juice	4 oz can	Green chilies, chopped (Old El Paso® preferred)

Combine all ingredients, except chilies, in a blender and process on high speed 1 to 2 minutes until smooth and creamy. Pour out into a bowl and stir in chilies. Garnish with a few diced tomatoes, fresh parsley and paprika.

Tip: Delicious as a spread on bread and crackers, or as a dip with chips and raw vegetables. Also great spread in pocket bread stuffed with falafels, shredded lettuce and tomatoes.

Yield: 3 cups

PEAS & PEANUTS
SALAD

3 c	Frozen "petite or early" peas, uncooked (16 oz bag)
1 c	Jicama, cut into ½ inch julienne style pieces
½ c	Onions, chopped
½ c	Lightly roasted peanuts, salted or unsalted
¼ c	Lightly roasted sunflower seeds, salted or unsalted
¼ c	Pepitas (green pumpkin seeds), raw or lightly roasted
½ tsp	McCormick® "Salt free" Garlic and Herb Seasoning
½ tsp	Onion salt
¼ tsp	Garlic salt
1 c	Sour Cream Supreme (see page 187)
4 leaves	Leafy green or red lettuce
1 stem	Green onion with top fringed, for garnish

Rinse frozen peas in a colander and drain well. Combine vegetables, peanuts, and seeds. Mix seasonings together and sprinkle evenly over the pea salad mixture. Add Sour Cream Supreme and stir all together until well mixed. Pour pea salad mixture into a decorative serving bowl. Border dish with leafy lettuce and garnish with green onion. Chill until ready to serve.

Yield: 6 ½ cups

SOUR CREAM SUPREME

1 ¼ c	Mori-Nu® Tofu, firm (10.5 oz)	1 tsp	Honey
¼ c	Sunflower oil or extra light olive oil	½ tsp	Salt
2 ½ T	Fresh lemon juice		

In a blender, combine all ingredients and process until smooth and creamy.

Yield: 1 ½ cups

PICNIC POTATO SALAD

2 lb	Red potatoes, boiled (about 1 qt)	1 c	Potato Salad Dressing (see below)
1 c	Onions, chopped		
¾ c	Celery, sliced or diced	1 tsp	Salt
½ c	Pickles, chopped	1 tsp	Dill weed

Cool potatoes (peeling is optional) and cut into bite size cubes. Add onions, celery, and pickles. Combine Potato Salad Dressing (recipe below), salt and dill weed and stir gently into potato mixture. Chill before serving.

Yield: 7 cups

POTATO SALAD DRESSING

1 c	Soymilk beverage, plain	½ tsp	Salt
¼ c	Olive oil, "extra light"	2 T	Instant Clear Jel® (instant food thickener)
2 T	Carrot, cooked		
1 ½ tsp	Onion powder	1 ½ T	Fresh lemon juice

In a blender, combine soymilk, oil, carrot, onion powder and salt. Process on high speed until carrots are liquefied. Add food thickener through the lid spout while blending on low speed. Increase speed as it thickens. Pour out into a bowl and add lemon juice. Stir until well mixed.

Yield: 1 ½ cups

QUICK ARTICHOKE PASTA TOSS

2 c	Rotinni (Veggie Spirals), uncooked
1 ⅓ c	Zesty Italian Dressing or "Fat-Free" Italian Dressing
8 oz	Canned artichoke hearts in water, drained and quartered
2 c	Broccoli florets
1 c	Fresh small button mushrooms (opt)
1 c	Cherry tomatoes, whole
1 can	Pitted whole black olives, small size
⅛ c	Fresh parsley, snipped

Cook noodles according to directions on package in salted water. While the noodles are cooking, prepare a double recipe of Zesty or "Fat-Free" Italian Dressing (see recipes below) and set 1 ⅓ cups aside. Drain and rinse noodles. Pour Italian dressing over hot noodles. Add vegetables and toss until well mixed. Cover and chill salad at least 6 hours before serving.

Yield: 10 cups

ZESTY ITALIAN DRESSING

Add to one 0.6 oz package of Good Seasons® "Zesty Italian" Dressing Mix:

3 T	Fresh lemon juice
3 T	Pineapple juice, concentrate
⅓ c	Water
¼ c	Olive oil, 'light"

Mix together in a cruet or an air-tight container. Close lid and shake well. Refrigerate 30 minutes before using. Shake again before serving.

Yield: 1 cup

"FAT-FREE" ITALIAN DRESSING

Add to one 1.05 oz package Good Seasons® "Fat-Free" Italian Dressing Mix:

¼ c	Fresh lemon juice
2 T	Frozen apple juice, concentrate
6 T	Pineapple juice
⅓ c	Water

Mix together in a cruet or an air-tight container. Close lid and shake well. Refrigerate 30 minutes before using. Shake again before serving.

Note: For a stronger Italian flavor, decrease water to ¼ cup.

Yield: 1 cup

MARINATED BEAN SALAD

2 c	Fresh green beans, cooked	½ c	Black olives, sliced
1 can	Wax beans, cut (15 oz)	¼ c	Green bell pepper, diced
1 can	Red kidney beans (15 oz)	¼ c	Red bell pepper, diced
1 can	Garbanzos or chick peas (15 oz)	1 c	Italian Dressing (p. 188)
1 c	Onion rings or slices		

Drain beans to remove juice. Combine all vegetables in a large bowl. Prepare Italian Dressing of choice. This step can be done ahead. Pour dressing over vegetables and mix thoroughly. Cover and marinate in refrigerator for several hours or overnight before serving.

Variation: Add 1 can artichoke hearts, quartered

Yield: 8 cups

TOFU GREEK SALAD

1 lb	Water-packed tofu, extra firm	½ lg	Red onion
6	Roma tomatoes	1 c	Black olives, pitted
3	Cucumbers	1 c	Herb Dressing (p. 215)

Cut tofu into ½ inch cubes. Cut tomatoes into wedges. Peel and slice cucumbers. Chop red onion. Leave the olives whole. Toss mixture with Herb Dressing (recipe on page 215) or Zesty Italian Dressing (recipe on page 188) and serve on a bed of leafy lettuce. For improved flavor, marinate tofu and vegetables in dressing 4–6 hours before lightly tossing.

Yield: 10 cups

CREAM CHEESY SPREAD

8 oz	Better Than Cream Cheese®, plain (Tofutti®)	⅛ tsp	Citric acid

Sprinkle citric acid evenly over cream cheese and stir until well mixed. Use mixture to stuff celery, or as a sandwich filling with sliced olives, cucumbers, and onions etc.

Yield: 1 cup

"QUICK BAKED" GOLDEN POTATO FRIES

Slice 2 large baking potatoes lengthwise into ½" wide sticks. Prepare a baking sheet with cooking spray. Spread potatoes out in a single layer. (To enhance flavor, drizzle 1 tsp olive oil over the potatoes and stir to coat evenly.) Sprinkle with any combination of seasonings to your taste i.e. dried parsley, herbs, chives, onion salt, garlic salt, Spike®, nutritional yeast etc. Broil on the top oven rack at 400° F. Stir after 10 minutes and then every 5 minutes for 15 minutes or until tender with golden brown crispy edges. You may also want to add onion rings to the fries during the last 5 minutes of baking time. Serve hot and, if desired, with Vinegarless Ketchup (see below) on the side.

Yield: 4 cups

"THICK & ZESTY" VINEGARLESS KETCHUP

12 oz	Tomato paste	1 tsp	Lime juice
1 c	Tomato sauce	1 tsp	Onion powder
¼ c	Pineapple juice, concentrate	1 tsp	Salt
¼ c	Fresh lemon juice	½ tsp	Garlic salt
2 T	Orange juice, concentrate	½ tsp	Paprika
3 T	Date butter (see p. 251)	¼ tsp	Citric acid crystals
2 T	Fructose or honey	⅛ tsp	Cumin, ground

Combine all ingredients in a blender and process until smooth. Refrigerate. The flavor improves after 2 days. Freeze extras not used within two weeks.

Yield: 3½ cups

"QUICK" VINEGARLESS KETCHUP

1½ c	Tomato sauce	2 T	Fruit-Fresh®, powder (or ⅛ tsp citric acid)
1 c	Tomato paste	1½ tsp	Salt
½ c	Pineapple juice	1 tsp	Onion powder
¼ c	Fresh lemon juice	½ tsp	Garlic salt
1 tsp	Lime juice	½ tsp	Paprika
3 T	Date butter (p. 251)	¼ tsp	Worcestershire sauce (opt) (Vegetarian brand)
2 T	Pineapple/orange juice (frozen concentrate)		
2 T	Fructose or honey		

Combine all ingredients in a blender and process until smooth. Refrigerate. Freeze extras not used within two weeks.

Variation: If thicker ketchup is desired, decrease tomato sauce to 1 cup and increase tomato paste to 1 ½ cups.

Yield: 4 cups

SIMPLY SMASHING STUFFED POTATOES

4 med	Russet potatoes, baked	¼ tsp	Salt (or more)
1 c	Mori Nu® Tofu, soft	1 ½ T	Dry bread crumbs, fine
¼ c	Green onions, diced	1 ½ T	SoyCo® Parmesan Cheese
1 ½ tsp	Chicken-style seasoning	1 tsp	Olive oil

Slice baked potatoes in half lengthwise and scoop out pulp, leaving a ¼ inch shell. Mash potatoes with a mixer. Add tofu, onion and seasonings and beat until light and fluffy. Add more tofu if necessary. Spoon potato mixture back into shells. Combine bread crumbs, grated parmesan cheese, and oil. Sprinkle evenly over potatoes. Place potatoes on an un-greased baking sheet. Bake at 350° F, 15 minutes or until heated through. Garnish with additional sliced green onions.

Yield: 8 stuffed potatoes

RANCH-STYLE DIP

2 c	Soy sour cream (see p. 187)	2 T	Dried or fresh chives
1 pkt	Ranch flavored "dip mix"		

Combine the soy sour cream and the packet contents. Stir in chives (reserve a few to garnish the top) and chill before serving. Delicious served with raw veggies or chips.

Note: Soy sour cream purchased from a health food store may be used in this recipe but I prefer the taste when made with either of the homemade sour cream recipes in this book.

Yield: 2 cups

VERY BERRY CREAM CHEESE SPREAD

4 oz	Better Than Cream Cheese®, plain (Tofutti®)
¼ c	All-fruit jam, (blueberry, strawberry or raspberry)

Gently stir or swirl mixture together. Spread on whole-wheat bagels or any whole grain bread of choice. Or, spread cream cheese on bread and top with jam.

Yield: ¾ cup

QUICK RICE PUDDING *with* MANGOS AND CREAM

½ c	Canned pear juice	⅓ c	Currants or raisins (opt)
½ c	Canned coconut milk	2 c	Fresh or canned fruit
½ c	Water		(i.e. mangos, pears,
3 T	Soymilk powder, plain		peaches, pineapple,
1½ c	Minute® Brown Rice, uncooked		bananas, apricots etc.)

Combine fruit juice, coconut milk, water and milk powder in a saucepan. Bring to a boil. Turn heat down to low setting and stir in rice. Cover and cook 5 minutes. Stir in currants or raisins, cover, and turn heat off. Wait 5 to 10 minutes before removing cover.

TO SERVE HOT:
Spoon into bowls, pour fruit over rice and add toppings as desired.

TO SERVE COLD:
Chill 1 to 2 hours before adding fruit and garnishes.

SUGGESTED TOPPINGS:
Grated coconut, granola and "Instant" Whipped Topping (see recipe below)

Yield: 5 cups

"INSTANT" WHIPPED TOPPING

1 ½ c	Water	⅓ c	Coconut milk, canned
⅔ c	Soymilk powder, plain*		("lite," unsweetened)
½ c	Blanched almonds (w/o skins)	2 tsp	Natural vanilla, flavoring
3 ½ T	Emes Kosher Jel® (plain)	¼ tsp	Salt
3 T	Fructose, powdered sugar or honey		Ice

In a blender, combine the water, milk powder, almonds and Emes Jel and process until the almonds are liquefied completely. Add remaining ingredients and process briefly. Finally, begin adding ice slowly through the lid spout and continue processing on high speed to make a total volume equal to 5 cups. Turn blender off and wait briefly. Mixture should now be light and fluffy. Best served immediately. If stored, and mixture becomes too firm, hand whip or beat gently with an electric beater before serving.

* Recommend Better Than Milk™ "Original."

Yield: 5 cups

SMOOTHIES

2 to 3 c	Frozen fruit of choice (Peaches, bananas, strawberries, blueberries, pineapple etc.)
1 c	Unsweetened 100% juice of choice, diluted or concentrate (Pineapple, apple, fruit blends etc.)
½ c	Vegan yogurt, any flavor (opt)
⅓ c	Soymilk powder, plain or vanilla (Better Than Milk™ "Original")
2 T	Fructose, honey, brown rice syrup or ¼ tsp Stevia extract (opt)

Combine all ingredients in a blender and process until smooth. Serve immediately.

Note: The ratio of fruit to juice can be adjusted according to your preference of thickness.

Yield: 4 cups (approx)

NATURALLY FRUITY "CREAM-SICLES"

1 lg	Banana, ripened	⅓ c	Soymilk, powder
½ c	Peaches	¼ c	Fruit juice concentrate, (peach or white grape)
2 lg	Strawberries	2 T	Fructose, granules (opt)
⅓ c	Pineapple chunks		

Combine all ingredients in a blender and process until smooth and creamy. Pour into popsicle containers and freeze.

Variation: Stir in bits of fresh fruit, chopped nuts or carob chips before freezing.

Tip: For best results and naturally sweet flavor, use fully ripened fruit.

Yield: 6 (3oz) cream-sicles

PEANUT BUTTER & BANANA "MILKSHAKE"

1 c	Cold soymilk, vanilla	½ tsp	Vanilla
2 T	Soymilk powder, plain or vanilla	1 lg	Ripe banana, frozen
⅓ c	Natural peanut butter	½ c	Crushed ice
1 T	Honey		

Combine soymilk, soymilk powder, peanut butter, honey and vanilla in a blender and process until well mixed. Add frozen banana and ice and blend again just until smooth.

Tip: For best results, pour into a chilled glass and serve immediately.

Yield: 2 ½ cups

STRAWBERRY BANANA "MILKSHAKE"

¾ c	Soymilk beverage, vanilla	1 c	Strawberries, frozen
½ c	Water-packed tofu, silken	1 med	Ripe banana, frozen
3 T	Maple syrup		

Combine soymilk, tofu and maple syrup in a blender and process until creamy. Add strawberries and banana and blend again just until smooth.

Yield: 3 cups

STRAWBERRY ICE CREAM

2 c	Frozen strawberries, packed	¼ c	Fructose, granules
2 c	Soymilk creamer, French vanilla (Silk®)	½ tsp	Strawberry extract
½ c	Soymilk powder, plain * (opt)		

Combine all ingredients in a blender and process until smooth and creamy. Pour into an ice cream maker and proceed according to the manufacturer's directions.

* Better Than Milk™ Soy "Original" is the recommended product.

Tip: This recipe can easily be doubled or tripled to fit the ice cream maker.

Yield: 1 quart

VANILLA ICE CREAM

2 c	Soymilk creamer, plain (Silk®)	1 c	Soymilk powder, plain*
2 c	Soymilk creamer, French vanilla (Silk®)	1 T	Clear vanilla, extract

Combine all ingredients in a blender and process until well mixed. Pour into an ice cream maker and operate according to manufacturers' directions.

* Better Than Milk™ Soy "Original" is the recommended product.

Tip: For a delicious treat, add ½ cup finely chopped carob chips and ¼ cup lightly toasted and finely chopped almonds (chilled) to the ice cream when nearly set or during the last 5 minutes of churning.

Note: This recipe can easily be doubled or tripled if necessary to fit the ice cream maker.

Yield: 1 quart

FRUIT KABOBS

Place on a skewer fresh cut fruits of choice.
(i.e. Bananas, grapes, strawberries, pineapple, kiwi and oranges.)

If not serving immediately, dip or brush fruit with pineapple juice to keep bananas and other fruits from turning dark. Enjoy kabobs plain or serve with Fresh Fruit Dressing (see recipe below).

SWEET & SOUR FRESH FRUIT DRESSING

1 c	Sour Cream Supreme	1 T	Frozen pineapple juice, (concentrate)
½ c	Crushed pineapple, well drained	2 tsp	Cook's® Vanilla powder
¼ c	Canned coconut milk, "lite" (unsweetened)	1 lg	Ripe banana
3 T	Better Than Milk™ powder	1 T	Instant Clear Jel®
3 T	Fructose or honey		

In a blender, combine Sour Cream Supreme (recipe on page 187) with all remaining ingredients, except Clear Jel®, and process until smooth and creamy. If desired, stir crushed pineapple into mixture rather than blending. Add 1 T Instant Clear Jel® through the lid spout while blender is running.

Note: May substitute Cook's® Vanilla powder with "clear" vanilla.

Yield: 3 cups

STRAWBERRY SHORTCAKE "BISCUIT-STYLE"

Shortcake:

1 ½ c	Unbleached white flour	½ tsp	Baking soda
1 c	Whole-wheat pastry flour	¾ c	Soymilk beverage (Silk®)
⅓ c	Fructose, granular	⅓ c	Smart Balance® "Light," melted (non-hydrogenated spread)
1 T	Baking powder	1 tsp	Lemon juice
1 tsp	Salt		

Strawberry topping:

1 qt	Strawberries, sliced	3 T	Fructose, granules
3 T	Water		

In a mixing bowl, combine dry ingredients. In a separate container, combine soymilk, Smart Balance® and lemon juice. Gently fold milk mixture into dry ingredients until evenly moistened. Prepare a heavy-duty baking sheet with cooking spray. For individual shortcakes, drop batter by large spoonfuls unto the baking sheet, allowing 1 inch between each shortcake. Flatten tops slightly. Bake in a pre-heated oven at 400° F, 10 minutes or until a light golden color on top and bottom. Meanwhile, prepare strawberries. Combine a portion of the sliced strawberries, (about 1 ½ cups) in a blender with the water and 2 T fructose and blend until puréed. Then sprinkle 1 T fructose over the remaining strawberries and lightly toss. Remove shortcakes from oven when ready and cool 2 or 3 minutes. Split shortcakes in half and cover with 2 or 3 tablespoons strawberry purée. Then top with remaining sliced strawberries and, if desired, favorite non-dairy whipped topping.

Variation: For pan shortcake, bake in an 8" square dish at 375° F, 20 minutes.

Tip: Instead of sliced strawberries alone, try a colorful mixture of fresh fruits. Our favorite mixture is peaches or mangos, strawberries, bananas and kiwi.

Yield: 8 shortcakes

"SWEET REFLECTIONS" BANANA-RASPBERRY DESSERT

4 c	Raspberries, unsweetened	4	Ripe bananas
6 oz	White grape juice concentrate	2 tsp	Pineapple juice
½ tsp	Fresh lemon juice	2 T	Almonds, slivered
2 T	Cornstarch or arrowroot		

If using frozen raspberries, place unopened raspberry package in a large bowl, add hot water to cover. Set aside to thaw. Drain thawed raspberries. Measure out ½ c raspberries and pour into a blender. Add the grape juice concentrate and lemon juice and process until smooth. Pour out into a saucepan and add cornstarch, arrowroot, or tapioca powder. Stir to dissolve thickener and bring mixture to a boil. Stir constantly and cook until syrup is thick and clear. Cool. Cut peeled bananas into diagonal slices ¼ inch thick. Arrange on four individual dessert plates in a sunburst pattern. Brush or drizzle bananas with the pineapple juice. Mound remaining raspberries in center of bananas, dividing equally. Spoon about ¼ cup raspberry juice syrup over raspberries on each plate, or divide equally. Before serving, sprinkle desserts with almonds.

Yield: 8 servings

COOKIE HAYSTACKS

3 c	Date pieces, softened	1 ½ c	Walnuts, chopped
1 ½ c	Raisins	¾ c	Whole-wheat flour
½ c	Orange or pineapple juice	⅓ c	Old-fashioned oats
⅛ c	Water	½ tsp	Salt
4 c	Unsweetened shredded coconut		

In a blender, combine dates, raisins, juice and water. Blend until smooth. Pour mixture out into a bowl. Add dry ingredients to the blender ingredients and mix lightly. Scoop up with a small ice cream scoop and drop onto an un-greased cookie sheet. Bake at 350° F, 20 to 30 minutes or until browned.

Variation: May use 2 cups dates and 3 cups shredded coconut.

Yield: 4 dozen

"QUICK & EASY" APPLE CRISP

Topping:

1 c	Quick oats
½ c	Unbleached white flour
½ c	Walnuts, chopped
¼ c	Old-fashioned oats
¼ c	Shredded coconut (opt)
¼ tsp	Salt
¼ tsp	Cinnamon, ground
3 T	Brown sugar, packed
3 T	Olive oil, "extra light"
1 T	Water
1 tsp	Vanilla extract

Combine all dry ingredients except brown sugar in a mixing bowl. Mix brown sugar with oil, water and vanilla. Combine the liquid and dry ingredients and stir until mixture is crumbly. Set aside.

Filling:

2 cans	Apple pie filling (21 oz each)
⅛ tsp	Cinnamon, ground
2 T	Smart Balance®, "Light" (non-hydrogenated spread)

Spray a 9" x 13" baking dish with cooking spray. Pour apple pie filling into the dish and spread it out. Sprinkle apples with cinnamon and dot evenly with Smart Balance®. Cover apple filling with topping. Bake at 350° F, 25 to 30 minutes until topping is golden brown.

Tip: Serve with favorite non-dairy whipped cream or vanilla ice cream.
Note: For a lower sugar version, use low-sugar apple pie filling available at grocery stores.

Yield: 7 cups

SOY-CREAMY DESSERT TOPPING

1 ¼ c	Water-packed tofu, silken
½ c	Soymilk beverage, plain (Better Than Milk™, "Original")
½ c	Fructose, granular
¼ tsp	Vanilla extract
⅛ tsp	Salt
2 T	Instant Clear Jel® (instant food thickener)

In a blender, combine all ingredients except Instant Clear Jel®. Process until smooth and creamy. Add Clear Jel® and blend again 5 to 10 seconds until thickened. Serve as a topping for desserts, as a layer in parfaits, or chill and serve alone for a pudding.

Yield: 1 ¾ cups

FRESH STRAWBERRY PIE

1 c	Water	1 box	Emes Kosher Jel®, (2 ½ oz) (strawberry flavor)
½ c	Fructose, granules	5 c	Fresh strawberries, sliced
2 T	Light corn syrup, (Karo®)	9-inch	Whole grain pie shell, baked
2 T	Cornstarch		

Combine water, fructose, corn syrup and cornstarch in a saucepan. Stir to dissolve cornstarch. Bring to a boil, stirring constantly. Reduce heat and simmer until mixture clears. Add strawberry Kosher Jel® and stir until dissolved. Set syrup aside to cool down to room temperature. Prepare strawberries. Pour syrup over the strawberries and stir lightly. Pour strawberries into a baked pie shell and smooth mixture out. (See page 272 and 273 for a selection of single pie crust recipes). Refrigerate until set. Serve with non-dairy whipped topping of choice.

Yield: 9-inch pie

FRESH FRUIT *with* PUDDING COMPOTE

Prepare (12 c) of fresh fruit combinations; i.e. peaches, bananas, strawberries, grapes, blueberries, pineapple and kiwi. Set aside.

2 c	Water	½ c	Spun "creamy" honey
1 c	Water-packed tofu, silken	½ c	White flour or tapioca
1 c	Cooked white rice	1 T	Fresh lemon juice
1 c	Coconut milk, canned ("lite," unsweetened)	2 tsp	Vanilla extract
		(opt)	Fresh mint leaves

In a blender, process water, tofu, rice, and coconut milk until smooth and creamy. Add remaining ingredients and blend until well mixed. Pour mixture into a saucepan and bring to a boil, stirring constantly until thick. Refrigerate pudding until cold before serving. Arrange half of fruit in a large serving bowl. Layer ¾ of pudding mixture over fruit. Cover with remaining fruit. Spoon remaining pudding on top and in the middle, allowing fruit to show around the edges. Place a whole strawberry or small cluster of grapes on top. Garnish with mint leaves if desired.

Yield: 16 cups

A Bit of Country

Featuring

Southern specialties guaranteed to give you that good old country feeling and a taste of Southern hospitality.

"CHICKEN" STYLE POTPIE

4 c	Potatoes, diced	2 T	Chicken-style seasoning (or) 1 ½ tsp salt
2 c	Carrots, diced	1 T	Nutritional yeast flakes
3 c	Water	1 ½ tsp	Onion powder
1 c	Onions, diced	⅛ tsp	Garlic powder
1 c	Celery, diced	1 c	Mushrooms, sliced
2 T	Olive oil	1 c	Frozen green peas
3 c	Soymilk beverage, plain	6 T	Unbleached white flour
¾ c	Soy cream (recipe below)	4 T	Water
2 c	Mock chicken, diced *		

Cook potatoes and carrots in water until nearly done. Drain. Set aside. Sauté onions and celery in oil until transparent. In a large pot, combine potatoes, carrots, onion, and celery with soymilk, soy cream, mock chicken, seasonings, mushrooms, and peas. Mix flour with water and stir until no longer lumpy. Add to the vegetable mixture and cook over medium heat to thicken. Pour mixture into a large casserole dish & cover with a whole grain pie-crust (see Wheat or Oat Potpie Crust recipes on page 203). Seal edges around dish. Bake at 350° F for 40 to 45 minutes or until browned and flaky. Or, make individual potpies but you may wish to use a bottom and a top crust for this method. Bake at 350° F for about 30 minutes for small potpies.

******Note:* I recommend using Worthington® "Chic-Ketts™" available in the frozen foods section of some health food stores.

Yield: 18 servings (cut 6 x 3)

SOY CREAM

½ c	Water	⅛ tsp	Garlic powder
¼ c	Soymilk powder (Soyagen®)	¼ c	Olive oil, "light"
¼ tsp	Salt	2 T	Fresh lemon juice
¼ tsp	Onion powder		

In a blender, combine water, soymilk powder, and seasonings and process until smooth. Remove lid spout and add oil slowly while blending. Pour mixture out into a bowl and fold in the lemon juice until well mixed.

Yield: 1 cup (scant)

WHEAT POTPIE CRUST

1 c	Whole-wheat pastry flour	6 T	Water
1 c	Unbleached white flour	¾ tsp	Salt
½ c	Olive oil, "extra light"		

Mix both flours in a bowl. Combine the oil, water and salt. Combine the flour and liquids and mix together lightly to form a ball. Place dough between two sheets of wax paper and roll out with a rolling pin.

Yield: 3 cups

OAT POTPIE CRUST

⅔ c	Mashed potatoes, cooked	1 tsp	Salt
1 ½ c	Oat flour	⅔ c	Water
½ c	Whole-wheat flour	⅓ c	Oil
2 T	Soymilk powder, plain		

Peel, cube and boil 2 potatoes. Mash enough potatoes to equal ⅔ cup and set aside. Combine flours, soymilk powder and salt. Mix water and oil together and pour into the dry ingredients. Stir until just moistened. Add mashed potatoes to the dough. Knead mixture together until a soft, pliable dough is formed. Let dough rest several minutes. Roll dough out on a floured surface.

Yield: 3 ½ cups

"CHICKEN" DIVAN

4 c	Water	1 T	Olive oil
2 c	Brown rice	2 pkt	Gravy Quik® (chicken-style)
1 tsp	Salt	2 c	Fresh broccoli florets
2 c	Mock chicken*	1 T	Fresh parsley, snipped
¼ c	Breading Meal # 2	1 T	Sesame seeds, lightly toasted

Cook rice with water and salt. Tear mock chicken into bite-size pieces and moisten with water. Place "chicken" and Breading Meal #2 (see page 206) in a plastic bag and shake to coat "chicken" evenly. Brown "chicken" in oil and set aside. Prepare gravy according to directions on the package except increase water to 1 ¼ cups. (May substitute ½ cup water with ½ c soymilk for a richer flavor.) Steam or microwave broccoli 3 minutes or until crisp-tender. Arrange rice on a large platter. Top with broccoli and "chicken" and pour the gravy over all evenly. Garnish with the parsley and sesame seeds.

**Note:* I recommend using Worthington® "Chic-Ketts™" available in the frozen foods section of some health food stores.

Yield: 10 cups

"CHICKEN" & RICE CASSEROLE

2 ½ c	Water	1 T	Chicken-style seasoning
2 c	Instant brown rice	½ tsp	Onion salt
1 c	Instant white rice		

Bring water to a boil. Add rice and seasoning. Cover and simmer 5 minutes and remove from heat. Pour rice into a large bowl and set aside.

1 c	Mock chicken	½ c	Jicama, julienned
1 c	Onions, chopped	½ c	Lightly roasted cashews
½ c	Celery, diced	¼ c	Green onions, sliced
1 T	Olive oil	¼ c	Fresh parsley, minced
1 ½ c	Jiffy Mushroom Soup (below)	1 T	Sesame seeds
½ c	Soy mayonnaise (p. 166 or 242)		

Tear mock chicken into bite size pieces and combine with onions, celery and oil in a skillet. Sauté until vegetables are tender. Stir mixture into rice. Add soup (see below), mayonnaise, and remaining ingredients. Mix well. Prepare a casserole dish with cooking spray. Spread rice mixture evenly into the casserole dish. If desired, garnish with additional cashews, green onions and sesame seeds. Cover and bake at 350° F, 30 minutes or until bubbly.

Yield: 9 x 13 casserole

JIFFY MUSHROOM SOUP

1 c	Fresh mushrooms, sliced	1 T	Cornstarch
1 ½ c	Water	1 T	Spectrum® Spread (opt)
½ c	Onions, chopped	1 tsp	Chicken-style seasoning
4 T	Soymilk powder, plain*	½ tsp	Salt
2 T	Unbleached white flour	½ tsp	Basil, dried

Sauté mushrooms in a skillet with 2 T water and ⅛ tsp salt until tender. Set aside. (May also microwave mushrooms with water and salt about 1 minute.) In a blender, combine remaining ingredients and process until smooth. Add mushrooms with liquids and flash blend a few times to break up mushrooms into pieces. Pour out into a saucepan and cook until thickened. Use this for recipes in place of canned soup. If necessary, add additional soymilk or water to thin mixture down to desired consistency.

Note: Recommend Better Than Milk™, "Original" for this recipe.

Variation: May substitute fresh mushrooms, 2 T water, and ⅛ tsp salt with 4 oz canned mushrooms, with liquid.

Yield: 2 ½ cups

VEGETARIAN "BEEF STEAKS" With GRAVY (Homemade Gluten)

GLUTEN:

1 c	Vital wheat gluten (Do Pep)	1 c	Water
¼ c	Unbleached white flour		

Combine flours and mix very well. Add water and quickly stir to make a ball of gluten. Let sit at least 20 minutes. While waiting, make the broth (see recipe below). When gluten is ready, form a long roll. Cut into 1-inch pieces. Flatten pieces out into a round shape and drop into boiling broth. Gluten will soon float if made properly. Simmer uncovered, 40 to 50 minutes, stirring occasionally. When done, cut gluten "steaks" into strips and coat with Breading Meal # 1 (see recipe below). Lightly coat a large non-stick frying pan with olive oil and heat on med-lo setting. Add gluten "strips" and spray "olive oil" cooking spray over gluten evenly. Fry until golden brown. Serve with ketchup or gravy. (See gravy recipes on pages 206 and 207)

Yield: 12 steaks

BROTH:

2 qt	Water	2 T	Bragg®, liquid aminos
½ c	Onion rings	½ T	Beef-style seasoning
½ c	Celery leaves	1 tsp	Celery salt
1 env	Onion-mushroom soup mix (Lipton®)	1 tsp	Garlic powder
4 lg	Basil leaves, chopped (or ½ tsp dried basil)	½ tsp	Cumin, ground
		2 lg	Bay leaves

Combine all ingredients in a large pot and bring to a boil.

Yield: 2 ½ quarts

BREADING MEAL #1

½ c	Unbleached white flour	1 tsp	Onion powder
½ c	Yellow corn meal	½ tsp	Garlic powder
2 T	Nutritional yeast flakes	1 T	Parsley, dried
2 tsp	Chicken-style seasoning	⅛ tsp	Salt
1 tsp	Garlic & Herb seasoning, "salt-free"		

Combine all ingredients and store in an air-tight container.

Yield: 1 ¼ cups

BREADING MEAL #2

½ c	Flour, wheat or white	1 T	Nutritional yeast flakes
¼ c	Cracker crumbs, finely blended	1 tsp	Onion powder
¼ c	Yellow corn meal	½ tsp	Salt
2 tsp	Beef or chicken-style seasoning	½ tsp	Garlic powder

Mix ingredients together and store in an air-tight container.

Yield: 1 ⅛ cups

CHOPLETS™ 'N GRAVY

1 can	Choplets™ (veggie chops) (or vegetarian gluten)	¼ c	Breading Meal #2
		1 recipe	Country Gravy

Slice Choplets™ into strips or bite-size pieces. Shake Choplets™ with Breading Meal #2 (recipe above) in a zip-lock bag to coat the pieces evenly. Brown in a small amount olive oil and cover with "Country Gravy" or gravy of choice (recipes following).

Yield: 3 cups

COUNTRY GRAVY

1 c	Onions, sliced	2 tsp	Beef-style seasoning
1 c	Fresh mushrooms, sliced	2 tsp	Chicken-style seasoning
½ c	Bell pepper, chopped	½ c	Hot water
1 tsp	Garlic purée	2 T	Unbleached white flour
2 T	Olive oil	1 c	Water

Sauté vegetables and garlic in 1 T oil. Remove from pan. Brown seasonings in remaining oil until dark brown. Dash in ½ cup hot water. Mix flour with remaining 1 cup water, pour into the pan and stir until thick. Stir in the sautéed vegetables. Pour over Choplets™ (recipe above) and serve.

Yield: 3 cups

MUSHROOM-ONION GRAVY

1 c	Mushrooms, sliced	2 tsp	Beef-style seasoning
½ c	Onions, sliced	2 tsp	Chicken-style seasoning
¼	Bell pepper, chopped (opt)	½ c	Hot water
½ tsp	Garlic, minced	2 T	Unbleached white flour
2 T	Olive oil	1 c	Water

Sauté vegetables in half the olive oil and remove from pan. Brown the beef and chicken flavored seasonings in remaining oil. When dark brown, dash in ½ cup hot water. Mix flour with remaining 1 cup water, pour into the pan and stir until thick. Add the sautéed vegetables.

Yield: 2 ½ cups

CREAMY CHICKEN-STYLE GRAVY

3 T	Unbleached all purpose flour	2 T	Chicken-style seasoning
1 c	Soymilk beverage, plain (Silk®)	⅛ tsp	Salt (or to taste)
1 c	Water	⅛ tsp	Sage, ground (opt)
¾ c	Water-packed tofu, silken	1 tsp	Fresh parsley, minced (opt)

Stir flour in a dry frying pan over med-hi heat until lightly browned. Cool. Combine flour with all remaining ingredients in a blender and process until smooth. Pour into a frying pan or saucepan and bring to a boil over med-hi heat, stirring constantly until thickened. If necessary, add more seasoning to taste. Remove from heat. Gravy will thicken more as it cools. If desired, sprinkle with parsley for garnish before serving.

Yield: 2 ¼ cups

"MINUTE" ONION-MUSHROOM GRAVY

1 env	Onion-mushroom soup mix (Lipton®)	2 c	Cold water
½ tsp	Beef-style seasoning	2 T	Unbleached white flour

Combine soup mix and seasoning in a saucepan. Combine a portion of the water (½ c) with the flour and stir to dissolve any lumps. Then add remaining water (1 ½ c) and mix well. Pour into saucepan with the soup mix. Bring to a boil over high heat, stirring constantly. Reduce heat and simmer gravy 3 to 5 minutes uncovered, stirring frequently until thickened.

Yield: 2 cups

VEGEBURGER WALNUT CASSEROLE

1 c	Onions, finely chopped	1 c	Water-packed tofu, silken
3 lg	Garlic cloves, finely minced	¼ c	Water
¼ c	Olive oil	¼ c	Bragg® Liquid Aminos
2 c	Vegetarian burger, frozen	2 ½ c	Corn bread stuffing mix
1 c	Walnuts, chopped	½ c	Vital wheat gluten
1 c	Water-packed tofu, extra firm		

Sauté onions and garlic in oil until softened. Add burger and brown lightly. Pour out into a large bowl. Stir in walnuts. Crumble tofu and add to mixture. Combine silken tofu, water and liquid aminos in a blender and process until creamy. Pour blended tofu mixture into burger mixture and stir until well mixed. Add the stuffing and gluten flour and mix well. Prepare a 9" x 13" or a 10" x 10" casserole dish with garlic or olive oil flavored cooking spray. Spread burger mixture out evenly into dish and pack down gently. Bake at 350° F, for 35 to 40 min. until evenly browned. Serve with gravy or ketchup.

Note: For vegeburgers, shape into 4-inch patties and brown on both sides in a frying pan generously coated with cooking spray. Makes 16 burgers.

Yield: 9 cups

OVEN-BAKED MACARONI AND "CHEESE"

1 ½ c	Regular elbow macaroni (Or use 2 c "large elbows")	1 ½ T	Cornstarch
		1 tsp	Salt
1 ½ c	Soymilk beverage, plain (Silk®)	2 T	Soy Parmesan cheese, grated
1 ½ c	Water-packed tofu, silken	2 ½ c	Soy cheddar cheese, shredded
2 tsp	Fresh lemon juice		

Boil macaroni in salted water until tender and doubled in size. Drain and rinse. Prepare a 10" square casserole dish with cooking spray. Spread cooked noodles into bottom of dish. Combine soymilk, tofu, lemon juice, cornstarch and salt in a blender and process until smooth and creamy. Pour the soy cream mixture over the noodles. Stir in the Parmesan cheese and only 2 cups grated soy cheese. Reserve the remaining cheese. Cover with glass lid and bake at 350° F, one hour. Garnish with remaining cheese and bake uncovered 8 to 10 min. more. Remove from oven. Allow to cool and set up 5 min. before serving.

Note: I prefer using the brand SoyCo® Lite & Less Parmesan Cheese Alternative and SoyaKass® Cheddar Cheese.

Yield: 8 cups

STOVE-TOP MACARONI 'N "CHEESE"

NOODLES:

2 c Macaroni elbows or spirals, uncooked

TOPPING:

¼ c Seasoned bread crumbs
3 T SoyCo® Parmesan Cheese Alternative
1 T Olive oil

Combine ingredients in a bowl and mix with fingers to make crumbs. Pour into a pie tin or spread on a cookie sheet and bake in a pre-heated oven at 300° F, about 10 minutes or until topping is crispy. Watch carefully to avoid browning.

AMERICAN "CHEESE" SAUCE:

1 ½ c Water
1 c Cooked white rice, or millet
½ c Mori-Nu® Tofu, firm
½ c Slivered almonds, (w/o skins)
½ c Cooked carrots, mashed
2 T Nutritional yeast flakes
1 ½ T Fresh lemon juice
1 ½ tsp Salt
1 tsp Onion powder
¼ tsp Garlic powder

In a blender, combine all ingredients and process on high speed until completely smooth and creamy. Bits of almonds or carrots should not be visible. Sauce will appear "shiny" when done. Heat in a saucepan, stirring constantly until hot.

METHOD:

Cook macaroni in boiling water until tender adding 1 tsp of salt to the water. While noodles are cooking, prepare and bake "Topping." Then prepare "American Cheese Sauce." Keep warm until ready to use. Drain and rinse cooked noodles well. Transfer to a bowl and pour 2 cups "cheese sauce" mixture over the hot noodles and toss lightly. Add soymilk or water to mixture if it seems too stiff. Pour into a shallow serving dish and sprinkle the topping evenly over the Macaroni & Cheese.

Variation: Add sautéed onions and/or bell peppers. Alternative toppings include a choice of crushed Pepperidge Farm Corn Bread Stuffing, crushed croutons, toasted sesame seeds or poppy seeds.

Yield: 6 cups

MAMA'S MASHED POTATOES

6 c	Potatoes, peeled & cubed	1 ½ tsp	Chicken-style seasoning
2 ½ c	Water	1 tsp	Onion powder
½ c	Soymilk beverage, plain (Silk®)	¾ tsp	Salt
½ c	Mori-Nu® Tofu, soft	¼ tsp	Garlic powder
3 T	Smart Balance®, "Light"		

Boil potatoes in water until tender. While potatoes are cooking, combine soymilk and tofu in a blender and process until creamy. Drain potatoes and transfer them to a large mixing bowl. Add Smart Balance®, seasonings, and blended cream to the potatoes and beat with an electric mixer until fluffy. Add more soymilk if necessary. Serve hot with gravy or Smart Balance®.

Yield: 5 cups

BLACK-EYED PEA STEW

2 c	Onions, chopped	2 cans	Diced tomatoes, plain (14.5 oz each)
½ c	Bell pepper, diced	1 can	Diced tomatoes, Italian (14.5 oz)
2 med	Garlic cloves, minced	1 ½ c	Frozen sliced okra, thawed
2 T	Olive oil		
2 c	Vegetarian Burger, canned		
4 c	Black-eyed peas, canned		

In a large pot, sauté onions, peppers, and garlic in oil until tender. Add burger and fry until lightly browned. Add remaining ingredients and simmer 10 to 15 minutes to blend flavors. Add water if necessary for desired thickness.

Yield: 12 cups

BLACK-EYED PEAS

2 c	Black eyed peas, dried	½ tsp	Salt or to taste (opt)
2 ¼ c	Water	1 T	Bac-O-Bits® (opt) (imitation bacon bits)
½ c	Onions, chopped		

Wash and sort peas. Cover peas with about 1 quart water and soak overnight or at least 4 hours. Drain. Simmer peas in water (2 ¼ cups), onions and salt until tender. Garnish with Bac-Os® if desired.

Yield: 3 cups

SAVORY KALE *with* PEPPERS & ONIONS

½ lb	Kale, tender young leaves	1 tsp	Olive oil
1 c	Onions, chopped	1 c	Water
¼ c	Red Peppers, diced	1 tsp	Chicken-style seasoning
2 lg	Garlic cloves, minced	(opt)	Salt

Soak and wash kale in water. Remove the large stems and discard any tough or discolored leaves. Stack 6 to 8 leaves at a time and cut crosswise into 1 inch strips. In a large saucepan, sauté onions, peppers and garlic in oil over medium heat until onions are translucent. Add water and kale, cover and simmer or steam 15 to 30 minutes. Add seasoning and salt to taste.

Variation: Replace kale with collards, Swiss chard or other greens.

Yield: 2 cups

FARM-STYLE CORN

16 oz	Yellow cut corn, frozen	2 T	Smart Balance®, "Light" (non-hydrogenated spread)
16 oz	Cream-style corn, frozen	⅛ tsp	Salt
3 T	Water		

Thaw corn. Combine all ingredients in a large saucepan and bring to a slow boil, stirring frequently. Reduce heat, cover and simmer 2-3 minutes. Serve.

Note: Not all brands of creamed corn are vegan. Check ingredients to look for any milk products listed.

Yield: 6 cups

SAVORY BABY LIMAS

1 lb	Baby limas, frozen (3 cups)	2 tsp	Chicken-style seasoning
2 ½ c	Water	1 ½ tsp	Nutritional yeast flakes
1 T	Red bell peppers, diced	½ tsp	Salt or to taste

Simmer beans in a covered pot with water about 45 minutes until "saucy" and well done. Add seasonings and simmer a few minutes longer until flavors mix through. Serve in soup cups, or over rice or toast.

Yield: 4 cups

SUMMER SQUASH & "CHEESE" CASSEROLE

1 c	Onions, chopped	½ tsp	Salt
1 T	Olive oil	¼ tsp	Onion salt
4 c	Yellow squash, chopped	¼ tsp	Lemon juice
1 c	Water	1 ½ c	SoyaKass® cheese, shredded (cheddar, jack or combo)
1 c	Water-packed tofu, silken		
½ c	Soymilk beverage, plain (Silk®)		

Sauté onions in oil in a large frying pan until soft. Add squash and water, cover and simmer until squash is tender. Mash squash into small pieces. Transfer ingredients to a prepared 10" square casserole dish. Combine tofu, soymilk, salts and lemon juice in a blender and process until creamy. Pour over squash and mix well. Work cheese through evenly, leaving some on top. Bake uncovered at 350° F, 30 to 35 minutes or until cheese begins to look bubbly and golden in color.

Variation: Use a mixture of zucchini and yellow squash.

Yield: 6 cups

SUMMER SQUASH STIR-FRY

1 sm	Onion, sliced	½ c	Frozen peas or pea pods
2 med	Yellow summer squash, sliced	1 tsp	Chicken-style seasoning
2 med	Zucchini, sliced	(opt)	Salt to taste
1 med	Carrot, cut diagonally	1 c	Shredded soy cheese (opt)

In a large skillet, sauté onions in a small amount olive oil or water. Add squash and carrots, with just enough water for simmering. Cover and cook until tender. Add thawed peas and simmer 2 to 3 more minutes. Season with chicken-style seasoning and/or salt to taste. Sprinkle with soy cheese if desired.

Yield: 6 cups

MESQUITE LENTILS

1 c	Onions, chopped	2 c	Brown lentils, dried
3 med	Garlic cloves	1 T	Beef-style seasoning
2 T	Olive oil	2 tsp	Salt
8 c	Water	2 ½ tsp	Mesquite Grill® seasoning

Sauté onions and garlic in oil until tender. Add water and seasonings, cover and cook until lentils are very soft.

Yield: 8 cups

SUCCOTASH

20 oz bag	Frozen lima beans	1 T	Flour or cornstarch
1 tsp	Salt	1 tsp	Marjoram, ground
1 c	Frozen cut corn	½ tsp	Chicken-style seasoning
¼ c	Water	¼ tsp	Onion powder
6 T	Soymilk powder, plain (Better than Milk™ "Original")	(opt)	Vegan butter flavoring

In a saucepan, add lima beans and enough water to just cover beans. Add salt, cover and simmer until almost tender. Add corn, return to a boil and simmer 5 more minutes. Combine ¼ c water with the remaining ingredients and mix until dissolved. Pour into vegetables and cook, stirring constantly until thick.

Yield: 3 cups

GERMAN POTATO CASSEROLE

8 c	Red or white potatoes, diced	1 c	Sauerkraut, drained
2 c	Onions, chopped	1 c	Golden Sauce (recipe below)
8	Veggie hot dogs, sliced	½ c	Golden delicious apple, shredded
1 T	Olive oil, "light"	1 tsp	Onion salt

In a large pot, cover potatoes with water and bring to a boil. Reduce heat, cover and simmer about 5 minutes. Drain. Sauté onions and veggie dogs in oil. In a large bowl, combine potatoes, onions and wieners. Combine remaining ingredients and stir gently into potato mixture. Prepare a large casserole dish with cooking spray. Spread mixture evenly into dish. Bake uncovered at 350° F, 45 minutes to 1 hour.

Yield: 15 cups

GOLDEN SAUCE

1 c	Mori-Nu® Tofu, firm	1 ½ tsp	Onion powder
¼ c	Olive oil, "light"	½ tsp	Salt
1 to 2 T	Cooked carrot	¼ tsp	Garlic powder

In a blender, combine above ingredients and process until carrots are no longer visible and mixture is smooth and creamy.

Yield: 1 ⅓ cups

"CHICKEN" & "SAUSAGE" GUMBO

2 c	Brown rice	4 oz	Canned green chilies (Old El Paso® chopped)
⅔ c	Unbleached white flour	1 ½ tsp	Lawry's® Seasoned Salt
1 c	Onions, chopped	1 tsp	Salt
1 c	Red onions, chopped	2 cubes	Vegetable bouillon (or 1 tsp powdered vegetable seasoning)
1 c	Green onions, sliced	12 oz	Sausage-style crumbles
1 c	Celery, diced	8 oz	Chic-Ketts™ (torn into bite size pieces)
¾ c	Bell pepper, diced	1 c	Frozen sliced okra, thawed
⅓ c	Fresh parsley, chopped		
4 med	Garlic cloves, minced		
¼ c	Olive oil, "light"		
4 c	Water		

Prepare rice according to directions on the package and set aside. Brown flour in a large frying pan over med/high heat stirring constantly until medium brown in color. Set aside. In a large pot, combine all onions, celery, peppers, parsley and garlic in oil and sauté until vegetables are tender. Add water, chilies, seasonings and browned flour and stir until well mixed. Stir in "chicken and sausage" meat substitutes and okra. Bring to a boil, then cover and reduce heat and simmer 10 minutes. Ladle gumbo into serving bowls and dollop 2 to 4 T rice into the center of the gumbo.

Yield: 14 cups

MAZIDRA
(A Lentil and Onion Lebanese Dish)

4 c	Water	1 tsp	Garlic purée
1 c	Brown lentils	1 tsp	Salt
1 ½ tsp	Mesquite Grill® Seasoning	2 T	Olive oil, "light"
½ tsp	Beef-style seasoning	1 lg	Onion, thinly sliced in rings

In a saucepan, combine water, lentils, seasonings, garlic and salt. Bring to a boil, reduce heat, cover and simmer 30 to 40 minutes or until lentils are tender. In a large non-stick frying pan, sauté onions in oil until translucent. (If crispier onions are desired, transfer sautéed onions to a baking sheet prepared with cooking spray. If needed, drizzle onions with 1 to 3 tsp additional olive oil and bake at 425° F, 5 to 10 minutes or until onions are lightly browned and edges begin to get crispy.) To serve, spoon lentils over cooked rice and cover with a generous portion of onion rings.

Yield: 6 cups

TOMATO-CUCUMBER SALAD WITH HERB DRESSING

3 c	Tomatoes, wedged	½ c	Onions, chopped
3 c	Cucumbers, sliced	½ c	Herb Dressing

Mix cold tomatoes, cucumbers and onions in a bowl. Pour Herb Dressing (see recipe below) over the vegetables and serve.

Yield: 7 cups

HERB DRESSING

Add to one 0.75 oz pkg. Good Seasons® "Garlic & Herb" Dressing Mix:

3 T	Fresh lemon juice	⅓ c	Water
3 T	Pineapple juice, concentrate	¼ c	Olive oil

Shake until well blended. Chill and shake again before serving.

Yield: 1 cup

CARROT-PINEAPPLE SALAD

3 c	Carrots, shredded	½ c	Pineapple tidbits, drained
¾ c	Raisins	½ c	Pecans, chopped

Combine above ingredients and chill. Stir in Creamy Dressing (see below) when ready to serve.

Yield: 5 cups

CREAMY DRESSING

½ c	Raw cashews, rinsed	½ tsp	Fresh lemon juice
½ c	Pineapple juice	¼ tsp	Salt (scant)
¼ c	Mori-Nu® Tofu, extra firm	1 tsp	Instant Clear Jel® (food thickener)
2 T	Apple juice, concentrate		
2 tsp	Pineapple juice, concentrate		

In a blender, combine all ingredients, except food thickener, and process until completely smooth and creamy. Add Clear Jel® and continue blending about 10 seconds more. Chill. Mix into salad when ready to serve.

Yield: 1 ¼ cups

FRESH KALE SALAD with OMEGA DRESSING

3 c	Fresh kale, finely chopped	¼ c	Water
12	Cherry tomatoes, quartered	3 T	Fresh lemon juice
½ c	Sweet onions, diced	2 T	Bragg® Liquid Aminos
⅓ c	Black olives, sliced	2 T	Flax oil or Omega oil blend
⅓ c	Pickling cucumber, diced	2 tsp	Honey
3 T	Sunflower seeds	½ tsp	Onion powder
2 T	Red bell pepper, diced	¼ tsp	Garlic powder
¼ c	Green onions, sliced		

Combine kale, tomatoes, onions, olives and cucumber in a serving bowl. Set aside the sunflower seeds, peppers, and green onions for later use. In a separate bowl or jar, combine water, lemon juice, liquid aminos, flax oil, honey and seasonings to make the "dressing" and mix well. Pour over salad and marinate in the refrigerator 2 hours. Add the sunflower seeds, red peppers and green onions just before serving.

Yield: 5 cups

MACARONI SALAD

4 c	Cooked elbow macaroni	¼ c	Sliced olives, black or green
¾ c	Red onions, chopped	½ c	Soy mayonnaise, (p. 165 or 166)
¾ c	Celery, sliced	½ tsp	Garlic salt
¾ c	Dill pickles, chopped	⅛ tsp	Celery salt

Combine all ingredients and mix lightly. Chill before serving.

Yield: 7 cups

WALDORF APPLE SALAD

4 c	Apples, diced	½ c	Nayonaise® (soy mayonnaise)
1 c	Seedless red grapes, halved	2 T	Fructose, granular
½ c	Celery, diced	1 c	Non-dairy whipped topping
½ c	Walnuts or pecans, chopped		(Cool Whip or similar product)

Combine apples, grapes and celery. Lightly toast nuts on a baking sheet at 250° F for 10 minutes. (This step can be done ahead in larger quantities. Store nuts in the freezer until ready for use.) Add nuts to fruit mixture. Combine Nayonaise® and fructose and gently stir into apple mixture. Fold whipped topping in last. Best if served immediately.

Yield: 6 cups

JIFFY CORNBREAD MUFFINS

1 ¼ c	Yellow corn meal, fine	1 ¼ c	Soymilk beverage, enriched
1 ¼ c	Unbleached white flour	⅓ c	Honey
4 tsp	Baking powder	¼ c	Water-packed tofu, silken
¾ tsp	Salt	3 T	Olive oil, "extra light"

Combine dry ingredients in a bowl. In a blender, combine soymilk, honey, tofu and oil and process until creamy. Pour mixture into dry ingredients (scrape blender jar as clean as possible) and stir gently until well mixed. Spoon batter evenly into a prepared heavy-duty muffin tin. Bake at 400° F, 15 to 18 minutes or until muffins are golden.

Variation: To make "Johnny Cake," spoon batter into a prepared 9-inch square baking dish. Bake at 350° F, 25 - 30 minutes until golden.

Yield: 12 muffins

CORNBREAD (Yeast-raised)

1 c	Warm water	1 ½ c	Unbleached white flour
3 T	Honey	¾ c	Yellow cornmeal, fine
2 T	Olive oil, "extra light"	3 T	Soymilk powder, plain
2 ½ tsp	Active dry yeast	1 tsp	Salt

Combine water, honey, oil and yeast. Let stand 3 minutes. Stir in remaining ingredients and mix well. Pour into an 8" square pan prepared with cooking spray. Let rise 30 minutes or until double. Bake at 350° F, 25 to 30 minutes until golden brown. Cool 10 min. before trying to remove cornbread from pan.

Variation: For "quick cornbread," replace yeast with 1 T non-aluminum baking powder (Rumford). Reduce salt to ½ tsp. Bake at 375° F, 20 to 25 minutes.

Yield: 8-inch square

OLD FASHIONED CORNBREAD

3 c	Yellow cornmeal, fine	2 T	Active dry yeast, rapid rise
1 c	Soy flour	2 T	Olive oil, "extra light"
2 c	Unbleached white flour	¼ c	Brown sugar or honey
2 tsp	Salt	2 ½ c	Warm water

Combine dry ingredients in a large bowl. In a separate bowl, mix oil, sweetener and water together and add to the dry ingredients. Mix well. Prepare bake ware with cooking spray. Pour into muffin tins, mini bread pans or cake pans, ¾ full, and let rise 10–15 minutes. Bake at 350° F, 20 minutes in muffin tins, 25 minutes in mini bread pans and 30–35 minutes in cake pans.

Yield: 18 muffins

GRANDMA'S HOME-STYLE BISCUITS

1 c	Warm water	2 c	Unbleached white flour
2 ½ tsp	Active yeast, rapid-rise	1 c	Whole-wheat flour
1 tsp	Honey	¼ c	Olive oil, "extra light"
¾ tsp	Salt	1 T	Wheat germ or oat bran

Dissolve yeast in warm water. Add honey, salt and unbleached white flour and mix well. Let rise until light and fluffy. Stir in remaining ingredients. Turn out on a floured surface and knead lightly until smooth (about 30 seconds). Roll out ¾ inches thick and cut with a 2-inch biscuit cutter. Place on an oiled cookie sheet and let rise in a draft free area 15 minutes. Bake at 350° F, about 20 minutes or until lightly browned.

Yield: 18 biscuits

HEARTY SOUTHERN BISCUITS

1 c	All purpose flour	½ c	Water
¾ c	Barley flour	¼ c	Olive oil, "extra light"
¼ c	Whole-wheat flour	1 T	Honey
1 T	Baking powder	½ c	Mori Nu® Tofu, soft
½ tsp	Salt		

Mix flours, baking powder and salt in a medium bowl. In a blender, combine water, oil, honey, and tofu and blend until smooth and creamy. Pour blender ingredients into dry ingredients. Stir quickly and briefly. Knead lightly on a floured surface. Roll dough out to 1-inch thickness. Cut with a biscuit cutter into 2-inch circles. Place side by side on a cookie sheet. Bake at 425° F, 13 to 15 minutes.

Yield: 1 dozen

"HEART- SMART" CORN BUTTER

1 c	Cold water	2 T	Olive oil, "light"
¼ c	Yellow corn meal	1 T	Emes Kosher Jel® (plain)
½ c	Mori-Nu® Tofu, extra firm	1 T	Cooked carrot (opt for color)
½ c	Warm water	1 tsp	Honey
¼ c	Almonds	1 tsp	Imitation butter flavored salt
3 T	Natural Butter Flavor, vegan (Spicery Shoppe®)	½ tsp	Salt
		pinch	Citric acid

Combine cold water and corn meal in a small saucepan and bring to a boil stirring constantly. Reduce heat to low, cover and simmer 10 minutes. Refrigerate mixture until completely cool and "set." In a blender, combine tofu, water, almonds, butter flavoring, oil and Emes. Process on high speed until no longer "gritty." Spoon chilled corn meal mush into the blender mixture and all remaining ingredients and process until smooth and creamy. Bits of carrot should not be visible. Refrigerate several hours before serving until "butter" thickens to a spreadable consistency.

Yield: 3 cups

HONEY BUTTER

½ c	Smart Balance® "Light," softened (non-hydrogenated spread)	¼ c	Spun honey (Sue Bee®)

Stir Smart Balance® and honey together until well mixed and serve promptly.

Tip: Serve with biscuits, corn bread or muffins.

Yield: ¾ cup

APRICOT JAM

2 c	Dried sulfured apricots, quartered	1 tsp	Fresh lemon juice
1 ½ c	Pineapple juice, unsweetened	1 T	Fructose, granular (opt)

Combine all ingredients in a saucepan and bring to a boil. Reduce heat and simmer 5 minutes. Cool. Pour into a blender and process on high speed until smooth. Chill.

Yield: 3 cups

PINEAPPLE - DATE JAM

1 c	Pitted dates	½ c	Crushed pineapple
¾ c	Water	1 tsp	Lemon juice

Combine dates and water in a saucepan and bring to a boil. Reduce heat and simmer 3 minutes. Cool. Pour into a blender and process on high speed until smooth. Pour out into a bowl and add pineapple and lemon juice. Stir until well mixed. Chill.

Yield: 2 cups

APPLE SPICE JAM

2 c	Dried apples, packed	½ c	Pineapple juice
2 c	Apple juice	½ tsp	Cinnamon, ground

Soak apples in water or juice 15 minutes. Pour into a blender and add remaining ingredients. Process on high speed until smooth. Chill.

Yield: 3 cups

SOUTHERN PEACH PRESERVES

12 oz	White grape juice, undiluted (frozen concentrate)	4 c	Fresh peaches, mashed (drain and reserve juice)
1 c	Water	½ tsp	Fresh lemon juice
4 T	Minute® Tapioca (or cornstarch)	2 T	Fructose, granular (opt)

In a saucepan, combine white grape juice, water and thickener of choice. (If using cornstarch, stir until dissolved.) Add reserved peach juice and lemon juice. Bring to a boil and simmer (about 15 minutes if using tapioca or 5 minutes for cornstarch) until juice is clear. Add mashed peaches and continue cooking a few more minutes. Cool and refrigerate.

Note: Purée peaches in a blender if you prefer a "jam" consistency. Or, follow the directions in "Blueberry Jam" if you prefer using fruit pectin.

Yield: 7 cups

GRAPE JAM

1 c	Golden raisins	1 ½ c	Water
7 oz	Purple grape juice, undiluted (frozen concentrate)	¼ c	Minute® Tapioca
½ c	Blueberries, frozen	2 T	Fructose, granular

Combine raisins, grape juice, and blueberries in a saucepan. Bring to a boil. Reduce heat, cover and simmer about 5 minutes until raisins are tender. Cool. Pour mixture into a blender and process until raisins are completely puréed. Return to the saucepan and add water, tapioca, and fructose. Cover and simmer, stirring frequently, until mixture clears and thickens or about 10 minutes. Refrigerate. Serve cold.

Yield: 3 cups

BLACKBERRY JAM

4 c	Blackberries	¼ c	Fructose, granular
12 oz	White grape juice, (frozen concentrate)	¼ c	Cornstarch, or tapioca powder
12 oz	Water	½ tsp	Fresh lemon juice

Purée blackberries in a blender. If desired, may strain puréed blackberries to remove seeds. In a saucepan, combine juice concentrate, water, fructose and thickener of choice and stir until well mixed. Bring to a boil and simmer until mixture clears. Add blackberry purée and lemon juice to the saucepan with the thickened juice and continue to cook stirring constantly until jam is thick. Cool and refrigerate.

Note: May also follow the directions for making "Blueberry Jam" if you prefer using fruit pectin.

Yield: 5 cups

STRAWBERRY TROPIC JAM

¾ c	Dried papaya or mango, diced	3 c	Strawberries, fresh (or frozen berries, thawed)
¼ c	Pineapple juice, unsweetened		

Combine dried fruit and pineapple juice in a saucepan, cover and simmer 5 to 10 minutes or until softened. Cool. Pour into a blender, add strawberries and process on high speed 3 to 5 minutes until smooth. Chill.

Yield: 4 cups

AUNT BEA'S OLD-FASHIONED APPLE PIE

8 c	Tart apples, thinly sliced	3 T	Minute® Tapioca
6 oz	Dole® "Orchard Peach" (frozen juice concentrate)	1 tsp	Cinnamon, ground
		¼ tsp	Salt
1 c	Date sugar or Sucanat®	1 tsp	Vanilla extract

Slice "Granny Smith" or "York" apples for a tart pie or use "Golden Delicious" apples if you prefer a sweeter and softer filling. Place apples in a bowl with the juice concentrate and coat the apples to prevent them from turning brown. Stir in remaining ingredients until well mixed. If using Granny Smith apples and you prefer a softer cooked apple, just microwave the apples with the juice for 2 to 3 minutes before adding the remaining ingredients. Prepare a double whole grain pie crust. (See selections of double pie crusts on page 276, or make a double recipe of one of the single pie crust recipes on page 273.) Prepare a 9-inch pie pan with dough for bottom crust. Pour filling into the pan and place dough over the filling for the top crust. Flute edges and slit crust evenly. Bake at 350° F, about 1 hour. Serve with choice of "Instant" Whipped Topping (below) or the "Vanilla Ice Cream" recipe on page 223.

Yield: 9-inch pie

"INSTANT" WHIPPED TOPPING

1 ½ c	Water	⅓ c	Coconut milk, canned ("lite," unsweetened)
⅔ c	Soymilk powder, plain*		
½ c	Blanched almonds (w/o skins)	2 tsp	Natural vanilla, flavoring
3 ½ T	Emes Kosher Jel® (plain)	¼ tsp	Salt
3 T	Fructose, powdered sugar or honey		Ice

In a blender, combine the water, milk powder, almonds and Emes Jel and process until the almonds are liquefied completely. Add remaining ingredients and process briefly. Finally, begin adding ice slowly through the lid spout and continue processing on high speed to make a total volume equal to 5 cups. Turn blender off and wait briefly. Mixture should now be light and fluffy. Best when served immediately. If stored, and mixture becomes too firm, hand whip or beat gently with an electric beater before serving.

* Recommend Better Than Milk™ Soy "Original."

Yield: 5 cups

BLUEBERRY PIE

9-inch	Whole-grain crust, double	1/16 tsp	Salt
4 c	Blueberries	¼ c	Water
¾ c	Water	3 T	Cornstarch
½ c	White grape, 100% juice (frozen concentrate, undiluted)	2 tsp	Fresh lemon juice
½ c	Fructose, granular	1 T	Smart Balance®, "Light" (non-hydrogenated spread)

Prepare a double crust recipe of choice. (See page 276 for selections) Place bottom crust in a 9-inch pie pan and set aside. Combine ½ cup blueberries with (¾ c) water and juice in a saucepan. Heat and simmer gently until berries are well cooked. Remove the berries. Add the fructose and salt to the juice. Dissolve cornstarch in (¼ c) water and also add to the juice. Bring to a boil, stirring constantly until the color of juice "clears." Remove from heat and cool 5 minutes. Stir in remaining blueberries and lemon juice. Pour filling into the pie shell. Dot with Smart Balance® spread. Cover with the top crust, trim and flute the edges of the top and bottom crust together. Bake at 450° F, 10 minutes. Make slits in the top crust and lower heat to 350° F. Bake an additional 30 minutes. Cool before cutting. Serve with "Instant" Whipped Topping (recipe on page 222) or "Vanilla Ice Cream" recipe below.

Yield: 9-inch pie

VANILLA ICE CREAM

2 c	Soymilk creamer, plain (Silk®)	1 c	Soymilk powder, plain*
2 c	Soymilk creamer, French vanilla (Silk®)	1 T	Clear vanilla, extract

Combine all ingredients in a blender and process until well mixed. Pour into an ice cream maker and operate according to manufacturer's directions.

* Better Than Milk™ Soy "Original" is the recommended product.

Tip: For a delicious treat, add ½ cup finely chopped carob chips and ¼ cup lightly toasted and finely chopped almonds (chilled) to the ice cream when nearly set or during the last 5 minutes of churning.

Note: This recipe can easily be doubled or tripled if necessary to fit the ice cream maker.

Yield: 1 quart

"LAZY DAISY" OATMEAL CAKE

3 ½ c	Water	1 tsp	Salt
2 c	Old fashioned oats	½ tsp	Allspice, ground
1 c	Maple syrup	2 c	Whole-wheat flour
1 c	Brown sugar, packed	1 ½ c	Whole-wheat pastry flour
½ c	Olive oil, "extra light"	2 T	ENER-G® Egg Replacer
1 T	Vanilla extract	1 T	Baking powder
¼ tsp	Maple flavoring	2 tsp	Baking soda
2 tsp	Cinnamon, ground		

Combine water and oats in a mixer, and beat with wire whips. Let stand while adding syrup, sugar, oil, flavorings and spices. Then continue beating at a low speed while adding flour, egg replacer, baking powder and soda. Increase speed and beat until well mixed. (Batter will be somewhat soupy.) Pour into a 9" x 13" prepared cake pan and bake at 350° F, 55 minutes until cake springs back to touch.

Yield: 9 x 13 sheet cake

DATE-NUT FROSTING

1 c	Pitted dates, packed	½ tsp	Salt
1 ½ c	Water	2 c	Pecans, chopped
½ c	Soymilk powder, plain*	2 c	Coconut, shredded
2 tsp	Natural vanilla, flavoring	¼ c	Vital wheat gluten (opt)

Simmer dates in water until soft. Cool 5 minutes. Transfer dates to a blender. Add milk powder, vanilla and salt and process until smooth. Return mixture to saucepan and fold in the nuts and coconut. If using frosting on a layered cake, it is necessary to add vital wheat gluten in order for the frosting to stick to the sides of the cake. If using frosting on a sheet cake, this step is not necessary. Spread frosting on cake while still warm. Sprinkle cake with additional shredded coconut for garnish and to improve appearance.

* Better Than Milk™ "Original" is the recommended product.

Yield: 5 cups

Broccoli "Cheese" Soup
"Chicken" Noodle Soup
Cheesy Delight Open Faced
Sandwich
Deluxe Lentil Vegetable Soup
Garden Oat Burger

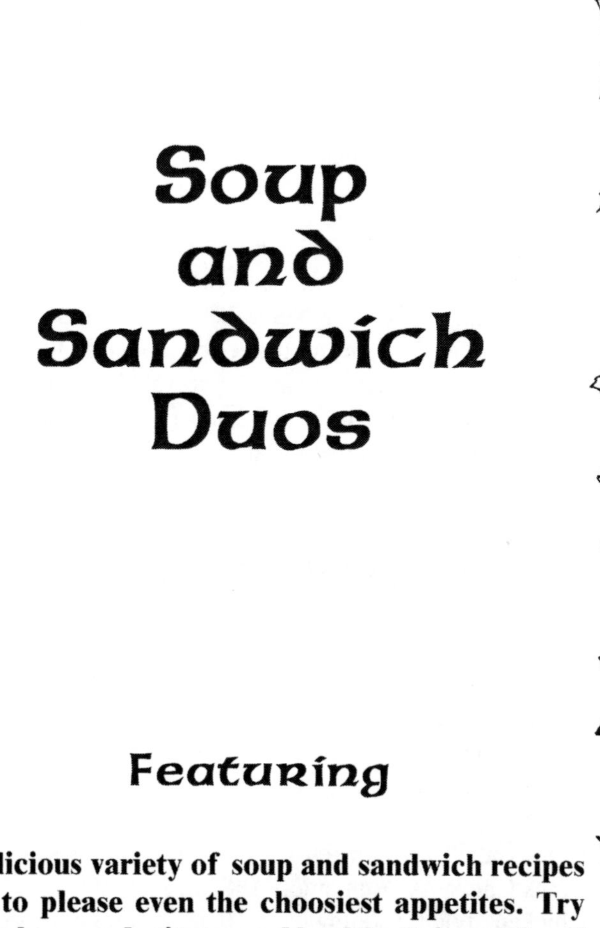

Soup and Sandwich Duos

Featuring

A delicious variety of soup and sandwich recipes sure to please even the choosiest appetites. Try tasty cheese substitutes and healthy "vinegarless" condiments to compliment all your favorite sandwiches. For special treats, you will enjoy the "ice creams" recipes made with fruit and soymilk. They are delicious and good for you too!

DELUXE LENTIL-VEGETABLE SOUP

1 c Brown lentils, dried
6 c Hot water
2 T Olive oil
2 med Garlic cloves, minced
2 c Onions, chopped
1 c Celery, diced
3 c Potatoes, cubed
1 ½ c Carrots, sliced
2 tsp Beef-style Seasoning
1 ½ tsp Spike® or Nature's Blend (p. 95)
¾ tsp Cumin, ground
½ tsp Basil, dried
½ tsp Coriander, ground
½ tsp Paprika
1 tsp Salt
2 tsp Honey or rice syrup
1 c Frozen peas (opt)
1 can Diced tomatoes (14.5 oz)
¼ c Fresh chopped herbs (parsley, chives, or green onions, etc.)

Place lentils in a bowl with hot water to soften while preparing vegetables. Sauté garlic, onions and celery in oil about 3 minutes. Add potatoes, carrots, Beef-style seasoning, Spike® or Nature's Blend, cumin, basil, coriander, and paprika and cook 2 to 3 more minutes over moderate heat stirring constantly. Add water and lentils, cover and simmer 20 to 25 minutes or until vegetables and lentils are tender. Add salt, honey, and peas (opt), cover and cook a few minutes more. Finally, add tomatoes and fresh herbs reserving a small amount for garnish.

Yield: 15 cups

CHICKEN NOODLE SOUP

1 c Onions, chopped
2 med Garlic cloves, minced
2 stalks Celery, sliced
1 med Carrot, diced
⅛ c Fresh parsley, minced
2 T Olive oil
1 c Chic-Ketts™ soy chicken
½ c Mock Chicken (Companion®)
3 T Chicken-style seasoning
2 T Nutritional yeast flakes
1 T Dried minced onion
1 tsp Spike® All Purpose Seasoning (or) Nature's Blend (p. 95)
1 tsp McCormick® Garlic and Herb ("Salt-free" Seasoning)
1 tsp Garlic salt
½ tsp Celery salt
8 c Water
6 oz Linguini noodles
1 c Frozen peas, thawed

In a large pot, sauté vegetables and parsley in olive oil until tender. Tear the Chic-Ketts™ ("white meat") into large bite-size pieces and the Mock Chicken ("dark meat") into small bite size pieces and add to the pot. Add the seasonings and spices. Add water and bring to a boil. Break the noodles into 4 inch pieces, add to boiling water, cover and simmer until noodles are done. Add peas, and cook 1 minute more.

Yield: 3 quarts

SEAFARER'S NAVY BEAN SOUP

1 c	Veggie hot dogs, sliced
1 c	Onions, chopped
½ c	Celery, chopped
½ c	Carrots, sliced
¼ c	Green peppers, diced
2 med	Garlic cloves, minced
1 T	Olive oil, "light"
2 cans	Navy beans, drained (15 oz each)
1 can	Diced tomatoes (14.5 oz)
2 c	Water
2 tsp	Chicken-style seasoning
½ tsp	Basil, dried
½ tsp	Lawry's® Seasoned Salt

In a large saucepan, sauté veggie dogs with vegetables in oil until vegetables are crisp-tender. Add remaining ingredients and simmer about 15 minutes. Serve with crackers.

Note: For a variation in flavor, replace hot dogs with Loma Linda® Tender Bits®, cut into bite size pieces.

Tip: For a "quick" version, replace onions, celery, peppers and garlic with a frozen vegetable "soup starter." Steam or microwave the carrots before adding to soup. Add beans, tomatoes and seasonings and simmer five more minutes before serving.

Yield: 8 cups

MINESTRONE SOUP

1 c	Onions, chopped
½ c	Celery, sliced
2 med	Garlic cloves, minced
1 T	Olive oil
6 c	Water
1 T	Chicken-style seasoning
2 tsp	Basil, (or) 2 T fresh basil
1 ½ tsp	Lawry's® Seasoned Salt
1 ½ tsp	Sucanat® sweetener
1 tsp	Onion powder
½ tsp	Coriander, ground
⅛ tsp	Oregano, dried (flakes)
1 sm	Bay leaf
1 ½ c	Kidney or red beans, canned
2 c	Diced tomatoes, canned
¾ c	Macaroni, elbow or shell
2 c	Zucchini, sliced or quartered
1 c	Carrots, sliced

In a large saucepan, sauté onions, celery and garlic in oil until tender. Add water, seasonings and beans. Bring to a boil. Lower heat, cover and simmer about 20 minutes. Add tomatoes and macaroni, cover and simmer about 10 minutes. Add zucchini and carrots and simmer 5 to 10 minutes more or until pasta and vegetables are tender. Remove bay leaf before serving.

Yield: 14 cups

SAVORY SPLIT PEA SOUP

STEP ONE:

3 ½ c Water
1 c Split peas, dried
1 c Potatoes, peeled and diced
2 tsp Chicken-style seasoning
2 tsp Bakon® Seasoning (opt) (or ¼ tsp liquid smoke)
½ tsp Salt
1 med Bay leaf (opt)

In a large saucepan, combine above ingredients and bring to a boil. Cover and simmer about an hour until peas are soft. Set aside. When cooled, discard bay leaf. Pour remainder into a blender and process until smooth and creamy. Set aside.

STEP TWO:

1 T Olive oil
1 c Onions, chopped
¼ c Celery, sliced
1 tsp Garlic purée

In the large saucepan, sauté above mixture in oil until onions are translucent and celery is tender.

STEP THREE:

1 c Water
½ c Carrots, diced
1 stem Green onion, diced
1 T Nutritional yeast flakes
½ tsp Basil, dried
½ tsp Parsley, dried
¼ tsp Celery salt
¼ tsp Lawry's® Seasoned Salt

Add above ingredients to the saucepan with the onion and celery mixture, bring to a boil, cover and simmer 15 minutes or until carrots are tender. Add the blended pea mixture and stir until hot. If desired, garnish with paprika, grated carrots, a dollop of soy sour cream and croutons.

Yield: 7 cups

"QUICK AS A WINK" VEGETABLE-RICE SOUP

1 qt	Water
4 tsp	Chicken-style Seasoning
1 tsp	Beef-style Seasoning
¼ tsp	Basil
⅛ tsp	Italian seasoning
1 c	Italian green beans (frozen)
1 c	Carrots, sliced
¼ c	Baby lima beans (frozen)
½ c	Instant brown rice, uncooked
¾ c	Zucchini, sliced
¾ c	Cauliflower, florets
1 can	Diced tomatoes (14.5 oz), seasoned with roasted garlic

Combine water and seasonings and bring to a boil. Add green beans, carrots, lima beans and rice. Return to a boil, reduce heat, cover and simmer 15 minutes. Add zucchini and cauliflower and simmer 3 to 5 minutes more or until tender. Add tomatoes, stir until heated through and serve.

Note: For an even quicker and easier recipe, replace fresh vegetables with one bag or up to 4 c of a frozen "Italian vegetable" mixture.

Variation: Add 1 cup Chic-Ketts™ (or favorite vegetarian protein) torn into bite size pieces. Add to broth before boiling the first time.

Yield: 10 cups

BROCCOLI CHEESE SOUP

1 ¼ c	Water
1 c	Cooked rice
1 c	Carrots, cooked
½ c	Raw cashews, rinsed
½ c	Mori Nu Tofu, firm
3 oz	Pimientos
2 T	Fresh lemon juice
2 T	Nutritional yeast flakes
2 T	Soymilk powder, plain
2 tsp	Chicken-style seasoning
2 tsp	Onion powder
1 ½ tsp	Salt
½ tsp	Garlic powder
2 c	Broccoli crowns

To prepare the cheese sauce, combine water, rice, carrots and cashews in a blender and process until very smooth and no longer "gritty." Add remaining ingredients, except broccoli, and blend again until creamy. Chop broccoli into bite size pieces and steam or microwave 2 to 3 minutes. Pour broccoli into a saucepan and cover with blended cheese sauce. Stir and if necessary, add additional water or soymilk to thin soup as desired. Heat again before serving.

Variation: Substitute broccoli with cauliflower or try a mixture. This cheese sauce recipe is also good over baked potatoes, rice and vegetables.

Yield: 6 ½ cups

"CREAM" OF POTATO SOUP

1 med	Onion, chopped	1 tsp	Onion salt
1 c	Celery, diced	½ tsp	Garlic and Herb seasoning
2 lg	Garlic cloves, minced	8 c	Water (approx)
1 T	Olive oil	½ c	Raw cashews, rinsed
8 c	Red potatoes, cubed	⅓ c	Unbleached white flour
2 T	Nutritional yeast flakes	1 c	Water
2 tsp	Chicken-style seasoning	1 stem	Green onion, minced
2 tsp	Salt	¼ c	Fresh parsley, minced

Sauté onions, celery and garlic in olive oil until tender. (May also sauté vegetables in water if preferred.) Add potatoes and spices with enough water to cover (about 8 cups) and simmer until potatoes are soft. In a blender, process cashews and flour with water (1 cup) until completely smooth and creamy. (Add up to 1 T more flour for thicker soup.) Stir cashew "cream" into soup and simmer until thickened. Garnish with green onions and fresh parsley as desired.

Variation: Add 2 cups frozen green peas to the soup just before adding the cashew cream and flour mixture. Avoid over cooking peas; they should remain bright green in color.

Yield: 5 quarts

CREAMY VEGETABLE SOUP

1 c	Onions, diced	¼ tsp	Basil, dried
¼ c	Celery, sliced	1 c	Potatoes, diced
1 lg	Garlic clove, minced	½ c	Carrots, sliced
2 tsp	Olive oil	1 c	Water
3 c	Water	⅓ c	Raw cashews, rinsed
2 T	Chicken-style seasoning	2 T	Unbleached white flour
½ tsp	Salt	1 c	Cauliflower, chopped
½ tsp	Onion powder	½ c	Peas or broccoli florets
½ tsp	Parsley, dried		

In a 3 quart pot, sauté onions, celery and garlic in olive oil until tender. Pour in (3 cups) water, add seasonings and bring to a boil. Add potatoes and carrots, reduce heat and simmer over low heat until nearly cooked. Combine (1 cup) water, cashews, and flour in a blender and process on high speed until smooth and creamy. Pour cashew cream into soup stock and bring to a boil, stirring constantly until thick. Add cauliflower and peas or broccoli, reduce heat and simmer 5 minutes before serving.

Yield: 8 cups

POZOLE SOUP

SOUP BASE:

1 T	Olive oil	1 qt	Water
1 clove	Garlic, minced	2 c	Crushed tomatoes, canned
1 stalk	Celery, thinly sliced	1 c	Tomato purée, canned
1 c	Onions, diced	1 c	Cilantro, chopped
1 c	Yellow squash, julienned	1T	Chicken-Style seasoning
1 c	Zucchini, julienned	1 tsp	Chili Powder Substitute (opt) (see page 132)
1 c	Carrots, diced		
1 ½ c	Hominy, canned	½ tsp	Salt

In a large pot, sauté garlic, celery, onions, squash and carrots in oil. Add remaining ingredients, (except hominy) and simmer until vegetables are tender. Add hominy just before serving to avoid overcooking. Fill soup bowls about half way with soup base before adding tortilla strips and garnishes listed below.

GARNISHES:

12	Corn tortillas strips, baked (see below)	1 c	Avocado, cubed
2 c	Purple cabbage, finely shredded	1 c	Olives, sliced
2 c	Tomatoes, diced	2	Limes, quartered
1 c	Green onions, sliced	2	Lemons, wedged
1 can	Black beans, rinsed	(opt)	Soy cheese, grated
1 c	Radishes, minced		

TORTILLA STRIPS: Stack tortillas and cut them into thin strips and then cut the strips in half. Prepare a baking sheet with cooking spray and spread tortilla strips out evenly. Bake at 250° F until crisp, turning as needed.

TO SERVE: Set baked tortilla strips and all garnishes out buffet style. Each person can then pick and choose. The tortilla strips should be added to the hot soup first followed by any or all of the garnishes. Lemon or lime juice squeezed over the top of the soup and garnish mixture adds a zesty flavor.

Yield: 3 quarts

CARROT BISQUE

1 sm	Onion, chopped
2 med	Garlic cloves, minced
1 tsp	Olive oil
3 c	Water
1 lb	Carrots, sliced
2 tsp	Honey or FruitSource®
1 tsp	Vege-Sal® (All Purpose Seasoning)
1 c	Raw cashew pieces

In a large pot, sauté onions and garlic in oil until translucent. Add water, carrots, honey and Vege-Sal and simmer until crisp-tender. Drain vegetable mixture, saving broth. In a blender, combine cashews with reserved soup broth and process until creamy. Add vegetable mixture and blend until smooth. Add additional seasoning if necessary to suit your taste. Reheat to serve. May garnish with fresh chopped chives, oyster crackers or croutons.

Variation: Replace honey with ½ cup cooked yams and blend with other ingredients.

Yield: 5 cups

JIFFY MUSHROOM SOUP

1 c	Fresh mushrooms, sliced
1½ c	Water
½ c	Onions, chopped
4 T	Soymilk powder, plain*
2 T	Unbleached all purpose flour
1 T	Cornstarch
1 T	Spectrum® Spread (opt)
1 tsp	Chicken-style seasoning
½ tsp	Salt
½ tsp	Basil, dried

Sauté mushrooms in a skillet with 2 T water and ⅛ tsp salt until tender. Set aside. (May also microwave mushrooms with water and salt about 1 minute.) In a blender, combine remaining ingredients and process until smooth. Add mushrooms with liquids and flash blend a few times to break up mushrooms into pieces. Pour out into a saucepan and cook until thickened. Use this for recipes in place of canned soup. If necessary, add additional soymilk or water to thin mixture down to desired consistency.

Note: Recommend Better Than Milk™, "Original" for this recipe.
Variation: May substitute fresh mushrooms, 2 T water, and ⅛ tsp salt with 4 oz sliced canned mushrooms, with liquid.

Yield: 2 ½ cups

TACO SOUP

1 c	Onions, chopped	1 can	Corn, un-drained (15 oz)
½ c	Celery, sliced	1 can	Green chilies, chopped(4 oz)
1 med	Garlic clove, minced	1 can	Vegetable broth (14.5 oz)
1 T	Olive oil	1 ½ c	Water
1 c	Vegetarian burger, frozen	½ c	Instant brown rice, uncooked
1 can	Kidney beans, (15 oz)	½ pkt	Taco seasoning
1 can	Black beans, (15 oz)	1 bag	Tortilla chips, unsalted
1 can	Vegetarian chili beans (15 oz)	12 oz	SoyaKass® cheddar cheese
1 can	Tomatoes, diced-unsalted (14.5 oz)		

In a large pot, sauté onions, celery and garlic in oil. Add burger and sauté until lightly browned. Add canned beans, tomatoes, corn and chilies and simmer 10 minutes. Add vegetable broth, water, rice and taco seasoning and simmer 10 minutes more. Break about 6 tortilla chips for each serving and place in the bottom of each bowl before spooning soup in. Shred soy cheese and sprinkle desired amount on top before serving.

Yield: 14 cups

INDIAN LENTIL SOUP

1 c	Red lentils, dried	1	Bay leaf
5 c	Hot water	1 c	Canned tomatoes, diced
1 c	Onions, chopped	1 ½ T	Tomato paste
1 c	Carrots, diced small	2 tsp	Salt
½ c	Celery, thinly sliced	¼ tsp	Cumin, ground
1 T	Olive oil	¼ tsp	Coriander, ground
1 lg	Garlic clove, minced	pinch	Cayenne pepper (to taste)
½ tsp	Fresh ginger, minced	⅓ c	Fresh parsley, minced

Rinse lentils. In a medium size pot, cover lentils with hot water to soak while preparing vegetables. Sauté onions, carrots and celery in oil until tender. Add garlic and ginger and sauté one more minute. Add mixture to lentils. Add the bay leaf and bring to a boil. Reduce heat, cover and simmer about 20 minutes. Add tomatoes, tomato paste, salt, cumin, coriander and cayenne pepper and simmer 10 minutes more or until lentils are soft. Remove bay leaf and stir in parsley just before serving.

Variation: Swirl 1 or 2 tablespoons "unsweetened" canned coconut milk into each bowl before serving.

Yield: 8 cups

INDIAN DHAL

1 c	Red lentils, dried	1 T	Olive oil
2 c	Water	1 T	Fresh garlic, minced
1 tsp	Salt	1 ½ tsp	Fresh ginger, minced
½ tsp	Turmeric, ground	2 T	Fresh cilantro, minced
¼ tsp	Coriander, ground	2 T	Water
⅛ tsp	Cayenne pepper	1 T	Tomato paste
⅔ c	Onions, diced	1 T	Cumin seed, toasted

Wash lentils in warm water until water is clear. Soak lentils in warm water 30 minutes and drain. In a medium size pot, combine lentils, 2 c water, salt, turmeric, coriander, and cayenne pepper. Simmer 30 minutes or until lentils are tender. Reduce heat to low and keep warm. In a frying pan, sauté onions in oil until golden in color. Add garlic and ginger and sauté 5 minutes. Add cilantro, 2 T water and tomato paste and mix well. Add sauce to lentils and stir well. In a small dry frying pan, toast cumin seed over med-hi heat, stirring constantly until aroma develops. Stir cumin seed into Dahl. Serve with Indian bread (chapatti or roti) or bread of choice.

Yield: 4 cups

MARIA'S WHOLE WHEAT CHAPATTIS

2 c	Whole-wheat flour	1 c	Quick oats
2 c	Unbleached white flour	¼ c	Sesame seeds
2 c	Water	½ tsp	Salt

Combine both flours in a bowl. Combine water, oatmeal, sesame seeds and salt in a blender and process until smooth. Pour blender ingredients into dry ingredients and knead well 10 to 12 minutes. Or, mix on "speed 2" in a Bosch bread machine 8 minutes. Divide dough into equal pieces, shape into balls and roll into circles. Bake on a hot griddle one minute on each side. No oil is necessary.

Yield: Variable, depending on size of chapatti

GARBANZO ROTI
(Indian Chapatti-Falafel style)

1 c	Garbanzo flour	½ tsp	Salt
1 T	Fresh parsley, minced	1/16 tsp	Cayenne pepper
1 T	Fresh cilantro, minced	¼ c	Water
2 tsp	Cumin seed, roasted and crushed	1 T	Olive oil
½ tsp	Coriander, ground		

Combine dry ingredients in a bowl. Mix water and oil and pour into flour mixture. Form into a ball. Oil hands and knead until smooth. (Dough will be slightly sticky.) Divide into 8 balls and roll out on a lightly floured board into thin round pancake shapes. Cook in a dry skillet on both sides until golden brown and springs back when pressed. Serve with Indian Dahl or lentil soup.

Tip: Roast cumin seed in a small frying pan over medium heat until browned and an aroma is present.

Yield: 8 pieces

JIFFY CORNBREAD MUFFINS

1 ¼ c	Yellow corn meal, fine	1 ¼ c	Soymilk beverage, enriched
1 ¼ c	Unbleached white flour	⅓ c	Honey
4 tsp	Baking powder	¼ c	Water-packed tofu, silken
¾ tsp	Salt	3 T	Olive oil, "extra light"

Combine dry ingredients in a bowl. In a blender, combine soymilk, honey, tofu and oil and process until creamy. Pour mixture into dry ingredients (scrape blender jar as clean as possible) and stir gently until well mixed. Spoon batter evenly into a prepared heavy-duty muffin tin. Bake at 400° F, 15 to 18 minutes or until muffins are golden.

Variation: To make "Johnny Cake," spoon batter into a prepared 9-inch square baking dish. Bake at 350° F, 25 to 30 minutes until golden.

Yield: 12 muffins

FALAFEL
(Pita Stuffers)

1 ½ c	Garbanzos, cooked	1 ½ tsp	Spike®, regular
½ c	Liquid from beans	1 tsp	Onion powder
1 T	Olive oil, "extra virgin"	1 tsp	Garlic powder
½ c	Cracker crumbs	1 tsp	Parsley, dried
2 T	Raw wheat germ	½ tsp	Coriander, ground
2 T	Dried minced onion	½ tsp	Cumin, ground
2 T	Potato flour	½ tsp	Chili powder, (opt)
1 T	Lemon or lime juice (opt)	2 cloves	Garlic, minced

Mash garbanzos with the bean liquid and oil until smooth. Add remaining ingredients and stir until well mixed. Shape into balls (1 ½ inch) and arrange on a baking sheet prepared with cooking spray. Bake at 350° F, for 30 minutes.

Tip: Serve in warmed or lightly toasted whole-wheat pita bread halves. For a complimentary spread, try using Hummus (see page 186) instead of mayonnaise. Garnish with shredded lettuce, tomato, alfalfa sprouts, sweet onions, olives etc. to create a great Middle Eastern pocket sandwich. For more flavor, drizzle with Tahini Dressing before serving. (See recipe below.)

Yield: 15 Falafels

TAHINI DRESSING

1 c	Sesame Tahini	1 T	Fresh parsley, finely chopped
⅔ c	Water	½ tsp	Salt
¼ to ⅓ c	Fresh lemon juice	¼ tsp	Cumin, ground (opt)
1 tsp	Garlic purée	⅛ tsp	Ginger, ground (opt)

Combine all ingredients and stir until well mixed and smooth. Serve over Falafels or steamed vegetables.

Yield: 2 cups

"QUICK BAKED" GOLDEN POTATO FRIES

Slice 2 large baking potatoes lengthwise into ½ inch wide sticks. Prepare a baking sheet with cooking spray. Spread potatoes out in a single layer. (To enhance flavor, drizzle 1 tsp olive oil over the potatoes and stir to coat evenly.) Sprinkle with any combination of seasonings to your taste i.e. dried parsley, herbs, chives, onion salt, garlic salt, Spike®, nutritional yeast etc. Broil on the top oven rack at 400° F. Stir after 10 minutes and then every 5 minutes for 15 minutes or until tender with golden brown crispy edges. You may also want to add onion rings to the fries during the last 5 minutes of baking time. Serve hot and, if desired, with Vinegarless Ketchup (see p. 243) on the side.

Yield: 4 cups

MULTI-PURPOSE VEGETABLE SEASONING

⅓ c	Potato flour
2 T	Nutritional yeast flakes
2 T	Onion powder
2 T	Salt
4 tsp	Parsley, dried
1 T	Fructose, granular
2 tsp	Turmeric, ground
2 tsp	Celery salt
2 tsp	Garlic powder
½ tsp	Marjoram, ground
¼ tsp	Savory, dried

Combine all ingredients in a blender and process on high speed until powdery. Store in an air-tight container in the freezer. Use to season soups and gravies.

Yield: 1 cup

CHEESY DELIGHTS (OPEN-FACED SANDWICHES)

Mix desired amount of diced green onion and/or sweet onion, sliced black and/or green olives, diced pimientos and Old El Paso® chopped mild green chilies into Pimiento Cheese (see page 243). Chill at least one hour or until partially set. Spread cheese mixture generously over English muffin halves, whole-wheat buns, rye bread or any favorite choice of bread. If desired, place a slice of tomato on top of cheese and garnish with minced parsley, basil, onion salt and SoyCo® Lite & Less™ Parmesan Cheese Alternative. Arrange sandwiches on a cookie sheet and broil at 400 to 425° F, about 10 minutes or until cheese is bubbly and bread becomes crispy around the edges. Watch carefully to prevent burning.

Yield: Up to 28 sandwiches

DELUXE GRILLED "CHEESE"

2 slices	Rye or whole wheat bread	¼ tsp	Garlic & Herb Seasoning
2 oz	SoyaKass® cheddar cheese	(opt)	Salt or onion salt (to taste)
2 slices	Tomato	2 tsp	Smart Balance®, "Light"
1 slice	Sweet onion		(non-hydrogenated spread)

Make sandwich with soy cheese, tomato and onion. Sprinkle with seasonings (to taste). Spread a thin layer of Smart Balance® on both sides of bread and grill on each side in a non-stick frying pan over medium heat until golden brown and cheese softens.

Tip: If you don't like the cooked tomato flavor, simply open sandwich after grilling and add tomatoes to keep them firm and fresh tasting.

Yield: 1 sandwich

VEGETARIAN REUBEN SANDWICH

2 slices	Rye bread	2 slices	Veggie bacon or beef
1 T	Nayonaise® or soy mayonnaise	2 oz	SoyaKass® cheddar cheese
1 tsp	Better Mustard (see page 241)	2 T	Sour kraut, drained

Toast bread. Prepare sandwich with remaining ingredients. Microwave on high about 30 seconds or until cheese melts.

Variation: Substitute "mayo and mustard" with Thousand Island Dressing (see page 77).

Yield: 1 sandwich

HOT ITALIAN OPEN FACED SUB SANDWICH

1	Whole-wheat hoagie bun	2 T	Black olives, sliced (opt)
1	Garlic clove, crushed (smooth)	¼ c	Soy cheese, shredded
½ c	Spaghetti or pizza sauce	1 tsp	Soy Parmesan cheese, grated

Split bun. Spread a thin layer of garlic over inside of bun. Cover with sauce, olives and cheeses. Bake open faced on a cookie sheet at 350° F, 10 to 15 minutes or until cheese is bubbly.

Yield: (2) open faced buns

GARDEN OAT BURGERS

1 c Onions, finely diced
1 c Fresh mushrooms (finely chopped)
½ c Carrots, shredded
3 med Garlic cloves, minced
1 T Olive oil
1 c Cooked cereal (Ralston®)
1 c Quick oats, uncooked
1 c Burger-style crumbles
½ c Black beans, mashed
½ c Cooked brown rice, soft
2 T Vital wheat gluten
4 tsp Beef-style seasoning
1 T ENER-G® Egg Replacer
2 tsp Maggi® liquid seasoning
1 tsp Garlic & Herb (McCormick®) ("salt-free" seasoning)
1 tsp Onion powder
¼ tsp Italian seasoning (opt)

Sauté onions, mushrooms, carrots and garlic in olive oil until tender. Pour into a large bowl. Add cooked Ralston (cracked wheat cereal), oats, burger crumbles, beans and rice. Mix well. Add remaining ingredients and mix well. Prepare a baking sheet with cooking spray. Spray the inside of a ¼ or ⅓ c "dry ingredient" measuring cup with cooking spray. Scoop up burger mixture and pack it in. Invert measuring cup and tap it on the baking sheet until burger mixture drops out. With the bottom of the measuring cup or a canning jar lid, press and shape burger into round patties. Bake at 350° F, 25 minutes. Turn over and bake 15 to 20 minutes more or until golden brown and firm enough to hold together.

Tip: Store leftover burgers in an air-tight container in the freezer. Thaw and reheat for a quick meal.

Yield: 12 to 14 burgers

SIZZLIN' SOY BURGERS

1 lb Vegetarian burger crumbles, frozen
1 env Onion-mushroom soup mix (Lipton®)
3 T Ortega® Taco Sauce, mild
2 T Water
⅓ c Unbleached white flour
⅓ c Vital wheat gluten

Thaw burger, and mix well with soup mix, taco sauce and water. Combine the two flours and stir into burger mixture. Form patties and fry on both sides over medium heat in a non-stick griddle or frying pan with a small amount of olive oil.

Yield: 8 burgers

VEGGIE "WHOPPERS"

2 ½ c	Water	2 ½ T	Beef-style seasoning
¼ c	Flax seed, whole	2 tsp	Kitchen Bouquet®
3 T	Tahini, sesame butter	¾ tsp	Sage, ground
2 T	Bragg® Liquid Aminos	1 ¼ c	Bulgur wheat
1 c	Onions, quartered	2 c	Burger-style crumbles
3 med	Garlic cloves, mashed	⅔ c	Gluten flour
⅓ c	Nutritional yeast flakes	⅓ c	Unbleached white flour

In a blender, combine half the water, flax seed, tahini and liquid aminos and process on high speed 20 to 30 seconds until flax seed is ground smooth. Add remaining water, onions, garlic and seasonings and blend about 10 seconds until onions are finely chopped. Pour into a sauce pan, add bulgur and simmer, covered, 20 minutes stirring occasionally until wheat is tender. Pour into a large bowl, add burger and mix well. Mix the gluten flour with the white flour and add to the bulgur/burger mixture. Stir until flour is mixed in well. Spray a ½ c "dry ingredient" measuring cup with olive oil or garlic flavored cooking spray. Or, for smaller burgers, use a ⅓ c measuring cup. Pack burger mixture into the measuring cup and level off. Invert cup and tap it firmly once or twice onto a baking sheet coated with cooking spray. When burger mixture drops out, use the bottom of the measuring cup to press burger mixture into a round patty ½ inch thick. Spray a light coating of cooking spray over each burger. Bake at 400° F, 15 minutes. Turn burgers over and spray a light coating of cooking spray on the other side. Bake 10 to 15 minutes more. Cool 5 minutes before serving.

Tip: Freezes well. Thaw and reheat on a barbecue grill or in a frying pan.

Yield: 12 (½ c burgers), or 15 (⅓ c burgers)

GARBANZO-MILLET BURGERS

1 ½ c	Onions, chopped	2 T	Bragg® Liquid Aminos
1 c	Cooked garbanzos, drained	1 T	Beef-style seasoning
2 med	Garlic cloves	1 tsp	Bernard Jensen's® Vegetable Seasoning
1 c	Cooked millet or rice	1 tsp	Spike® Seasoning
1 c	Pecans	1 tsp	Basil, dried
1 can	Pitted olives, drained	½ tsp	Cumin, ground
2 c	Vegetarian burger	½ tsp	Thyme, dried
1 ½ c	Quick oats	1 T	ENER-G® Egg Replacer
⅓ c	Gluten flour	3 T	Water
¼ c	Nutritional yeast flakes		

In a food processor, combine onions, garbanzos, garlic, millet or rice, pecans, and olives. Chop mixture well. Pour out into a bowl and add burger, oats, flour, and spices and stir until well mixed. Whisk egg replacer with water until foamy. Gently fold egg substitute into the burger mixture. Form into patties and cook slowly over low to medium heat, browning both sides. For best results, use a non-stick frying pan and spray it with a coating of cooking spray or olive oil to speed up the process.

Variation: Omit liquid aminos, Bernard Jensen's seasoning, Spike®, basil, cumin and thyme. Replace with 1 envelope Lipton® Onion Soup.

Yield: 24 burgers

BETTER MUSTARD

¾ c	Water	½ tsp	Salt
⅓ c	Fresh lemon juice	1 clove	Garlic, mashed
¼ c	Unbleached white flour	½ tsp	Maggi® Seasoning
2 tsp	Turmeric	¼ c	Olive oil, extra "light"

In a blender, process first 5 ingredients on high until creamy. Pour into a saucepan and cook at boiling point temperature stirring constantly until thickened. Cool. Return to blender and add garlic and Maggi® Seasoning. Process on high, and slowly drizzle in oil through the lid spout. Continue to blend for one more minute. Spoon into a glass storage container. Chill before serving.

Yield: 1 ½ cups

BETTER 'N MAYONNAISE

1 box	Mori-Nu® Tofu, firm (12.3 oz)	1 tsp	Prepared mustard
⅓ c	Olive oil, "extra light"	½ tsp	Onion powder
¼ c	Soymilk beverage, plain (Silk®)	¼ tsp	Citric acid
2 T	Corn syrup, light (Karo®)	1 T	Instant Clear Jel® (instant food thickener)
1 ¼ tsp	Salt		

Combine all ingredients except Instant Clear Jel® in a blender and process until smooth and creamy. Lower the blender speed, remove the lid spout and add the Instant Clear Jel® while the blender is running. Blend until thickened. Keep refrigerated.

Note: If desired, substitute mustard with Better Mustard (see page 241) in this recipe. If the mayonnaise becomes too runny after 3 or 4 days, simply return mayo to a blender and add more Instant Clear Jel®, 1 tsp at a time to achieve desired consistency.

Yield: 2 ¼ cups

TOFU MAYONNAISE

1 c	Water	⅛ tsp	Citric acid crystals
½ c	Soymilk powder (plain)	2 ½ T	Instant Clear Jel® powder (or 3 T cornstarch dissolved in 2 T water)
½ c	Almonds (w/o skins)		
½ c	Tofu, firm		
⅓ c	Olive oil, "extra light"	¼ c	Pineapple juice
1 ½ tsp	Salt	¼ c	Fresh lemon juice
½ tsp	Onion powder	1 T	Frozen O.J. concentrate
¼ tsp	Garlic powder		

Combine water, milk powder, nuts and tofu in a blender and process on high speed until completely smooth. Reduce blender speed to lowest setting and drizzle oil in slowly. Then add salt, onion powder, garlic powder, and citric acid. Resume a high speed, remove lid spout and add Instant Clear Jel® powder one tablespoon at a time. It may be necessary to stop the blender often and stir mixture to assist the blending process. Continue blending until completely smooth. (Or, add cornstarch/water to mayonnaise mixture, blend briefly and pour out into a saucepan and simmer until thick.) Pour into a bowl and gently stir in pineapple, lemon juice and orange juice concentrate. (Do not add juices to the blender. It must be stirred in by hand.) Refrigerate 1 to 2 hours before serving to enhance flavor.

Yield: 3 cups

"QUICK" VINEGARLESS KETCHUP

- 1 ½ c Tomato sauce
- 1 c Tomato paste
- ½ c Pineapple juice
- ¼ c Fresh lemon juice
- 1 tsp Lime juice
- 3 T Date butter (p. 251)
- 2 T Pineapple/orange juice (frozen concentrate)
- 2 T Fructose or honey
- 2 T Fruit-Fresh® powder (or) ⅛ tsp citric acid
- 1½ tsp Salt
- 1 tsp Onion powder
- ½ tsp Garlic salt
- ½ tsp Paprika
- ¼ tsp Worcestershire sauce (opt) (Vegetarian brand)

Combine all ingredients in a blender and process until smooth. Refrigerate. Freeze extras not used within two weeks.

Variation: For a thicker ketchup, decrease tomato sauce to 1 cup and increase tomato paste to 1 ½ cups.

Yield: 4 cups

PIMIENTO CHEESE

- 1 ¼ c Water
- 1 c Cooked rice
- 4 T Emes Kosher Jel® (plain)
- ½ c Water-packed tofu, extra firm
- ½ c Raw cashews, rinsed
- 3 T Nutritional yeast flakes
- 4 oz Pimientos, canned
- 2 T Lemon juice
- 2 tsp Onion powder
- 2 tsp Salt
- ½ tsp Garlic powder

In a blender, combine water, rice, Kosher Jel, tofu and cashews. Process on high speed until completely smooth and creamy. Add remaining ingredients and blend well. Pour into a container coated with cooking spray. Refrigerate several hours until set. Gently shake out of container to slice cheese.

Note: To shred cheese easily, freeze mixture at least 2 hours first. For a creamy sauce to serve over vegetables or noodles, do not refrigerate mixture after blending, but heat and serve immediately. Or, if using previously "set" leftovers, heat mixture slowly until cheese melts.

Yield: 3 cups

MOZZARELLA CHEESE

1 c	Soymilk beverage, plain (or water)	4 tsp	Fresh lemon juice
1 c	Cooked rice, brown or white	1 ½ tsp	Salt
¾ c	Water-packed tofu, extra firm	1 tsp	Onion powder
½ c	Raw cashews, rinsed	¼ tsp	Garlic powder
4 T	Emes Kosher Jel® (plain)		

In a blender, combine all ingredients and process on high speed, stopping and stirring as necessary, until completely smooth and creamy (3 to 5 minutes). The sauce will heat up and appear "shiny" when completed. Pour into a container coated with cooking spray. Refrigerate 2 to 4 hours until set. Gently shake out to slice cheese.

Note: To shred cheese easily, freeze mixture at least 2 hours first. For a creamy sauce to pour over vegetables or noodles, do not refrigerate mixture after blending, but heat and serve immediately. Or, if using previously "set" leftover cheese, heat mixture slowly over low to medium heat, stirring frequently until melted.

Tip: May substitute cashews with slivered blanched almonds (w/o skins).

Yield: 3 cups

TUNA-STYLE SALAD

1 c	Vegetarian tuna, frozen *	3 T	Celery, diced
⅓ c	Nayonaise®, (eggless mayonnaise)	3 T	Dill pickles, chopped
¼ c	Sweet onions, finely chopped (opt)		

Thaw vegetarian tuna and add measured amount into a small mixing bowl. Add remaining ingredients and stir gently. Spread desired portion between two slices of whole grain bread or in a bun. Add lettuce and alfalfa sprouts if desired.

* "Tuno®" by Worthington® is recommended.

Yield: 2 cups

THREE GRAIN "NO-OIL" BREAD

2 c	Warm water	2 T	Wheat germ
2 c	Warm applesauce	2 T	Vital wheat gluten
3 T	Honey or brown sugar	½ c	Rye flour
2 T	Active dry yeast	6 c	Whole-wheat flour
1 T	Salt	1 c	Unbleached white flour
¼ c	Quick oats	1 c	Unbleached white flour (for kneading)
⅓ c	Wheat bran		

In a large bowl, combine water, applesauce, honey or sugar, and yeast. Set aside for 10 minutes until bubbly. Add salt, oats, wheat bran, wheat germ and vital wheat gluten. Allow to rest 5 minutes. Then stir in rye and wheat flour. Gradually add 1 cup unbleached flour until it becomes too difficult to stir. Oil hands or spray hands with cooking spray. Turn dough out unto a floured board or counter and knead in remaining 1 cup flour. Add more flour if dough is too sticky, but take care not to add any more than is necessary. Knead well up to 10 minutes. When texture is correct, dough should spring back when pressed. Place in a clean, oiled bowl in a warm place and cover with a towel. Let rise until doubled, 25 to 30 minutes. Punch down and divide dough into 2 equal parts for large loaves or 3 parts for medium size loaves. Knead lightly, shape loaves and place in bread pans coated with cooking spray. Cover with a towel and let rise again until doubled in size. Bake in a pre-heated oven at 350° F, 40 to 45 minutes. Bread should sound hollow when tapped when it is done. Remove from pans, cover with a towel and cool on a wire rack.

Yield: 2 to 3 loaves

AUTOMATIC BREAD MACHINE
Whole Wheat Bread Recipe

1 c	Warm water	2 ½ tsp	Active yeast, "rapid-rise"
2 T	Oil	2 c	Whole-wheat flour
2 T	Honey	⅔ c	Unbleached white flour
1 ¼ tsp	Salt	2 T	Vital wheat gluten

Combine water, oil, honey, salt and yeast in the bread machine bowl. Then add flours and set the machine for automatic bread according to directions.

Note: If making bread on a delayed time setting, it is important to place yeast on top of the flour to keep it dry until the processing begins.

Variation: For higher fiber content, use 2 ⅓ cup whole-wheat flour to ⅓ c unbleached white flour.

Yield: 1 loaf

SPROUTED WHEAT BREAD

STEP ONE:

1 c Hard winter wheat berries
2 c Water (for soaking)

Cover berries with water and soak uncovered 24 hours. Then place berries in the refrigerator and soak 24 hours more. Drain and discard water after 48 hours is completed.

STEP TWO:

3 c Warm water
2 T Active dry yeast
3 c Whole-wheat flour

In a blender, combine soaked wheat berries and half the water (1 ½ c) and process 2 minutes on high speed. Pour blended berries out into a large bowl. Mixture should be stringy. Add remaining water and yeast. Using a slotted spoon, stir until well mixed. Add flour to make a "sponge," hand whipping 2 or 3 minutes.

STEP THREE:

1 T Salt
⅓ c Brown sugar or honey
¼ c Oil
2 T Vital wheat gluten
4 c Whole-wheat flour
1 c Flour (for kneading)

Add each ingredient, (except kneading flour), one at a time into the center of the sponge, but don't mix until all ingredients have been added. Then mix in a folding motion. Use hands to turn dough toward the center of the bowl until stiff. When dough becomes sticky, add ½ cup flour around the edges of the bowl. Dust hands with flour as needed. Turn dough out onto a floured counter or bread board. While kneading, handle bread as lightly as possible and dust with flour as needed. Knead about 10 minutes. To test if dough is done, gently pull a small piece apart. If it resists breaking, it is done. Place dough into an oiled bowl in a warm, draft free spot and cover with a clean cloth. Let rise until double. Punch down and knead again briefly. Divide into 2 or 3 equal portions. Shape into loaves and place into bread pans prepared with cooking spray. Let rise until 1 inch above the top of the pan. Bake at 350° F, 40 to 45 minutes. Bread should sound hollow when tapped. Remove from pans and allow to cool on a bread rack or by standing bread on end.

Yield: 2 large loaves (or) 3 small loaves

BOSCH BREAD MACHINE
Whole Wheat Bread Recipe

STEP ONE:

6 c	Warm water	3 T	Active dry yeast
½ c–⅔ c	Honey	3 c	Whole-wheat flour
½ c–⅔ c	Oil		

Combine above ingredients in bread bowl with dough hooks assembled, place both lids on bowl and turn machine on to speed "2" and mix for 2 minutes.

STEP TWO:

¼ c	Vital wheat gluten	2 T	Salt
1 tsp	Citric acid (or) 1T lemon juice		

Turn machine off. Add above ingredients. Then resume mixing, speed "2."

STEP THREE:

1 c	Quick oats	3 c	Unbleached white or bread flour
⅔ c	Rye flour	6 c	Whole-wheat flour (plus or minus)
½ c	Wheat bran		

Remove "center" lid and add above ingredients slowly while continuing to operate on speed "2." Continue adding flour until dough pulls away from side of the bowl and is wiped clean. Then replace center lid and continue mixing for 8 minutes.

STEP FOUR:
Remove dough from bowl and place on a floured surface. Using a large knife, divide dough into 4 equal parts for large loaves, or 5 equal parts for medium size loaves. Knead briefly, flatten and roll dough up and shape into loaves. Place into bread pans and let rise to 90% of full size. Bake in a pre-heated oven at 350° F, 35 to 40 minutes or until loaf sounds hollow when tapped. Remove loaves from oven, turn out on bread racks, cover with a tea towel and let cool.

Yield: 4 to 5 loaves

SPELT BREAD

2 c	Water	⅛ tsp	Cinnamon
2 c	Spelt flour	¼ c	Soy flour
2 T	Active yeast, dry	4 c	Spelt flour
¼ c	Brown sugar or honey	½ c	Spelt flour (for kneading)
¼ c	Olive oil, "extra light"		
2 tsp	Salt		

In a large bowl, combine water, spelt flour (2 cups) and yeast. Whip 1 to 2 minutes to make a sponge. Add the sweetener, oil, salt, cinnamon and soy flour. Whip 2 more minutes. Cover and let sit in a warm place 30 minutes or until double. Stir in remaining spelt flour (4 cups.) Turn onto a floured (½ c) board and knead until smooth or about 5 minutes. Keep as light as possible. It will not have quite as much elasticity as other breads. Divide dough and shape into a two loaves. Place in oiled loaf pans, cover with a damp cloth and let rise in a warm place until double in size, approximately 30 minutes. Bake at 350° F for 35 to 40 minutes or until a golden brown color.

Note: Spelt flour mimics whole-wheat flour in taste and appearance. Spelt bread is generally an acceptable substitute for people with wheat allergies.

Yield: 2 loaves

GARBANZO-OLIVE SANDWICH SPREAD

1 can	Garbanzos, drained (15 oz)	¼ tsp	Garlic salt
1 c	Black olives, chopped	¼ tsp	Basil, dried
⅓ c	Green onions, finely diced	⅓ c	Better 'n Mayonnaise (see page 242)
¼ tsp	Chicken-style seasoning		

Mash garbanzos until soft. Add olives and seasonings and mix well. Add mayonnaise to moisten spread. Add more or less to suit taste. Serve as a sandwich spread or with crackers.

Variation: Substitute garbanzos with pinto beans and add ¾ tsp McKay's® Beef-style seasoning. For variety, add finely chopped walnuts and/or mild green chilies.

Yield: 2 ½ cups

TAHINI HONEY SPREAD

1 c	Tahini, sesame butter	½ c	Spun honey (Sue Bee®)

Stir tahini until well mixed. Add honey and mix until creamy. Store in the refrigerator. Spread on bread or crackers.

Variation: Substitute tahini with peanut butter.

Yield: 1 ½ cups

WALNUT & OLIVE "CREAM CHEESE" SPREAD

8 oz	Soy cream cheese, (Tofutti®) (French onion or plain flavor)	3 T	Celery, finely chopped
½ c	Black olives, chopped	½ tsp	Onion powder
¼ c	Walnuts, finely chopped	⅛ tsp	Garlic powder
¼ c	Sweet onions, finely diced	⅛ tsp	Salt
		⅛ tsp	Citric acid

Combine all ingredients and stir gently until well mixed. (Be extra careful to sprinkle citric acid evenly over entire mixture before mixing to assure evenness of flavor.) If desired, garnish with finely diced red bell peppers or tomatoes. Serve with raw veggies or crackers. Also delicious as a sandwich spread on bread with lettuce, tomatoes, onions, and alfalfa sprouts.

Yield: 2 cups

VERY BERRY CREAM CHEESE SPREAD

4 oz Better Than Cream Cheese®, plain (Tofutti®)
¼ c All-fruit jam, (blueberry, strawberry or raspberry)

Gently stir and swirl mixture together. Spread on whole-wheat bagels or any whole grain bread of choice. Or, spread cream cheese on bread and top with jam.

Yield: ¾ cup

CRISPY SESAME-OAT CRACKERS

5 c	Quick oats	⅓ c	Sesame seeds
1 ½ c	Whole-wheat flour	1 ½ c	Water
½ c	Brown sugar or Sucanat®	½ c	Olive oil, extra "light"
½ c	Ground almonds or pecans	2 tsp	Salt

In a large bowl, combine oats, flour, sweetener, nuts and sesame seeds. In a separate bowl, combine water, oil and salt. Combine liquid and dry ingredients and stir until well mixed. Prepare a cookie sheet with cooking spray. Pour mixture onto the cookie sheet and roll out to the edges with a rolling pin (or a cooking spray can). Bake 1 hour at 250° F. Take out of oven and score into 2 or 3 inch squares. Return to oven and bake 30 minutes more. Cool and break into squares.

Note: These lightly sweetened crackers are good eaten with sweet spreads like "Very Berry Cream Cheese" or "Honey Tahini Spread." They're also great eaten alone as a snack.

Yield: 5 dozen crackers

WHOLE-GRAIN CRACKERS

2 ¼ c	Quick oats	¾ c	Water
1 ½ c	Whole-wheat pastry flour	½ c	Olive oil, "extra light"
¾ c	Wheat germ, raw	3 T	Brown sugar
¾ tsp	Salt		

Combine oats, flour, wheat germ and salt in a mixing bowl. Combine water, oil and brown sugar in a "2 cup" measuring cup and stir to dissolve sugar. Pour into dry ingredients and mix quickly. Prepare a heavy-duty cookie sheet with cooking spray. Spread dough mixture out evenly on the cookie sheet and press dough down with hands. Use a cooking spray can as a "rolling pin" to flatten and pack the dough down. Cut into 2-inch squares before baking. Bake at 325° F, for 30 minutes. Turn oven off and let crackers cool completely in the oven. (Crackers will continue to bake several minutes.)

Variation: For "Wheat Thins," prepare crackers according to recipe but divide dough between 2 cookie sheets and cut into 1-inch squares. Bake at 325° F, 20 min. Turn oven off and let crackers cool completely in oven. Makes 140 "Wheat Thins."

Yield: 35 crackers

OATMEAL-DATE COOKIES

½ c	Date butter (see below)	½ c	Olive oil, "extra light"
2 c	Quick oats	⅓ c	Honey or fructose
1 c	Old-fashioned oats	⅓ c	Apple juice, undiluted (frozen concentrate)
1 c	Whole-wheat flour	1 T	ENER-G® Egg Replacer, mixed in 4 T water
½ c	Unbleached white flour	1 tsp	Vanilla extract
½ c	Soymilk powder, plain	½ tsp	Maple flavoring
½ c	Walnuts, chopped		
1 tsp	Salt		

Prepare date butter according to directions below and set aside. Combine dry ingredients. Combine liquids and pour into the dry ingredients and mix well. Use ⅔ of cookie mixture and drop by heaping tablespoonfuls on a baking sheet and gently shape into cookies. Take care not to press mixture together too much. Press a small "well" into the center of each cookie. Spoon 1 tsp date butter into each "well" and top with enough cookie dough to just cover. Bake in a preheated oven at 350° F, 16–18 minutes or until lightly browned. Cool slightly then place in a covered air-tight container.

Note: Make **DATE BUTTER** by combining 1 cup pitted dates with ½ cup water and simmering 2 to 3 minutes until soft. Cool. Mash dates well with a fork or pour into a blender and process until dates are smooth and creamy. (Yield: 1 cup)

Variation: For a delicious low-fat version, substitute half or all oil with equal proportions of WonderSlim® Fat & Egg Substitute.

Yield: 2 dozen

FROZEN FRUIT ICE CREAM

Freeze 4 cups fresh or canned fruit, in any combination. In a blender, process the frozen fruit with ½ cup Better Than Milk™ "Original" soymilk powder. Add a small amount of fruit juice concentrate, only if necessary to assist in the blending process. For a sweeter taste, add fructose or a few drops of Stevia extract. Serve at once as soft ice cream or return to the freezer several hours for firmer ice cream. Scoop up, garnish with toppings and serve immediately.

Toppings: Sprinkle desired portions of grated coconut, chopped nuts, carob chips, sunflower seeds, or fresh chopped fruit on top for added flavor.

Yield: 3 cups

NUTTY OATMEAL COOKIES

1 c	Quick oats	⅓ c	Nut butter, creamy (Cashew, almond or peanut)
1 c	Whole-wheat pastry flour	⅓ c	Soymilk beverage, plain
⅔ c	Fructose or light brown sugar	2 T	Olive oil, "extra light"
⅓ c	Walnuts, chopped	2 tsp	Vanilla extract
⅓ c	Carob chips, sweetened		
½ tsp	Salt		

In a mixing bowl, combine oats, flour, sugar, walnuts, carob chips and salt. In a separate bowl, combine nut butter with remaining ingredients and stir until well mixed. Add nut butter mixture to the dry ingredients and stir just until evenly moistened. For tender cookies, avoid over mixing the dough. Prepare a heavy-duty baking sheet with cooking spray. Drop dough by large spoonfuls (2 T) onto the baking sheet. Spray fingertips with cooking spray and gently press dough into 2 ½ inch round shapes. Avoid flattening the dough. Bake at 350° F, 15 to 17 minutes until set and tops begin to look golden. Let cool on the baking sheets 5 minutes before removing cookies to wire racks to cool completely.

Yield: 15 cookies

MOCHA-BANANA NUT ICE CREAM

1 c	Water	2 or 3 T	Pure maple syrup
½ c	Raw cashews	1 T	Natural vanilla, flavoring
½ c	Soymilk powder, plain	1 tsp	Natural maple flavoring
2 T	Carob powder	5 or 6	Ripe bananas, frozen
⅛ tsp	Roma® (coffee substitute)		

In a blender, combine water and cashews and process until completely liquefied. Add dry ingredients and flavorings and blend until smooth. Break bananas into chunks and add through the lid spout while blending on high speed until total volume equals 5 cups. Serve immediately for soft ice cream or for firm ice cream, pour into a shallow container and freeze several hours before scooping. Serve plain or garnish with choice of sliced almonds, chopped pecans or walnuts, grated coconut, carob shavings, raspberries, strawberries, or mint leaves.

Variation: Increase cashews up to 1 cup if a richer, creamier taste is desired.

Yield: 5 cups

TOLL HOUSE COOKIE "LOOK-A-LIKES"

- 1 c Whole-wheat flour
- 1 c Unbleached white flour
- 1 tsp Salt
- ½ tsp Baking soda
- 8 oz Smart Balance® "Light" (non-hydrogenated spread)
- 1 c Light brown sugar, packed
- ½ c Mori-Nu® Tofu, firm
- 2 tsp Vanilla extract
- 1 c Walnuts, chopped
- ⅔ c Carob chips

Combine flours, salt and baking soda in a bowl and set aside. In a large mixing bowl, beat Smart Balance® (softened at room temperature), sugar, tofu, and vanilla at "cream" setting until smooth and creamy (about 1 minute). Lower speed and gradually beat in flour mixture. Resume high speed and beat 1 minute more. Stir in walnuts and carob chips. Drop by heaping tablespoons onto a cookie sheet prepared with cooking spray. Allow 1 inch between cookies. Bake in a pre-heated oven on the center oven rack at 375° F, 14 minutes or until golden brown. Cool for 2 minutes. Using a spatula, transfer cookies to a wire rack to cool completely before storing.

Tip: For best results, use a heavyweight cookie sheet and bake only one pan full at a time.

Yield: 3 dozen

VANILLA ICE CREAM

- 2 c Soymilk creamer, plain (Silk®)
- 2 c Soymilk creamer, French vanilla (Silk®)
- 1 c Soymilk powder, plain*
- 1 T Clear vanilla, extract

Combine all ingredients in a blender and process until well mixed. Pour into an ice cream maker and operate according to manufacturer's directions.

* Better Than Milk™ Soy "Original" is the recommended product.

Tip: For a delicious treat, add ½ cup finely chopped carob chips and ¼ cup lightly toasted and finely chopped almonds (chilled) to the ice cream when nearly set or during the last 5 minutes of churning.

Note: This recipe can easily be doubled or tripled if necessary to fit the ice cream maker.

Yield: 1 quart

"ICE CREAM" BIRTHDAY CAKE

9-inch	Whole-grain pie crust, single	¾ c	Soy sour cream (Tofutti®)
3 pints	Non-dairy ice cream (Tofutti®) (mixture of berry flavors)	⅓ c	Mori-Nu® Tofu, firm
		1 c	Carob chips, sweetened
3 med	Bananas, thinly sliced	2 T	Soymilk beverage
¼ c	Pineapple juice	¼ c	Walnuts, finely chopped
⅓ c	Rice syrup	(opt)	Raspberries
¾ c	Soy cream cheese (Tofutti®)	(opt)	Mint leaves

Prepare a single recipe pie crust. Place it in the bottom of a 10-inch spring form pan and trim the edges. Pierce the crust evenly with a fork. Bake at 425° F, 10 to 15 minutes or until lightly browned. Cool. Slice bananas and toss gently with the pineapple juice. Arrange a layer of bananas over the crust. Thaw the ice cream just long enough to be able to pour out into a bowl and stir together. Spread ice cream over the bananas and freeze until firm. Combine rice syrup, soy cream cheese, soy sour cream and tofu in a blender and process until smooth and creamy. Pour over ice cream layer and freeze again. Combine carob chips and soymilk in a saucepan and heat slowly, stirring often until melted. Drizzle or swirl carob sauce over the top of the cake. Sprinkle with walnuts. Cover and keep frozen until ready for use. Take the frozen cake from freezer and remove the sides of the pan. Slice as soon as able (5 minutes) and if desired, garnish with raspberries and mint leaves.

Yield: 10-inch cake

STRAWBERRY ICE CREAM

2 c	Frozen strawberries, packed	¼ c	Fructose, granules
2 c	Soymilk creamer, French vanilla (Silk®)	½ tsp	Strawberry extract
½ c	Soymilk powder, plain * (opt)		

Combine all ingredients in a blender and process until smooth and creamy. Pour into an ice cream maker and proceed according to the manufacturer's directions.

* Better Than Milk™ Soy "Original" is the recommended product.

Tip: This recipe can easily be doubled or tripled to fit the ice cream maker.

Yield: 1 quart

BLUEBERRY YUM YUM

BLUEBERRY FILLING:

4 c	Fresh or frozen blueberries	½ c	Water
1 ½ c	Grape juice, frozen concentrate	½ c	Cornstarch
2 T	FruitSource® or honey		

In a saucepan, combine berries, grape juice and FruitSource® and bring to a boil. Reduce heat to simmering point. Dissolve cornstarch in water and pour into saucepan, stirring constantly. Cook until mixture thickens and clears. Remove from heat. Refrigerate until cold.

YUMMY FILLING:

¾ c	Water	⅓ c	Mori-Nu® Tofu, firm
⅓ c	Better Than Milk™ powder	2 T	FruitSource® or honey
¼ c	Almond slivered	1 tsp	Natural vanilla, flavoring
3 T	Emes Kosher Jel® (plain)	⅛ tsp	Salt
½ c	Soy cream cheese (Tofutti®) (Better Than Cream Cheese®)	2 c	Crushed ice (approx)

In a blender, combine water, milk powder, almonds and Emes. Process until completely liquefied. Add remaining ingredients, except ice, and blend until smooth. Add ice through the lid spout and continue blending until mixture become thick and fluffy.

QUICK GRAHAM CRUST:

1 ½ c	Graham cracker crumbs	3 T	Smart Balance® or Spectrum® (Margarine alternatives)
½ c	Freshly ground pecans		

Combine crust ingredients (adding a little water if necessary) and press into a 9-inch pie pan. Bake at 350° F, 10 minutes. Cool before adding fillings.

METHOD #1

To assemble, pour alternate layers of Blueberry filling and Yummy filling into the graham cracker crust, ending with Yummy filling. Garnish with blueberries or graham cracker crumbs. Chill until set before serving.

METHOD #2

Spoon alternate layers of graham cracker crumbs or granola, Blueberry filling and Yummy filling into parfait glasses, ending with Yummy filling. Garnish with blueberries and a mint leaf on top.

Yield: 9-inch pie (or) 12 parfaits

OLD-FASHIONED APPLE CRISP

Topping:

1 c	Quick oats
½ c	Unbleached white flour
½ c	Walnuts, chopped
¼ c	Old-fashioned oats
¼ c	Shredded coconut (opt)
¼ tsp	Salt
¼ tsp	Cinnamon, ground
3 T	Brown sugar, packed
3 T	Oil
1 T	Water
1 tsp	Vanilla extract

Combine all dry ingredients except brown sugar in a mixing bowl. Mix brown sugar with oil, water and vanilla. Combine the liquid and dry ingredients and stir until mixture is crumbly. Set aside.

Filling:

8 c	Tart apples, peeled and chopped
6 oz	White grape/peach, 100% juice (frozen concentrate, undiluted)
1 c	Fructose or light brown sugar
3 T	Minute® Tapioca
1 tsp	Cinnamon, ground
1 tsp	Vanilla, extract
⅛ tsp	Salt (see note below)

Mix apples with juice, sugar, tapioca, cinnamon and vanilla. Sprinkle salt evenly over the apples and stir until well mixed. Prepare a 9" x 13" baking dish with cooking spray. Pour apples into the dish and spread out evenly. Cover apple filling with the topping. Bake at 350° F, 25 to 30 minutes until topping is golden brown.

Tip: Serve with favorite non-dairy whipped cream or vanilla ice cream.

Note: May substitute salt with (2 T) Smart Balance® "Light." Dot evenly over the apple filling before covering with topping.

Variation: Substitute half the apples with pears for a great new taste.

Yield: 8 cups

Holiday Burger Loaf
Yams with Orange Glaze
Non-Dairy Pumpkin Pie
Crescent Rolls

A Thanksgiving Tradition

Featuring

A vegetarian Thanksgiving dinner complete with "Turkey" and all the trimmings. A feast that's sure to please.

HOLIDAY "TURKEY"

GLUTEN BASE:

4 c	Vital wheat gluten (Do-Pep®)	2 T	Nutritional yeast flakes
1 c	All purpose flour	4 T	Soy sauce
2 pkg	George Washington Broth®	4 c	Water

Combine ingredients and knead gluten into a ball. Take off a piece of the gluten about the size of your fist and set aside to be used later for the turkey skin.

FILLING:

3 lg	Onions, quartered	1 ½ c	Walnuts or pecans
4 stalks	Celery	1 c	Herb stuffing mix *
6 cloves	Garlic		

Take the big ball of gluten and push it through a meat grinder a little at a time with the above filling ingredients. Use half the stuffing mix to work the gluten through the grinder and then use the last half at the end to clean any remaining gluten out of the grinder. Pour mixture into a bowl.

SPICES:

3 T	Chicken-style seasoning (McKay's®)	2 tsp	Sage (opt)

Stir spices into the above gluten mixture.

PROCEDURE:

Take the gluten you saved for the skin and press it out as thin as possible into a large rectangle. Put the ground turkey mixture in the center and wrap the skin around it making an oblong shape like a turkey breast. Now wrap turkey in several layers of cheesecloth. See that the cheesecloth is wrapped quite firmly around the turkey and sew securely with a needle and thread across the top seam and on both ends. Cook "turkey gluten" in broth (see recipe on next page).

* Note that not all stuffing mixes are vegetarian. Read ingredients listed on the package carefully.

Continued on next page

BROTH:

2 med	Onions, chopped	3 c	Tomato juice or tomato sauce
6 cloves	Garlic, minced	½ c	Soy sauce
2 stalks	Celery, chopped	2 env	Onion-mushroom soup mix (Lipton)
2 sm	Bell peppers, chopped	1 T	Chicken or beef-style seasoning
¼ c	Olive oil		

In a large saucepan, sauté onions, garlic, celery and peppers in oil until half tender. Add remaining ingredients. Place "turkey gluten" and broth in a roaster and cover. Set oven on 250° F, and simmer turkey 3 to 4 hours. Baste turkey every 30 minutes with the broth and turn turkey over half way through cooking time. Then turn heat off and leave turkey in the oven to soak 6 to 8 hours. Remove the turkey from the oven and cut off the cheesecloth wrapper. Serve on an oval platter and garnish with dressing or rice and vegetables. If not eaten the same day, just freeze leftover turkey until needed and thaw in the refrigerator before re-heating.

Yield: 1 Vegetarian turkey

VEGETARIAN MEATLOAF

12 oz	Water-packed tofu, extra firm	6 oz	Italian tomato paste
1 ½ c	GranBurger® (or TVP-beef flavor)	¼ c	Fresh parsley, chopped
1 ½ c	Pepperidge Farm® Stuffing	¼ c	Nutritional yeast flakes
1 c	Quick oats	¼ c	Vital wheat gluten
1 can	Mock duck, finely chopped	2 T	ENER-G® Egg Replacer, (mixed in ¼ c water)
1 env	Onion soup mix (Lipton®)	1 tsp	Beef-style seasoning
½ c	Pecans, chopped	1 tsp	Sage, dried
1 med	Onion, chopped	½ c	Ketchup (or vinegarless)
1 stalk	Celery, diced	⅓ c	Crushed pineapple
2 large	Garlic cloves, minced	2 or 3 T	Brown sugar
⅓ c	Bell pepper, chopped		
¼ c	Ketchup (or vinegarless—p. 243)		

Prepare a large loaf pan with cooking spray. Mix all ingredients together except ½ c ketchup, pineapple and brown sugar. Squeeze the pineapple dry and add the ketchup and brown sugar. Pour the pineapple mixture into the bottom of the pan. Press loaf mixture into the pan over the pineapple mixture. Bake at 350° F, 1 hour and 5 minutes. Let cool at least 15 minutes before removing loaf. Invert loaf onto an oval platter dressed with a lettuce bed. Garnish with carrot curls, crushed pineapple, and fresh parsley on top. Arrange a border around the loaf with potatoes, broccoli, cherry tomatoes and orange twists.

Yield: 1 (oversized) loaf

HOLIDAY BURGER LOAF *with* SWEET 'N SOUR GLAZE

3 T	Olive oil, "extra virgin"	1 T	Beef-style seasoning
2 c	Onions, diced	1 tsp	McCormick® Garlic & Herb ("Salt-free" Seasoning)
1 c	Carrots, grated	1 tsp	Sage
½ c	Fresh mushrooms, chopped	1 tsp	Maggi® Seasoning
⅓ c	Red and/or green bell peppers, diced	¾ tsp	Kitchen Bouquet®
3 med	Garlic cloves, minced	½ tsp	Onion salt
4 c	Fresh bread crumbs, wheat	3 T	Water
1 can	Vegetarian Burger® (20 oz) (Worthington®)	2 T	ENER-G® Egg Replacer
		½ c	Vital wheat gluten (Do-Pep®)

In a large skillet, add oil, onions, carrots, mushrooms, peppers and garlic. Sauté over med heat until vegetables are tender. Pour mixture out into a large bowl. Break up about 2 slices of bread at a time, add to a blender and process until crumbly. Pour into a measuring cup and continue procedure to equal 4 cups. Add bread crumbs and burger to the vegetable mixture and mix well. In a small bowl, combine all seasonings with the water and egg replacer and whisk until well mixed. Add to the burger mixture and stir until evenly moistened. Last, add vital wheat gluten flour and mix well. Set aside.

GLAZE:

½ c	Ketchup (or "Quick" Vinegarless p. 243)	3 T	Water
3 T	Brown sugar		

Combine all ingredients and stir to dissolve sugar. Prepare a loaf pan with cooking spray. Pour two-thirds of glaze mixture into the bottom of the pan. Pack the burger mixture into the loaf pan and smooth out until level. Pour remaining glaze over burger. Bake at 350°F, 60 to 65 minutes or until sides begin to pull away from the pan and the glaze has darkened to a deep red color. Cool about 10 minutes before attempting to turn out of pan. If desired, garnish loaf with a swirl of additional ketchup, and a border of parsley or other greenery, cherry tomatoes & cooked vegetables. (See picture next to p. 257.)

Note: If unable to use Vegetarian Burger®, replace it with 2 cups Mock Duck or beef-flavored gluten finely ground and ¾ cup TVP re-hydrated in ¾ cup hot water.

Tip: Leftover "Burger Loaf" makes a great sandwich filling!

Yield: 1 (9 x 5) loaf

COMPANY LOAF

2 c	Water	2 tsp	Onion powder
1 lg	Onion, quartered	2 tsp	Kitchen Bouquet®
1 ½ c	Fresh mushrooms, chopped	1 tsp	Salt
2 med	Carrots, cut in thirds	½ tsp	Sage, ground
3 lg	Garlic cloves, crushed	¼ tsp	Thyme, dried flakes
½ c	Nutritional yeast flakes	1 ½ c	Bulgur wheat
¼ c	Bragg® Liquid Aminos	1 c	Fresh bread crumbs
1 T	Tahini, sesame butter	1 c	Walnuts, finely chopped
1 T	Beef-style seasoning	½ c	Vital wheat gluten
1 T	Olive oil	½ c	Whole-wheat flour

In a blender, combine all ingredients except bulgur, bread crumbs, walnuts and both flours. Blend on med/hi speed about 10 seconds or long enough to finely chop the vegetables. Pour blended vegetables into a pot with the bulgur wheat. Simmer 10 minutes or just long enough to absorb the liquids. Stir in the bread crumbs and walnuts. (For improved nutty flavor, toast walnuts before chopping. Spread on a cookie sheet and bake at 250° F, 10 to 15 minutes.) Mix the two flours together well and add to the bulgur. Stir until well mixed. Coat a 9" x 5" loaf pan with cooking spray. Spoon bulgur mixture into the pan and gently pack it down. Bake at 350° F, one hour. Cool 15 minutes before turning loaf out onto an oval serving platter. Garnish with fresh parsley and cherry tomatoes. Delicious served with gravy or ketchup.

Yield: 1 (9 x 5) loaf

"GIBLET" DRESSING

1 c	Onions, chopped	½ tsp	Sage, dried
1 c	Celery with tops, finely diced	¼ tsp	Marjoram, ground
⅓ c	Olive oil	⅛ tsp	Coriander, ground
1 can	Mock Duck, (10 oz)	⅛ tsp	Thyme, dried
4 c	Herb flavored stuffing mix	⅛ tsp	Savory, dried
4 c	Whole wheat bread cubes, dried	¼ c	Fresh parsley, snipped
1 ½ c	Black olives, sliced	2 ⅓ c	Soymilk beverage, plain
4 tsp	Chicken-style seasoning		

Sauté onions and celery in oil. Pinch off pieces of the mock duck and add it to the sauté mixture. Crush the stuffing mix and combine it with the bread, olives and seasonings in a large bowl. Add the sautéed mixture to the stuffing. Heat milk and pour over the dressing mixture and stir lightly but thoroughly. Spoon dressing into a large baking dish prepared with cooking spray. Bake at 350° F, 45 minutes to 1 hour.

Yield: 10 cups

DINNER ROAST

1 lb	Water-packed tofu, extra firm	2 T	Olive oil, "extra virgin"
1 c	Burger-style crumbles	1 tsp	McCormick® Garlic & Herb (Salt-free Seasoning)
¾ c	Mozzarella Cheese Sauce (see page 264)	½ tsp	Beef-style seasoning
1 env	Onion-mushroom soup mix	2 T	ENER-G® Egg Replacer
½ c	Pecans, chopped	4 T	Water
½ c	Onions, chopped	4 c	"Product 19®," dry cereal (or similar cold cereal)
½ c	Olives, chopped		

Squeeze as much excess water out of tofu as possible. Or, freeze tofu and thaw to create a bean curd that allows you to squeeze most of the water out. (Some tofu brands are not suitable for this method. If tofu becomes like a dry tough sponge, avoid this step.) In a large bowl, crumble tofu and burger. Add cheese sauce (this should be made ahead or use leftovers), soup mix, pecans, onions, olives and oil. Add seasonings and stir evenly through the tofu-burger mixture. Whip Egg Replacer in water until foamy and fold gently into mixture. Last, add cereal and stir lightly until well mixed. Pour into a casserole dish prepared with cooking spray. Spread mixture out evenly but lightly. (Do not pack down.) Bake at 350° F, 40 minutes. Serve with gravy of choice (see selections following).

Variation: May add 1 cup seasoned cooked rice.

Yield: 9 cups

HOLIDAY HERB GRAVY

1 ½ c	Onions, chopped	2 tsp	Fresh thyme, minced (⅛ tsp dried)
1 c	Fresh mushrooms, sliced	2 tsp	Fresh sage, minced (⅛ tsp dried)
1 T	Olive oil	3 ¾ c	Water
1 T	Beef-style seasoning	5 T	Unbleached white flour
1 T	Chicken-style seasoning		

Sauté onions and mushrooms in oil over med heat 2 minutes. Cover, reduce heat to med/lo and cook, stirring occasionally 5 more minutes or until mushrooms release liquids. Add fresh herbs and sauté briefly. Combine part of the water (¾ cup) with the flour and stir to dissolve any lumps. Then add remaining (3 cup) water and mix well. Pour into the onion/mushroom and herb mixture. Bring to a boil stirring constantly. Reduce heat and simmer, stirring occasionally until thickened.

Yield: 4 cups

CASHEW GRAVY

2 ½ c	Hot water	2 T	Liquid aminos or "lite" soy sauce
½ c	Raw cashews, rinsed	1 T	Nutritional yeast flakes
¼ c	Soymilk powder, plain	2 tsp	Chicken-style seasoning
2 T	Cornstarch	2 tsp	Onion powder

In a blender, combine half the hot water with cashews and process until very smooth. Add remaining water and all remaining ingredients and continue blending until thoroughly mixed. Pour out into a saucepan and bring to a boil stirring constantly until thick.

Variation: Sauté fresh mushrooms, minced chives or green onions and add to gravy before boiling.

Yield: 2 ½ cups

COUNTRY GRAVY

1 c	Onions, sliced	2 tsp	Beef-style seasoning
1 c	Fresh mushrooms, sliced	2 tsp	Chicken-style seasoning
½ c	Bell peppers, chopped	½ c	Hot water
1 tsp	Garlic purée	2 T	Unbleached white flour
2 T	Olive oil	1 c	Water

Sauté onions, mushrooms, peppers and garlic in half the oil (1 T). Remove from pan. Brown seasonings in remaining oil (1 T) until dark brown. Dash in ½ c hot water. Mix flour with remaining water, pour into the pan and stir until thick. Stir in the sautéed vegetables.

Yield: 3 cups

RICH BROWN GRAVY

2 T	Water	¾ c	Cold water
2 T	Beef-style seasoning	3 T	Unbleached white flour
2 tsp	Olive oil	1 tsp	Nutritional yeast flakes
1 ½ c	Hot water	1 tsp	Kitchen Bouquet®

Mix 2 T water with the beef-style seasoning and brown mixture in a frying pan with olive oil. Dash in water and stir to dissolve seasoning. Combine cold water with remaining ingredients and whisk until smooth. Pour into the frying pan mixture and bring to a boil, stirring constantly until thickened.

Yield: 2 cups

"QUICK" VINEGARLESS KETCHUP

1 ½ c	Tomato sauce	2 T	Fruit-Fresh®, powder (or ⅛ tsp citric acid)
1 c	Tomato paste	1 ½ tsp	Salt
½ c	Pineapple juice	1 tsp	Onion powder
¼ c	Fresh lemon juice	½ tsp	Garlic salt
1 tsp	Lime juice	½ tsp	Paprika
3 T	Date butter (p. 251)	¼ tsp	Worcestershire sauce (opt) (Vegetarian brand)
2 T	Pineapple/orange juice (frozen concentrate)		
2 T	Fructose or honey		

Combine all ingredients in a blender and process until smooth. Refrigerate. Freeze extras not used within two weeks.

Variation: For thicker ketchup, decrease tomato sauce to 1 cup and increase tomato paste to 1 ½ cups.

Yield: 4 cups

MOZZARELLA CHEESE

1 c	Soymilk beverage, plain (or water)	4 tsp	Fresh lemon juice
1 c	Cooked rice, brown or white	1 ½ tsp	Salt
¾ c	Water-packed tofu, extra firm	1 tsp	Onion powder
½ c	Raw cashews, rinsed	¼ tsp	Garlic powder
4 T	Emes Kosher-Jel® (plain)		

In a blender, combine all ingredients and process on high speed, stopping and stirring as necessary, until completely smooth and creamy (3 to 5 minutes). The sauce will heat up and appear "shiny" when completed. Pour into a container coated with cooking spray. Refrigerate 2 to 4 hours until set. Gently shake out to slice cheese.

Note: To shred cheese easily, freeze mixture at least 2 hours first. For a creamy sauce to pour over vegetables or noodles, do not refrigerate mixture after blending, but heat and serve immediately. Or, if using previously "set" leftover cheese, heat mixture slowly over low to medium heat, stirring frequently until melted.

Tip: May substitute cashews with slivered blanched almonds (w/o skins).

Yield: 3 cups

CRANBERRY SAUCE

½ c	Pineapple juice concentrate	1 T	Brown sugar
½ c	Chiquita® "Raspberry Passion" (frozen juice concentrate)	12 oz	Fresh cranberries
		1 tsp	Orange zest, grated
¼ c	Honey		

Bring juices and sweeteners to a boil. Add cranberries, reduce heat and boil gently 5 to 10 minutes until all the skins pop. Remove from heat when sauce is thick. Let cool slightly before adding orange zest. Cool completely and refrigerate until needed.

Yield: 2 ¼ cups

YAMS WITH ORANGE GLAZE

4 med	Yams or sweet potatoes	2 T	Fructose, granular (opt)
1 c	Orange juice	1 tsp	Orange zest, grated
1 ½ T	Cornstarch	½ tsp	Lemon zest, grated
⅓ c	Pure maple syrup	¼ tsp	Salt
2 T	Smart Balance®, "Light" (opt)	1 tsp	Fresh parsley, snipped

Cook yams until tender, peel and slice into a baking dish. Combine half the orange juice with cornstarch in a saucepan and stir to dissolve starch. Add remaining orange juice and all other ingredients (except the parsley) and bring to a boil, stirring constantly. Simmer mixture until thick and clear. Pour glaze over yams and serve. Garnish with parsley before serving.

Yield: 6 cups

GREEN "PETITE" PEAS *with* PEARL ONIONS

16 oz	Petite green peas, frozen	1 tsp	Chicken-style seasoning (or ½ tsp onion salt)
1 c	Pearl onions, frozen		
¼ c	Water	1 T	Smart Balance®, "Light"

In a saucepan, combine all ingredients except Smart Balance®. Bring to a boil, cover and reduce heat. Simmer 1 or 2 minutes. Turn off heat. Wait 2 minutes and remove from heat. Drain if necessary and dot with Smart Balance®.

Yield: 4 cups

BROCCOLI With CHEESY SAUCE

4 c	Broccoli crowns	1 ½ tsp	Fresh lemon juice (or 1/16 tsp citric acid)
¾ c	Water	2 tsp	Cornstarch
½ c	Mori-Nu® Tofu, firm	2 tsp	Chicken-style seasoning
2 ½ T	Pimientos	½ tsp	Salt
2 T	Cashews	½ tsp	Onion powder
1 ½ T	Nutritional yeast flakes	⅛ tsp	Garlic powder
1 T	Oil		

Steam or cook broccoli and set aside. In a blender, combine remaining ingredients and process until smooth and creamy. Pour into a saucepan and bring to a boil, stirring constantly until thickened. Pour over broccoli and serve.

Yield of sauce: 1 ⅓ cups

SWEET POTATO MOUNDS

3 med	Sweet potatoes, unpeeled	1 c	Pineapple juice, unsweetened
8 oz	Crushed pineapple, undrained	2 T	Pure maple syrup
2 T	Pure maple syrup	2 tsp	Cornstarch
1 tsp	Cinnamon, ground	8	Pecan halves
1 can	Pineapple slices, (20 oz)		

Bake sweet potatoes until tender. When cooled, peel off skin. Mash sweet potatoes with crushed pineapple, syrup and cinnamon and set aside. Drain pineapple slices, reserving juice for glaze. In a small saucepan, combine 1 cup pineapple juice with syrup and cornstarch. Stir to dissolve. Bring to a boil, stirring constantly to make a glaze. Prepare a 9" x 13" casserole dish with cooking spray. Pour half of the glaze into the dish to cover the bottom. Arrange the pineapple rings on the glaze in 2 rows of 4 rings each. Using an ice cream scoop, mound a rounded scoop of the potato mixture on each ring. Bake at 350° F for 15 minutes. Remove from oven and place a pecan half on top of each scoop of potato. Spoon remaining glaze evenly over each potato mound and pineapple ring. Bake an additional 5 minutes.

Yield: 8 mounds

ORZO® TRIO with CANADIAN WILD RICE

½ c	Onions, chopped	14 oz	Canned vegetable broth (plus water to equal 2 c)
½ c	Celery, diced	1 ⅓ c	Orzo®, Tri-Color Pasta
1 ½ tsp	Olive oil	1 T	Smart Balance®, "Light" (non-hydrogenated spread)
1 c	Water	⅓ c	Sliced almonds, toasted
⅓ c	Wild rice, uncooked		
2 tsp	Chicken-style seasoning		

In a non-stick saucepan, sauté onion and celery in oil until tender. Add water, rice and chicken seasoning and bring to a boil. Reduce heat, cover and simmer 35 minutes. Add broth/water mixture, Orzo®, and Smart Balance® and return to a boil. Reduce heat, cover and simmer 10 minutes more, stirring occasionally. Lightly toast almonds and gently stir them in just before serving.

Yield: 5 cups

MAMA'S MASHED POTATOES

6 c	Potatoes, peeled & cubed	1 ½ tsp	Chicken-style seasoning
2 ½ c	Water	1 tsp	Onion powder
½ c	Soymilk beverage, plain(Silk®)	¾ tsp	Salt
½ c	Mori-Nu® Tofu, soft	¼ tsp	Garlic powder
3 T	Smart Balance®, "Light"		

Boil potatoes in water until tender. While potatoes are cooking, combine soymilk and tofu in a blender and process until creamy. Drain potatoes and transfer them to a large mixing bowl. Add Smart Balance®, seasonings, and blended cream to the potatoes and beat with an electric mixer until fluffy. Add more soy milk if necessary. Serve hot with gravy or Smart Balance®.

Yield: 5 cups

MASHED POTATOES DELUXE

8 med	Red potatoes, with skins	1/3 c	Soymilk powder, plain
1 c	Water	6 T	Smart Balance®, "Light"
2/3 c	Raw cashews, rinsed	½ c	Fresh parsley, snipped

Cook or microwave potatoes until tender. Do not peel. In a blender, process water with cashews and soy milk powder until creamy. Whip hot potatoes in the large bowl of an electric mixer. Add cashew cream, Smart Balance®, parsley and salt to taste and whip until smooth. Add more water as necessary.

Yield: 6 cups

MANDARIN-ALMOND HOLIDAY SALAD

CARAMELIZED ALMONDS:

½ c	Sliced almonds	¼ c	Fructose, granular

Caramelize by cooking over medium heat, stirring occasionally until fructose melts, and sticks to nuts. Remove immediately from heat, cool in a pan and break into small pieces. This step can be done ahead.

ITALIAN DRESSING:
Add to one 0.7 oz package of Good Seasons® "Italian" Dressing mix:

3 T	Fresh lemon juice	⅓ c	Water
3 T	Pineapple juice concentrate	¼ c	Olive oil, "light"
2 T	Fresh parsley, minced	3 T	Honey

Mix together in a cruet or an air-tight container. Shake well and refrigerate. Shake again before serving.

SALAD:

1 head	Romaine lettuce	20 oz	Mandarin oranges, drained
2 c	Celery, chopped	4 stems	Green onions, finely diced

Just before serving, assemble salad. Toss with dressing. Sprinkle ½ cup almonds over top.

Variation: Sprinkle salad with crispy Ramen® noodles just before serving.

Yield: 12 cups

FRESH HERBED SAVORY GARLIC BREAD

Prepare or purchase "whole-wheat" French bread. Slice diagonally into 1 inch wide pieces. Spread the following mixture on each slice.

5 T	Spectrum® Naturals Spread (or Smart Balance® "Light")	1 stem	Green onion, finely chopped
1 T	Fresh parsley, minced	¼ tsp	Garlic powder
2 tsp	Fresh basil, minced (½ tsp dried)	⅛ tsp	Salt (to taste)

Wrap loaf in foil and bake at 400° F, 15 minutes. Open foil and bake an additional 3 to 5 minutes for a crispy crust.

Yield: 1 loaf

CRESCENT ROLLS

¾ c	Warm water	1 c	Whole-wheat flour
2 T	Brown sugar	4 T	Quick oats
2 T	Olive oil, "light"	1 T	Soymilk powder, plain
1 ½ tsp	Active dry yeast	1 T	Wheat germ
1 c	All purpose flour	1 tsp	Salt

Combine the warm water, brown sugar, oil and yeast in a measuring cup and set aside. Combine remaining dry ingredients in a mixing bowl. Pour yeast mixture into dry ingredients and mix together to form a ball. Turn the dough out onto a floured surface and knead 5 to 8 minutes until the dough becomes like elastic. Return dough to an oiled bowl and turn to coat lightly. Cover with a clean, dry towel and place in a warm draft-free spot to rise until doubled. Punch down and roll dough out into a 12-inch circular shape, ¼ inch thick. Cut into 12 wedges. Start with the wider side and roll wedges inward. Prepare a baking sheet with cooking spray and arrange rolls on the sheet two inches apart. Shape rolls into a crescent. Allow rolls to rise until double. Bake at 375° F, 15 to 18 minutes.

BASIC WHOLE WHEAT ROLLS

SPONGE:

2 ¾ c	Warm water	3 c	Whole wheat flour
½ c	Warm applesauce	¼ c	Vital wheat gluten
	(or) ¼ c oil	1 ½ T	Active dry yeast

In a mixing bowl, combine the above ingredients and beat well with a wooden spoon to make a sponge. Let stand 10 minutes.

ADD:

2 tsp	Salt	1 T	Lemon juice
3 to 4 c	Whole-wheat flour		

Stir enough flour into the sponge to form a ball, but avoid getting too stiff. Turn out onto a lightly floured surface and knead at least 10 minutes until smooth and elastic. To reduce sticking, oil or coat your hands with cooking spray. Pinch off pieces of dough and shape dough into rolls and place side by side on a 11" x 15" pan. (For loaves, shape into 2 equal loaves and place in loaf pans prepared with cooking spray.) Let rise in a warm oven 25 to 30 minutes or until doubled. Do not remove rolls from oven. Raise temperature to 350° F. Bake rolls 30 minutes. (Or bake loaves 40 to 45 minutes until golden brown.) Remove from pans and cool on a wire rack. May brush tops lightly with oil while still warm.

Yield: 2 dozen rolls or 2 loaves

"HEART-SMART" CORN BUTTER

1 c	Cold water	2 T	Olive oil, "light"
¼ c	Yellow corn meal	1 T	Emes Kosher-Jel® (plain)
½ c	Mori-Nu® Tofu, extra firm	1 T	Cooked carrot (opt for color)
½ c	Warm water	1 tsp	Honey
¼ c	Almonds	1 tsp	Imitation butter flavored salt
3 T	Natural Butter Flavor, vegan (Spicery Shoppe®)	½ tsp	Salt
		pinch	Citric acid

Combine cold water and corn meal in a small saucepan and bring to a boil stirring constantly. Reduce heat to low, cover and simmer 10 minutes. Refrigerate mixture until completely cool and "set." In a blender, combine tofu, water, almonds, butter flavoring, oil and Emes. Process on high speed until no longer "gritty." Spoon chilled corn meal mush into the blender mixture and all remaining ingredients and process until smooth and creamy. Bits of carrot should not be visible. Refrigerate several hours before serving until "butter" thickens to a spreadable consistency.

Yield: 3 cups

ORANGE HONEY BUTTER

Add the following to 1 cup of cold, pre-set Corn Butter (see above):

½ tsp	Orange zest, grated
1 T	Orange juice, frozen concentrate
2 T	Creamy "spun" honey (SueBee® or similar brand)

Whip at high speed until fluffy. Refrigerate before serving.

Yield: 1 ¼ cups

RASPBERRY BUTTER

1 c	Corn Butter (recipe above)	¼ c	Raspberry Jam, seedless

Gently swirl jam into cold, pre-set and pre-whipped "Corn Butter." Place in freezer 30 minutes. Scoop mixture out with a melon ball spoon and arrange butter on a small plate. Return to freezer until 5 minutes before serving.

Variation: Add cranberry sauce instead of the raspberry jam.

Yield: 1 ¼ cups

SOY "E-Z" PUMPKIN PIE

1 can	Libby's® Pumpkin Pie "Mix" (30oz)	⅛ tsp	Cinnamon, ground
⅓ c	Cornstarch	1 ¼ c	Soymilk beverage (Silk® or West Soy® Plus)
⅛ tsp	Allspice, ground	9-inch	Whole-grain pie crust
⅛ tsp	Cloves, ground		

Preheat oven to 425° F. Pour about 1 cup of the pumpkin pie mix into a large bowl. Set remainder aside. Add cornstarch to pumpkin and stir until cornstarch is dissolved. Next, stir in the spices. Then add remaining pumpkin and soymilk and gently stir until well mixed. Pour into an unbaked 9-inch whole grain pie crust. (See "Two-Grain," "Pastry Wheat," or "Cashew-Barley" pie crust recipes on page 272 or 273.) Bake pie at 425° F, 15 minutes. Reduce heat to 350° F and continue baking 1 hour more. Allow to cool completely until set before cutting and serving.

Tip: For best results, cover edges of crust with foil or a pie crust shield after baking 30 minutes.

Yield: 9-inch pie

"SOY SIMPLE" PUMPKIN PIE

2 c	Pumpkin, solid pack	1 tsp	Cinnamon
⅓ c	Cornstarch	½ tsp	Salt
¾ c	Light brown sugar	1 ½ c	Soymilk, vanilla (Silk®)
1 ½ tsp	Pumpkin pie spice	9-inch	Whole-grain pie crust

Combine pumpkin and cornstarch in a mixing bowl and stir until starch dissolves. Add sugar and spices and mix well. Pour in soymilk about ½ c at a time, stirring gently after each addition until well mixed. Pour into an unbaked 9-inch whole grain pie crust. (See "Cashew-Barley," "Two-Grain" or "Pastry Wheat" pie crust recipes following.) Bake at 425° F, for 10 minutes. Then lower heat to 350° F and bake an additional 50 minutes. Allow to cool completely until set before cutting pie and serving.

Variation: For a mild delicate flavor, substitute pumpkin pie spice with ½ tsp allspice, ¼ tsp nutmeg and ⅛ tsp ginger. Or, decrease pie spice to ½ tsp and add ¼ tsp nutmeg and ¼ tsp allspice. The cinnamon and salt are the same as above for all recipes.

Tip: For best results, cover edges of crust with foil or a pie crust shield after baking 30 minutes.

Yield: 9-inch pie

NON-DAIRY PUMPKIN PIE

2 ½ c	Mori-Nu® Tofu, extra firm	⅓ c	Brown sugar
½ c	Honey	2 or 3 tsp	Pumpkin Pie Spice
15 oz	Pumpkin, solid pack (Libby's®)	¼ tsp	Salt

Process tofu and honey in a blender until smooth and creamy. Add remaining ingredients and blend well. Pour into a deep dish 9 or 10-inch unbaked whole grain pie shell. (See pie crust selections following.) Bake at 400° F, 1 hour or until toothpick comes out clean. For best results, cover edges of crust after 30 minutes with foil or pie crust shields to prevent over-browning. Cool completely before slicing.

Variation # 1: May substitute pumpkin pie spice with 2 tsp cinnamon, ½ tsp nutmeg, ¼ tsp allspice, ¼ tsp ginger and ⅛ tsp cloves.

Variation # 2: Decrease pumpkin pie spice to 1 tsp. Add 2 tsp cinnamon.

Yield: 10-inch pie

PECAN TOPPING
(For pumpkin pie)

1 c	Pecan pieces	2 T	Smart Balance® "Light," melted (non-hydrogenated spread)
⅓ c	Light brown sugar		

Mix ingredients together and sprinkle over a cooked pumpkin pie. Broil 5 inches from heat for 1 or 2 minutes until bubbly.

Yield: 1 cup

CASHEW-BARLEY CRUST
(Single, 9-inch)

½ c	Barley flour	¼ c	Raw cashew butter
½ c	All purpose flour	¼ c	Hot water
1 T	Wheat germ (opt)	3 T	Olive oil, "extra-light"
½ tsp	Salt		

Combine flours, wheat germ and salt. In a separate bowl, mix the cashew butter, water and oil together and heat until very warm. Pour into flour and stir until dough is moist. Knead into a ball. Roll dough out into a large circle between 2 pieces of wax paper. Press into a 9" pie plate. Trim and flute edges.

Yield: 9-inch (single) crust

LIGHT AND FLAKY TWO-GRAIN PIE CRUST (Single, 9-inch)

¾ c	Whole-wheat pastry flour	½ tsp	Salt
½ c	Unbleached all purpose flour	⅓ c	Olive oil, "extra light"
¼ c	Oat flour	¼ c	Water

Spoon flours into measuring cups and combine in a mixing bowl. Add salt and stir until well mixed. Mix oil and water together, pour into flour mixture and stir lightly to form dough. Then knead gently to form a smooth ball. Place dough between two sheets of wax paper and roll out 2 inches larger than the pie plate. Remove top layer of wax paper, invert into pie plate and remove the other sheet of wax paper. Trim if necessary and flute edges. Fill with pie filling of choice.

Note: Double recipe for pies requiring a double crust.

Hint: If regular whole-wheat flour is used in place of whole-wheat "pastry" flour, additional water is necessary to compensate for the differences in the flours. A pastry wheat crust will also be lighter and flakier.

Tip: If a pre-baked crust is needed, pierce crust evenly with a fork before baking at 425° F, 12-15 minutes or until lightly browned.

Yield: 9- inch (single) crust

PASTRY-WHEAT PIE CRUST (Single, 9-inch)

¾ c	Whole-wheat pastry flour	⅓ c	Olive oil, "extra light"
¾ c	Unbleached all purpose flour	¼ c	Water
½ tsp	Salt		

Spoon flours into measuring cups and combine in a mixing bowl. Add salt and stir until well mixed. Mix oil and water together, pour into flour mixture and stir lightly to form dough. Then knead gently to form a smooth ball. Place dough between two sheets of wax paper and roll out 2 inches larger than the pie plate. Remove top layer of wax paper, invert into pie plate and remove the other sheet of wax paper. Trim if necessary and flute edges. Fill with pie filling of choice.

Note: Double recipe for pies requiring a double crust.

Yield: 9-inch (single) crust

"MINCE-NUT" PIE

CRUST:

1 c	Rolled oats	⅓ c	Olive oil, "extra-light"
1 c	Unbleached white flour (or whole-wheat pastry flour)	⅓ c	Pure maple syrup, (or use ⅓ c water with ½ tsp maple flavoring)
½ tsp	Salt	1 tsp	Vanilla extract
¼ tsp	Nutmeg, ground	½ tsp	Lemon zest, grated
¼ tsp	Cardamom, ground		

Grind rolled oats in a blender or food processor to make a coarse flour. Place ground oats in a mixing bowl, add flour, salt and spices. (If using a food processor, add these ingredients to ground oats; crust can be made in the processor). Add oil and remaining ingredients. Mix until dry ingredients are well coated. Place dough between two pieces of waxed paper and roll out into an 11-inch circle. Chill for at least two hours. Coat a 9-inch pie plate with cooking spray. Remove wax paper from one side of dough, invert into pie plate and then remove the other side. Press gently to cover bottom and sides of pan. Flute edges. Prick crust several times with a fork. Bake crust in a pre-heated oven at 350° F, 20 minutes or longer until completely baked.

FILLING:

2 c	Pecan pieces or halves	2 T	Frozen orange juice, (concentrate)
1 c	Pitted dates	2 tsp	Vanilla extract
½ c	Raisins or currants	1½ tsp	Fresh lemon juice
2 c	Apple, orange or pear juice, regular strength	¼ tsp	Each of ground allspice, nutmeg, cardamom, & ginger
2 T	Emes Kosher-Jel®, plain	pinch	Salt
¼ c	Cold water		

Spread pecans over a large baking tray or cookie sheet. Roast at 250° F, 10 to 12 minutes or until pecans turn slightly darker and taste lightly roasted. Remove from the oven and set aside. Place dates and raisins or currants in a saucepan. Add juice, bring to a boil, cover, lower heat and simmer for 10 to 15 minutes, until dried fruit is very soft. Soften Emes gelatin in cold water, add to hot fruit mixture. Remove from heat and stir in frozen orange juice concentrate, vanilla, lemon juice, spices and salt. Purée mixture in a blender or food processor until very smooth. Pour out into a bowl. Add only 1 ½ c pecans to the date mixture. Stir and pour into pie crust. Garnish the top of the pie with the remaining ½ c of pecans. Refrigerate until set. Serve with "Instant Whipped Topping" (see page 222) or "Vanilla Ice Cream" (see page 253) if desired.

Yield: 9-inch pie

SOUTHERN-STYLE PECAN PIE

9-inch	Whole grain crust, single	1 T	Vanilla extract
2 c	Pecan pieces, toasted	⅛ tsp	Ginger, powder
1 c	Dark corn syrup (Karo®)	½ c	Soymilk beverage, plain
½ c	Light brown sugar, packed	⅓ c	Cornstarch
2 T	Smart Balance®, "Light" (non-hydrogenated spread)	¾ c	Flax Seed Jell (recipe below)

Prepare crust of choice. (See "Two-Grain" or "Pastry Wheat" single pie crust recipes on p. 273 for options). Place prepared dough in a 9-inch pie pan, flute edges and chill while preparing filling. Spread pecans evenly on a baking sheet and bake at 250° F, 10 minutes. Set aside to cool. In a medium saucepan, combine corn syrup, brown sugar, Smart Balance®, vanilla and ginger. Bring to a boil, lower heat and simmer gently 5 minutes, uncovered. Remove from heat to cool. Combine soymilk and cornstarch and stir to dissolve cornstarch. Add to the syrup and mix well. In a small saucepan, prepare flax seed jell according to recipe below. Measure and pour ¾ cup jell into the syrup mixture and hand beat with a wire whip until mixture is the consistency of beaten eggs. Spread pecans into the bottom of the pie shell. Pour syrup over the pecans. Bake at 350° F, for 40 to 45 minutes or until bubbly. Cool completely 2 hours, then refrigerate several hours or until set before cutting.

Yield: 9-inch pie

FLAX SEED JELL

2 c	Water	6 T	Flaxseed, whole

In a medium saucepan, bring water to a boil. Add flax seed, reduce heat and simmer 5 minutes only. Remove from heat and immediately pour mixture through a large fine meshed sieve to separate the jell from the seeds.

Note: The jell becomes thick very quickly once removed from heat so the straining process must be done quickly or it will not separate from the seeds.

Tip: To use left over flax seeds, combine seeds with ¾ cup water in a blender and process on high speed until seeds are ground. Keep refrigerated and add to casseroles or whole grain bread recipes.

Yield: ¾ cup

MIXED BERRY PIE

⅓ c	Honey	3 ½ T	Minute® Tapioca
¼ c	Chiquita® "Caribbean Splash" (frozen juice concentrate)	⅛ tsp	Salt
2 tsp	Fresh lemon juice	6 c	Berries Supreme® (frozen berry mixture)

Stir honey and juice together until well mixed. Add lemon juice, tapioca and salt. Gently fold into berries. Prepare a double pie crust. (See selections below.) Pour filling into a 9-inch unbaked pie shell. Arrange top crust & flute edges. Bake at 425° F, 10 minutes. Slit top crust. Lower heat to 350° F, and bake for an additional 35 minutes. Serve with topping of choice.

Yield: 9-inch pie

PASTRY-WHEAT PIE CRUST
(Double, 9-inch)

1 ½ c	Whole-wheat pastry flour	⅔ c	Olive oil, "extra light"
1 ½ c	Unbleached all purpose flour	½ c	Water
1 tsp	Salt		

Spoon flours into measuring cups and combine in a mixing bowl. Add salt and stir until well mixed. Mix oil and water together, pour into flour mixture and stir lightly to form dough. Then knead gently to form a smooth ball. Divide dough into two balls, one larger. Place each ball between two sheets of wax paper and roll out 2" larger than the pie plate. Remove top layer of wax paper, invert dough into pie plate and remove the other sheet of wax paper. Fill with pie filling of choice and adjust top crust. Trim if necessary and flute edges. Bake according to directions.

CASHEW-BARLEY CRUST
(Double, 9-inch)

1 c	Barley flour	½ c	Raw cashew butter
1 c	Unbleached white flour	⅓ c	Oil
2 T	Wheat germ (opt)	½ c	Hot Water
1 tsp	Salt (scant)		

Combine flours, wheat germ and salt. In a separate bowl, mix the cashew butter, oil and water together. Heat mixture in a microwave or on the stovetop. Pour into flour and stir until dough is moist. Knead into a ball. Divide into two balls, one larger than the other. Roll out each ball between 2 pieces of wax paper. Remove wax paper and press the larger crust in the bottom of a 9" pie plate. Add the filling and top crust. Bake according to directions.

Variation: Replace cashew butter with raw almond butter.

PEACHES and "CREAM" HOLIDAY PUNCH

2 c	Orange juice, unsweetened	2 T	Fructose, granular
2 c	Frozen peach slices	1 tsp	Cook's® Vanilla Powder (or use clear vanilla)
1 c	Soymilk beverage, plain (Better Than Milk™ Original)	¼ tsp	Nutmeg, ground (opt)
½ c	Peach nectar, canned juice		

Combine all ingredients except nutmeg in a blender and process until smooth. Chill. Pour into glasses over crushed ice and sprinkle nutmeg on top, if desired. May also serve from a punch bowl with a peach ice ring.

Variation: Make an ice ring by pouring additional punch into a mold and freeze. Before serving, turn the ring out into a punch bowl.
Garnish with orange peel "roses," mint leaves and cranberries.

Yield: 5 ½ cups

SPARKLING GRAPE JUICE

12 oz	White grape/peach, 100% juice (frozen concentrate, undiluted)	4 ½ c	Club soda, chilled (or a 1 liter bottle)

Mix juice concentrate with club soda. Best when chilled and served very cold or over ice cubes.

Note: Any flavor 100% juice concentrate may be used in this recipe.

Yield: 48 oz

ROMA® CAPPUCCINO

½ c	Soymilk beverage, plain (Silk®)	1 tsp	Carob powder
½ c	Water	¼ tsp	Vanilla extract
1 ½ tsp	Fructose or Sucanat®	⅛ tsp	Maple flavoring
1 tsp	Roma®, rounded		

Combine all ingredients in a blender and process on low speed until well mixed. Heat in a saucepan on the stovetop, or in a microwave oven.

Yield: 1 cup

Jingle Bells Buffet

Featuring

An assortment of appetizers, breads, salads and Christmas "goodies" perfect for your holiday drop-in parties. When entertaining family and friends, give them the special gift of deliciously healthy treats.

SPINACH-POTATO PUFFS

10 oz	Fresh spinach, chopped	2 T	Nutritional yeast flakes
1 c	Raw potatoes, finely shredded	1 T	ENER-G® Egg Replacer
1 c	Water-packed tofu, firm (mashed)	2 tsp	Chicken-style Seasoning
½ c	Onions, chopped	1 tsp	Salt (or ½ tsp-see below)
1 c	Mozzarella cheese, shredded (opt) (see page 264)	½ tsp	Onion powder
		¼ tsp	Savory, dried
½ c	Corn bread stuffing mix, (Pepperidge Farm®)	¼ tsp	Garlic powder
		⅛ tsp	Rosemary
6 T	Vital wheat gluten		

Remove large stems, rinse and steam or cook spinach until blanched. Cool and squeeze out excess liquid. (May also use 10 oz frozen spinach, thawed and squeezed dry.) Combine spinach with potatoes, tofu, onions and mozzarella cheese (opt). (If cheese is used, reduce salt listed above to ½ tsp.) In a separate bowl, combine stuffing mix with gluten flour, yeast flakes, egg replacer and all seasonings. Pour dry ingredients evenly over the spinach mixture. Stir or use hands if necessary to work mixture together well. Form into 1 ½ inch balls and arrange on a baking sheet prepared with cooking spray. Cover with a cookie sheet (up side down) or a foil "tent" and bake at 400° F, 25 to 30 minutes. Uncover and bake 10 more minutes until slightly browned. Serve plain or cover with Tomato & Herbs Italian Sauce (see recipe below).

Variation: May also use a commercial shredded soy cheese in place of the Mozzarella Cheese recipe on p. 264, but reduce the salt to ¾ tsp.

Yield: 28 balls

TOMATO & HERBS ITALIAN SAUCE

½ c	Onions, chopped	½ tsp	Oregano, dried
1 T	Olive oil	½ tsp	Basil, dried
1 can	Hunt's® Diced Tomatoes (14.5 oz)	¼ tsp	Thyme, dried (opt)
½ tsp	Garlic powder	⅛ tsp	Salt

In a saucepan, sauté onions in oil until translucent. Add tomatoes and spices. Bring to a boil. Cook about 10 minutes, stirring frequently. Pour sauce over the cooked Spinach-Potato Puffs (see recipe above) and serve.

Yield: 2 cups

NUT RISSOLES

BREAD:
1 recipe "Crescent Rolls" (see recipe below)

FILLING:

1 c	Vegetarian burger, canned	1 tsp	Beef-style seasoning
½ c	Onions, chopped	½ tsp	Garlic powder
¼ c	Celery, diced	⅛ tsp	Sage, dried
¼ c	Fresh mushrooms, chopped	¾ c	Olives, chopped
2 tsp	Olive oil	¼ c	Pecans, finely chopped
1 T	Nutritional yeast flakes	1 T	Fresh parsley, minced

Sauté burger, onion, celery, and mushrooms in oil until vegetables are tender and burger is browned. Add all remaining ingredients and mix together well. Spoon 1 T of burger mixture onto the wide end of each crescent roll wedge, roll up and fold ends under and place on a cookie sheet. Allow rolls to rise until doubled. Bake at 375° F, 18 minutes or until golden brown.

Variation: Place half a veggie wiener or a small "breakfast link" and half a slice of soy cheese (cut diagonally) inside each crescent roll and bake as directed above for a quick appetizer or meal.

Yield: 12 Rissoles

CRESCENT ROLLS

¾ c	Warm water	1 c	Whole-wheat flour
2 T	Brown sugar	4 T	Quick oats
2 T	Olive oil, "light"	1 T	Soymilk powder, plain
1 ½ tsp	Active dry yeast	1 T	Wheat germ
1 c	All purpose flour	1 tsp	Salt

Combine warm water, brown sugar, oil and yeast in a measuring cup and set aside. Combine remaining dry ingredients in a mixing bowl. Pour yeast mixture into dry ingredients and mix together to form a ball. Turn the dough out onto a floured surface and knead 5 to 8 minutes until the dough becomes like elastic. Return dough to an oiled bowl and turn to coat lightly. Cover with a clean, dry towel and place in a warm draft-free spot to rise until doubled. Punch down and roll dough out into a 12-inch circular shape, ¼ inch thick. Cut into 12 wedges. Start with the wider side and roll wedges inward. Prepare a baking sheet with cooking spray. Arrange rolls on the sheet two inches apart. Shape rolls into a crescent and allow rolls to rise until double. Bake at 375° F, 15 to 18 minutes.

Tip: Use a Bosch Bread machine for excellent results. Yield: 12 rolls

RATATOUILLE

1 med	Onion, chopped	1 sm	Zucchini, diced
2 cloves	Garlic, minced	1 tsp	Salt
1 med	Green pepper, chopped	½ tsp	Oregano, dried
2 T	Olive oil	¼ tsp	Basil, dried
1 med	Eggplant, peeled and diced	⅛ tsp	Thyme, dried(opt)
4 oz	Mushrooms, sliced and un-drained	⅛ tsp	Onion salt
1 can	Tomato sauce, herb flavored (14.5 oz)		

In a large saucepan, sauté onions, garlic and green pepper in olive oil until tender. Add remaining ingredients and simmer about 45 minutes or until vegetables are tender. Spoon into baked Pastry Cups, baked wonton wrappers, (see below) or over a brown and wild rice mixture and serve immediately.

Note: To prepare wonton wrappers, press one wrapper into a muffin tin prepared with cooking spray. Spray wrappers directly with cooking spray and bake at 350° F, 5 minutes. Remove from heat and place wrappers on a cookie sheet. Fill each wrapper with the Ratatouille mixture and return to the oven and bake an additional 5 minutes. Sprinkle with SoyCo® Parmesan Cheese Substitute before serving if desired. Serve hot.

Yield: 6 cups

POTATO-CHEESE PINWHEELS

4 c	Red potatoes, cubed	½ tsp	Onion powder
1 ½ c	Water	½ tsp	Salt
½ c	Nayonaise® (eggless mayonnaise)	1 c	Onions, chopped
¼ c	Water-packed tofu, silken	1 lg	Garlic clove, minced
1 c	Soy cheddar cheese, shredded	1 T	Olive oil
2 tsp	Chicken-style seasoning	½ c	Veggie wieners, chopped
2 tsp	Dried chives	9-inch	Pastry crust, double

Boil potatoes (unpeeled for added color) in water until tender. Drain, reserving water. Mash potatoes. Add Nayonaise® and tofu and beat until creamy. Stir in soy cheese and seasonings. In a frying pan, sauté onions and garlic in oil. Add veggie wieners and cook until lightly browned. Stir sauté mixture into potatoes. Prepare crust recipe of choice. Divide dough into two balls and roll each out into a rectangle. Divide potato mixture. Spoon potatoes onto dough 3 inches from the front edge and from side to side. Roll potatoes up in dough. Cut one inch slices off the roll and place on a baking sheet prepared with cooking spray. Bake at 375° F, 25-35 minutes or until golden. Best served hot.

Yield: 30 pinwheels

HUMMUS
(A Middle Eastern Chickpea Puree)

2 ½ c	Cooked garbanzos, drained, (reserve broth)	4 cloves	Garlic
½ c	Tahini (sesame seed butter)	1 ½ tsp	Onion powder
7 T	Garbanzo broth or water	1 tsp	Salt
6 T	Fresh lemon juice	4 oz	Canned chilies, chopped (Old El Paso® preferred)

Combine all ingredients, except chilies, in a blender and process on high speed 1 to 2 minutes until smooth and creamy. Pour out into a bowl and stir in chilies. Garnish with a few diced tomatoes, fresh parsley and paprika.

Tip: Delicious as a spread on bread and crackers, or as a dip with chips and raw vegetables. Also great spread in pocket bread stuffed with falafels, shredded lettuce and tomatoes.

Yield: 3 cups

STUFFED MUSHROOMS

½ lb	White stuffing mushrooms	½ tsp	Onion salt
¼ c	Onions, finely chopped	2 T	Fresh parsley, chopped
2	Garlic cloves, minced	¼ c	Dry bread crumbs, fine
1 T	Olive oil		

Clean mushrooms well. Remove stems and hollow out each mushroom. Mince stems and sauté with onions and garlic in oil until mushrooms are tender and onion is translucent. Sprinkle mixture evenly with the onion salt. Add parsley, stir briefly and remove from heat. Stir in bread crumbs. Mound each mushroom cap with stuffing mixture and arrange in a shallow baking dish or on a cookie sheet prepared with cooking spray. Bake at 425° F, 5 to 10 minutes or until thoroughly heated.

Variation: Stuff at least 1 lb of mushrooms, (24 or more) with the "Dinner Roast" recipe (page 262) and bake at 400° F, 20 minutes or until well done.

Yield: 12 stuffed mushrooms

WALNUT & OLIVE "CREAM CHEESE" SPREAD

8 oz	Soy cream cheese, (Tofutti®) (French onion or plain flavor)	3 T	Celery, finely chopped
½ c	Black olives, chopped	½ tsp	Onion powder
¼ c	Walnuts, chopped	⅛ tsp	Garlic powder
¼ c	Sweet onions, finely diced	⅛ tsp	Salt
		⅛ tsp	Citric acid

Combine all ingredients and stir gently until well mixed. (Be extra careful to sprinkle citric acid evenly over entire mixture before mixing to assure evenness of flavor.) If desired, garnish with finely diced red bell peppers or tomato. Serve with raw veggies or crackers. Also delicious when used to stuff celery or as a sandwich spread on bread with lettuce, tomato, sliced onion, and alfalfa sprouts.

Yield: 2 cups

STUFFED SHELLS

1 ½ c	Water	¼ c	Green pepper, chopped
½ c	Brown lentils, dried	1	Green onion, diced
¼ tsp	Salt	2 T	Fresh parsley, minced
1 med	Tomato, diced	½ c	Sour Cream Supreme (p. 288)
¾ c	Broccoli, finely chopped	12	Jumbo shells, cooked

Rinse and drain lentils. In a small saucepan combine water, lentils and salt. Bring to a boil, cover saucepan, reduce heat and simmer 20 to 25 minutes or until the lentils are tender. Drain. Cover and chill until ready to serve. Prepare vegetables. In a large bowl, toss the chilled lentils with all the vegetables except parsley. Combine the parsley and sour cream. Stir half the sour cream mixture into the lentil mixture. If necessary, season with additional salt to taste. Stuff each shell with 2 to 3 T of the lentil mixture. Garnish with a spoonful of the remaining sour cream on top of each shell. Serve shells "open side up" on a lettuce bed with a border of sliced tomatoes.

Note: For a quick alternative, use canned lentils.

Yield: 12 shells

"CHEESY" ARTICHOKE DIP

⅔ c	Cheese Sauce (see recipe below)	¼ c	Cornbread stuffing mix (Pepperidge Farm®)
1 c	Onions, chopped	2 T	Fresh parsley, minced
2 med	Garlic cloves, minced	½ tsp	Lawry's® Seasoned Salt
2 T	Olive oil	⅛ tsp	Salt
½ c	Tofu, firm	⅛ tsp	Oregano powder
2 T	Fresh lemon juice	8 oz can	Artichoke hearts, chopped

Make the Cheese Sauce recipe first and set aside ⅔ c. Sauté onions and garlic in oil until onions are translucent. In a blender, process tofu and lemon juice until smooth and creamy. Pour out into a bowl. Add stuffing mix, parsley and spices and mix well. Add artichokes, sauté mixture and cheese sauce to the tofu mixture and mix well. Spoon into an 8" x 8" pan. Bake at 350° F, 30 min.

Tip: For an attractive gourmet dip, hollow out the center of a round loaf of sour dough or pumpernickel bread. Scoop the artichoke mixture out of the pan and mound it into the hollowed out center of the bread. Serve on a large round platter and surround loaf with chunks of bread or crackers.

Yield: 3 cups

CHEESE SAUCE

1 c	Hot water	1 T	Fresh lemon juice
1 c	Cooked brown rice	1 ½ tsp	Salt
¾ c	Raw cashews, rinsed	1 tsp	Onion powder
¼ c	Sliced carrots	¼ tsp	Garlic powder
2 T	Nutritional yeast flakes		

In a blender, combine water, rice, cashews and carrots and process until smooth and creamy. Add remaining seasonings and blend well.

Yield: 3 cups

PEANUT BUTTER PATE

2 c	Tomato juice, canned	2 stalks	Celery, diced
1 c	Peanut butter, creamy (Jif®)	½ c	Cornstarch
1 sm	Onion, diced	¼ tsp	Salt
4 oz	Pimiento, finely diced		

Combine all ingredients. Pour into a double boiler, prepared with cooking spray. Steam 4 hours. Invert on a platter covered with lettuce. Garnish with cherry tomatoes and parsley. Serve with crackers or as a sandwich spread.

Yield: 4 cups

GOURMET "CREAM CHEESE" BALL

16 oz	Soy cream cheese, French onion	4 tsp	Instant Clear Jel® (instant food thickener)
8 oz	Soy cream cheese, plain (Tofutti®)	½ tsp	Salt
½ c	Raw onions, minced	⅛ tsp	Citric acid crystals (opt)
4 oz	Diced pimientos, drained	1 ½ c	Pecans, chopped
2 oz	Pimientos, crushed or puréed		
4 tsp	Dried chives		

Combine soy cream cheese, onions and pimientos, chives and stir until well mixed. Combine food thickener, salt and citric acid and sprinkle over cheese mixture evenly and mix well. Shape into a round ball and chill until firm enough to roll in chopped pecans. Press pecans gently into cheese until all sides are covered. Chill until ready to serve. Serve on a round platter with crackers or use mixture to stuff celery.

Variation: Add 1 tsp liquid smoke to the recipe to mimic a "smoked salmon" cream cheese flavor.

Tip: Spray the inside of a Jello mold with cooking spray, cover cheese ball with pecans and press into the mold. Refrigerate until firm and turn out onto serving dish.

Yield: 5 cups

PARTY "CHEESE" RING

1 ¼ c	Water	2 tsp	Onion powder
1 c	Cooked rice	2 tsp	Salt
½ c	Tofu, extra firm	½ tsp	Garlic powder
½ c	Raw cashews, rinsed	1 c	Black olives, sliced
4 T	Emes Kosher Jel® plain	½ c	Raw onions, minced
4 oz	Pimientos, drained	4 oz	Canned chilies, chopped (Old El Paso®)
3 T	Nutritional yeast flakes	2 oz	Pimientos, diced (drain)
2 T	Lemon juice		

In a blender, combine water, rice, tofu, cashews, Emes and pimientos. Process on high speed until completely smooth and creamy. Add yeast flakes, lemon juice and dry seasonings and blend again until well mixed. Pour mixture out into a bowl and stir in olives, onions, chilies and pimientos. Spray the inside of a ring-shaped jello mold with cooking spray. Pour cheese mixture into ring mold and refrigerate until set (about 3 or 4 hours). Turn out onto a round platter. Garnish inside of ring with parsley. Place about 6 cherry tomatoes and sprigs of parsley around the outside of the ring for added color. Serve with crackers.

Yield: 5 cups

LAYERED BEAN DIP

16 oz	Vegetarian refried beans	½ c	Soy sour cream
4 oz	Canned chilies, chopped	⅓ c	Soy cheddar cheese
1 T	Taco seasoning mix	½ c	Salsa, mild
¾ c	Soy cheddar cheese	¼ c	Tomatoes, diced
½ c	Guacamole, prepared	¼ c	Black olives, sliced

Combine refried beans, chilies and taco seasoning in a bowl and mix well. Shred soy cheddar cheese and fold into beans. Spread mixture on a round serving platter. Microwave 1–2 minutes until heated through and cheese is melted. Spread guacamole on top of bean/cheese mixture. Spread soy sour cream on top of guacamole. Top with additional cheese, salsa, tomatoes and olives. Garnish with tortilla chips tucked under the beans around the perimeter of the platter.

Yield: 5 cups

VEGETABLE DIP

10 oz	Frozen spinach, chopped	2 c	Sour Cream Supreme (p.288)
1 pkg	Knorr's® Vegetable Soup mix	½ c	Soy mayonnaise (Nayonaise®)
8 oz	Water chestnuts, chopped	½ c	Red bell pepper, chopped (opt)
3 stems	Green onions, chopped		

Thaw spinach and squeeze dry. Stir spinach together with remaining ingredients. Add salt to taste if needed. Cover and refrigerate 2 hours before serving. Stir again just before serving.

Variation: Replace water chestnuts with jicama, chopped.

Yield: 5 cups

RANCH-STYLE DIP

2 c	Soy Good Sour Cream (see p. 298)	2 T	Dried or fresh chives
1 pkt	Ranch flavored "dip mix"		

Combine the soy sour cream and the packet contents. Stir in chives (reserve a few to garnish the top) and chill before serving. Delicious served with raw veggies or chips.

Note: Soy sour cream purchased from a health food store may be used in this recipe but I prefer the taste when made with either of the homemade sour cream recipes in this book.

Yield: 2 cups

STRAWBERRY SURPRISE SALAD

1 ¼ c	Hot water	2	Ripe bananas, mashed
¾ c	Chiquita® "Calypso Breeze" (frozen juice concentrate)	1 c	Walnuts, chopped
¼ c	Emes Kosher Jel® (plain)	1 c	Soy sour cream, (see choices below)
16 oz	Birds Eye® Strawberries in "lite" syrup		

In a large bowl, mix water with juice concentrate and set aside. Pour ½ cup Calypso Breeze mixture into a small sauce pan, add Emes Jel® and heat stirring constantly until dissolved. Pour back into bowl of juice. Thaw strawberries and chop into smaller pieces. Add strawberries with juice, bananas and walnuts to the juice mixture. Divide mixture in half. Pour half into a large jello mold coated with cooking spray. Chill until set. Meanwhile, prepare sour cream recipe of choice and chill. Spread 1 cup sour cream over set layer of jello. Pour remaining jello mixture over sour cream and chill again until set.

Yield: 7 cups

SOUR CREAM SUPREME

1 ¼ c	Mori-Nu® Tofu, firm (10.5 oz)	1 tsp	Honey
¼ c	Sunflower oil or extra light olive oil	½ tsp	Salt
2 ½ T	Fresh lemon juice		

In a blender, combine all ingredients and process until smooth and creamy.

Yield: 1 ½ cups

"SOY GOOD" TOFU SOUR CREAM

1 box	Mori-Nu® Tofu, firm (12.3 oz)	¼ tsp	Salt
3 T	Sunflower oil or extra light olive oil	¼ tsp	Honey
¼ tsp	Citric acid crystals		

In a blender, combine all ingredients and process until smooth and creamy.

Variation: Add 1 tsp fresh lemon juice for a stronger sour taste.

Yield: 1 ½ cups

RASPBERRY JELLO FLUFF

16 oz	Frozen raspberries	¼ c	Emes Kosher Jel® plain
12 oz	Chiquita® "Raspberry Passion" (frozen juice concentrate)	1 ½ c	Instant Whipped Topping (recipe below)

Thaw raspberries and reserve juice. Stir Emes Jel into reserved juice. Heat mixture up slightly to dissolve the gelatin. Add to raspberries. Combine raspberry mixture, frozen juice concentrate and water if necessary to equal 3 ½ cups. Add ¼ cup pre-set whipped topping to the Jello mixture and hand whip until well blended. Pour half of the raspberry mixture into a Jello mold coated with cooking spray. Chill until set. Pour enough of the remaining whipped topping over Jello to measure about ½ inch thick, and return to refrigerator until set. Top with remaining raspberry mixture and chill several hours until set.

Note: If an alternative whipped topping is used in this recipe, you must add an extra tablespoon of Emes Kosher Jel® to the recipe.

Yield: 5 cups

"INSTANT" WHIPPED TOPPING

1 ½ c	Water	⅓ c	Coconut milk, canned (lite, unsweetened)
⅔ c	Soymilk powder, plain*		
½ c	Blanched almonds (w/o skins)	2 tsp	Natural vanilla, flavoring
3 ½ T	Emes Kosher Jel®, plain	¼ tsp	Salt
3 T	Fructose, powdered sugar or honey		Ice

In a blender, combine the water, milk powder, almonds and Emes Jel and process until the almonds are liquefied completely. Add remaining ingredients and process briefly. Finally, begin adding ice slowly through the lid spout and continue processing on high speed to make a total volume equal to 5 cups. Turn blender off and wait briefly. Mixture should now be light and fluffy. Best served immediately. If stored, and mixture becomes too firm, hand whip or beat gently with an electric beater before serving.

* Recommend Better Than Milk™ "Original."

Yield: 5 cups

ORANGE JELLO FLUFF

11 oz	Mandarin oranges, canned	1 box	Mori-Nu® tofu, firm (12.3 oz)
8 oz	Crushed pineapple, canned	¼ c	Soy cream cheese, plain (Tofutti®)
¼ c	Soymilk beverage, plain	¼ c	Fructose, granular
5 oz	Emes Kosher Jel®(orange flavor) (or 2 boxes, 2 ½ oz each)	½ tsp	Vanilla extract

Drain juices of oranges and pineapple into a small saucepan. Set fruit aside. Add soymilk to the juice and heat mixture until very hot. Pour into a blender, add Kosher Jel and process on a low speed 5 to 10 seconds until Kosher Jel dissolves. Add half the oranges and all of the pineapple and blend well. Add tofu, soy cream cheese, fructose and vanilla and blend again until creamy. Last, add remaining oranges and flash blend 2 or 3 times until oranges are coarsely chopped. Pour into a 5 cup Jello mold and refrigerate until set.

Yield: 4 ½ cups

CHRISTMAS ORANGE SALAD

6	Oranges (Valencia)	2 med	Bananas, sliced
½ c	Pecans, chopped	1 med	Red apple, cubed
½ c	Frozen coconut, grated		

Cut chilled oranges into slices. Remove seeds and cut orange sections away from peelings over a bowl in order to save the juice. Add remaining ingredients and toss lightly. Serve immediately.

Yield: 8 cups

PUMPKIN MOUSSE DESSERT

1 T	Emes Kosher Jel® (plain)	1 tsp	Pumpkin pie spice
⅓ c	Cold water	1 T	ENER-G® Egg Replacer dissolved in 4 T water
¾ c	Canned pumpkin, solid pack	2 c	"Instant" Whipped Topping (see recipe on page 289)
½ c	Honey	⅓ c	Pecans, chopped
½ c	Mori Nu® Tofu, firm (blended)		
½ tsp	Salt		

In a saucepan, soften gelatin in water. Stir over low heat until dissolved. Add pumpkin, honey, tofu, salt and pie spice. Cook over med. heat, stirring constantly until thoroughly heated. Cool. Whisk Egg Replacer with water until foamy. Fold into pumpkin mixture. Alternate layers of pumpkin mixture, pecans and pre-set whipped topping in parfait glasses. Chill before serving.

Yield: 6 to 8 parfaits

TOFU-BANANA BREAD #2

BLENDER INGREDIENTS:

½ c	Mori Nu® Tofu, firm	¼ c	Olive oil, "extra light"
½ c	Brown sugar, packed	¼ c	Honey
⅓ c	Soymilk beverage, plain	2 tsp	Vanilla extract
1 ½ c	Ripened bananas	2 tsp	ENER-G® Egg Replacer

DRY INGREDIENTS:

1 c	Whole-wheat flour	2 T	Wheat germ
1 c	All purpose flour	2 tsp	Baking powder
1 c	Pecans or walnuts, chopped	¾ tsp	Salt
½ c	Grape Nuts® (cold cereal)	½ tsp	Baking soda

Combine blender ingredients and process until smooth. In a large bowl, combine all dry ingredients. Pour blender ingredients into the dry mixture and stir gently until well blended. Pour into a loaf pan prepared with cooking spray. Bake at 350° F, approximately 55 minutes.

Variation: To make Banana-Nut Muffins; increase baking powder to 1 T. Fill muffin cups ¾ full, sprinkle additional finely chopped nuts on top and bake at 375° F, 25 minutes.

Yield: 1 loaf or 12 muffins

CRANBERRY BREAD

1 ½ c	All purpose flour	½ c	Walnuts
1 c	Whole-wheat pastry flour	½ c	Apple juice, concentrate
2 tsp	Baking powder	½ c	Honey
½ tsp	Baking soda	¼ c	Olive oil, "extra light"
½ tsp	Salt	½ c	Mori Nu® Tofu, firm
1 ½ c	Fresh cranberries	1 T	ENER-G® Egg Replacer

Combine dry ingredients. Chop walnuts and cranberries in a food processor and add to the dry mixture. Combine liquid ingredients, tofu and egg replacer in a blender and process until smooth. Pour into dry ingredients. Stir gently until well mixed. Pour into a loaf pan prepared with cooking spray. Bake at 350° F, 55 minutes.

Yield: 1 loaf

CAROB FUDGE

2 c	Carob chips, date or malt sweetened	1 tsp	Natural vanilla, flavoring
¼ c	Soy or almond milk	½ c	Dry coconut, grated and unsweetened, (opt)
1 c	Walnuts or pecans, chopped		
½ c	Almond, cashew or peanut butter		

Combine carob chips and milk in a saucepan. Cook over lo-med heat stirring constantly until chips are melted. (A double boiler also works well for this.) Stir in walnuts and nut butter until well mixed. Stir in vanilla last. Pour into an oblong pan, and sprinkle with coconut if desired. Chill until firm. Cut into squares and store in an air-tight container.

Yield: 3 ½ cups

TOLL HOUSE COOKIE "LOOK-A-LIKES"

1 c	Whole-wheat flour	1 c	Light brown sugar, packed
1 c	Unbleached white flour	½ c	Mori-Nu® Tofu, firm
1 tsp	Salt	2 tsp	Vanilla extract
½ tsp	Baking soda	1 c	Walnuts, chopped
8 oz	Smart Balance® "Light" (non-hydrogenated spread)	⅔ c	Carob chips

Combine flours, salt and baking soda in a bowl and set aside. In a large mixing bowl, beat Smart Balance® (softened at room temperature), sugar, tofu, and vanilla at "cream" setting until smooth and creamy (about 1 minute). Lower speed and gradually beat in flour mixture. Resume high speed and beat 1 minute more. Stir in walnuts and carob chips. Drop by heaping tablespoons onto a cookie sheet prepared with cooking spray. Allow 1 inch between cookies. Bake in a pre-heated oven on the center oven rack at 375° F, 14 minutes or until golden brown. Cool for 2 minutes. Using a spatula, transfer cookies to a wire rack to cool completely before storing.

Tip: For best results, use a heavyweight cookie sheet and bake only one pan full at a time.

Yield: 3 dozen

CARROT RAISIN COOKIES

2 c	Whole-wheat flour	½ c	Grated coconut
2 c	All purpose flour	1 c	Grated carrots
1 c	Date sugar	8 oz	Crushed pineapple
1 c	Raisins	⅓ c	Olive oil, "extra light"
1 c	Walnuts, chopped	⅓ c	Honey
1 tsp	Baking powder	2 tsp	Vanilla extract
½ tsp	Baking soda	⅔ c	Apple juice, undiluted (frozen concentrate)
½ tsp	Cinnamon, ground		
1 tsp	Salt		

In a large bowl, mix together all dry ingredients. In a separate bowl combine coconut, carrots, pineapple (un-drained), and remaining liquid ingredients. Pour mixture into dry ingredients and stir until well mixed. Spoon onto a cookie sheet prepared with cooking spray and shape with oiled fingers. Bake 20 minutes at 350° F. Cool slightly, cover and store.

Yield: 4 dozen

OATMEAL RAISIN COOKIES

2 c	Quick oats	½ c	Water-packed tofu, silken
½ c	Whole-wheat flour	½ c	Light brown sugar, packed
¼ c	Unbleached white flour	½ c	Smart Balance®, "Light" (non-hydrogenated spread)
½ tsp	Cinnamon		
¼ tsp	Salt	¼ c	Fructose, granules
½ c	Pecans or walnuts, (opt)	2 T	Molasses, mild
⅓ c	Raisins	1 tsp	Vanilla extract

Combine dry ingredients (oats thru raisins) in a medium bowl. In the large bowl of an electric mixer, combine tofu, brown sugar, Smart Balance®, fructose, molasses and vanilla and beat until creamy. Add dry ingredients and stir until evenly mixed. Prepare a heavy-duty baking sheet with cooking spray. Drop dough by spoonfuls unto the baking sheet and gently form into cookie size shapes. Bake at 350° F, 20 minutes or until lightly browned. (If using an "air-bake" sheet, increase temperature to 375° F.) Cool on a baker's rack.

Yield: 18 cookies

OATMEAL-DATE COOKIES

½ c	Date butter (see below)	½ c	Olive oil, "extra light"
2 c	Quick oats	⅓ c	Honey
1 c	Old-fashioned oats	⅓ c	Apple juice, undiluted (frozen concentrate)
1 c	Whole-wheat flour	1 T	ENER-G® Egg Replacer, mixed in 4 T water
½ c	Unbleached white flour	1 tsp	Vanilla extract
½ c	Soymilk powder, plain	½ tsp	Maple flavoring
½ c	Walnuts, chopped		
1 tsp	Salt		

Prepare date butter according to directions below and set aside. Combine dry ingredients. Combine liquids and pour into the dry ingredients and mix well. Use ⅔ of cookie mixture and drop by heaping tablespoonfuls on a baking sheet and gently shape into cookies. Take care not to press mixture together too much. Press a small "well" into the center of each cookie. Spoon 1 tsp date butter into each "well" and top with enough cookie dough to just cover. Bake in a preheated oven at 350° F, 16-18 minutes or until lightly browned. Cool slightly then place in a covered air-tight container.

Note: Make **DATE BUTTER** by combining 1 cup pitted dates with ½ cup water and simmering 2-3 minutes until soft. Cool. Mash dates well with a fork or pour into a blender and process until dates are smooth and creamy. (Yield: 1 cup)

Variation: For a delicious low-fat version, substitute half or all of the oil with equal proportions of WonderSlim® Fat & Egg Substitute.

Yield: 2 dozen

FRUIT "NUTTY" BALLS

2 c	Pitted dates	4 c	Nuts, (walnuts, almonds or pecans)
1 c	Raisins	4 c	Shredded coconut
1 c	Dried apricots		

Chop or grind dried fruits through a food processor or a grinder. Place mixture in a bowl and set aside. Then process nuts until finely chopped. Add nuts to the dried fruit mixture. Stir in 2 cups of coconut and mix well. With hands, form into 1-inch balls and roll them in remaining 2 cups of coconut. Place in an air-tight container and refrigerate until ready to serve.

Variation: Add 1 ½ T carob powder to mixture.

Yield: 60 balls

CAROB-BANANA CAKE

2 c	Whole-wheat flour	2 c	Water
1 c	Unbleached white flour	1 c	Ripened banana, mashed
½ c	Date sugar	½ c	Olive oil, "extra light"
½ c	Carob powder	½ c	Honey
2 tsp	Roma® (coffee substitute)	2 T	Lemon juice
2 tsp	Baking powder	1 T	Vanilla extract
2 tsp	Baking soda	1 T	ENER-G® Egg Replacer
1 tsp	Salt		

Combine flours, date sugar, carob powder, Roma®, leavening agents and salt. In a blender, process water with banana, oil, honey, lemon juice, vanilla and egg replacer until smooth. Combine wet and dry ingredients, stir just until moistened. Pour into two 8-inch or 9-inch cake pans prepared with cooking spray. Bake at 350° F, 30 to 35 minutes or until toothpick comes out clean and cake springs back after touch. Spread icing of choice (see below or page 296) on the completely cooled cake.

Note: Bake a 9" x 13" cake at 350° F, 50 minutes.
To make brownies, increase baking powder to 1 T, omit soda, add 1 cup chopped walnuts and bake at 350° F, 45 minutes.

Variation: May substitute date sugar with brown sugar. Decrease the amount of brown sugar to 1 ¾ cup and decrease the water to 1 ½ cups, increase baking powder to 1 T and decrease Roma® to 1 tsp.

Yield: 9" x 13" or 2 layer cake

NON-DAIRY COCONUT ICING

2 c	Better Than Milk™, beverage	⅓ c	Honey (or fructose, granular)
1 box	Mori-Nu® Tofu, extra firm	4 T	Instant Clear Jel®
2 tsp	Cook's® Vanilla, powdered (or use clear vanilla)	2 c	Frozen coconut, shredded
		2	Bananas, sliced lengthwise

Combine first 4 ingredients in a blender and process until smooth. Add the Instant Clear Jel® through the lid spout while blender is on high speed, 1 T at a time until mixture is thick. Pour icing into a bowl and stir in 1½ cups coconut. Chill. When completely cooled, slice cakes in half horizontally. Layer in order: 1) Cake 2) Sliced banana, (may dip bananas in pineapple juice to preserve color) 3) Icing 4) Repeat. Cover outside of cake with icing. Garnish top and sides of cake with remaining coconut. Chill until ready to serve.

Yield: 6 cups

DATE-NUT FROSTING

1 c	Pitted dates, packed	½ tsp	Salt
1 ½ c	Water	2 c	Pecans, chopped
½ c	Soymilk powder, plain*	2 c	Coconut, shredded
2 tsp	Natural vanilla, flavoring	¼ c	Vital wheat gluten (opt)

Simmer dates in water until soft. Cool 5 minutes. Transfer dates to a blender. Add soymilk powder, vanilla and salt and process until smooth. Return mixture to saucepan and fold in the nuts and coconut. If using frosting on a layered cake, it is necessary to add vital wheat gluten in order for the frosting to stick to the sides of the cake. If using frosting on a sheet cake, this step is not necessary. Spread frosting on cake while still warm. Sprinkle cake with additional shredded coconut for garnish and to improve appearance.

* Better Than Milk™ "Original" is the recommended product.

Yield: 5 cups

RICH 'N CREAMY CAROB ICING

1 ¼ c	Raw almond butter	¼ c	Carob powder
1 ¼ c	Sucanat® sweetener	1 T	Vanilla, extract
⅔ c	Mori-Nu® Tofu, extra firm	¼ tsp	Roma®(coffee substitute)
¼ c	Almond, rice or soymilk		

Combine all ingredients in a small mixing bowl and beat with an electric mixer until creamy. May refrigerate unused portion up to 2 weeks.

Tip: Spread the icing leftovers between graham crackers for a really quick and delicious treat kids love!

Yield: 3 cups

LITE 'N LUSCIOUS CAROB ICING

2 c	Mori-Nu® Tofu, extra firm	¼ c	Carob powder
1 c	Sucanat®, sweetener	¼ c	Cornstarch
⅔ c	Almond or soymilk, vanilla flavor	2 tsp	Vanilla extract

In a blender, combine all ingredients and process until smooth and creamy. Pour into a saucepan and cook over medium heat stirring constantly until thick. Refrigerate until cold. Cake should be cooled before spreading icing.

Yield: 3 ½ cups

BANANA CAKE

1 ½ c	Ripe bananas	1 ¾ c	Whole-wheat pastry flour
1 ¼ c	Light brown sugar, packed	1 ¾ c	Unbleached white flour
¾ c	Olive oil, "extra light"	1 T	ENER-G® Egg Replacer
⅔ c	Water-packed tofu, silken	2 tsp	Baking powder
⅓ c	Water	2 tsp	Baking soda
1 T	Vanilla extract	1 tsp	Salt

In a blender, combine bananas, sugar, oil, tofu, water and vanilla and process until smooth and creamy. In a separate bowl, combine dry ingredients. Pour blender ingredients into dry ingredients and mix well. Prepare a 9" x 13" baking dish with butter flavored cooking spray. Pour batter into dish and bake at 350° F, 35 minutes or until cake springs back to touch. Cool completely before frosting.

Note: Frost with "White Chiffon Icing" (see below) and sprinkle chopped pecans over the top. Or, cut into squares and dollop "Lemon Topping" on top (see recipe on page 298) and garnish with a small lemon twist, a slice of banana, grated coconut or chopped pecans.

Variation: Divide batter into (2) 9-inch cake pans. Bake at 350° F, 25 to 30 minutes until cake springs back to touch.

Yield: 9 x 13 sheet cake

WHITE CHIFFON ICING

12.3 oz	Mori-Nu® Tofu, extra firm	½ c	Smart Balance®, "Light" (non-hydrogenated spread)
¼ c	Soymilk beverage, plain		
8 oz	Soy cream cheese, plain (Tofutti®)	2 T	Instant Clear Jel® (instant food thickener)
1 c	Fructose, granules		

Combine tofu and soymilk in a blender and process until very smooth. Combine soy cream cheese, fructose and Smart Balance® in a mixing bowl and beat with an electric mixer on high speed until creamy. Add the tofu mixture and Instant Clear Jel® and beat again until the icing is a smooth chiffon texture. Place in the refrigerator to chill. Spread on a completely cooled cake.

Tip: This icing is a nice compliment for banana cake, carrot cake or yellow cake.

Yield: 3 cups

LEMON CHIFFON TOPPING

1 box	Mori-Nu® Tofu, extra firm (12.3 oz)	1 tsp	Vanilla, natural
¾ c	Ripened banana, mashed	¼ tsp	Lemon zest
3 oz	Pineapple juice (frozen) concentrate	1/16 tsp	Salt
1 T	Fruit Fresh® powder	1 tsp	Instant Clear Jel® (food thickener)
1 T	Powdered sugar, (opt)		

In a blender, combine all ingredients (except the instant food thickener) and process until smooth and creamy. Add the food thickener and blend 15 seconds more until pudding thickens. Chill. Yield: 2 ½ cups

HONEY-NUT SESAME STICKS

1 c	Sesame seeds	½ tsp	Salt
1 c	Almonds, finely ground	⅓ c	Honey
½ c	Whole-wheat flour	¼ c	Pure maple syrup
4 tsp	Wheat germ	1 tsp	Vanilla extract

Combine dry ingredients. Combine sweeteners, pour into dry ingredients and stir until well mixed. Spray hands or a spatula with cooking spray and press mixture out into the center of a cookie sheet until ¼ inch thick. Square edges and score nearly through into ½ inch wide by 1½ inch long sticks. Bake at 350° F, 10 to 11 minutes. Cool until sticks harden and gently break or cut into pieces at the scored marks. Yield: 60 pieces

CAROB CRISPIES

1 c	Carob chips, sweetened	4 c	Granola, dry
1 c	Peanut butter, natural	1 c	Currants or raisins
½ c	Maple syrup or honey	½ c	Nuts, chopped (walnuts, pecans, peanuts)
1 tsp	Roma®, coffee substitute	½ c	Dried coconut, grated (opt)
1 tsp	Vanilla extract		
½ tsp	Maple flavoring		

Combine carob chips, peanut butter, sweetener of choice, Roma® and flavorings in a small saucepan. Warm over medium heat stirring frequently until carob chips are melted. Mix granola, fruit and nuts together in a large bowl. Pour carob sauce over granola mixture and stir until well mixed. Prepare a 9" x 13" baking dish with cooking spray. Spread the warmed carob/granola mixture into the dish evenly and press mixture down. Spray a knife with cooking spray and cut mixture into squares. Refrigerate until cold. Break the squares apart and store in an airtight container in the refrigerator until ready to serve. Yield: 48 squares

JEAN'S CHRISTMAS FRUIT CAKE

2 c	Flax jell (see below)	6 c	Walnuts, coarsely chopped
1 T	Vanilla extract	3 c	Dried papaya, chopped
2 tsp	Almond extract (opt)	3 c	Dried cranberries (opt)
3 c	Unbleached white flour (sifted)	2 c	Dried pineapple, chopped
1 ½ c	Dark brown sugar	2 c	Raisins
1 tsp	Salt	2 c	Soft dates, chopped

Prepare flax jell according to recipe below. Strain into a bowl. Then repeat process using the same seeds the second time. Strain second batch into first recipe and add vanilla and almond flavoring to the jell before chilling overnight. Combine flour, sugar and salt in a large bowl. Add flax jell mixture and mix to make a batter. Gently work in remaining nuts and dried fruits with your hands. Line the bottom and sides of four 7-inch bread pans with parchment paper or brown paper bags cut to fit. Grease paper well with oil or cooking spray. Fill pans with cake mixture and press down to fill corners. (Or use two 9-inch round spring form pans. Cut parchment paper to fit the bottom of the pans and spray inside with cooking spray. Divide cake mixture between the 2 pans). Cover pans lightly with foil and bake at 300° F, 1 hour. Remove foil and continue to bake 10 to 20 minutes more. Remove from oven. As soon as cool enough to handle, invert bread pans to remove cakes or remove the sides of the spring-form pan. Peel off paper liners and wrap up with plastic wrap or wax paper. Then wrap in aluminum foil or any air-tight container. Keep refrigerated. (Stores good enough to eat all year long!)

Yield: 4 (7-inch x 4-inch) cakes

FLAX JELL

2 c	Water	6 T	Flax seeds, whole

Bring water a boil. Add seeds and boil 5 minutes only. Strain through a fine sieve immediately to separate the seeds from the jell. Thickens quickly as it cools.

Yield: ¾ to 1 cup

CHRISTMAS PUNCH

40 oz	Welch's® "White Grape Juice"
12 oz	Welch's® "Cran-Apple," frozen juice concentrate, diluted
12 oz	Chiquita® "Raspberry-Passion," frozen juice concentrate, diluted

Dilute frozen juices according to directions. Mix and serve from punch bowl. For a decorative addition, garnish with a frozen ice ring mold made with red grapes and holly leaves inside.

Yield: 17 cups

SPARKLING GRAPE JUICE

12 oz	White grape/peach, 100% juice (frozen concentrate, undiluted)	4 ½ c	Club soda, chilled (or a 1 liter bottle)

Mix juice concentrate with club soda. Best when chilled and served very cold or over ice cubes.

Note: Any flavor 100% juice concentrate may be used in this recipe.

Yield: 48 oz

ROMA® CAPPUCCINO

½ c	Soymilk beverage, plain (Silk®)	1 tsp	Carob powder
½ c	Water	¼ tsp	Vanilla extract
1 ½ tsp	Fructose or Sucanat®	⅛ tsp	Maple flavoring
1 tsp	Roma®, rounded		

Combine all ingredients in a blender and process on low speed until well mixed. Heat in a saucepan on the stovetop, or in a microwave oven.

Yield: 1 cup

Glycemic Index

What follows is a brief discussion of the principles of glycemic index. For a more detailed understanding visit the ADA website at www.eatright.org.

Glycemic index (GI) evaluates the effect of carbohydrate on blood sugar levels. High GI foods raise blood insulin and sugar levels quickly and higher than desirable. GI is determined by feeding various carbohydrate foods and comparing their rise in glucose levels compared to equal amounts of sugar (or white bread) eaten on a previous day. Eating high glycemic meals, compared to lower glycemic meals, results in:

- Higher 24-hour blood sugar levels
- Higher insulin levels
- Higher glycosylated hemoglobin levels (HbA1c)
- Increased hunger following reactive low blood sugar

Higher glycemic index meals also results in an increased risk for diabetes, obesity, and coronary heart disease.

It was reported in the *Journal of the American Medical Association* on May 8, 2002, that obese children who ate either instant oatmeal or steel-cut oats (instant has a high glycemic index) had different glycemic responses. The amount of calories eaten were identical for breakfast and lunch. However at supper, they ate *at lib.* After eating instant oatmeal, they ate 53% more calories at supper than after they ate the steel-cut oats. The same study reported that rats fed a high glycemic diet compared to rats fed a low glycemic diet develop marked obesity in 32 weeks. In 16 human studies, 15 studies found lower satiety, increased hunger, and higher voluntary food intake after eating high vs. low glycemic index meals.

Glycemic Index of Selected Foods

Foods	Glycemic Index*	Foods	Glycemic Index*
White Bread	***100***	Oatmeal	82
Cornflakes	130	Brown rice	79
Instant white rice	129	Whole wheat bread	73
Baked Potato	121	Pasta	71
Waffle	109	Pinto beans	55
Cheerios®	106	Apple, raw	52
White rice	91	Skim milk	46
Banana	88	Soy milk	43
Pizza	86	Fructose	32
Table sugar or honey	84	Peanuts	20
Bran Chex®	83	Broccoli	20

Glycemic Load

A better indicator of glycemic meals is to calculate the glycemic load of food items. Glycemic load is measured by multiplying the foods glycemic index as a percentage times the carbohydrate content of that food.

- **For Example:** the glycemic index of mashed potatoes = 122
- ½ cup mashed potatoes has 20 g of carbohydrate
- **Glycemic load = 20 X 1.22 = 24.4**

Summing the glycemic load of all foods in a day gives the daily glycemic load. In the Nurses Health Study, a daily glycemic load greater than 150 was linked to a higher risk of heart disease. This was reported in the American Journal of Clinical Nutrition in 2000.

Glycemic Load of Common Foods

Food	Glycemic* Index	Glycemic* Load	Food	Glycemic* Index	Glycemic* Load
Raisins, 2/5 cup	9	28	Apple juice, 8 oz.	57	12
Baked potato, sm.	121	26	Banana, 1	74	12
Instant rice, ½ cup	129	25	Pinto beans, 7/8 c	55	10
Cranberry juice, 8 oz	97	24	Waffle, 1	109	10
Rice Chex®, 1 ¼ cup	127	23	Lima beans, ½ c	46	10
White rice, 1 cup	91	23	Corn, 1 ear	78	9
Corn flakes, 2/3 cup	130	21	Popcorn, plain, 2 c	103	8
White bread, 1 slice	102	21	Apple, 1 fresh	52	8
Spaghetti, ½ cup	64	21	Soy milk, 8 oz.	63	8
Brown rice, ¾ cup	79	18	Grapes, 25	66	8
Doughnut, 1 med	108	17	WW bread, 1 sl.	73	7
Rolled oats, 1 cup	83	17	Orange, 1 med	60	5
Muffin, blueberry, 1	84	17	Peaches, 1 med	60	5
Corn chips, 2 oz.	90	17	Lentils, ½ cup	41	5
Ice cream, ½ cup	130	16	Cantaloupe, 3 sl.	93	4
Soft drink, 8 oz.	90	16	Carrot, 1 med	68	3
Pretzels, 5 twists	119	16	Green peas, ½ cup	68	3
Pastry, 1	84	15	Cashews, 1.75 oz.	31	3
Yams, 1 cup	53	13	Strawberries, 10	57	1
Cheerios®, 1 cup	106	15	Peanuts, 1.75 oz.	21	1
Orange juice, 8 oz.	71	13	Broccoli, ½ cup	20	<1

The Glycemic Load Principle

In general, high glycemic load foods are refined, lower in fiber and include the following:

- Snack foods
- Fast foods
- Pastry, cookies
- Sweets
- Soda pop
- White bread/rice
- Refined carbohydrates
- Potatoes

In general, low glycemic load foods are unrefined whole foods, higher in fiber and include the following:

- Fresh fruit & Vegetables
- Legumes, peas, beans, garbanzos, soy, tofu
- Nuts
- Whole-grain breads and cereals including oatmeal and brown rice
- Protein rich foods
- Healthy fats

It also helps to look at the effect of glycemic index and dietary fiber on the risk of diabetes as reported in the *Journal of the American Medical Association* on February 12, 1997.

In the Women's Health study, women who ate the least fiber were twice as likely to get diabetes as those who ate the most fiber. Women with the highest glycemic index were 51% more likely to get diabetes then women who ate the lowest glycemic index diet. The overall risk was 2.5 times higher on the low fiber, high GI diet. In summary decreasing the fiber in the diet leads to an increasing glycemic index.

* *American Journal of Clinical Nutrition*, 2002, Kaye Foster-Powell at al, International Table of Glycemic Index and Glycemic Load Values.

Notes

The Beauty of Antioxidants

Ever want to turn back the hands of time? Just as a nail rusts or ages from oxidizing when left in water, our bodies will age and succumb to disease from the oxidative exposure to free-radicals. To combat this process, we turn to "anti-oxidants" that act as tiny internal policemen working hard to keep us healthy by protecting us from excessive free-radical damage.

To understand this process, we must first understand the nature of oxygen. The oxygen we breathe is bound in a double molecule form as two atoms of oxygen called O2 and is vital for all life. But sometimes oxygen exists in a form that is harmful. Free radicals, or unstable oxygen molecules, consist of single atoms of oxygen constantly trying to convert to the stable O2 form. To do this they seek to join up with anything that will accept them, especially any site where there is a deficiency of oxygen. Therefore, low oxygen organisms, such as bacteria, fungus and yeasts get sizzled by frantic singlet oxygen free radicals that try to join up with them. Even cancer cells or damaged cells will be killed by this process. This is a good thing, but at the same time, we need to make sure healthy cells have a way of protecting themselves from the over zealous free radicals. The internal police force that saves healthy cells from free radical damage, aging or disease is therefore called "anti-oxidants."

Much in the same way that a beekeeper wears a protective suit to prevent being stung by thousands of angry bees, the healthy cells need a protective outer membrane made up of millions of delicate antenna-like sugar molecules called polysaccharides, a type of antioxidant. Therefore, the thicker the beekeepers suit, the better the protection. The more anti-oxidants we have, the better the free radical protection.

We can also reduce the number of free-radicals we are exposed to. Some free-radicals are unavoidable. They are in the air that we breathe, and in the toxins and chemicals on the food that we eat and they are even in the sunshine we are exposed to daily. But we can reduce our free-radical exposure by avoiding cigarette smoke, pollution, fried fats, micro-waved foods, stress, excessive sun, and toxins and chemical found in most skin care and home care products.

There are five types of damage to the cells caused by free-radicals.

1) Lipid peroxidation or damage to fat compounds in the body. A growing body of evidence suggests that the LDL "bad" cholesterol damages arteries only when it has been oxidized (combined with oxygen).
2) Cross-linking or when free radicals cause protein and/or DNA molecules to fuse together. In the skin, this is seen as a wrinkle. In the

retina, degenerative changes occur. And in the brain, amyloidal tissue forms causing Alzheimer's.

3) Membrane damage of cells destroys the integrity of the cell which in turn interferes with the cell's ability to take in nutrients and expel wastes effectively.
4) Lyposome damage results from the rupture of the digestive particles in the cell membranes causing premature death of the cell.
5) Accumulation of the pigment in skin causing "age spots" resulting from free-radical interference of cell chemistry.

There are many antioxidants found in our foods, especially in the plant based food groups. Many are classified as vitamins such as Vitamin A, C and E. Others are found in supplement forms like CoEnzyme Q10, or as OPC's found in grape seeds and in functional beverages high in polysaccharides. There are powerful antioxidants called polyphenols found in green tea, and isoflavones called genistein and diadzein in soy. But some of the most generous helpings of antioxidants belong to the most colorful vegetables and fruits (especially berries). The U.S. Department of Agriculture has developed a way to determine the antioxidant value of a food with the Oxygen Radical Absorbance Capacity Test. This test determines how well a food acts as a sponge to soak up the free radicals. Those foods that occupy and express the highest values on this scale are fruits, particularly the red and blue berries.

Antioxidants are working hard to keep us feeling young and looking young so that we may enjoy life to the fullest. Ensure that your diet includes the recommended servings of fruits and vegetables daily. If your diet is lacking, you should consider supplementing your diet with a vegetarian, pharmaceutical grade, multiple vitamin. To reduce you exposure to free radicals, look for manufactured foods free from artificial colors, flavors and preservatives. Also, consider switching to organic skin care and home care products that are free from toxic chemicals, including artificial coloring agents, artificial fragrances, petroleum based ingredients, foaming agents (bubbles), lye and man-made preservatives. For information on how to order quality supplements and safe products for you and your family, email Kathryn at: tastefullyvegan@aol.com.

Understanding the Mystery of Glyconutrients

Putting the terms “sugar and “health” together seems almost like a paradox. Most people think of sugar as being bad for you, but there are actually two kinds of sugars. One is refined or “extracellular” simple sugars which have long been associated with human disease. The other sugars are “intracellular” or complex in nature which can be found in fruits and vegetables and provide the body with the nutrition it needs. Emerging evidence shows that it is these complex types of sugars- commonly called polysaccharides or glyconutrients, are biologically active and are responsible for fighting off disease and maintaining overall health. Unlocking the mystery of glyconutrients may be one of the most important discoveries of this past century for understanding the immune system.

Glyconutrients are not vitamins, minerals, enzymes or herbals. They do not cure or heal alone, but they give your body what it needs to repair, correct and heal itself at a cellular level. There are eight essential cell sugars necessary for optimal health. Only two of these, glucose and galactose, are commonly found in foods we frequently eat.

Glyco means “sweet” and when describing a sugar or carbohydrate molecule, sugar, carbohydrate and saccharides are used interchangeably.

Glycoforms are large complex sugar molecules that combine with proteins and become glycoproteins or fats to become glycolipids which attach and coat the cell membrane surface of virtually every cell in the human body that contains a nucleus. As they dock at specific receptor sites, they appear much like little antennas that send signals and instructions to the inner workings of the cell or act as bar codes on the surface for the purpose of identification of nutrients. As the cells touch each other, they communicate their needs for nutrients, repair, hormones, and everything necessary to the cell for life. Therefore, glycoforms function as cellular recognition molecules that communicate what the body needs to remain healthy. If you are deficient in these surface sugars, the cells eventually will lack the communication system necessary to remain healthy. Even lacking tiny amounts of these sugars could have a profound effect on the immune system. If your cells can’t talk to each other or are not communicating effectively, sickness and disease could result. In some cases, the cells may become so confused that they may decide to attack healthy good cells resulting in autoimmune diseases such as MS, Lupus, fibromyalgia, and arthritis, while bad cells like cancer are left to grow and multiply because the killer cells are confused. Hormones could be misdirected, leaving you with physical and emotional problems and cells may not know which vitamins and minerals they need to absorb. Many researchers who study cellular communication proclaim it to be the most important discover in the history of modern medicine.

In test after test conducted at leading institutes around the world, polysaccharides have been shown to lower cholesterol, increase lean muscle mass, increase energy and endurance, regulate blood pressure, decrease body fat, accelerate wound healing, ease allergy symptoms, improve quality of sleep, alleviate anxiety and stress, promote cheerfulness, improve weekend digestion, and allay autoimmune diseases such as arthritis, psoriasis, and diabetes. Even viruses respond--from the common cold to the flu. The debilitating symptoms of chronic fatigue syndrome and fibromyalgia frequently abate after adding polysaccharides. And, for cancer patients, polysaccharides mitigate the toxic effects of radiation and chemotherapy--while augmenting their cancer-killing effects, resulting in prolonged survival and improved quality of life. The more doctors learn about glyconutrients, the more excited they become about their long-term fundamental health benefits…the key to a long healthy life.

We believe the polysaccharide bioactivity of the Goji berry of Himalayan origin, scientifically known as Lycium Barbarum Polysaccharides (LBP's), to be the leading whole food provider of all essential cell sugars necessary for optimal health. Goji berries contain numerous polysaccharides, with 4 primary bioactive polysaccharides newly identified in the Goji berries. Scientists determined their structural composition to be unique peptide-bound acidic heteropolysaccharides of a type never before encountered in any of the world's tens of thousands of botanical species. In fact, not only does LBP contain these 4 unique polysaccharides, but it may also be the richest source of glyconutrients and the most nutritionally dense whole food on the planet. LBP fortifies the immune system as it commands and controls many of the body's most important biochemical defense systems. To read about the medical studies and the latest research that has been reported from use of Goji berries, visit www.pubmed.com and search for Lycium Barbarum Polysaccharide.

For more information on how to order a delicious tasting nutritional beverage containing the juice of more than 2 pounds of Goji berries per liter bottle, (98% Goji berry juice of Himalayan origin, 2% grape, pear and apple concentrates) visit: www.TasteGoji.com.

References: *Sugars That Heal*, Emil Mondoa, MD
Goji, The Himalayan Health Secret, Dr. Earl Mindell, R.Ph., M.H. Ph.D.
Scientific American, January 2002 & July 2002
Science Magazine, March 23, 2001

Painting Your Plate with Colors

Remember when your Mom used to tell you to eat lots of fruit and all your vegetables every day? There are as many nutritious plant foods available for us to eat year round as there are colors in a rainbow. Colorful foods do much more for you than just looking picturesque on your plate. A diet that consists of a variety of rich colors, including ruby red, bright orange, dark green, brilliant yellow and deep purple is a good recipe for prevention. These colors are made of phytochemicals called *carotenoids*. Research has proven the more vibrant the color, the more powerful the antioxidant protection to the body.

Carotenoids, of which there are hundreds available to us, are becoming a matter of interest to researchers because of their health-promoting benefits. The carotenoids can be divided into two groups: the *carotenes* (alpha-carotene, beta-carotene, and lycopene) and the *xanthophylls* (astaxanthin, cryptoxanthin, lutein, and zeaxanthin). Carotenoids have proven to have protective effects against many chronic diseases, including heart disease, cancer, and blinding eye diseases increasingly common among seniors such as macular degeneration and glaucoma. In recent years, new studies have shown much promise that carotenoids may even inhibit tumor growth by boosting immunity in ways that assist the body in suppressing the growth of cancer cells.

Foods painted in "energetic bold red" colors not only catch your eye and look pretty on your plate, they are champions when it comes to disease fighting foods. Red is a must-have when choosing fruits and vegetables. Out of the top 20 disease fighting foods listed, 7 were red fruits and vegetables. The winners were: 1) Strawberries 2) Raspberries 3) Cranberries 4) Cherries 5) Red grapes 6) Red bell peppers and 7) Tomatoes.

Second, color your diet with "heart smart orange/yellow." You'd be hard pressed to find a group of foods that work so hard to protect your heart as well as the orange/yellow fruits and vegetables. This includes the citrus group, which also contains excellent sources of Vitamin C, known for protecting you against cancer and heart disease (by lowering homocysteine), and working as an anti-aging antioxidant. Citrus also assists in the proper absorption of many nutrients in other foods. Besides containing carotenoids, citrus foods also contain a plant dye called hesperetin. Hesperetin pigment not only adds an orange-yellow color to foods, it acts like a non-stick coating for the millions of tiny platelets in your blood which helps to keep the platelets from forming clots. This in turn helps cut the risk of heart attack and stroke. Next, we must give recognition to carrots. We already know that carrots are rich sources of alpha and beta carotenes which protect our eyes. Carrots are also effective in short-circuiting cancer cells.

Third, you must make room for the "green giants" on your plate. Dark green vegetables are among the best disease-fighters around. Eight green fruits and vegetables made the top 20 USDA list of antioxidant foods. When it comes to cancer protection, the National Cancer Institute ranks broccoli as No. 1. Broccoli is a member of the cruciferous family, as is kale, cauliflower, cabbage and brussels sprouts. Greens also contain lutein which protects the eyes from macular degeneration. And of course, we always think of spinach for providing us with iron and leafy vegetables like kale and collards for giving us rich sources of calcium for strong bones.

Finally, improve your brain power and "feast on the blues!" Blue and purple foods are superstars at protecting the body from the damage of free radicals by destroying them before they can do harm. Because they are like tiny powerhouses of antioxidant and anti-inflammatory protection, they rank at the top on the list of 20 disease fighting foods. Besides fighting heart disease and cancer, they exhibit remarkable anti-aging benefits to the brain. Eating just ½ to 1 cup of blueberries each day can improve and sharpen your memory, coordination and balance. It doesn't matter if they are fresh or frozen, blended or eaten whole, just eat them daily to feed your brain and stay mentally young longer.

But let's not forget the protective phytochemicals or plant chemicals found in whole grains, such as wheat, rice, and oats shown to reduce the risk of two of the greatest killers worldwide—cancer and cardiovascular diseases (including heart attacks and strokes) These protective phytochemicals are concentrated within the bran and germ—parts usually removed in the refining process. The germ is the life of the grain and is the area that sprouts when planted. It is rich in B Vitamins, fiber and amino acids. Refined wheat, for example, contains about 200 to 300 times *less* of these protective phytochemicals! Because of this, we can achieve the greatest health benefits by choosing whole grains, like whole wheat and brown rice, instead of refined grain products containing white flour and white rice.

Make sure that you are getting plenty of carotenoids by putting as many colors as possible on your plate at each meal. The next time you plan a meal, try a baked sweet potato (rich in alpha-carotene) with some steamed broccoli (rich in beta-carotene, and lutein). And how about some yellow sweet corn (rich in zeaxanthin) and a crisp green salad (rich in beta-carotene) topped with tomatoes, (rich in lycopene) with an olive oil and lemon dressing. Finish it off with fresh nectarines (cryptoxanthin), raspberries and blueberries for dessert.

Glossary of Ingredients

Almonds, blanched: Drop whole almonds into boiling water for not more than one minute or they will discolor. Pour into a colander and rinse under cold water. Drain. Skins will now pop off easily. Slivered almonds have already had the skins removed and usually are already blanched when purchased.

Almond butter: Almonds ground to the same consistency as peanut butter. This can be purchased at most natural food stores. You can also do this at home with a Champion Juicer. Be sure almonds are lightly roasted and you may prefer to remove the skins before grinding if almond butter is used in a pie-crust recipe.

Almond Mylk™: Manufactured by Wholesome and Hearty Foods, Inc. A rich creamy dairy milk alternative made from almonds in regular or vanilla flavor. Available at most natural food stores.

Arrowroot: Starchy flour from a tropical tuber used for thickening. Usually less processed than cornstarch. Can be substituted in equal proportions for cornstarch.

Bakon Seasoning®: Turula yeast with a natural "hickory smoke" flavor. Great on Scrambled Tofu, Hot Oatmeal or as a flavor enhancer in sandwich spreads.

Barley flour: A white, mild-flavored whole grain flour that performs well as a substitute for all purpose white flour in recipes such as pie crust, cakes, muffins and cookies. The gluten content is lower than wheat flour.

Better Than Milk™: Manufactured by Fuller Life, Inc. A dairy milk substitute made from soy, available powdered or ready to drink. Located in most health food stores. The "Original" plain (casein-free) powdered and ready to drink formulas are the products used most often in this book.

Bernard Jensen's Seasoning®: ("Natural Vegetable Seasoning and Instant Gravy"). A delicious seasoning made from soybeans, alfalfa, corn and whole wheat. It adds a savory taste to gravy, soups, patties, casseroles, etc. Available at many natural food stores.

Bragg® Liquid Aminos: An unfermented soy sauce substitute made from soybeans. It is high in amino acids and minerals, but a little lower in sodium than regular soy sauce. Look for it in natural food stores and most Adventist health food stores.

Bulgur wheat: A nutritious and easy to prepare, precooked cracked wheat. Gives a meaty texture to some entrees. Also used in salads, soups and casseroles.

Brown rice syrup: A thick, sweet syrup used interchangeably with honey or other liquid sweeteners. Available in most natural food stores.

Cardamom: A relative of ginger and native to India, this aromatic spice is used widely in Scandinavian and Indian cooking. The small black seeds have a spicy-sweet flavor. Available ground or in whole seed form.

Carob powder: A dark brown cocoa-like powder made from the highly nutritious locust bean pod, also called St. John's Bread. It is naturally sweet and high in calcium, phosphorus, potassium, iron, and magnesium. Carob is reminiscent of chocolate; however it contains no caffeine or theobromine and has half the fat of chocolate.

Cashew butter: Cashews ground to the same consistency as peanut butter. This can be purchased at most natural food stores. You can also do this at home with a Champion Juicer. Be sure cashews are lightly roasted before grinding.

Chic-Ketts®: Chicken flavored vegetable protein made by Worthington Foods, Inc. Does not contain egg whites. Look for it in the freezer section of Adventist health food stores.

Choplets®: Beef flavored vegetable protein, canned. Does not contain egg whites. Available at Adventist health food stores and some supermarkets.

Cilantro: Bright green lacy leaves and stems of the coriander plant. Used in Asian , Italian and Mexican cuisine. It is also called Chinese parsley.

Citric acid crystals: An extremely tart flavoring derived from citrons, lemons, oranges, or similar fruits. Available at some supermarkets, pharmacies and most health food stores.

Cook's® Vanilla Powder: Real vanilla in a white powder form. Available at some supermarkets and bakery supply stores. If you are unable to find this, substitute with clear vanilla found in supermarkets.

Couscous: A versatile tiny pasta originating from North Africa. The whole grain durum wheat variety is recommended as a delicious high fiber main or side dish. Since it can be prepared in minutes, its popularity continues to grow.

Date butter: Made from dates that have been simmered in water until soft and then blended until smooth. Used as a natural sweetener in several recipes. Also a delicious spread on bread, or muffins.

Date sugar: This whole food sweetener is made from ground and dried dates and is used as an excellent substitute for brown sugar. Because it is less refined, it provides less sugar grams per tsp when compared to refined sweeteners. Delicious in most cookie, cake and pie recipes.

Do-Pep®: A commercial brand for "vital wheat gluten". This flour has the highest gluten content available. Used in bread recipes to restore elasticity when the gluten content of the ingredients is low. Also works as a binder in recipes that call for eggs and is used to make meat substitutes.

Emes Kosher Jel®: An all-vegetable gelatin containing carageenan, locust bean gum, and cottonseed gum. Available plain and unsweetened, or in several flavored and sweetened varieties. Dissolves in liquids when heated and will gel as it cools. Available at most Adventists Book Centers. To locate the ABC nearest you call 1-800-235-3000.

ENER-G® Baking Powder: Made simply of calcium carbonate and citric acid. Use it in proportions 2 times that of regular baking powder and bake soon after mixing as the rising begins as soon as it is mixed. Carried in some natural food stores or mail order from Ener-G Foods, Inc., PO Box 24723, Seattle, WA, 98124, 206-767-6660.

ENER-G® Baking Soda: Consists only of calcium carbonate. Follow instructions given for Ener-G Baking Powder.

ENER-G® Egg Replacer: A non-dairy powdered leavening and binding agent used as a substitute for eggs in baked goods. It is made from tapioca flour, potato starch and natural leavening and is available at natural food stores.

Fructose: Commonly called fruit sugar because it is the main sugar in many fruits. Fructose can also be produced from corn syrup. Available in granular or liquid form.

FruitSource®: A substitute for honey. It is a natural sweetener made from grapes and grains in both liquid and granulated form. Available in most natural food stores.

Garbanzos: Also called chickpeas. In the legume family easily recognized by their pea shape with a protruding shoot, beige color and nutty flavor. Available dried or canned. Traditionally used in hummus, falafel and salads.

Garbanzo flour: Made from dry garbanzos, which have been ground into flour. Available at some natural food stores or can be made at home with a Magic Mill II flour mill.

GranBurger®: Dehydrated vegetable protein granules with an artificial beef flavor by Worthington Foods, Inc. Used as a substitute for ground beef. Available at natural food stores and Adventist health food stores.

Instant Clear Jel®: A commercially prepared pre-cooked Amioca starch derived from waxy corn. It thickens almost immediately upon contact with liquids and therefore does not require cooking. To prevent lumping, it is necessary to mix it with liquids in an electric blender. Made by National Starch and Chemical Corporation and available from bakery wholesalers or health food stores and retail bakeries. You may also call the Product Orders/Shipping Dept. at 916-637-4111, Ext. 7410 or Ener-G Foods, Inc. at 800-331-5222.

Jicama: A beet shaped root vegetable with thin brown skin and crisp, white flesh. Usually eaten raw in salads but is also delicious in stir-fry vegetables or Oriental cooking. Containing 90% water, the texture is between an apple and a pear but not as sweet. Use firm small tubers free from scrapes. Once peeled, best if eaten within 3 days.

Kitchen Bouquet: A liquid browning and seasoning sauce used in gravies and casseroles to give a rich brown color. Available in supermarkets.

Lecithin: A thick oily liquid derived from soy and used in salad dressings or baked goods. Can also be used to brush onto bake ware to provide an effective non-stick coating. Mix two parts liquid lecithin into one part vegetable oil.

Liquid smoke: Bottled hickory smoke flavoring. Available in supermarkets.

Maggi® Seasoning: A dark brown liquid seasoning similar to soy sauce used to improve the flavor of vegetables, gravies, soups and casseroles. Available in supermarkets.

McKay's® "Chicken-Style or Beef-Style" Instant Broth and Seasoning: An excellent all-vegetarian seasoning widely used to give chicken or beef flavorings to recipes. The "no-MSG, no-lactose and no-whey" variation is recommended. To order: Send requests to Tastefullyvegan@ aol.com.

Millet: Small golden whole grain kernels with a sweet nutty flavor. Rich in minerals and can be used like rice.

Mock Abalone: Also called "Cha'i-Pow-Yü" braised canned gluten by Companion®. Available in oriental food stores and many health food stores.

Mock Duck: Also called "Mun-Cha'i-Ya" braised canned gluten. Available in most oriental food stores and Adventist health food stores. Most common brand is Companion®.

Mori Nu® Silken Tofu: A smooth textured, custard-like tofu made from the soybean. It is sold in aseptic packages as a non-perishable, which gives it the advantage over water-packed tofu. It is available in soft, firm and extra-firm textures and as regular or lower fat ("lite") versions. Available at health food stores and most supermarkets.

Nutritional Yeast Flakes: An edible food yeast or "dead yeast" high in many of the B vitamins. Good tasting yeast flakes are yellow in color and have a cheese-like flavor. Common brands are KAL® (my first choice but a bit more expensive) and Red Star®.

Oat bran: Fiber-rich bran derived from the outer shell of the oat grain. Adds moisture and a hearty flavor to baked goods. Known for its distinct benefits of improving health.

Oat flour: Commercially available in most health food stores and some supermarkets. Make your own by blending 2 cups oatmeal in a blender until very fine.

Olive oil: The oil highest in mono-unsaturated fat. Delicious in Italian cooking, salads and sautéed vegetables where its distinctive flavor enhances the recipe.

Pam®: A vegetable cooking spray that can be applied to frying pans and baking dishes providing a non-stick coating. Butter, garlic and olive oil flavors are available as flavor enhancers when sprayed directly on foods before cooking.

Rice Dream®: A non-dairy milk substitute made from brown rice. Available in a variety of formulas and ready to drink. The calcium-added formula is recommended, especially for children.

Silk® Soymilk: A delicious ready to use soymilk beverage manufactured by White Wave. Available in most supermarkets and health food stores.

Smart Balance® "Light": A low fat vegan butter or margarine substitute. It contains no processed hydrogenated fats. Thus, it is naturally free of trans-fatty acids. Note that only the "light" version of Smart Balance® is vegan and the product of choice in our recipes.

SoyaKass® Cheese: Commercially prepared soy cheese available in a variety of flavors. Available at many health food stores and many health food stores.

SoyCo® "Lite & Less" Grated Parmesan Cheese Alternative: A delicious substitute for parmesan cheese. Available soy or rice based. Contains the milk protein casein.

Soy Protein Isolate: A powder from soy bean that has been defatted and has most of the carbohydrates removed. It is about 90% pure protein and is rich in iso-flavones.

Spelt: A forgotten non-hybridized wheat that has been cultivated for thousands of years. Spelt has a unique type of gluten with high water solubility that is easier to digest than gluten in common wheat. Spelt flour can be substituted in recipes to make bread, pasta and cereal.

Stevia: A dietary supplement extracted from the leaves of the stevia plant grown in South America. This intensely sweet sugar alternative can be used in hot drinks, fruit ice creams, smoothies, cookies and cakes. Available in health food stores in liquid extract, powdered and crushed leaf preparations.

Sucanat®: Made from organic sugar cane juice in granulated form. Unrefined and retains all of the vitamins and minerals provided by nature. An excellent substitute for brown sugar and can be used interchangeably in baked goods or for any recipe that calls for brown sugar sweetening.

Tahini: A thick, smooth paste or sesame butter made from ground sesame seeds. A staple of Middle Eastern cuisine high in omega fatty acids.

Tofu: Fresh soybean curd. White easily digestible curd made from cooked soybeans. High in protein. Available in Japanese-style silken (softest) tofu in shelf-stable aseptic packages often referred to as "boxed tofu". Most common name brand is Mori-Nu®. Also available in Chinese-style water-packed tubs in the refrigerated section of supermarkets. Often referred to as "fresh tofu" and available in 12, 14 or 16 oz sizes. Both types come in soft, firm and extra-firm styles. The "boxed" styles are also available as fat-reduced.

Textured Vegetable Protein or TVP: Very low fat meat substitute made from defatted soy flour that is compressed until the protein fibers change in structure. Sold in dehydrated granular or chunk form. Available in beef, chicken or unflavored varieties. Must be re-hydrated before use. Popular in recipes requiring burger, like chili, spaghetti sauce or Sloppy Joes, or in chunk form for stews. Available in most health food stores and food cooperatives.

Turmeric: An orange colored herb powder used to give a natural yellow color and a unique flavor to tofu, rice, curries and sauces. Commonly used in middle eastern and Indian cuisine.

Vanilla, Natural Flavor: An alcohol-free non-bitter vanilla made with organic vanilla beans. Perfect for flavoring recipes that do not require boiling or baking.

Vegetarian Burger Substitute: Beef flavored vegetable protein hamburger substitute available frozen, canned or dried.

Vegetarian Oyster Sauce: A delicious vegetarian mushroom sauce, which replaces oyster sauce in oriental recipes. Unfortunately, this may be very difficult to find in America. Try looking for it in oriental food stores.

Vegetarian Worcestershire Sauce: Same as the original minus the anchovies. Available in most health food stores.

Vital Wheat Gluten: This is derived from whole wheat and is the glutinous part of the grain that causes bread to be light and elastic. See also Do-Pep®.

West-Soy® "Plus" Soymilk: A delicious non-dairy beverage made from soybeans. Available in most natural food stores and some supermarkets.

Wheat bran: Derived from the outer shell of the wheat kernel. A good source of protein, B vitamins, iron and phosphorus. Adds fiber content and bulk.

Wheat germ: The most vital part of the wheat kernel - the heart. It is rich in protein, iron, vitamin B1 and vitamin E. Available raw or toasted.

Whole-wheat flour: Flour containing all of the wheat including the bran and the germ. Contains high amounts of fiber and nutrients.

Whole-wheat pastry flour: Made from "soft wheat" and has a lower gluten content. The best flour to use for most non-yeasted or "quick-raised" baked goods such as muffins, scones, cookies, cakes and pie crusts.

WonderSlim® Fat & Egg Substitute: Replaces high-fat shortenings or oil in the recipe. It is made from plums and is becoming widely available in natural food stores. Other similar brands are Lighter Bake® or Just Like Shortnin'™.

Notes

Recommended Newsletters & Journals

These journals and newsletters are not all promoters of vegetarianism however the food and nutrition information is sound. Visit their sites on the Internet for ordering information. Most are inexpensive. Some are free. While this list is not all-inclusive it is representative of all that is available.

Scientific Health and Medical Journals

1. American Journal of Clinical Nutrition (AJCN), **www.ajcn.org**
2. American Journal of Epidemiology, **www.jhsph.edu/Publications/JEPI**
3. British Medical Journal (BMJ), **www.bmj.com**
4. CA – A Cancer Journal for Clinicians, **www.ca-journal.org**
5. Circulation, **http://circ.ahajournals.org/**
6. Journal of the American Dietetic Association(JADA),**www.eatright.org**
7. Journal of the American Medical Association (JAMA), **www.jama.com**
8. Journal of the National Cancer Institute, **http://jnci.oupjournals.org**
9. Medicine and Science in Sports and Exercise, **www.acsm-msse.org**
10. New England Journal of Medicine (NEJM), **www.nejm.com**
11. PUBMED, **www.ncbi.nlm.nih.gov/PubMed**

Health Journals for the General Public

1. Health and Fitness, **www.acsm-healthfitness.org**
2. Health News by the New England Journal of Medicine (NEJM)
3. Journal of Health and Healing, **www.tagnet.org/wildwood**
4. Nutrition Action, **http://www.cspinet.org**
5. Vibrant Life, **www.vibrantlife.com**

Government Health Agencies

1. Agency for Healthcare Research and Quality (AHRQ) **www.ahcpr.gov**
2. Centers for Disease Control and Prevention CDCP) **www.cdc.gov/cdc**
3. Food And Drug Administration (FDA) **www.fda.gov**
4. National Institutes of Health (NIH) **www.nih.gov**
5. National Cholesterol Educational Program (NCEP) **www.nhlbi.nih.gov/about/ncep/index**
6. National Center for Health Statistics **www.cdc.gov/nchs/default.htm**
7. National Heart Lung and Blood Institute **www.nhlbi.nih.gov/index.htm**
8. US Department of Health and Human Services (DHHS) **www.hhs.gov**
9. United States Department of Agriculture (USDA) **www.usda.gov**

Health Letters

1. **The American Institute for Cancer Research Newsletter,** 1759 R Street NW, Washington, DC, 20009. Free. www.aicr.org

2. **Clinical Pearls News, A Health Letter on Current Research in Nutrition and Preventive Medicine**, www.clinicalpearls.com

3. **Harvard Health Letter**, Subscription Department, PO Box 420299, Palm Coast, FL, 32142-9858. http://www.health.harvard.edu/

4. **Harvard Heart Letter**, P.O. Box 420235, Palm Coast, FL 32142 www.health.harvard.edu

5. **Health After 50**, published by Johns Hopkins Medical Letter, www.hopkinsafter50.com

6. **Healthy Choices Newsletter**, LifeLong Health, 15431 SE 82nd Dr., Suite G, Clackamas, OR 97015-0569, (503) 557-9545, http://www.lifelonghealth.org

7. **Mayo Clinic Nutrition Letter**, www.mayo.edu/healthinfo/public

8. **Nutrition Action Health Letter**, Center For Science in the Public Interest, 1875 Connecticut Ave NW, Suite 300, Washington DC USA, 20009-5728. www.cspinet.org

9. **Sloan-Kettering Cancer Letter,** www.mskcc.org

10. **Vegetarian Nutrition and Health Letter,** 1707 Nichol Hall, School of Public Health, Loma Linda University, Loma Linda, CA 92350, 888-558-8703 vegletter@sph.llu.edu

Other Reprints

1. **Current Issues in Vegetarian Nutrition: Proceedings of an International Conference, 1996,** Edited by Winston Craig, PhD, RD, Department of Nutrition, Andrews University, Berrien Springs, MI 49104-0210.

2. **Nutrition 2000, Proceedings of an International Vegetarian Conference, 1994,** edited by Winston Craig, PhD, RD, Department of Nutrition, Andrews University, Berrien Springs, MI 49104-0210.

3. **Third International Congress on Vegetarian Nutrition, March 24–26, 1997, Supplement to The American Journal of Clinical Nutrition,** September 1999, Volume 70, Number 3(S).

Nutritional Analysis[1]

Recipe	Serv Size	Cal	Prot gm	Carb gm	Fiber Total gm	Fat Total gm	Fat Sat gm	Fat Mono gm	Fat Poly gm	Vit B12 mcg	Vit D mcg	Ca mg	Fe mg	Na mg	Zn mg
Almond Apple Bar	1	131	2.9	17.8	1.6	5.7	0.5	3.3	1.5	0.7	0.0	68	0.8	84	0.2
Almond Barley Crust	1/12	179	3.8	16.1	1.9	12.3	1.0	7.6	2.9	0.0	0.0	31	0.8	179	0.3
Almond Broccoli Stir-Fry	1 c	152	10	15	5.0	7.7	1.0	3.8	2.2	0.0	.08	153	4.1	146	0.8
Almond Cheesecake Delight	¼ c	172	5.4	19.1	.95	8.8	.9	4.9	2.4	.08	0.0	110	2.4	99	.82
Almond Cream	1/3 c	50	1.7	1.5	1.05	4.0	0.0	0.0	0.0	0.0	0.0	20.6	0.3	44	.026
Almond Pie Crust	1/12	88	1.8	7.8	.93	6.1	.5	3.81	1.43	0.0	0.0	15.4	.41	89	.16
Alpine Cheese	1 T	19	0.48	2.41	0.21	0.84	0.17	0.48	0.15	0.0	0.0	8.17	0.17	93	0.15
American Cheese Sauce	2 T	28.6	1.33	2.87	0.31	1.47	0.16	0.80	0.43	0.0	0.0	16.3	0.62	103	0.16
Apple Butter	2 t	14.6	.09	3.7	.15	.02	.01	0.0	.01	0.0	0.0	1.83	.07	1.07	.01
Apple Crisp, Old Fashioned	½ c	202	2.0	38	3.0	5.0	1.0	2.0	2.0	0.0	0.0	23	1.0	58	tr
Apple Crisp Quick & Easy	½ c	200	3.0	34	2.0	7.0	1.0	3.0	3.0	0.0	0.0	13	1.0	91	tr
Apple Spice Butter	2 t	5.1	.02	1.34	.15	.01	0.0	0.0	0.0	0.0	0.0	.7	.03	1.4	.01
Apple Spice Jam	1 T	11.4	0.04	3.0	0.2	0.02	0.0	0.0	0.01	0.0	0.0	1.6	0.07	2.6	0.01
Apricot Jam	1 T	27	0.35	7.0	0.7	0.05	0.01	0.02	0.01	0.0	0.0	5.6	0.45	1.0	0.1
Arroz Mexicano	½ c	115	2.0	21	2.0	3.0	tr	2.0	tr	0.0	0.0	17	1.0	243	tr
Asparagus Almond Crepes	1	109	5.2	12.1	3.3	4.8	0.06	0.01	0.09	0.0	0.0	50.4	1.19	384	0.78
Auto Bread Machine Bread	1 sl	99	3.6	16.4	2.1	2.2	0.2	1.1	0.5	0.0	0.0	7.0	1.0	167	0.07
Baby Limas, Savory	½ c	80	4.0	15	3.0	tr	tr	tr	tr	0.0	0.0	23	1.0	328	tr
Baked Corn Fritters	1	128	2.8	23	1.5	2.8	0.2	1.5	0.8	.08	0.0	57	1.2	206	0.3
Baked Egg Rolls	2	111	5.7	15.7	1.9	3.0	0.4	1.3	0.7	0.0	0.0	33	0.9	396	0.3
Baked Eggplant Parmesan	2	157	3.8	21.3	2.8	7.2	1.3	2.7	2.8	0.0	.08	46.3	1.9	761	.59
Barbecue Sauce	1 T	16	0.4	4.0	0.3	0.02	0.0	0.0	0.01	0.0	0.0	13	0.4	151	0.03
Barley Nut Waffles	1	273	8.5	45.3	9.6	7.9	0.9	4.2	2.2	0.04	0.0	74	2.7	284	2.4
Basic Nut Milk	1 c	117	3.6	6.6	1.7	9.3	0.9	6.0	2.0	0.0	0.0	4.8	0.7	91	0.5

[1] This table is only an approximate guide to the nutrient content of the ingredients used in these recipes. tr = trace

Recipe	Serv Size	Cal	Prot gm	Carb gm	Fiber Total gm	Fat Total gm	Fat Sat gm	Fat Mono gm	Fat Poly gm	Vit B12 mcg	Vit D mcg	Ca mg	Fe mg	Na mg	Zn mg
Better Mustard	1 t	8.6	0.06	0.44	0.03	0.77	0.05	0.47	0.21	0.0	0.0	0.36	0.04	17.7	0.0
Better Than Milk Combo	1 c	112	2.0	22	0.0	0.8	0.0	0.0	0.0	0.4	0.4	427	0.05	152	0.0
Black Eyed Pea Stew	1 c	159	11	22	6.3	3.6	0.7	2.1	0.7	0.6	0.0	111	1.9	252	1.1
Black Eyed Peas	½ c	58.4	1.9	12.3	2.97	0.23	0.06	0.02	0.1	0.0	0.0	73.1	0.65	2.6	0.6
Blackberry Jam	2 t	10	0.06	2.5	0.22	0.03	0.01	0.0	0.01	0.0	0.0	2.01	0.04	0.28	0.02
Blue Ribbon Baked Beans	½ c	39.3	.84	7.3	.92	.92	.13	.63	.1	0.0	0.0	13.4	.41	42	.19
Blueberry Oat Bran Muffins	1	180	2.6	28.2	1.7	7.2	.64	3.97	2.07	0.0	.18	101	1.2	320	.34
Blueberry Jam	2 t	21	tr	5.0	tr	tr	tr	tr	tr	0.0	0.0	1.0	tr	2.0	tr
Blueberry Topping	2 T	24.7	.17	6.4	.5	.08	.01	.02	.05	0.0	0.0	2.1	.06	2.3	.02
Blueberry Yum Yum	1/12	287	6.6	47	2.4	8.6	1.2	3.9	1.6	0.1	0.0	127	1.8	185	0.6
Bosch Whole Wheat Bread	1 sl	114	3.6	21	2.9	2.2	0.2	1.1	0.7	0.0	0.0	9.3	1.2	205	0.7
Breading Meal #1	1 T	26	0.86	5.4	0.61	0.13	0.02	0.02	0.05	0.0	0.0	3.03	0.34	73.2	0.12
Breading Meal #2	1 T	25	.71	4.9	.25	.27	.05	0.0	.06	0.0	0.0	3.7	.31	134	.05
Bread, Spelt	1 sl	221	8.0	48	10	3.0	tr	1.0	1.0	0.0	0.0	4.0	2.0	179	tr
Breakfast Banana Crisp	½ c	254	7.0	42.5	4.4	6.8	2.6	1.6	2.0	0.04	0.0	57	2.0	214	1.7
Breakfast Scones	1	102	2.6	16.8	1.6	2.8	0.2	1.5	0.8	0.05	0.0	41	1.0	100	0.1
Broccoli Cheese Rice Ring	½ c	93	3.5	16	2.3	2.0	0.4	0.9	0.5	0.0	0.0	41	1.2	232	0.6
Broccoli Cheese Soup	1 c	77	2.7	10.9	1.15	2.74	0.51	1.46	0.47	0.05	0.0	49.6	0.96	355	0.48
Broccoli in Lemon Sauce	½ c	40.2	1.3	3.3	1.2	2.8	.19	1.65	.79	.03	0.0	35.2	.37	60	.15
Broccoli with Cheese Sauce	½ c	49	3.0	4.0	1.0	3.0	tr	1.0	1.0	0.0	0.0	39	1.0	247	tr
Burritos Supreme	1/3	193	9.0	25	3.0	7.0	1.0	3.0	1.0	0.0	0.0	57	2.0	518	tr
Cabbage & Walnut Stir-Fry	½ c	30	1.0	3.3	1.3	1.7	0.2	0.6	0.85	0.0	0.0	16	0.2	60	0.1
Cake, Banana	1/48	95	2.0	15	1.0	4.0	tr	2.0	1.0	0.0	0.0	40	tr	119	tr
Cake, Oatmeal, Lazy Daisy	1/48	100	1.5	18	1.5	2.5	tr	1.5	1.0	0.0	0.0	57	0.5	131	0.5
Carob Banana Cake	1/24	88	1.22	16.5	1.75	2.45	0.19	1.4	0.68	0.0	0.0	24.9	0.49	113	0.21
Carob Chip Cookies	1	123	2.3	16.1	1.3	5.9	0.7	2.6	2.2	0.04	0.0	47.5	0.6	49	0.2
Carob Crispies	1/48	131	3.0	16	2.0	7.0	2.0	2.0	2.0	0.0	0.0	17	1.0	3.0	tr
Carob Fudge	1 T	72	1.7	5.0	0.8	5.4	0.9	2.7	1.5	0.08	0.0	46	0.3	13	0.25
Carob Pecan Milk	1 c	159	3.6	18.4	0.9	8.2	1.6	4.7	1.4	0.3	0.0	196	1.2	158	1.0

Recipe	Serv Size	Cal	Prot gm	Carb gm	Fiber Total gm	Fat Total gm	Fat Sat gm	Fat Mono gm	Fat Poly gm	Vit B12 mcg	Vit D mcg	Ca mg	Fe mg	Na mg	Zn mg
Carrot Bisque	1 c	222	5.4	22.8	3.4	13.8	2.67	8.16	2.32	0.0	0.0	45.6	2.28	356	1.86
Carrot Cake with Frosting	1/36	159	2.2	20.8	1.6	7.9	1.7	3.6	2.3	0.0	0.0	32	0.8	200	0.4
Carrot Pineapple Salad	½ c	135	2.8	18	1.6	6.6	0.9	3.8	1.6	0.0	0.0	34	1.4	58	0.8
Carrot Raisin Cookie	1	105	1.2	18	1.2	3.5	.52	1.3	1.5	0.0	0.0	17	.73	68	.3
Carrots & Orange Sauce	1/3 c	42.4	.55	10.5	1.04	.09	.01	.01	.03	0.0	0.0	13.7	.25	58.1	.01
Cashew Apple French Toast	1	165	4.1	24	1.8	6.4	1.4	3.5	1.1	0.0	0.1	24	1.7	233	0.9
Cashew Banana French Toast	1	185	5.7	28	2.9	6.8	1.4	3.7	1.2	0.0	0.07	34	2.1	391	1.4
Cashew Barley Crust	1/12	179	4.2	17.8	1.8	11.3	1.4	6.7	2.5	0.0	0.0	6.8	1.09	0.35	0.75
Cashew Gravy	¼ c	53	1.6	4.7	0.25	3.2	0.6	1.9	0.5	0.0	0.0	6.0	0.5	194	0.4
Cashew Jack Cheese	2 T	45	1.19	5.62	.53	2.1	.42	1.2	.38	0.0	0.0	25.2	.4	232	.37
Casserole, Angel Hair Pasta	½ c	125	7.0	16	2.0	4.0	tr	1.0	1.0	0.0	0.0	47	1.0	374	1
Casserole, Vege Walnut	½ c	198	15	77	2.0	11	1.0	4.0	4.0	0.9	0.0	79	2.0	407	1.0
Cereal 2-Grain Hot	1 c	176	7.0	32	6.0	3.0	tr	tr	1.0	0.0	0.0	15	2.0	188	1.0
Champagne Chicken	1 c	183	10	14	1.6	9.6	1.0	3.6	0.9	0.2	0.4	143	1.0	604	0.7
Chapatti, Garbanzo Roti	1 ea	68	2.0	11	2.0	2.0	tr	1.0	tr	0.0	0.0	12	1.0	135	tr
Chapatti, Whole Wheat	1 ea	133	5.0	26	3.0	2.0	tr	1.0	1.0	0.0	0.0	31	1.0	69	1.0
Cheese Enchiladas	1	186	13	13.6	2.0	10.2	1.6	4.0	4.0	0.0	0.0	174	8.4	775	1.4
Cheese Ring, Party	¼ c	31	1.0	4.0	1.0	1.0	tr	1.0	tr	0.0	0.0	13	tr	138	tr
Cheese Sauce	1 T	24	.84	2.2	.44	1.4	.11	.85	.34	0.0	0.0	1.4	.08	73	.06
Cheesy Artichoke Dip	1 T	11	0.36	1	0.29	0.67	0.08	0.42	0.11	0.0	0.0	1.97	0.05	31.1	0.02
Cheesy Delights	½	82	3.5	14.2	3.4	1.9	0.3	0.87	0.53	0.0	0.0	92	1.4	282	0.63
Cheesy Hashbrown Casserol	½ c	102	2.2	19.4	1.1	1.4	.14	.43	.30	0.0	0.0	24	.48	187	.07
Chicken & Rice Casserole	1/24	98	3.5	12.9	0.9	3.6	0.5	1.3	0.4	0.02	0.02	21.6	0.6	174	0.3
Chicken & Sausage Gumbo	½ c	171	8.9	21.6	3.13	5.5	0.54	2.57	2.02	0.32	0.0	62.5	2.24	509	0.73
Chicken Enchiladas	1	98	4.5	12.3	.93	3.5	.19	.92	.17	.01	.01	58	.38	152	.07
Chicken Kelaguen	½ c	130	9.4	4.3	2.4	8.8	4.1	1.6	2.8	0.82	0.0	17	1.5	412	0.51
Chicken Mushroom Crepes	1	202	9.95	16.7	2.2	10.7	1.5	4.8	3.6	0.81	0.38	134	1.7	721	0.51
Chicken Noodle Soup	1 c	144	9	15.3	2.48	5.39	0.47	1.69	0.3	0.0	0.0	22.3	0.95	626	0.38
Chicken Style Pot Pie	1/30	190	6.9	21.3	2.8	9.0	0.6	4.2	1.8	0.0	0.04	22	1.0	380	0.4

Recipe	Serv Size	Cal	Prot gm	Carb gm	Fiber Total gm	Fat Total gm	Fat Sat gm	Fat Mono gm	Fat Poly gm	Vit B12 mcg	Vit D mcg	Ca mg	Fe mg	Na mg	Zn mg
Carrot Bisque	1 c	222	5.4	22.8	3.4	13.8	2.67	8.16	2.32	0.0	0.0	45.6	2.28	356	1.86
Carrot Cake with Frosting	1/36	159	2.2	20.8	1.6	7.9	1.7	3.6	2.3	0.0	0.0	32	0.8	200	0.4
Carrot Pineapple Salad	½ c	135	2.8	18	1.6	6.6	0.9	3.8	1.6	0.0	0.0	34	1.4	58	0.8
Carrot Raisin Cookie	1	105	1.2	18	1.2	3.5	.52	1.3	1.5	0.0	0.0	17	.73	68	.3
Carrots & Orange Sauce	1/3 c	42.4	.55	10.5	1.04	.09	.01	.01	.03	0.0	0.0	13.7	.25	58.1	.01
Cashew Apple French Toast	1	165	4.1	24	1.8	6.4	1.4	3.5	1.1	0.0	0.1	24	1.7	233	0.9
Cashew Banana French Toast	1	185	5.7	28	2.9	6.8	1.4	3.7	1.2	0.0	0.07	34	2.1	391	1.4
Cashew Barley Crust	1/12	179	4.2	17.8	1.8	11.3	1.4	6.7	2.5	0.0	0.0	6.8	1.09	0.35	0.75
Cashew Gravy	¼ c	53	1.6	4.7	0.25	3.2	0.6	1.9	0.5	0.0	0.0	6.0	0.5	194	0.4
Cashew Jack Cheese	2 T	45	1.19	5.62	.53	2.1	.42	1.2	.38	0.0	0.0	25.2	.4	232	.37
Casserole, Angel Hair Pasta	½ c	125	7.0	16	2.0	4.0	tr	1.0	1.0	0.0	0.0	47	1.0	374	1
Casserole, Vege Walnut	½ c	198	15	77	2.0	11	1.0	4.0	4.0	0.9	0.0	79	2.0	407	1.0
Cereal 2-Grain Hot	1 c	176	7.0	32	6.0	3.0	tr	tr	1.0	0.0	0.0	15	2.0	188	1.0
Champagne Chicken	1 c	183	10	14	1.6	9.6	1.0	3.6	0.9	0.2	0.4	143	1.0	604	0.7
Chapatti, Garbanzo Roti	1 ea	68	2.0	11	2.0	2.0	tr	1.0	tr	0.0	0.0	12	1.0	135	tr
Chapatti, Whole Wheat	1 ea	133	5.0	26	3.0	2.0	tr	1.0	1.0	0.0	0.0	31	1.0	69	1.0
Cheese Enchiladas	1	186	13	13.6	2.0	10.2	1.6	4.0	4.0	0.0	0.0	174	8.4	775	1.4
Cheese Ring, Party	¼ c	31	1.0	4.0	1.0	1.0	tr	1.0	tr	0.0	0.0	13	tr	138	tr
Cheese Sauce	1 T	24	.84	2.2	.44	1.4	.11	.85	.34	0.0	0.0	1.4	.08	73	.06
Cheesy Artichoke Dip	1 T	11	0.36	1	0.29	0.67	0.08	0.42	0.11	0.0	0.0	1.97	0.05	31.1	0.02
Cheesy Delights	½	82	3.5	14.2	3.4	1.9	0.3	0.87	0.53	0.0	0.0	92	1.4	282	0.63
Cheesy Hashbrown Casserol	½ c	102	2.2	19.4	1.1	1.4	.14	.43	.30	0.0	0.0	24	.48	187	.07
Chicken & Rice Casserole	1/24	98	3.5	12.9	0.9	3.6	0.5	1.3	0.4	0.02	0.02	21.6	0.6	174	0.3
Chicken & Sausage Gumbo	½ c	171	8.9	21.6	3.13	5.5	0.54	2.57	2.02	0.32	0.0	62.5	2.24	509	0.73
Chicken Enchiladas	1	98	4.5	12.3	.93	3.5	.19	.92	.17	.01	.01	58	.38	152	.07
Chicken Kelaguen	½ c	130	9.4	4.3	2.4	8.8	4.1	1.6	2.8	0.82	0.0	17	1.5	412	0.51
Chicken Mushroom Crepes	1	202	9.95	16.7	2.2	10.7	1.5	4.8	3.6	0.81	0.38	134	1.7	721	0.51
Chicken Noodle Soup	1 c	144	9	15.3	2.48	5.39	0.47	1.69	0.3	0.0	0.0	22.3	0.95	626	0.38
Chicken Style Pot Pie	1/30	190	6.9	21.3	2.8	9.0	0.6	4.2	1.8	0.0	0.04	22	1.0	380	0.4

Creamy Italian Dressing	2 T	63	3.0	3.0	tr	5.0	1.0	3.0	1.0	0.0	0.0	54	1.0	69	tr
Creamy Mushroom Sauce	¼ c	54.3	1.3	7.9	0.48	1.9	0.25	1.25	0.17	0.1	0.16	72.1	0.4	274	0.09
Creamy Vegetable Soup	1 c	106	3.0	15	1.8	4.8	0.7	2.4	0.6	0.0	0.0	22.7	0.9	458	0.6
Crescent Rolls	1	97	3.0	17.5	1.7	1.7	0.2	0.8	0.4	0.03	0.0	25	1.1	184	0.09
Crispy Corn Chips	4	24	.5	4.75	0.0	.25	0.0	0.0	0.0	0.0	0.0	20	0.1	1.25	0.0
Curried Garbanzos	½ c	110	4.0	17	3.0	3.0	tr	2.0	1.0	0.0	0.0	37	1.0	419	1.0
Date & Walnut Bread	1 sl	167	3.4	31	3.4	4.6	.44	1.5	2.4	0.0	0.0	84	1.2	303	.71
Date Nut Frosting	2 T	86.1	1.02	6.82	1.3	6.61	2.56	2.62	1.02	0.06	0.0	45	0.31	40.3	0.42
Date Pecan Pie	1/12	345	4.7	43	3.2	18.9	1.5	11.5	4.9	0.0	0.0	33	1.7	118	1.6
Dessert Topping, Soy	2 T	50	2.0	9.0	tr	1.0	tr	tr	1.0	0.0	0.0	24	1.0	23	tr
Dinner Roast	1/24	98	5.0	8.0	0.5	5.6	0.7	2.7	1.6	1.3	0.2	61	5.4	220	3.0
Dip, Layered Bean	1 T	13	1.0	1.0	tr	1.0	tr	tr	tr	0.0	0.0	3.0	tr	57	tr
Dip, Ranch-Style	2 T	5.0	tr	1.0	tr	tr	0.0	0.0	0.0	0.0	0.0	tr	tr	210	tr
Enchilada Sauce	1	23	.84	4.4	.94	.63	.08	.3	.12	0.0	0.0	20	.83	305	.18
Enchilada, Spinach Cheese	1/2	74	4.0	9.0	1.0	3.0	tr	1.0	1.0	0.0	0.0	37	1.0	341	tr
English Trifle	½ c	189	7.0	39	3.5	1.8	0.3	0.4	1.9	0.04	0.0	106	2.8	78	0.3
Falafel	2 ea	135	4.0	22	3.0	3.0	tr	2.0	1.0	tr	0.0	43	2.0	466	1.0
Fat-Free Italian Dressing	2 T	22.9	.08	6.3	.05	.03	.01	0.0	.01	0.0	0.0	3.03	.06	259	.02
Flax Seed Jell	1 T	24	1.0	2.0	1.0	2.0	tr	tr	1.0	0.0	0.0	10	tr	3.0	tr
French Dressing	2 T	21	0.22	5.25	0.2	0.06	0.01	0.0	0.03	0.0	0.0	4.2	0.16	151	0.04
French Onion Soup	1 c	109	1.87	12.5	1.75	5.5	0.75	3.86	0.52	0.0	0.0	25.1	0.37	692	0.27
French Tarts	1	144	2.8	21	1.23	6.3	1.02	3.5	1.3	0.04	0.0	65.2	0.77	122	0.47
Fruit Pudding Compote	1 c	161	4.2	32	2.5	3.1	1.04	.38	.94	0.0	0.0	43	2.3	6.4	.48
Fresh Spring Rolls	1	69	3.9	11	1.2	1.5	0.2	0.3	0.7	0.0	0.0	54	2.3	116	0.36
Frozen Fruit Ice Cream	½ c	105	1.7	23.8	1.7	.62	.07	.05	.12	.3	0.0	209	.37	61.4	.14
Fruit Filled Sweet Rolls	1	173	4.2	31.8	3.4	4.1	0.4	1.3	1.9	0.0	0.0	18	1.5	135	0.2
Fruit Nutty Balls	1	98	2.5	9.5	1.51	6.6	1.9	1.15	3.15	0.0	0.0	9.5	0.57	203	0.38
Fruit Sweetened Granola	½ c	220	5.7	26.3	3.7	6.4	0.9	2.8	2.1	0.0	0.0	30	10.2	92	1.0

Creamy Italian Dressing	2 T	63	3.0	3.0	tr	5.0	1.0	3.0	1.0	0.0	0.0	54	1.0	69	tr
Creamy Mushroom Sauce	¼ c	54.3	1.3	7.9	0.48	1.9	0.25	1.25	0.17	0.1	0.16	72.1	0.4	274	0.09
Creamy Vegetable Soup	1 c	106	3.0	15	1.8	4.8	0.7	2.4	0.6	0.0	0.0	22.7	0.9	458	0.6
Crescent Rolls	1	97	3.0	17.5	1.7	1.7	0.2	0.8	0.4	0.03	0.0	25	1.1	184	0.09
Crispy Corn Chips	4	24	.5	4.75	0.0	.25	0.0	0.0	0.0	0.0	0.0	20	0.1	1.25	0.0
Curried Garbanzos	½ c	110	4.0	17	3.0	3.0	tr	2.0	1.0	0.0	0.0	37	1.0	419	1.0
Date & Walnut Bread	1 sl	167	3.4	31	3.4	4.6	.44	1.5	2.4	0.0	0.0	84	1.2	303	.71
Date Nut Frosting	2 T	86.1	1.02	6.82	1.3	6.61	2.56	2.62	1.02	0.06	0.0	45	0.31	40.3	0.42
Date Pecan Pie	1/12	345	4.7	43	3.2	18.9	1.5	11.5	4.9	0.0	0.0	33	1.7	118	1.6
Dessert Topping, Soy	2 T	50	2.0	9.0	tr	1.0	tr	tr	1.0	0.0	0.0	24	1.0	23	tr
Dinner Roast	1/24	98	5.0	8.0	0.5	5.6	0.7	2.7	1.6	1.3	0.2	61	5.4	220	3.0
Dip, Layered Bean	1 T	13	1.0	1.0	tr	1.0	tr	tr	tr	0.0	0.0	3.0	tr	57	tr
Dip, Ranch-Style	2 T	5.0	tr	1.0	tr	tr	0.0	0.0	0.0	0.0	0.0	tr	tr	210	tr
Enchilada Sauce	1	23	.84	4.4	.94	.63	.08	.3	.12	0.0	0.0	20	.83	305	.18
Enchilada, Spinach Cheese	1/2	74	4.0	9.0	1.0	3.0	tr	1.0	1.0	0.0	0.0	37	1.0	341	tr
English Trifle	½ c	189	7.0	39	3.5	1.8	0.3	0.4	1.9	0.04	0.0	106	2.8	78	0.3
Falafel	2 ea	135	4.0	22	3.0	3.0	tr	2.0	1.0	tr	0.0	43	2.0	466	1.0
Fat-Free Italian Dressing	2 T	22.9	.08	6.3	.05	.03	.01	0.0	.01	0.0	0.0	3.03	.06	259	.02
Flax Seed Jell	1 T	24	1.0	2.0	1.0	2.0	tr	tr	1.0	0.0	0.0	10	tr	3.0	tr
French Dressing	2 T	21	0.22	5.25	0.2	0.06	0.01	0.0	0.03	0.0	0.0	4.2	0.16	151	0.04
French Onion Soup	1 c	109	1.87	12.5	1.75	5.5	0.75	3.86	0.52	0.0	0.0	25.1	0.37	692	0.27
French Tarts	1	144	2.8	21	1.23	6.3	1.02	3.5	1.3	0.04	0.0	65.2	0.77	122	0.47
Fruit Pudding Compote	1 c	161	4.2	32	2.5	3.1	1.04	.38	.94	0.0	0.0	43	2.3	6.4	.48
Fresh Spring Rolls	1	69	3.9	11	1.2	1.5	0.2	0.3	0.7	0.0	0.0	54	2.3	116	0.36
Frozen Fruit Ice Cream	½ c	105	1.7	23.8	1.7	.62	.07	.05	.12	.3	0.0	209	.37	61.4	.14
Fruit Filled Sweet Rolls	1	173	4.2	31.8	3.4	4.1	0.4	1.3	1.9	0.0	0.0	18	1.5	135	0.2
Fruit Nutty Balls	1	98	2.5	9.5	1.51	6.6	1.9	1.15	3.15	0.0	0.0	9.5	0.57	203	0.38
Fruit Sweetened Granola	½ c	220	5.7	26.3	3.7	6.4	0.9	2.8	2.1	0.0	0.0	30	10.2	92	1.0

Recipe	Serv Size	Cal	Prot gm	Carb gm	Fiber Total gm	Fat Total gm	Fat Sat gm	Fat Mono gm	Fat Poly gm	Vit B12 mcg	Vit D Mcg	Ca mg	Fe mg	Na mg	Zn mg
Homemade Muesli	½ c	158	14.3	23.5	3.3	6.5	1.6	2.5	2.0	0.28	0.3	22	1.4	49	1.4
Honey Butter	1 T	53	tr	6.0	tr	4.0	1.0	1.0	1.0	0.0	0.0	tr	tr	64	tr
Honey Granola	½ c	349	8.4	50.4	4.7	13.5	1.3	7.3	4.0	0.24	0.0	221	2.4	51	1.3
Hot Herbed Garlic Br Spread	1 t	6.5	0.02	0.06	0.02	0373	0.16	0.0	0.0	0.0	0.0	.55	0.01	19.2	0.0
Huevos Rancheros Salsa	1 T	3.2	.11	.66	.16	.01	0.0	0.0	0.0	0.0	0.0	3.7	.0	24	.01
Hummus	2 T	61	2.5	6.3	1.5	3.3	0.4	1.2	1.4	0.0	0.0	24	0.8	109	0.8
Ice Cream Cake	1/24	264	3.0	33	2.0	13	3.0	tr	2.0	0.0	0.0	19	tr	207	tr
Ice Cream, Strawberry	½ c	163	tr	34	1.0	4.0	tr	3.0	0.5	0.0	0.0	7.0	tr	21	tr
Ice Cream, Vanilla	½ c	240	2.0	32	0.0	10.5	0.0	7.5	2.8	0.24	0.0	80.0	0.0	180	0.0
Icing, White Chiffon	1 T	51	1.0	7.0	tr	2.0	1.0	tr	1.0	tr	0.0	13	tr	39	tr
Indian Dahl	½ c	108	7.0	16	8.0	2.0	tr	1.0	1.0	0.0	0.0	28	3.0	289	1.0
Instant Whipped Topping	¼ c	63	3.4	7.2	0.3	2.3	0.8	0.9	0.3	0.2	0.0	114	0.3	64	0.1
Italian Bread Sticks	1	136	4.0	18.7	1.9	5.4	0.9	2.9	1.1	0.0	0.0	16.8	1.6	91	0.6
Italian Style Meatless Balls	2	111	5.4	8.6	1.6	6.7	.77	3.6	1.9	.56	0.0	45	2.2	253	1.03
Italian Style Pizza	1/12	97	2.92	16.6	1.4	2.4	.36	1.46	.34	0.0	.05	16.1	1.4	242	.22
Jack Cheese Sauce	2 t	40.4	1.2	4.6	0.53	2.11	0.42	1.21	0.38	0.0	0.0	5.3	0.4	229	0.37
Jiffy Mushroom Soup	1 c	77	2.0	15.3	0.7	0.4	0.03	0.02	0.06	0.3	0.3	210	0.5	403	0.2
Juice, Sparkling Grape	1 c	161	0.0	40	0.0	0.0	0.0	0.0	0.0	0.0	0.0	9.0	0.0	56	tr
Juice, Tomato, Snappy	1/2 c	25	1.0	6.0	1.0	tr	tr	tr	tr	0.0	0.0	11	1.0	602	tr
Kabob Sauce	1 T	7.6	.26	1.74	.13	.02	0.0	0.0	.01	0.0	0.0	1.5	.08	105	.03
La Fiesta Splash	1 c	98	.9	24.9	2.42	.34	.08	.08	.06	0.0	0.0	20	.34	3.65	.12
Lemon Chiffon Pie	1/12	143	4.6	26	0.4	2.8	0.5	1.6	0.5	0.1	0.0	81	0.7	52	0.4
Lemon Chiffon Topping	1 T	12.3	.68	2.1	.05	.12	0.0	0.0	0.0	0.0	0.0	1.9	.03	11.9	.01
Lemon Custard Pie	1/12	130	1.5	26	0.4	2.8	0.5	1.6	0.5	0.10	0.0	79	0.6	44	0.4
Lemon Pudding	1 T	24	1.5	3.0	0.1	0.8	0.1	0.2	0.4	0.0	0.0	20	1.0	8.0	0.2
Lemon Wonton Soup	1 c	114	3.3	21	1.3	1.7	0.2	0.7	0.6	0.0	0.1	31	1.3	635	0.4
Lentil Vegetable Soup	1 c	86	2.5	15.2	2.21	2.01	0.28	1.36	0.23	0.0	0.0	26.5	1.15	348	0.38
Lite & Luscious Carob Icing	1/24	34.4	1.0	7.59	0.09	0.2	0.0	0.0	0.0	0.0	0.06	5.6	0.06	14.5	0.02
Lite Italian Dressing	2 T	78.2	.11	4.5	.04	6.8	.91	4.9	.57	0.0	0.0	3.04	.09	320	.03

Loaf, Company	1/12	272	18	130	0.7	9.0	1.0	3.0	5.0	1.0	0.0	67	.0	712	2.0
Macaroni & Cheese	½ c	152	5.7	21.6	1.2	4.98	0.59	2.8	1.3	0.0	0.0	45.6	2.2	304	0.62
Macaroni & Cheese, Oven	½ c	85	7.0	6.0	tr	4.0	tr	1.0	2.0	0.0	0.0	52	tr	344	tr
Macaroni Salad	½ c	80	2.2	13.3	1.0	2.0	0.08	0.23	0.15	0.0	0.0	16.6	0.7	233	0.3
Mafalda Surprise	½ c	213	8.5	36	3.0	5.0	1.0	7.0	3.0	1.3	0.0	96	2.0	308	tr
Maja Blanka	¼ c	96	354	16.6	.31	3.4	2.1	.03	.02	0.0	0.0	1.3	.14	69	.09
Mayonnaise, Better 'N	2 T	21	tr	1.0	tr	2.0	tr	1.0	tr	0.1	0.0	23	tr	64	tr
Mandarin Salad	1 c	139	1.9	20	1.3	6.7	0.8	4.7	0.9	0.0	0.0	39	0.9	237	0.5
Marinated Bean Salad	½ c	56	2.9	9.9	2.8	.9	.12	.4	.24	0.0	0.0	26	1.3	86.5	.46
Mama's Mashed Potatoes	½ c	99	3.0	18	1.0	2.0	1.0	1.0	1.0	0.1	0.0	50	1.0	297	tr
Mazidra	½ c	80	5.0	10.0	.2	2.5	0.2	1.4	0.7	0.0	0.0	10	1.5	291	0.6
Mesquite Lentils	½ c	85	6.0	12	6.0	2.0	tr	1.0	tr	0.0	0.0	15	2.0	437	1.0
Mexican Enchiladas	1	149	4.9	22.8	2.15	5.2	.65	2.5	.75	0.0	0.0	99	2.22	424	.58
Milkshake, p'nut butter &ban	1¼ c	448	16	45	4.0	25	5.0	12	6.0	1.5	1.5	221	1.0	111	1.0
Milkshake, Strawberry-banan	8 oz	193	4.0	43	3.0	2.0	tr	tr	1.0	0.7	1.2	194	1.0	24	tr
Millet Porridge	½ c	193	4.5	36	2.8	3.4	2.1	0.3	0.7	0.0	0.0	8.7	1.0	184	1.3
Minestrone Soup	1 c	70	2.8	12	2.4	1.1	0.15	0.7	0.2	0.0	0.0	26	1.2	264	0.4
Mixed Berry Pie	1/12	220	3.3	32	5.3	10.0	0.8	5.9	2.8	0.0	0.0	28	1.3	203	0.7
Mixed Vegetable Quiche	1/16	113	6.3	11.8	2.1	4.9	.35	2.6	1.01	0.0	0.0	31	.42	410	.21
Mocha Banana-nut Ice cream	½ c	140	2.5	25	1.5	3.7	0.7	1.9	0.6	0.24	0.0	170	0.7	2.4	0.6
Mock Duck Blk Bean Sauce	½ c	72	5.8	7.2	1.75	2.4	0.5	1.0	0.14	0.0	0.0	14.5	0.39	257	0.10
Mock Egg Salad	¼ c	70	4.8	3.0	0.3	4.9	0.5	1.4	1.5	0.0	0.0	67	3.2	229	0.5
Mozzarella Cheese	2 T	39	1.8	3.8	0.3	2.0	0.4	0.9	0.6	0.0	0.0	31	1.0	149	0.3
Muffins, Jiffy Cornbread	1 ea	165	3.0	29	1.0	4.0	tr	2.0	1.0	0.3	0.0	134	1.0	305	tr
Oriental Mushroom Gravy	2 T	5.8	0.3	1.13	0.03	0.01	0.0	0.0	0.0	0.0	0.03	0.69	0.03	92	0.01
Mushroom Onion Gravy	2 T	16.3	0.19	1.2	0.13	1.2	0.16	0.83	0.1	0.0	0.05	1.25	0.08	74.4	0.03
Nachos, Pueblo	3 ea	55	3.0	4.0	tr	3.0	tr	1.0	1.0	0.0	0.0	tr	tr	254	tr
Navy Bean Soup	1 c	252	16.4	34	11.7	5.9	0.8	2.1	2.6	0.0	0.0	104	3.5	571	1.6
Non-Dairy Coconut Icing	1/24	77	1.7	9.9	1.22	3.9	3.2	0.16	0.05	0.05	0.0	49.3	0.32	28	0.15

Recipe	Serv Size	Cal	Prot gm	Carb gm	Fiber Total gm	Fat Total gm	Fat Sat gm	Fat Mono gm	Fat Poly gm	Vit B12 mcg	Vit D Mcg	Ca mg	Fe mg	Na mg	Zn mg
Non-Dairy Oat crepes	1	73	2.2	12.3	1.4	1.7	0.15	0.82	0.48	0.1	0.0	80	0.51	109	0.38
Non-Dairy Parmesan Cheese	1 t	16.3	.65	1.2	.19	1.05	.1	.66	.22	.02	0.0	18.6	.17	20.3	.06
Non-Dairy Pumpkin Pie	1/12	229	9.9	30.0	1.7	9.7	0.6	1.0	2.5	0.0	0.0	121	5.7	234	0.8
Nut Rissoles	1	64	3.5	5.03	1.63	3.6	0.37	2.33	0.6	0.0	0.03	33.6	1.18	225	0.39
Oat Crust for Quiche	2 T	55	1.2	6.6	.91	2.7	.19	1.6	.75	.02	0.0	15.4	.57	71	.23
Oat Pot Pie Crust	1/12	110	2.4	13.2	1.82	5.4	0.38	3.2	1.5	0.04	0.0	30.8	1.14	142	0.46
Oat Waffles	1	157	5.0	24	3.2	5.6	0.8	2.8	1.6	0.0	0.0	21	1.5	208	0.7
Oatmeal, Apple Walnut	½ c	194	7.0	27	4.0	8.0	1.0	2.0	4.0	0.0	0.0	31	2.0	89	1.0
Oatmeal Raisin Cookie	1	106	2.0	18	2.0	3.0	1.0	1.0	1.0	0.0	0.0	31	1.0	75	tr
Oatmeal Date Cookie	1	222	4.9	31.5	2.8	9.18	0.71	4.49	3.33	0.13	0.0	109	1.23	148	0.79
Old Fashioned Cornbread	1	175	5.2	32	2.3	3.4	0.3	1.4	1.4	0.0	0.0	14	1.2	245	0.7
Orange Honey Butter	1 t	11	.28	1.3	.07	.57	.04	.34	.14	0.0	0.0	2.11	.04	23	.02
Orange Jello Fluff	½ c	164	4.0	31	2.0	4.0	1.0	tr	2.0	0.1	0.0	78	1.0	40	1.0
Orange Tofu Topping	1 T	11	0.5	2.0	0.02	0.1	0.0	0.0	0.0	0.0	0.0	6.8	0.01	22	0.01
Oriental Dressing	1 T	26	.04	2.23	.03	2.01	.15	1.2	.59	0.0	0.0	1.73	.4	.01	.01
Orzo with Wild Rice	½ c	143	5.0	21	2.0	5.0	1.0	3.0	1.0	0.0	0.0	26	1.0	414	1.0
Pancakes, Brown Rice	1 ea	184	4.0	37	3.0	2.0	tr	1.0	1.0	0.0	0.0	76	1.0	309	1.0
Pancakes, Buck Wheat	1 ea	114	5.0	20	1.0	2.0	tr	tr	1.0	0.0	0.0	152	2.0	391	1.0
Pancakes, Oat Bran	1 ea	156	6.0	28	5.0	3.0	tr	1.0	1.0	0.6	0.0	79	2.0	274	1.0
Pancakes, Wheat 'n Bran	1 ea	214	11	42	8.0	3.0	tr	tr	1.0	0.0	0.0	301	3.0	653	2.0
Pancakes, Whole Grain	1 ea	116	5.0	22	2.4	1.0	tr	tr	1.0	0.5	0.0	202	2.0	413	1.0
Pao	1	107	5.6	17	1.8	2.1	0.36	0.7	0.4	0.0	0.0	7.03	0.9	240	0.29
Pasta Primavera	1 c	242	6.8	30	4.2	8.68	1.69	3.64	2.71	.2	0.0	167	6.03	401	.96
Peach Nut Bread	1 sl	330	7.3	52	3.3	12.0	.07	4.4	5.9	0.0	0.0	116	2.7	236	2.13
Peach Raspberry Crisp	1/20	151	2.5	25.8	2.3	4.9	.88	1.8	1.9	0.0	0.0	16.4	.94	88	.41
Peaches & Cream Punch	1 c	121	1.5	30	1.5	0.2	0.01	0.03	0.04	0.1	0.0	86	0.2	25	0.2
Peanut Butter Pate	1 T	92	3.3	7.5	1.3	6.1	0.85	3.02	1.9	0.0	0.0	12.9	0.56	116	0.47
Peas & Peanuts Salad	½ c	116	5.2	9.8	4.2	6.9	.88	2.1	3.4	0.0	0.0	19.6	.95	200	.95
Pecan Topping	1 T	62	1.0	4.0	1.0	5.0	1.0	3.0	1.0	0.0	0.0	5.0	tr	13	tr

Peking Noodle Stir-Fry	1 c	282	16.0	31.1	3.7	11.5	1.5	4.8	4.3	0.0	0.08	169	8.1	250	2.0
Picnic Potato Salad	½ c	78	1.6	15.2	1.6	1.4	.11	.77	.38	0.0	.07	19.7	.35	189	.24
Pie, Aunt Bea's Apple	1/12	128	3.0	16	1.0	6.0	1.0	4.0	1.0	0.0	0.0	11	1.0	89	tr
Pie Crust, Pastry Wheat	227	139	3.0	17	2.0	7.0	1.0	4.0	2.0	0.0	0.0	14	1.0	89	tr
Pie Crust, Two Grain	2.02	123	1.0	29	1.0	1.0	tr	1.0	tr	0.0	0.0	5.0	tr	35	tr
Pie, Blueberry	43.4	207	1.0	41	tr	5.0	1.0	2.0	1.0	tr	0.0	16	1.0	160	tr
Pie, Lemon	2.5	107	1.0	22	2.0	1.0	tr	tr	tr	0.3	0.0	33	tr	109	tr
Pie, Pumpkin, Soy Easy	6.4	75	1.0	16	tr	1.0	tr	tr	tr	0.4	0.0	54	1.0	110	tr
Pie, Pumpkin Soy Simple	0.54	111	1.0	27	2.0	1.0	tr	tr	tr	0.0	0.0	10	tr	15	tr
Pie, Strawberry	3.82	282	3.0	37	3.0	15	1.0	9.0	5.0	0.1	0.0	36	1.0	64	1.0
Pie, Southern Pecan	1/12	262	3.0	37	3.0	15	1.0	9.0	5.0	0.1	0.0	36	1.0	64	1.0
Pimiento Cheese	2 T	20	0.9	2.4	0.6	0.9	0.2	0.5	0.2	0.0	0.0	4.9	0.4	148	0.2
Pinakbet	½ c	51	2.7	6.2	2.02	2.2	0.31	1.05	0.66	0.0	0.0	41	1.5	224	0.31
Pineapple Date Jam	1 T	17	0.14	4.5	0.5	0.03	0.01	0.01	0.0	0.0	0.0	2.4	0.09	0.2	0.02
Pistachio Ice Cream	½ c	244	9.7	27.2	4.4	11.1	1.5	6.0	3.2	0.0	0.0	214	2.5	81	0.3
Posole	1 c	168	4.9	27	4.8	5.4	0.7	3.0	0.0	0.0	0.0	87	1.8	413	0.4
Potato Casserole, Shredded	½ c	100	2.0	12	2.0	5.0	1.0	2.0	1.0	0.3	0.0	57	tr	317	0.0
Potato Cheese Pinwheels	1 ea	52	3.0	5.0	tr	2.0	tr	1.0	tr	0.1	0.0	11	tr	185	tr
Potato Crust	2 T	58	.92	7.1	.3	2.65	.18	1.6	.73	.02	0.0	14	.64	71	.06
Potato Salad Dressing	1 T	26	.19	1.1	.03	2.4	.15	1.41	.62	0.0	.13	17.5	.02	49	.01
Pumpkin Mousse Dessert	1	177	1.68	25.8	1.27	7.5	0.27	2.08	0.82	0.0	0.0	37.5	0.35	148	0.32
Purple Passion Fruit Salad	½ c	58	.34	14.8	.92	.17	.04	.02	.06	0.0	0.0	5.4	.19	1.4	.06
Quesadillas	1/4	135	3.27	22.6	.86	3.5	.39	1.5	.49	0.0	0.0	123	1.43	248	.24
Quesadillas, Chicken Style	1/4	206	12	21	2.0	8.0	1.0	2.0	2.0	0.5	0.0	46	2.0	471	tr
Quick 3 Bean Chili	1 c	152	10	26	9.0	0.8	0.3	0.2	0.12	0.0	0.0	60	3.3	512	0.55
Quick Artichoke Pasta Toss	½ c	46	1.4	6.7	1.4	1.8	.3	1.2	.21	0.0	.06	20	.9	124	.2
Quick Vinegarless Ketchup	1 T	11	0.2	2.7	0.2	0.05	0.01	0.01	0.02	0.0	0.0	2.5	0.2	91	0.04
Raisin Bran Muffins	1	224	5.8	36.4	6.9	9.2	.81	3.8	3.8	0.0	0.0	114	2.4	241	1.4
Ranch Dressing Quick/Easy	2 T	43	0.9	1.2	0.01	3.8	0.5	2.6	0.3	0.0	0.0	3.2	0.02	125	0.01

Recipe	Serv Size	Cal	Prot gm	Carb gm	Fiber Total gm	Fat Total gm	Fat Sat gm	Fat Mono gm	Fat Poly gm	Vit B12 mcg	Vit D Mcg	Ca mg	Fe mg	Na mg	Zn mg
Ranch Style Dressing	1 T	27	1.51	.76	.04	2.19	.29	.41	1.38	0.0	0.0	21	1.02	95	.15
Raspberry Bran Muffin	1	158	4.0	28	5.0	5.0	1.0	3.0	1.0	.02	0.0	129	1.0	217	tr
Raspberry Butter	2 t	1.4	0.03	1.6	0.08	0.04	0.0	0.02	0.01	0.0	0.0	1.3	0.02	1.3	0.01
Raspberry Jam	2 t	9.7	.06	2.4	.18	.03	0.0	0.0	.02	0.0	0.0	1.4	.04	.28	.02
Raspberry Jello Fluff	1/3 c	77	0.39	15.7	1.07	1.55	0.03	0.02	0.1	0.0	0.0	24.4	0.23	3.62	0.15
Raspberry Vinaigrette	2 T	28	0.09	7.6	0.06	0.04	0.01	0.0	0.01	0.0	0.0	1.7	0.03	291	0.02
Ratatouille	½ c	54	1.4	8.1	2.6	2.45	0.34	1.68	0.27	0.0	0.09	13.1	0.67	400	0.23
Rice Barley Pilaf	½ c	147	3.6	20	2.75	4.92	0.62	3.0	1.02	0.0	0.0	26	2.95	229	1.03
Rice, Perfect	½ c	118	3.0	25	1.0	1.0	tr	tr	tr	0.0	0.0	12	tr	237	1.0
Rice Pudding with Mango	½ c	165	3.04	34.2	2.1	2.01	0.79	0.32	0.32	0.09	0.0	74.2	0.66	22.3	0.64
Rice Vermicelli	1 c	191	13.9	23.4	3.5	4.9	0.84	1.1	2.2	0.32	0.0	148	6.5	587	0.67
Rich & Creamy Carob Icing	1/24	69.5	1.4	7.8	0.48	4.22	0.39	2.7	0.87	0.0	.02	20.8	0.31	5.3	0.23
Rigatoni with Pesto Sauce	½ c	176	7.0	19	1.0	8.0	1.0	4.0	1.0	0.0	0.0	9.0	1.0	156	tr
Reuben Sandwich, vegetarian	½ ea	162	11	17	2.0	5.0	tr	1.0	2.0	0.4	0.0	59	2.0	634	tr
Roma Capaccino	1 c	89	4.0	19	0.0	1.0	0.0	0.0	0.0	1.5	0.0	150	tr	79	tr
Salad, Tuna Style	2 T	69	3.0	2.0	1.0	5.0	1.0	tr	tr	0.6	0.0	13	1.0	281	tr
Salad, Fresh Kale	1 c	145	4.0	131	3.0	10	1.0	1.0	2.0	0.0	0.0	81	2.0	362	1.0
Salad, Waldorf Apple	½ c	110	1.0	13	1.0	6.0	tr	1.0	2.0	0.0	0.0	10	tr	85	tr
Salsa, Sassy	1 T	4.0	Tr	1.0	tr	tr	tr	tr	tr	0.0	0.0	3.0	tr	25	tr
Sausage Style Gravy	¼ c	36	2.0	3.5	0.6	1.7	0.3	0.9	0.3	0.0	0.0	12	0.5	207	0.3
Sausage/Mush Onion Quiche	1/16	79	7.1	1.04	.62	2.5	.24	1.3	.2	0.0	.16	22	.34	375	.12
Savory Kale	½ c	60	2.5	10.6	2.5	1.6	0.2	0.9	0.3	0.0	0.0	88	1.1	101	0.4
Savory Lentils	½ c	35	1.5	3.9	.78	1.8	.24	1.3	.18	0.0	0.0	13.2	.84	342	.2
Savory Split Pea Soup	1 c	150	8.0	25	3.4	2.4	0.3	1.5	0.3	0.0	0.0	33	1.8	314	1.0
Scones, Honey Wh. Currant	1 ea	330	8.0	61	5.0	8.0	1.0	4.0	2.0	0.0	0.0	143	2.0	324	tr
Scones, Maple Pecan	1 ea	287	7.0	50	5.0	8.0	1.0	3.0	2.0	0.0	0.0	145	2.0	386	tr
Scrambled Tofu Eggs	½ c	107	9.4	4.5	0.4	6.7	1.0	2.4	3.0	0.0	0.08	122	6.2	217	1.0
Scrambled Tofu Eggs Curry	1 c	231	12	21	2.0	12	1.9	5.9	3.5	0.2	1.1	256	6.8	484	1.8
Seafarer's Navy Bean Soup	1 c	231	14.6	32.6	10.6	5.2	0.7	1.79	2.2	0.68	0.0	96.1	3.48	405	1.41

Recipe	Serv Size	Cal	Prot Gm	Carb gm	Fiber Total gm	Fat Total gm	Fat Sat gm	Fat Mono gm	Fat Poly gm	Vit B12 mcg	Vit D mcg	Ca mg	Fe mg	Na mg	Zn mg
Seasoned Brown Rice	½ c	29.6	.61	6.3	.46	.21	.04	.07	.07	0.0	0.0	3.7	.14	152	.16
Sesame Chicken	1 ea	187	12	19	2.0	7.0	1.0	1.0	1.0	0.6	0.0	60	2.0	612	trace
Sesame Oat Crackers	1	65	1.5	7.8	1.1	3.3	0.3	1.8	1.0	0.0	0.0	14	0.6	72	0.1
Sesame Sticks, Honey-nut	3 ea	123	3.0	13	2.0	7.0	1.0	4.0	2.0	0.0	0.0	95	2.0	56	1.0
Shortcake, Strawberry	1/16	155	4.0	32	3.0	2.0	1.0	1.0	1.0	0.0	0.0	68	1.0	299	trace
Siew Mai	2	87	3.0	12	0.5	1.9	0.35	0.6	0.7	0.0	0.0	12	0.6	232	0.15
Simply Smash. Stuff. Potato	1	93	3.4	17.3	1.6	1.2	.12	.5	.13	0.0	0.0	18.6	0.97	164	.23
Smoothies	1 c	107	1.6	24.3	1.5	0.6	0.05	0.05	0.12	0.32	0.0	221	0.39	66.2	0.11
Sour Cream Supreme	1 T	68.9	0.01	10.4	0.01	2.3	0.3	0.4	1.5	0.0	0.0	0.16	0.0	57	0.0
Southern Peach Preserves	2 t	18	0.23	4.43	0.25	0.5	0.01	0.01	0.01	0.0	0.0	2.62	0.05	0.27	0.03
Soy Burger, Sizzlin	½ ea	68	10	6.0	1.0	tr	tr	tr	tr	0.9	0.0	16	1.0	380	tr
Soy Cream	1 T	42	0.42	1.2	0.01	1.04	0.24	2.25	0.99	0.0	0.0	8.3	0.1	49.6	0.0
Soy Good Tofu Sour Cream	1 T	38	2.5	0.8	0.02	3.0	0.4	0.6	1.9	0.0	0.0	32	1.7	24	0.3
Soy Mayonnaise	2 t	22.4	.3	1.9	.05	1.5	.1	.89	.37	.04	.05	35	.03	54	.02
Soy Oat Waffles	1	196	7.6	31.4	4.6	5.5	0.7	2.3	1.8	0.0	0.0	46	3.3	411	0.7
Spaghetti Florentine	1 c	111	9.9	12.4	4.8	3.0	0.4	1.0	1.2	0.0	0.0	99	3.6	713	0.9
Spicy Vinegarless Ketchup	1 T	10.5	0.3	2.53	.32	.07	.01	.01	.02	0.0	0.0	3.3	.21	54	.06
Spinach & Pasta Salad	1 c	52	2.71	10.5	2.47	.34	.05	.02	.14	0.0	0.0	53	1.68	62.9	.40
Spinach Potato Crepe	1	528	1.25	5.8	0.88	3.01	0.46	2.0	.036	0.0	0.0	26.7	0.87	207	0.27
Spinach Potato Puffs	2	33	2.93	3.85	0.56	0.89	0.12	0.18	0.45	0.0	0.0	40.23	1.23	117	0.27
Spinach Potato Quiche	1/16	123	6.4	13.1	2.4	5.5	.43	3.04	1.09	0.0	.08	50	.93	460	.37
Sprouted Wheat Bread	1 sl	107	3.67	20.4	2.9	1.99	0.18	1.0	0.60	0.0	0.0	8.9	1.02	179	0.74
Stew, Chicken & Curry	1 c	232	16	13	5.0	14	6.0	1.0	trace	1.2	0.0	27	3.0	817	trace
Soup, Taco	1 c	214	16	33	7.0	3.0	tr	1.0	1.0	0.6	0.0	43	4.0	704	1.0
Soup, Indian Lentil	1 c	122	8.0	20	9.0	2.0	tr	1.0	trace	0.0	0.0	46	3.0	623	1.0
Strawberry Rasp. Topping	2 T	25.9	.18	6.5	.64	.08	.01	.01	.04	0.0	0.0	3.9	.13	.54	.04
Strawberry Surprise Salad	1/3 c	102	2.86	10.4	0.89	6.17	0.61	2.42	2.79	0.0	0.0	36.3	1.24	36.7	0.38
Strawberry Tropic Drink	1 c	63	.6	15.3	.48	.15	.02	.02	.05	0.0	0.0	12	.32	3.5	.1
Strawberry Tropic Jam	1 T	20	0.14	5.3	0.12	0.08	0.0	0.0	0.01	0.0	0.0	2.7	0.06	0.09	0.01

Stroganoff, Mushroom	½ c	113	5.0	29	1.0	3.0	tr	1.0	1.0	0.0	0.0	41	1.0	170	tr
Stuffed Mushrooms	1	25	0.75	2.8	0.4	1.3	0.2	0.9	0.2	0.0	0.4	8.1	0.4	108	0.2
Stuffed Prunes	2	104	1.9	12	2.0	6.3	0.6	1.5	3.9	0.0	0.0	18	0.7	1.7	0.4
Stuffed Shells	1	79	4.1	12.5	1.7	1.6	0.19	0.24	0.96	0.0	0.0	12.8	1.2	787	0.46
Sub Sandwich	1 ea	188	10	19	2.0	8.0	1.0	3.0	4.0	0.0	0.0	51	1.0	848	1.0
Succotash	1/3 c	112	5.52	21.8	4.7	0.39	0.05	0.01	0.1	0.2	0.0	153	1.38	313	0.41
Summer Squash Casserole	½ c	45	3.0	2.0	1.0	3.0	tr	1.0	1.0	0.0	0.0	38	tr	179	tr
Summer Squash Stir-Fry	½ c	26.2	1.3	5.6	1.8	0.18	0.03	0.01	0.07	0.0	0.0	18.3	0.48	41.2	0.26
Sweet & Sour Chicken	1 c	173	9.2	22	3.9	6.2	0.35	1.7	0.32	0.0	0.0	45	0.88	431	1.17
Sweet & Sour Dip	1 T	15	Tr	3.0	tr	tr	tr	tr	tr	0.0	0.0	2.0	tr	34	tr
Sweet & Sour Fresh Fruit Dr.	2 T	43.3	0.65	6.7	0.15	1.6	0.29	0.21	0.87	0.04	0.0	31	0.05	39	0.02
Sweet & Sour Sauce	1/3 c	91	1.1	19.3	1.2	1.8	0.24	1.3	0.18	0.0	0.0	17.0	0.43	27	0.14
Sweet Potato Mounds	1 ea	151	1.0	35	3.0	1.0	tr	1.0	trace	0.0	0.0	39	1.0	9.0	trace
Sweet Reflections Banana	1 c	152	1.8	34.9	3.9	1.8	0.25	0.78	0.5	0.0	0.0	26.4	0.71	2.9	0.47
Syrup, Coconut	2 T	57	tr	9.0	tr	3.0	2.0	tr	tr	0.0	0.0	tr	tr	15	tr
Syrup, Maple, Topping	2 T	62	tr	16.0	tr	tr	tr	tr	tr	0.0	0.0	21	tr	4.0	tr
Tabouli Salad	½ c	109	2.4	13.7	3.5	5.8	0.8	4.0	0.6	0.0	0.0	22	1.0	224	0.4
Tahini Dressing	2 T	91	3.0	4.0	1.0	8.0	1.0	3.0	4.0	0.0	0.0	66	1.0	84	1.0
Tahini Spread, Honey	2 T	162	3.0	16	2.0	11	1.0	4.0	5.0	0.0	0.0	86	2.0	24	1.0
Tamale Pie	1/12	185	7.5	28	6.0	5.0	0.5	2.0	0.5	0.0	0.0	113	2.2	645	0.4
Tangy Mayo Kabob Dressing	1 T	26.3	.24	1.07	.12	2.4	.16	1.4	.64	0.0	.12	17	.17	37	.02
Tartar Sauce	1 T	16	0.2	1.0	0.1	1.3	0.0	0.0	0.1	0.0	0.0	4.2	0.03	92	0.01
Tartar Sauce, Quick	1 T	25	Tr	1.0	tr	2.0	tr	tr	tr	0.0	0.0	1.0	tr	106	tr
Teriyaki Sauce	1 t	18	.14	4.7	.02	0.0	0.0	0.0	0.0	0.0	0.0	2.4	.05	38	.02
Tex Mex Enchiladas	1	238	14.4	23.8	1.6	11.3	1.52	3.9	4.1	0.0	0.0	229	8.7	633	1.5
Thick & Zesty Ketchup	1 T	14.2	0.35	3.4	.33	.1	.01	.01	.03	0.0	0.0	3.4	.21	52	.06
Thousand Island Dressing	2 T	36	0.4	3.4	0.2	2.4	0.01	0.01	0.02	0.0	0.0	6.5	0.1	136	0.04
Three Grain No Oil Bread	1 sl	105	3.8	22.9	3.22	0.57	0.10	0.08	0.22	0.0	0.0	10.3	1.17	179	0.78
Toast, Breakfast	1 sl	184	7.0	21	3.0	9.0	2.0	4.0	3.0	0.0	0.0	28	1.0	151	1.0

	Size		gm	Gm	Total gm	Total gm	Sat gm	Mono gm	Poly gm	B12 mcg	D Mcg	mg	mg	mg	mg
Tofu Banana Bread #1	1 sl	222	5.0	31	2.23	9.9	.82	3.9	4.3	0.0	0.0	54	1.3	194	.56
Tofu Banana Bread #2	1 sl	271	5.9	38.9	2.98	11.5	0.98	4.3	5.3	0.26	0.16	98.3	1.66	297	0.93
Tofu Fish Sticks	2	192	14.4	20.5	1.3	7.12	1.03	1.57	3.93	0.0	0.0	165	9.1	179	1.47
Tofu Foo Yung	1	129	10.8	10.8	1.6	5.8	0.83	1.7	2.9	0.0	0.07	135	6.6	148	1.06
Tofu Greek Salad	½ c	67	4.2	4.6	.79	4.2	.6	2	1.4	0.0	0.0	60	2.8	116	.49
Tofu Lasagna	1 c	224	13.4	30.1	3.2	7.4	.95	2.43	2.5	.4	0.0	128	6.2	587	1.01
Tofu Mayonnaise	1 T	28	.72	1.3	.15	2.3	.19	1.4	.68	0.0	0.0	9.0	.34	68	.08
Tomato Cheese Polenta	1/9	181	11	19	2.0	7.0	1.0	2.0	4.0	0.0	0.0	16	1.0	800	tr
Tomato Cuc Salad w Herb	1 c	99.6	1.6	11.2	1.6	6.2	0.85	4.26	0.69	0.0	0.0	17.3	0.79	12.8	0.25
Tomato & Herb Ital. Sauce	1 T	7.6	0.15	0.8	0.15	0.43	0.06	0.31	0.04	0.0	0.0	3.5	0.14	38.7	0.01
Tropical Fruit Soup	½ c	82	0.6	20	0.95	0.2	0.04	0.02	0.3	0.0	0.0	16	0.3	5.7	0.09
Veg Meatballs in BBQ Sauce	3	258	40	26	13	4.5	0.4	2.4	0.6	0.0	0.0	214	6.9	187	3.6
Veg. Rice- Mushroom Soup	1 c	85	3.0	14	1.7	2.0	0.3	1.3	0.3	0.0	0.16	19	0.8	473	0.7
Vegetable Dip	1 T	16.5	0.53	1.1	0.31	1.19	0.13	0.34	0.62	0.0	0.0	7.1	0.92	47	0.03
Vegetable Fried Rice	½ c	183	10.2	24.3	3.3	5.1	1.01	2.05	0.86	0.0	0.0	42	1.09	371	0.77
Vegetable Rice Soup	1 c	54	2.0	11.4	2.5	0.3	0.02	0.01	0.04	0.0	0.0	24	0.6	255	0.1
Vegetarian Beef Steaks	1	25	1.9	3.9	0.53	0.17	0.01	0.01	0.01	0.0	0.0	4.1	0.2	245	0.03
Vegetarian Fajitas	1	133	4.0	19	1.4	5.2	0.4	2.0	0.4	0.0	0.05	42	1.6	274	0.2
Vegetarian Goulash	1 c	163	7.4	26	3.0	3.0	0.5	1.5	0.8	1.2	0.0	52	2.2	356	0.5
Veggie-Whoppers	½ c	224	21	73	7.0	4.0	tr	1.0	2.0	1.3	0.0	55	3.0	844	1.0
Very Berry Cream Cheese	1 T	39	0.4	3.3	0.2	2.7	1.0	1.0	0.7	0.0	0.0	0.4	0.08	68	0.02
Very Berry Fruit Soup	½ c	73	0.5	18	1.5	0.2	0.04	0.03	0.06	0.0	0.0	9.8	0.3	1.7	0.1
Virgin Pina Colada	1 c	131	1.09	21.8	.94	5.2	3.8	.12	.06	0.0	0.0	19.3	.55	4.6	.21
Virgin Strawberry Daiquiri	1 c	163	.69	42.4	2.09	.26	.02	.02	.01	0.0	0.0	23	1.3	4.9	.20
Waffles, Millet	1 ea	252	7.0	50	7.0	2.0	tr	tr	1.0	0.0	0.0	16	2.0	360	1.0
Waffles, Rice	1 ea	204	3.0	44	2.0	2.0	tr	tr	1.0	0.0	0.0	17	tr	181	1.0
Wheat Potpie Crust	1/12	138	2.04	12.4	0.98	9.3	0.62	5.6	2.5	0.0	0.0	1.97	.042	0.33	0.0
Whole Wheat Rolls	1	109	4.8	20.8	3.6	0.8	0.2	0.01	0.0	0.0	0.0	13	1.5	178	0.03
Yams with Orange Glaze	1/3 c	47	0.5	11.4	0.8	0.05	0.01	0.0	0.01	0.0	0.0	12	0.2	34	0.3

Index of Recipes

Appetizers & Dips

Beverages

Breads & Muffins

Crackers & Flat Breads

Quick-Raised

Yeast-Raised

Breakfast Dishes

Breads & Cereals

Fruit

Pancakes

Tofu & Potatoes

Waffles

Cheese Substitutes

Condiments

Desserts

Cakes & Icings

Cookies

Frozen Desserts

Fruit Desserts

Pies

Puddings & Jell-O

Toppings

Dressings

Entrees & Main Dishes

Beans

Crepes

Main Dishes

Pasta

Milks

Salads

Sandwiches

Sauces

Savory Spreads

Seasonings

Soups

Vegetables & Side Dishes

Notes

The World's Most Powerful Anti-Aging Food!

Did you know that in some remote places in this world, a life expectancy of more than 100 years is not uncommon?

Research has shown that many of the world's longest living people consume regular daily helpings of a tiny red fruit that may just be the world's most powerful anti-aging food—**the goji berry.**

FreeLife™ is the first company to perfect a difficult and demanding proprietary extraction process and create the only standardized form of this incredible plant available in the world today: **HIMALAYAN GOJI™ JUICE.**

Goji - The Himalayan Health Secret™

If you have not yet heard of goji, you are not alone. While it has occupied an important place in traditional Asian medicine for countless generations, the secrets of its nutritional benefits have remained a mystery to most of the world.

Through the ages, legends abound about this miraculous fruit. There are festivals held to celebrate its goodness, and a poem was written in its honor.

The First Healers

It is said that the Himalayans were the first natural healers, and that they shared their wisdom with the ancient herbalists of China, Tibet, and India. One of their most prized secrets was the fruit of the native goji vine, which had been flourishing in the Himalayan valleys since the beginning of time. Those who came there to learn took the goji home with them and planted it in their own valleys, thus spreading the legend of this most marvelous and healthful fruit.

Since its discovery in the Himalayas, those who know of the remarkable goji berry are awed by its unmatched health-promoting powers.

Dr. Earl Mindell's Most Important Health Discovery Ever!

Widely regarded as the world's #1 nutritionist, Dr. Earl Mindell's research has resulted in many important health discoveries.

- He was largely responsible for creating the "nutritional revolution" with the publication of the *Vitamin Bible*; the biggest-selling nutritional book ever.

- He was the first to introduce to the world the remarkable health benefits of soy, with his best-selling *Soy Miracle* book.

- He brought the power of MSM to mainstream America.

- He teamed up with FreeLife International®, lending his vast experience and expertise to the formulation of an exclusive and diverse line of all-natural nutritional supplements—the most comprehensive, synergistic nutritional products available on the market today.

Dedicated to helping others optimize their health and well-being for over 40 years, it is a dream come true for Dr. Mindell to bring the miraculous goji berry to the world.

A Dream Come True

"As a pharmacist and nutritionist dedicated to helping others optimize their health and well-being, it is a dream come true to bring the miraculous goji to the world. I believe that Himalayan Goji Juice will have more powerful benefits on health, well-being, and anti-aging than any other product I have seen in the last 40 years" Dr. Earl Mindell

In Search of the True Goji

Just as there are many varieties of grapes for wine making, there are many varieties of goji—as many as 41 species growing in Tibet alone!

Dr. Mindell knew that he must exhaustively analyze the dozens of varieties to find the one true goji—the one that had been discovered by the early Himalayan healers, and which, from ancient times, had been praised in legend.

In the same way that human fingerprints can be used to distinguish one person from all others on the planet, a spectrometer can detect even subtle differences between berries at the molecular level. This technique results in the generation of a graph, a unique fingerprint for whatever is being tested—a Spectral Signature.

Thanks to years of dedicated scientific research, FreeLife™ is the only company in the world to have developed a Spectral Signature to identify, isolate, and harvest only those special goji berries with the exact nutrient profile of the legendary goji from the Himalayas.

Goji's Master Molecules

Working together, FreeLife and Dr. Mindell have been pioneers in the research of goji polysaccharides. Goji's four unique polysaccharides, or phytonutrient compounds, work in the body as directors and carriers of the instructions that cells use to communicate with each other. These polysaccharides are "Master Molecules" and command and control many of the body's most important defense systems.

Goji of Himalayan quality exhibits a balanced polysaccharide profile and a uniquely potent Spectral Signature. It is the true descendant of the original goji of legend.

100% Goodness in Every Bottle, Every Time - Himalyan Goji™ Juice

- Proprietary, 100% juice product, patterned after the ancient recipes and practices of the Himalayans.
- 100% all-natural juice flavoring system gives a consistently delicious flavor, and works synergistically with the product to enhance its already remarkable benefits. Never any added sugar, artificial sweeteners, colors, or flavors.
- Proprietary technology for extracting the juice without destroying goji's delicate, but extremely powerful nutrients.
- Exclusive recipe and proprietary chill-blending technology.
- Each one-liter bottle contains the equivalent of more than 2 pounds of fresh goji berries!
- Carefully standardized to deliver a consistently high level of perfectly balanced and fully active polysaccharides, the Master Molecules that your body needs to replenish on a daily basis for optimal health and longevity. (These Master Molecules are unique to goji—they are not found in any other plant on earth.)
- Made only with berries that exhibit the ideal Himalayan Spectral Signature—your assurance of potency, purity, and authenticity in every bottle.
- Strict seven-step quality manufacturing process ensures that you and your family experience the same nutritional value with every sip.

You and your entire family will enjoy the energizing health benefits from this nutrient rich, 100% juice beverage.

For overall good health, we suggest that you start with one ounce of HIMALAYAN GOJI™ JUICE daily. Current research indicates that the greatest benefit may be realized by drinking up to four ounces per day. HIMALAYAN GOJI™ JUICE can be taken as is, or mixed with your favorite hot or cold beverage.

Frequently Asked Questions

Is it okay for children to drink Himalayan Goji Juice?
Yes, Himalayan Goji Juice is great for the entire family.

Is Himalayan Goji Juice only made with goji berries from the Himalayas?
Although they grow in the wild, goji berries are not cultivated in the Himalayas in sufficient quantity for large-scale distribution. The berries used in Himalayan Goji Juice are selected from the world's best-known growing regions. These include Inner Mongolia, as well as Ningxia and Xinjiang in the pristine Heavenly Mountains of western China. We use only those berries that conform to the precise Spectral Signature fingerprint and balanced polysaccharide profile of the original *Lycium barbarum* (goji) of the Himalayas.

Will FreeLife have difficulty sourcing goji berries?
We have several sources of supply for goji berries and we have no concerns about difficulty in sourcing them.

Are the 4 polysaccharides unique to Himalayan Goji Juice?
The 4 polysaccharides are unique to goji, but can vary in quality depending on the ancestry of the plant and the growing conditions for a particular region in a particular year. FreeLife is the only company that has developed a Spectral Signature to ensure that you always receive the same high potency polysaccharides in exact balance when you drink Himalayan Goji Juice.

What's all the fuss about ORAC?
ORAC (Oxygen Radical Absorbance Capacity) is a non-official, non-governmental, private for-pay service that puts a product through a simple test that results in a number that represents what they call "total antioxidant power." There are many different classes of antioxidants, however, and they each work differently. To a scientist, the ORAC number means little because it does not give specific information about what kinds of antioxidants are present. Because the test is so limited in what it measures, we have never done an ORAC test on Himalayan Goji Juice.

While Himalayan Goji Juice does have antioxidant power, its true power comes from another source: its unique Master Molecule Polysaccharides, which simply cannot be found in any other plant on earth. Dozens of published scientific studies have confirmed that these polysaccharides are the most important bioactive components, and are responsible for the incredible health benefits of the goji berry. The list of the benefits of these polysaccharides can be found in Dr. Earl Mindell and Rick Handel's book, *Goji, The Himalayan Health Secret*, and we sincerely believe that they are nothing less than astounding.

So if you want optimal antioxidant power, take FreeLife's Basic Mindell Plus, the most comprehensive antioxidant supplement we have ever seen. If you want the benefits of the miraculous goji berry, drink Himalayan Goji Juice.

How much Himalayan Goji Juice should someone drink on a daily basis?
FreeLife recommends 1–3 ounces daily. There are no known side effects from drinking more than that (other than smiling too much!).

How long does it take before an improvement is seen with Himalayan Goji Juice?
Everyone will receive benefits within different time periods depending upon their body's nutritional needs, however, most people will begin to see noticeable results within the first month.

How does FreeLife ensure the quality of Himalayan Goji Juice?
FreeLife has a Seven-Step Quality Manufacturing Program to ensure that you receive the same consistent, standardized quality in every liter of Himalayan Goji Juice. Our Spectral Signature is your assurance of potency, purity, and authenticity in every bottle.

How do I measure an ounce of Himalayan Goji Juice?
An ounce of Himalayan Goji Juice is about one capful, or 2 tablespoons.

How is Himalayan Goji Juice different from other "juices"?
There is never any added sugar, artificial sweeteners, artificial colors or flavors in Himalayan Goji Juice, and goji is the only plant that has the 4 unique polysaccharides—the Master Molecules that are so important to your body' defense systems.

How many pounds of goji berries are in a bottle of Himalayan Goji Juice, and why are fresh berries better than dried berries?
One liter of Himalayan Goji Juice contains the polysaccharides equivalent of 2.2 pounds of fresh goji berries. As an alternative, we suppose that one could simply eat dried goji berries. However, our research indicates that the quality of commercially-available dehydrated berries can vary tremendously, and

there's also a high probability that the polysaccharides in dried berries may have oxidized and degraded. FreeLife will not offer dried goji berries until it can be scientifically proven that they can deliver a consistent health benefit.

Is Himalayan Goji Juice organic?
Although Himalayan Goji Juice is not certified organic, it is produced to the highest standards of ecological and environmental responsibility. While the remoteness of the goji growing regions has presented many challenges, we are working toward a cooperative program of organic certification for our indigenous Asian growers. Until then, you can be assured that, like every FreeLife product, Himalayan Goji Juice is certified to be free of detectable pesticide and herbicide residues. Also, Himalayan Goji Juice contains no added sugar, artificial colors, sweeteners, or flavors.

Why does FreeLife not emphasize the vitamins and 18 amino acids that are in goji?
Himalayan Goji Juice is a high-tech functional food, specifically designed to preserve the content and balance of the goji berry's delicate and highly protective polysaccharides. It is standardized to a consistently high level of polysaccharides, in perfect balance. Dozens of published scientific studies have confirmed that these polysaccharides are the most important bioactive components, and are responsible for much of the benefit of the goji berry. That is why we have chosen to focus on this aspect of the goji, rather than emphasize the other nutritional aspects of this remarkable plant.

Are preservatives necessary in Himalayan Goji Juice and, if so, are they natural?
Yes. Freshness preservation is required to keep this chill-blended product from spoiling. We use less than one-tenth of 1% of naturally-derived sodium benzoate and potassium sorbate in Himalayan Goji Juice. Potassium sorbate is the potassium salt of sorbic acid. Sorbic acid is a natural constituent of many fruits and vegetables. Sodium benzoate is the sodium salt of benzoic acid. Benzoic acid is a natural component of berries. Both ingredients are two of the safest preservatives that can be used in food products. They are so safe that they are even on the FDA's GRAS (Generally Recognized as Safe) list. The only way to totally avoid preservatives would be to hot-fill the product in glass bottles. Hot filling would destroy our delicate active ingredients—the bioactive polysaccharides.

Why are other fruit juices added to Himalayan Goji Juice?
Our proprietary recipe incorporates a small amount of other fruit juices to ensure uniformity, and to help bring out the best flavor from the goji berry.

How soon should Himalayan Goji Juice be consumed after it is opened?
It is recommended that you consume Himalayan Goji Juice within 30 days after opening and refrigerating the bottle.

After Himalayan Goji Juice is opened, how long can it stay out of refrigeration and still remain effective?
For best-keeping qualities, keep Himalayan Goji Juice refrigerated after opening. It should not be left out for any more than a couple of hours, the same steps you would take for any food or beverage that must be refrigerated after opened.

The Right Positioning - Explosive Growth

HIMALAYAN GOJI™ JUICE is part of the explosive functional foods industry. This market segment has been experiencing incredible growth since 1996, and leading industry analysts expect it to explode at a growth rate of at least 15% per year as consumers become more and more health conscious, and baby boomers search for ways to halt the aging process.

"The market for functional foods has been estimated at $20 billion annually in the U.S. alone, according to the reports. It is expected to grow at some 15 percent each year."
—CNNmoney, February 10, 2000
(from the editors of CNN and MONEY Magazine)

"Functional beverages...are becoming a multi-billion dollar industry."
—CBSNews.com, July 30, 2002

"In the U.S., baby boomers who started turning 50 in 1996 are doing so at a rate of 300,000 per month. The interest in retarding the aging process and remaining healthy will continue to drive the market demand for functional food products."
—Agriculture & Agri-Food Canada

HIMALAYAN GOJI™ JUICE is the first dietary supplement of its kind. It is readily identified as a true category creator.

Legendary Health Benefits

Many of the legendary health-giving properties of *lycium barbarum* (goji's Latin name) are today being confirmed in modern scientific studies, and this has led to the possibility of even more far-reaching benefits. Some of the studies are shown below:

Enhanced Immune Response

A polysaccharide-protein complex from Lycium barbarum upregulates cytokine expression in human peripheral blood mononuclear cells. Eur J Pharmacol 2003 Jun 27;471(3):217–22

Gan L, Zhang SH, Liu Q, Xu HB.

Institute of Pharmacy, Huazhong University of Science and Technology, Wuhan 430074, People's Republic of China. ganlu07@163.com

The production of cytokine is a key event in the initiation and regulation of an immune response. Many compounds are now used routinely to modulate cytokine production, and therefore the immune response, in a wide range of diseases, such as cancer. Interleukin-2 and tumor necrosis factor-alpha are two important cytokines in antitumor immunity. In this study, the effects of Lycium barbarum polysaccharide-protein complex (LBP(3p)) on the expression of interleukin-2 and tumor necrosis factor-alpha in human peripheral blood mononuclear cells were investigated by reverse transcription polymerase chain reaction (RT-PCR) and bioassay. Administration of LBP(3p) increased the expression of interleukin-2 and tumor necrosis factor-alpha at both mRNA and protein levels in a dose-dependent manner. The results suggest that LBP(3p) may induce immune responses and possess potential therapeutic efficacy in cancer.

PMID: 12826241 [PubMed - indexed for MEDLINE]

Anti-Fatigue Effects

Isolation and purification of Lycium barbarum polysaccharides and its antifatigue effect. Wei Sheng Yan Jiu, 2000 Mar 30;29(2):115–7

[Article in Chinese]

Luo Q, Yan J, Zhang S.

Department of Hygiene, Hubei Medical University, Wuhan 430071, China.

A purified component of lycium barbarum polysaccharide (LBP-X) was isolated from lycium barbarum L. by DEAE ion-exchange cellulose and sephacryl gel chromatography. LBP-X was tested on five different doses (5, 10, 20, 50 and 100 mg.kg-1.d-1) in mice. The results showed that LBP-X induced a remarkable adaptability to exercise load, enhanced resistance and accelerated elimination of fatigue. LBP-X could enhance the storage of muscle and liver glycogen, increase the activity of LDH before and after swimming, decrease the increase of blood urea nitrogen (BUN) after strenuous exercise, and accelerate the clearance of BUN after exercise. The dosage of LBP-X 10 mg.kg-1.d-1 was the best amount among the five tested doses.

PMID: 12725093 [PubMed— indexed for MEDLINE]

Weight Loss

Study on the composition of Lycium barbarum polysaccharides and its effects on the growth of weanling mice. Wei Sheng Yan Jiu, 2002 Apr;31(2):118–9

[Article in Chinese]

Zhang M, Wang J, Zhang S.

Food Science Department, Huazhong Agricultural University, Wuhan 430070, China.

In order to observe the effects of lycium barbarum polysaccharides (LBP-4) on the growth of weanling mice and the absorption of some metals in the their body, the composition of LBP-4 is determined. 120 female weanling mice are divided in random into 4 groups. They are fed on LBP-4 at the dose of 5, 10 and 20 mg/(kg.d) respectively. The taken feed weight and the body weight of mice are recorded everyday. After 21 days, the content of calcium, magnesium, zinc and iron in pygal muscles and femora of mice is determined. The results showed that LBP-4 is composed of six kinds of monosaccharides that can enhance food conversion rate and the content of zinc and iron in body of mice, and reduce the body weight.

PMID: 12561548 [PubMed - indexed for MEDLINE]

Free-Radical Prevention

Experimental research on the role of Lycium barbarum polysaccharide in anti-peroxidation. Zhongguo Zhong Yao Za Zhi, 1993 Feb;18(2):110–2, 128

[Article in Chinese]

Zhang X.

Beijing Military General Hospital.

In this work, the changes in electrical parameters of cell membrane of Xenopus Oocytes were determined using routine microelectrode electrophysiological technique after incubation of the cells in frog Ringer solution containing free radical producing system for 6 hours. It was observed that the resting membrane potential was raised, and the membrane resistance and time constant were decreased. The effects of free radical on the cells can be prevented and reversed by incubation with superoxide dismutase or Lycium barbarum polysaccharide.

PMID: 8323695 [PubMed—indexed for MEDLINE]

The astounding benefits of goji have been reported over time in many prestigious journals and magazines:

- *Journal of Chinese Herbal Medicine*
- *Journal of Ethnopharmacology*
- *China Pharmacology and Toxicology*
- *Chinese Herb News magazine*
- *Research Communications Molecular Pathology and Pharmacology*
- *Chinese Patent Herbs*
- *Chinese Herbs*
- *Nature Reviews Drug Discovery*
- *Chinese Oncology Magazine*
- *Hygiene Research*
- *Physiology Academic Journal*
- *Chinese Stomatology*
- And many more

New Food Pyramid

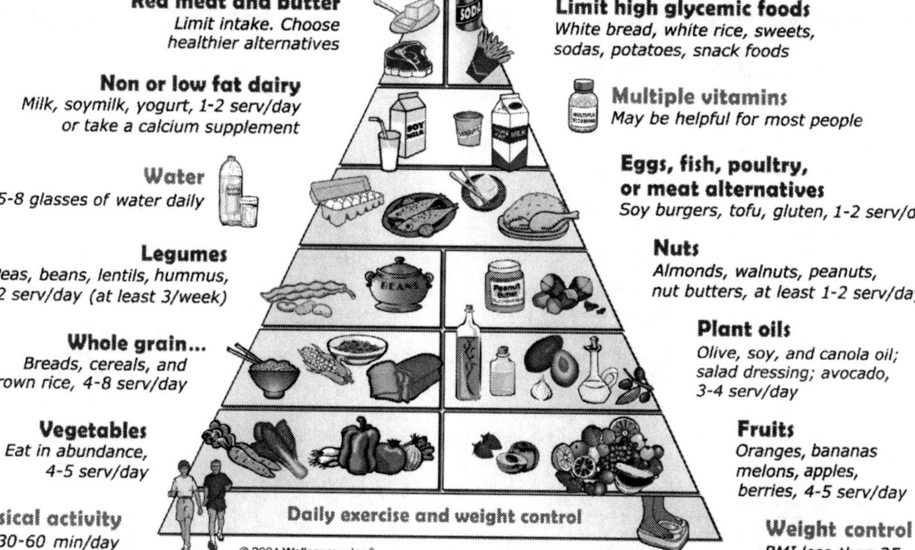

The new food pyramid is designed to assure good nutrition and to help prevent disease. Notice the number of servings recommended daily. Adjust if needed to maintain a healthy weight.

Serving Sizes

Red meat— 2 oz. lean meat or 1 T butter. Limit intake if eaten at all. Choose healthier alternatives.

Dairy— 1 C milk or yogurt, 1 oz. low fat cheese, ½ C cottage cheese, 1 C soymilk (should be 8+ g protein/ serving)

Legumes— ½ C cooked beans, peas, lentils, or garbanzos, ⅓ C hummus

Vegetables— 1 C lettuce or salad, 1 C fresh or ½ C cooked vegetables, 6 oz. vegetable juice

Whole grains— 1 slice bread, ½ to ⅔ C dry cereal, ½ C cooked cereal, pasta, brown rice

High glycemic foods— 1 slice bread or small bun; ½ C cooked white rice; 1 can soda pop; ½ C low-fat frozen yogurt; 2 T sugar, jam, or syrup; ½ C potatoes or 10 French fries

Eggs, fish, poultry, and plant proteins— 1 egg, 2 oz. fish or meat, 1 soy or Gardenburger®, ¼ block tofu, 1 gluten steak (6–8+ g protein/serv)

Nuts— 1 oz. nuts, 2 T peanut or almond butter, 2 T sunflower seeds

Fruit— 1 medium fruit (apple, banana, orange), ½ C canned fruit, 1 C fresh berries or melon, 6 oz. pure fruit juice

Plant oils— 1 tsp oil or trans-fat free margarine, 2 tsp salad dressing or mayo, 1 T low fat mayo or margarine, 8 medium olives, 2 T or ⅕ avocado

Source: Adapted by DR Hall, DrPH, from Harvard's New Food Pyramid (Scientific American Dec 17, 2002), The DASH Diet, NHLBI of NIH, Health Information Center, 2003, and Dietary Guidelines for Americans, 2000.

Other Nutrition and Health Guidelines

Physical activity— Aim for 30–60 minutes of moderate activity/ day, such as brisk walking.

Water— Drink plenty of water, at least 5–8 glasses daily.

Salt— Use salt moderately. Limit sodium to 1500 mg/day; especially important if blood pressure is high.

Multiple vitamins— Most persons may benefit from a daily supplement. Calcium may also be helpful for non-dairy users.

Plant foods— Eating a variety of whole grains, fruits, and vegetables is the basis of healthy eating. (US Dietary Guidelines)

Weight— Maintain a healthy weight, BMI <25, Waist <33 women, <35 men

Healthy Eating Self Test

Instructions: How healthy are your eating habits? Take this quick nutrition self test to see. Mark the box in the column that best describes your usual eating pattern. Write the individual score beside the box you marked in the right column.

Eating Practices	Column A	Column B	Column C	Scor
1. Breakfast *How often do you eat breakfast?*	[ ] 0 Occasionally or never	[ ] 3 Most days (5 or more times/week)	[ ] 5 Every day	
2. Whole-grain bread/cereal *Number of servings you eat daily?* (serv = 1 sl bread, ¾ C dry cereal, ½ C cooked cereal or brown rice	[ ] 0 0 to 2 per day	[ ] 5 At least 3 per day	[ ] 10 4 or more per day	
3. Fruits and vegetables *Number of servings you eat daily?* (serv = 1 fruit, 1 cup fresh, ½ cup cooked, 2/3 cup juice)	[ ] 0 0 to 4 servings per day	[ ] 5 5 to 6 servings per day	[ ] 10 7 or more servings/day	
4. Spreads and other fats *What kinds do you usually eat?*	[ ] 0 Primarily use butter or stick margarine, and shortening	[ ] 5 Primarily use soft tub margarine and vegetable oils	[ ] 10 Only use vegetable oils and trans fat free margarine	
5. Meats/Protein foods *What kinds of protein foods do you typically eat?*	[ ] 0 Regularly eat red meat including steak, hot dogs, hamburger, and/or sausage	[ ] 5 Seldom eat meat or limit it to only lean meat, skinless poultry, or fish	[ ] 10 Eat primarily peas, beans, lentils, nuts, soy proteins, tofu, and other plant based protein foods	
6. Dairy products *What kind of dairy products do you typically use?*	[ ] 0 Use regular milk, cheese, cottage cheese, and yogurt	[ ] 3 Use only lowfat milk, cheese, cottage cheese, or yogurt	[ ] 5 Use only nonfat milk, cheese, or yogurt or use soymilk	
7. Legumes, dry beans/peas *How often do you eat them?*	[ ] 0 0 to 2 times/week	[ ] 3 3-6 times per week	[ ] 5 Daily	
8. Nuts, seeds, nut butters *How often do you eat them?*	[ ] 0 0 to 3 times per week	[ ] 5 4 to 5 times per week	[ ] 10 Daily	
9. Salt and salty foods *How much do you eat?*	[ ] 0 Always salt food at meal time and often eat salty foods	[ ] 3 Occasionally add additional salt to food or eat salty foods	[ ] 5 Use salt sparingly and limit intake of salty foods	
10. High glycemic foods *How often do you eat* white bread, white rice, sugary dry cereals, pastry, and snack foods?	[ ] 0 Eat some of these foods most every day	[ ] 3 Limit these foods, only eat them a few times in a week	[ ] 5 Seldom eat high glycemic foods or eat in small amounts	
11. Sodas/Sweets *How often do you eat/drinkt soda* pop, punch, ice cream, candy, sugar, jam, and other sweets?	[ ] 0 Love sweets, eat them every day	[ ] 3 Limit sweets, only eat sweets occasionally or in small amounts	[ ] 5 Seldom eat sugar rich foods, and eat primarily fresh fruit and pure fruit juices	
12. Body mass index (BMI) Mark your BMI value **or** waist girth (see BMI chart on back).	[ ] 0 BMI 30 or higher Waist 37"+ in women., 39"+ men	[ ] 5 BMI 25 to 29.9 Waist 33"+ women, 35"+ men	[ ] 10 BMI 18.5 to 24.9 Waist <33" women, <35" men	
13. Physical activity level *How often do you get 30+ min of physical activity in a day?* walk, bike, jog, dance, garden, hike.	[ ] 0 Never or seldom exercise	[ ] 3 3-4 days per week	[ ] 5 5-7 days per week	
14. Water *Number of glasses of water you normally drink each day?*	[ ] 0 Less than 5 glasses per day	[ ] 3 5 to 7 glasses daily	[ ] 5 8 to 10+ glasses daily	

Scoring: Sum all of the scores in the right hand column to arrive at your total score or *Nutrition Index*. Compare your results with the norms on the right. Put an 'X' on the Nutrition Scale that corresponds with your score.

Your Nutrition Index (0-100)

Nutrition Scale (0-100) a high score is desirable.

|--------|--------|--------|--------|--------|--------|--------|--------|--------|--------|

0 10 20 30 40 50 60 70 80 90 100

Needs Improving Doing Well Excellent

Interpreting Your Nutrition Index Score

	Nutrition Index	% of population
Excellent	80 -100	18%
Doing well	54 - 79	22%
Needs Improving	less than 55	43%
Poor eating habits	less than 35	17%

For more information on nutrition and health see www.MakingHealthyChoices.info Rev. 6-25-03 DRH

Healthy Eating Guidelines

Eating should be enjoyable and keep you healthy. Here are 10 key guidelines to help you eat well and live a long, healthy life.

1. Eat predominantly from whole, plant based foods
The U.S. Dietary Guidelines state[1], "Eating a variety of whole grains, fruits, and vegetables is the basis of healthy eating." These foods are packed with nutrients and phytochemicals that protect the body from disease. They are cholesterol free and low in calories. Emphasize plant-based foods in your diet.

2. Maintain a healthy weight
Try these eating tips to assist you in this lifetime goal:

- Learn to eat lower calorie foods (fruits, vegetables, salads)
- Limit high calorie desserts (ice cream, cheese cake, etc.)
- Drink water in place of soda pop, lemon aide, or fruit punch
- Limit fast food and high calorie restaurant food
- Keep portion sizes moderate and limit second helpings
- Eliminate junk foods and typical snack foods
- Eat slowly and enjoy your meals
- If needed, join a weight loss support group or see a dietitian

A healthy weight is defined as a body mass index (BMI) less than 25 or a waist girth < 33" for women and < 35" for men. Check your BMI on the following chart.

Body Mass Index (BMI) Chart

Height	Healthy BMI 23	OverWt BMI 25	Obese 1 BMI 30+	Obese 2 BMI 35+
4' 10"	110	119+	143+	167+
5' 0"	118	128+	153+	179+
5' 2"	126	136+	164+	191+
5' 4"	134	145+	174+	204+
5' 6"	142	155+	186	216+
5' 8"	151	164+	197+	230+
5' 10"	160	174+	209+	243+
6' 0"	169	184+	221+	258+
6' 2"	179	194+	233+	272+
6' 4"	189	205+	246+	287+

Source: NIH, NHLBI, National Obesity Initiative, 2003

3. Aim for 30-60 minutes of physical activity daily.
Physical activity balances calorie intake to help you maintain a healthy weight. Choose moderate activities you enjoy such as brisk walking, biking, active gardening, aerobics to music, and sports. If you have health problems, get your doctor's specific guidance before initiating an exercise program.

4. Eat fresh fruits and vegetables in abundance
They help maintain your weight and promote good health. The new NIH DASH Diet[3] recommends eating 8 to 10 servings of fruits and vegetables daily. Include a wide variety of vegetables, greens, and salads. Eat citrus, melons, berries, grapes, apples, and other fresh fruits in abundance.

5. Choose healthy fats
Not all fats are bad. Some are essential for health. Eat some healthy fats each meal. Examples include:

- Unhydrogenated vegetable oils (Canola, olive, soy, corn)
- Trans fat free margarine (read the food label)
- n-3 fatty acids (found in flax meal, walnuts, and soy
- Olives, avocado, nuts, and nut butters
- Limit saturated fat (animal fats) to less than7% of calories
- Avoid trans fats found in partially hydrogenated fats (e.g. margarine, shortening, pastry, cookies, cake, baked goods)

6. Eat whole grains
Whole wheat bread, brown rice, oatmeal and other whole grains lower the risk of heart attacks, strokes, diabetes, and certain cancers. Eat at least 3 servings of whole grains daily.

7. Eat nuts/legumes daily
Legumes and nuts are good sources of protein, fiber, and healthy fats. Eat them daily for best health.

8. Choose healthy protein foods
Limit red meats. Healthier protein foods include legumes, tofu, soy, nuts, and other vegetable protein foods that are cholesterol free and low in saturated fat. Skinless poultry and fish are also healthier alternatives to red meat.

9. Limit high fat dairy products
Limit butter, cream, and high fat cheese. Use low fat dairy or soymilk (be sure soy has at least 7-8 g of protein/serving).

10. Choose healthy carbohydrates
Limit high glycemic foods such as snack foods, sugar, soda pop, white bread, white rice, and potatoes. They raise blood sugar and insulin levels, and increase the risk for obesity, diabetes, and heart disease. Choose unrefined carbohydrates high in fiber.

Other Nutrition Guidelines

- Drink plenty of water (it's good for body and brain)
- Use salt moderately, no more than 2400 mg of sodium/day
- Eat plenty of dietary fiber, women 25 g and men 38 g per day
- Eat a good breakfast daily (avoid skipping meals)
- Use the New Food Pyramid[7] to help you plan healthy meals

What is a Serving Size?

Dairy 1 C milk or yogurt, ½ C cottage cheese, 1.5 oz low fat cheese

Plant oils 1 tsp vegetable oil or trans fat free margarine,

Vegetables 1 C salad, 1 C fresh veggies, ½ C cooked, 6 oz juice

Legumes ½ C cooked beans

Grains bread 1 slice, dry cereal 2/3 C, cooked cereal, rice, or pasta ½ C

Protein foods 1 egg, ½ C tofu, 1 soy or garden burger, 2 oz meat

Fruit 1 medium fresh fruit, 1 C berries or melon, 6 oz fruit juice

Nuts 1 oz nuts, 2T nut butter

References

1. HHS. Dietary Guidelines, 2000
2. NAS, Inst. of Medicine, DRIs, 2002
3. JAMA 289:2083-93, Apr 23/30, 2003
4. NIH, ATP3 Heart Report, 2000
5. Amer J of Clin Nutr 70:412-19, '99
6. British Medical Journal, Nov 14, '98
7. Willett, Rebuilding the food pyramid, Scientific American Dec 17, 2002

We invite you to view the complete selection of titles we publish at:

www.LNFBooks.com

or write or e-mail us your thoughts, reactions, or criticism about this or any other book we publish at:

TEACH Services, Inc.
P.O. Box 954
Ringgold, GA 30736

info@TEACHServices.com

or you may call us at:

800-367-1844